Research Methodology

Research Methodology

for the Business and Administrative Sciences

2ND EDITION

jc welman
sj kruger

OXFORD
UNIVERSITY PRESS

Great Clarendon Street, Oxford OX2 6DP

Oxford University Press is a department of the University of Oxford.
It furthers the University's objective of excellence in research, scholarship, and education by publishing worldwide in

Oxford New York

Auckland Bangkok Buenos Aires Cape Town Chennai
Dar es Salaam Delhi Hong Kong Istanbul Karachi Kolkata
Kuala Lumpur Madrid Melbourne Mexico City Mumbai Nairobi
São Paulo Shanghai Singapore Taipei Tokyo Toronto

with an associated company in Berlin

Oxford is a registered trade mark of Oxford University Press
in the UK and certain other countries

Published in South Africa
by Oxford University Press Southern Africa, Cape Town

Research Methodology: for the Business and Administrative Sciences Second Edition

ISBN 0 19 578046 9

First published 1994 by Southern Book Publishers (Pty) Ltd

Designer: Mark Standley

Published by Oxford University Press Southern Africa
PO Box 12119, N1 City, 7463, Cape Town, South Africa

Set in 11 pt on 12 pt Dante Mt by RHT desktop publishing cc, Durbanville
Reproduction by RHT desktop publishing cc, Durbanville
Cover reproduction by The Image Bureau, Cape Town
Printed and bound by Clyson Printers, Maitland

Abridged table of contents

1	The aims of research	1
2	The research topic, title and research problem	10
3	Literature review	32
4	Research design: Population and sampling types	45
5	Types of quantitative research designs	68
6	Validity of conclusions	96
7	Data-collecting methods and measuring instruments in quantitative research	126
8	Qualitative research design	177
9	Data analysis and interpretation of results	193
10	Report writing	221
11	The research proposal	245
	Appendices	272
	References	287
	Internet resources	292
	Index	297
	User guide for MoonStats	309

Contents

Preface xvii
Learning matrix for research standards xix

1 The aims of research 1

1.1 Introduction: What is research? 2
1.2 Scientific as opposed to non-scientific knowledge 3
1.2.1 Sources of non-scientific knowledge 3
1.2.1.1 Authority 3
1.2.1.2 Opinions of peers 3
1.2.1.3 Traditions 4
1.2.1.4 Debating 4
1.2.1.5 Accidental observation 4
1.2.2 Scientific knowledge 5
1.2.2.1 Systematic observation 5
1.2.2.2 Control 5
Research Example I 6
1.2.2.3 Replication 6
Self-evaluation questions 6
1.3 Quantitative and qualitative research cycles 6
Summary 9
Multiple choice and true/false questions 9

2 The research topic, project title and research problem 10

2.1 Introduction 11
2.2 Statement of the research problem/question and its variables 11

Research Example II 14
Activity 2.1 15
Self-evaluation question 16
2.2.1 The origin of research problems 16
2.2.1.1 Practical problems 16
2.2.1.2 Previous research 17
2.2.1.3 Theories 17
2.2.2 The purpose of research 18
Activity 2.2 20
2.2.3 The purpose of other forms of research 20
2.2.3.1 Historical research (Records) 20
2.2.3.2 Case study research 21
2.2.3.3 Action research 21
2.3 Research hypotheses 22
2.3.1 Formulating the research hypothesis 22
2.3.2 Formalising the research hypothesis in terms of operationalised constructs 23
2.3.3 The construct validity of the operationalisation of the independent variable and of the measurement of the dependent variable 26
Activity 2.3 27
Activity 2.4 27
2.4 The cyclic progress of the scientific expansion of knowledge 28
Self-evaluation questions 30
Summary 30
Multiple choice and true/false questions 31

3 Literature review 32
3.1 Introduction 33
3.2 Literature searches 33
3.2.1 Previous research 33
3.2.2 Tracing and recording relevant literature 33
3.2.3 Planning the literature search 34
3.3 Compiling a literature review 35
3.3.1 Integrating the studies 35
3.3.2 Primary and secondary sources 35
3.3.3 Quotations 36
3.4 The reference system 36

3.4.1 References in the text 37
3.4.2 Alphabetical order of sources in the reference list 38
3.4.3 Language of reference 38
3.4.3 Journal articles in the list of references 39
3.4.5 Books and chapters in books 39
3.4.6 Other sources 39
Activity 3.1 40
Activity 3.2 41
Literature sources 42
Electronic sources 43
Summary 43
Multiple choice and true/false questions 44

4 Research design: Population and sampling types 45
4.1 Introduction 46
4.2 Sampling 46
4.2.1 The sampling frame 47
Activity 4.1 52
Self-evaluation questions 53
4.2.2 Random sampling 53
4.2.2.1 Simple random sampling 53
4.2.2.2 How to use a table of random numbers 54
4.2.2.3 Stratified random sampling 55
4.2.2.4 The advantages of a stratified random sample 56
4.2.3 Other types of probability sampling 56
4.2.3.1 Systematic sampling 58
4.2.3.2 Cluster sampling 60
4.2.4 Non-probability sampling 61
4.2.4.1 Accidental sampling (incidental sampling) 62
4.2.4.2 Purposive sampling 63
4.2.4.3 Quota sampling 63
4.2.4.4 Snowball sampling 63
4.2.5 Sample size (*n*) 63
Activity 4.2 65
Self-evaluation questions 66
Multiple choice and true/false questions 66

5 Types of quantitative research designs 68

5.1 Introduction 69
5.2 Experimental research 69
5.2.1 Characteristics of true experimental research 70
5.2.1.1 Control over the independent variable 70
5.2.1.2 Random assignment of units of analysis to groups 70
5.2.1.3 Nuisance variables 72
5.2.2 Causality in the human behavioural sciences 73
5.2.2.1 Correlation between variables 73
5.2.2.2 Cause must precede the effect 74
5.2.2.3 Control of the third variable 74
5.2.3 Laboratory versus field studies 77
Activity 5.1 78
Activity 5.2 78
5.3 Quasi-experimental research 79
5.3.1 The non-equivalent control group design 79
5.3.2 The interrupted time-series design 80
Activity 5.3 83
5.4 Non-experimental research 83
Research Example III 84
5.4.1 Survey designs (relationships between variables) 84
Activity 5.4 85
5.4.2 Non-experimental research designs involving measurements at a single time 85
5.4.2.1 Correlational design 85
5.4.2.2 The criterion-groups design 86
5.4.2.3 Cross-sectional design 86
5.4.3 Longitudinal designs 86
Research Example IV 87
5.4.3.1 Panel designs 87
5.4.3.2 Cohort designs 88
5.4.3.3 Trend design 88
Activity 5.5 89
5.4.4 Prediction studies 89
5.4.4.1 The retrospective design 89
5.4.4.2 The prospective design 91
Activity 5.6 91
5.4.5 Opinion polls 91

Research Example V 92
Self-evaluation questions 93
Summary 94
Multiple choice and true/false questions 94

6 Validity of conclusions 96

6.1 Introduction 97
6.2 Suitability of research designs 97
6.3 Internal validity and threats 97
6.3.1 Introduction 97
6.3.2 Factors beyond the researcher's control 99
6.3.2.1 History 100
6.3.2.2 Spontaneous change (development, maturation, recovery or deterioration) 100
6.3.2.3 Other third-variable problems 101
Activity 6.1 105
Activity 6.2 105
6.3.3 Factors that influence the researcher's control 106
6.3.3.1 The subject effect 107
Research Example VI 109
6.3.3.2 The experimenter effect 110
6.3.3.3 Pretest sensitisation 111
6.3.4 Measurement problems 112
6.3.4.1 Measurement reactivity 112
6.3.4.2 Instrumentation 112
6.3.5 Group differences 113
6.3.5.1 Selection 113
6.3.5.2 Interaction between selection and spontaneous change 113
6.3.6 Random assignment to groups 114
6.3.7 Matching 114
6.3.7.1 Precision control 115
6.3.7.2 Nuisance variable 115
6.3.7.3 Frequency distribution control 116
6.3.8 Unplanned developments within and between groups 116
6.3.8.1 Communication between treatment groups 117
6.3.8.2 Differential attrition of participants 117
Self-evaluation questions 117

6.4 External validity and threats 118
6.4.1 Introduction 118
6.4.2 Population validity 118
6.4.3 Ecological validity 120
Activity 6.3 121
Self-evaluation questions 124
Summary 124
Multiple choice and true/false questions 125

7 Data-collecting methods and measuring instruments in quantitative research 126
7.1 Introduction 127
7.2 Systematic observation and quantitative measurement 128
7.3 Measurement theory 128
7.3.1 The nature of measurement 130
7.3.2 The levels of measurement 130
7.3.2.1 Nominal measurement 132
7.3.2.2 Ordinal measurement 132
7.3.2.3 Interval measurement 132
7.3.2.4 Ratio measurement 133
Activity 7.1 133
Activity 7.2 134
7.4 Validity (Construct validity of the dependant variable) 135
7.4.1 Construct validity 135
7.4.2 Criterion-related validity 137
7.5 Reliability 138
7.5.1 Estimating reliability 139
7.5.1.1 Test-retest reliability 139
7.5.1.2 Parallel-forms reliability 140
7.5.1.3 Internal consistency 140
7.5.1.4 Interrater/intercoder/tester/test or measurement-scorer reliability 141
7.6 Pilot studies in the development of an instrument 141
7.7 Measuring instruments 142
7.7.1 Introduction 142
7.7.2 Unobtrusive measurement 143
7.7.2.1 Physical traces 143

7.7.2.2 Personal documents and mass media material 144
7.7.2.3 Official statistics and archival sources 144
7.7.3 Group contacts 145
7.7.3.1 Survey questionnaires and postal dispatch 146
Activity 7.3 148
7.7.3.2 Standardised tests 149
7.7.3.3 Attitude scales 149
Activity 7.4 152
7.7.3.4 Rating scales and situational tests 153
7.7.3.5 Response styles and how to prevent them 155
Activity 7.5 157
7.7.4 Personal visits and communication by telephone 158
7.7.4.1 Personal visits 158
7.7.4.2 Telephonic interviews 159
7.7.4.3 Structured interviews 160
7.7.4.4 Unstructured interviews 160
7.7.4.5 Semi-structured interviews 161
7.7.5 Individual apparatus (measurements/tests) 162
7.7.6 Direct observation (checklists) 162
7.8 Developing and constructing questionnaires, interview schedules and attitude items 165
7.9 Ethical considerations 171
Research Example VII 171
Activity 7.6 172
Self-evaluation questions 173
Summary 174
Multiple choice and true/false questions 174

8 Qualitative research design 177
8.1 Introduction 178
8.2 Historical research 178
8.2.1 The principles of historical research 179
8.2.1.1 Primary versus secondary sources 179
8.2.1.2 Stringent criticism 179
8.2.1.3 Causal explanations 179
8.3 The phenomenological approach 181
8.3.1 The role of the researcher 181

8.3.2 The importance of the context of the study 181
8.3.3 The aims of research 181
8.3.4 Research design and methods 182
8.4 Qualitative methods 182
8.4.1 Case study research 182
8.4.2 Participant observation 184
8.4.2.1 Degrees of participation 185
8.4.2.2 The process/course of participant observation 185
Research Example VIII 185
8.4.3 Unstructured and in-depth interviews (and focus-groups) 187
8.4.3.1 Nature 188
8.4.3.2 Process/course of the interview(s) 188
8.4.3.3 Sampling 189
8.4.3.4 Analysis 189
8.4.3.5 Reporting 190
8.4.4 Participatory research 190
8.4.4.1 Action research 190
Activity 8.1 191
Summary 191
Multiple choice and true/false questions 191
Self-evaluation questions 192

9 Data analysis and interpretation of results 193
9.1 Introduction 194
9.2 Content analysis 195
Research Example IX 195
9.2.1 Steps in performing a content analysis 195
9.3 Statistical validity and techniques 197
9.3.1 Statistical validity 197
9.3.2 The sensitivity of a research design 199
9.3.2.1 Eliminating rival hypotheses 199
9.3.2.2 Eliminating the variance 200
9.3.2.3 Complex experimental research designs 200
9.4 Statistical techniques (and coding) 200
9.4.1 Descriptive statistics 208
9.4.1.1 Histograms/bar diagrams 208
9.4.1.2 Mean/average and variability 208

Activity 9.1 209
9.4.1.3 Correlations and cross-tabulation 209
9.4.2 Inferential statistics 212
9.4.2.1 Chi-square (X^2) analysis 213
9.4.2.2 *t*-tests 213
9.4.3 Using computers in statistical analysis (use the CD-ROM) 213
9.5 Presenting the results 216
Activity 9.2 216
Summary 216
Multiple choice and true/false questions 218
Self-evaluation questions 219

10 Report writing 221
10.1 Introduction 222
10.2 The sections of a research report 222
10.2.1 The title 223
10.2.2 The abstract 223
10.2.3 The introduction 224
10.2.4 The literature review 224
10.2.5 Problem statement and hypotheses 224
10.2.6 Methods and procedures 224
10.2.7 The results 226
10.2.7.1 Presenting the results 227
10.2.8 The discussions and conclusions 228
Activity 10.1 229
Activity 10.2 232
10.2.9 The list of references 233
10.2.10 Appendices or annexures 233
10.3 Conventions, grammar and style 234
10.3.1 Conventions 234
10.3.2 Grammar and style 234
10.4 Evaluation criteria for a research report 236
Self-evaluation questions 239
Summary 244

11 The research proposal 245
11.1 Introduction 246
11.2 Requirements of a research topic 247

11.3 Designing a research project 249
11.4 Sections of a research proposal 252
11.4.1 The introduction 252
11.4.2 The statement or formulation of the research problem 253
11.4.3 The proposed method, procedures and statistical analysis 253
11.4.3.1 Research method and procedures 253
11.4.3.2 Statistical analysis 254
11.4.4 The list of references 254
11.5 Evaluation criteria for a research proposal 254
11.6 The student-study supervisor role 256
11.7 Research proposal evaluation example 257
Activity 11.1 268
Activity 11 2 270
Summary 271

Appendices 272
Appendix A: A laboratory study of the effects of situation redefinition on spatial crowding 272
Appendix B: Answers to some self-evaluation questions 273
Appendix C: Table of random numbers 275
Appendix D: Case Studies A to E 276
Appendix E: Answers to multiple choice and true/false questions 285

References 287
Internet resources 292
Index 297
User guide for MoonStats 309

Preface

If you are an undergraduate or doctoral student and you need to know how to conduct research, you must read this book *Research Methodology for the Business and Administrative Sciences*. It can be used by researchers and students dealing with individuals, groups of people, organisations, products or systems, activities or events, and who want to conduct research on problems in fields such as:

corporate and business administration; correctional services and policing; cost and management accounting; credit management; human resource management; information technology; internal auditing; library and information studies; public management; public relations; purchasing management; real estate; safety management; taxation; and others

because the principles of scientific research stay the same and examples relating to the above-mentioned fields are given throughout the book.

The book is organised according to the typical STEPS you would follow IN DOING RESEARCH, namely:

establishing the aim of your research (CHAPTER 1) by stating the problem to be investigated and formalising hypotheses from that (CHAPTER 2). By doing a literature review you will read what problems and answers other researchers have en-countered in their research (CHAPTER 3). This usually helps you to decide on what research design to use (CHAPTER 4, 5 AND /OR 8), keeping in mind all factors that may influence the sampling method and the validity of your conclusions (CHAPTER 6). Then the data must be collected (CHAPTER 7 AND/OR 8), analysed and interpreted (CHAPTER 9) before you write a report (CHAPTER 10) in which you draw conclusions about the value and significance of addressing the research problem.

For those researchers and students who have to write a research proposal, the last chapter in the book (CHAPTER 11) provides guidelines WITH REFERENCES TO RELEVANT SECTIONS in the rest of the book on how to do it.

If your research problem lends itself to be studied by a QUANTITATIVE APPROACH (Sect. 1.3), we recommend that you read chapters:

1, 2, 3, 4, 5, 6 and 8, ending with chapter 10 – the writing of the report.

For those whose research problem lends itself to be studied by a QUALITATIVE APPROACH (Sect. 1.3), we recommend that you read chapters:

1, 2, 3, 4, 6, 8 and 9, ending with chapter 10 – the writing of the report.

If you need to submit only a LITERATURE STUDY for partial fulfilment of a degree or for an assignment, we recommend that you read Chapters 1, 2 and 3 first. Then proceed with your study keeping the guidelines in Chapter 6 in mind. Before finishing you may find the recommendations in Chapter 10, in conjunction with your own academic institution's regulations, helpful.

In the light of the increasing importance of the electronic media in research, we also include information on using the Internet as a research tool. A list of useful websites appears at the back of the book. Also included is a CD-ROM containing *MoonStats*, a statistical software programme. This programme provides the tools for data exploration and description. It enables students of statistics and research to gain a solid foundation in statistics, and allows them to confidently manage basic statistics.

This book has one final outcome as its purpose – to convey and ensure a clear understanding of the nature of research to its readers in an attempt to help them find an answer to their specific problem by providing practical guidelines, exercises and activities with case studies on how to do research.

Welman and Kruger

Learning matrix for research standards

Learning Area	Levels					
Outcomes	**Outputs**	**Support**	**Operational**	**Co-ordination**	**Implementation**	**Strategic**
Project design and proposal	A research proposal is compiled		Consult related disciplines, do literature review to gain preliminary knowledge	Conceptualise appropriate research of inter-disciplinary value	Formulate research design based on a sound methodology and theoretical framework	Write research proposals
Identify research needs and set objectives	Hypothesis/ Objectives/ Questions are compiled as a result of problem identification and need analysis	Determine type of research	Determine relevant resources and methods	Formulate purpose, needs, objectives and link to design	Identify problem and determine objectives and hypotheses	Formulate and link hypotheses to research problem, objectives and needs
Conduct research (Adopt a critical objective approach to problem solving to reach conclu-sions and make projections)	An appropriate research method-ology is applied		Review various methodologies	Choose appropriate methodology	Operationalise the method	
Collect information using techniques relevant to the discipline	State of the art overview of empirical data exists	Identify and locate potentially useful information resource centres/ environments and retrieve relevant information sources		Acquire basic library skills	Use a variety of information sources and information gathering techniques	Apply cognitive information literacy skills in conducting the literature study
Interpret data *(Adapted from Technikon SA workshop papers)*	Explanation of results within theoretical framework		Identify various methods to analyse data using technology	Analyse data by using appropriate data analyses and/or qualitative techniques (with technology)	Interpret and integrate findings by using data interpretation techniques	Draw valid conclusions through interpreting data

1 The aims of research

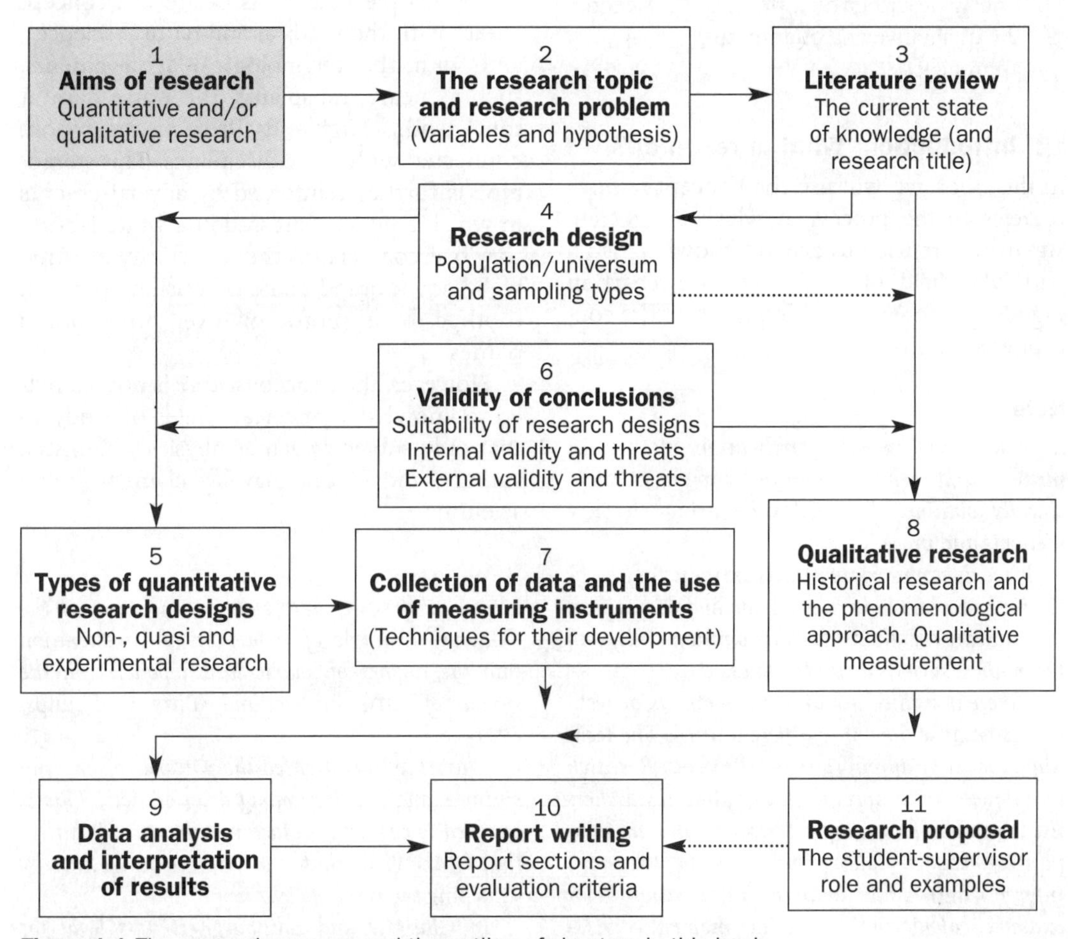

Figure 1.1 The research process and the outline of chapters in this book

Learning Outcomes

After studying this chapter, you should be able to:

1. differentiate between research methodology as opposed to research methods and techniques
2. name the three key characteristics (core features) of scientific knowledge that differentiate it from common human inquiry
3. explain how research produces scientific knowledge
4. illustrate the research process diagrammatically
5. briefly describe the differences between the qualitative and quantitative approaches.

1.1 Introduction: What is research?

In this book we will use the concept *research* to refer to the process in which SCIENTIFIC METHODS are used to expand knowledge in a particular field of study. The flowchart in Figure 1.1 can serve as a definition of the concept RESEARCH.

Note

RESEARCH involves the application of various methods and techniques in order to create scientifically obtained knowledge by using objective methods and procedures.

It seems appropriate at this introductory stage to briefly explain how research methodology differs from research methods, such as opinion polls, and techniques, such as attitude scales.

Different studies use different methods or techniques because they have different aims. The techniques must be appropriate for the tasks. Research techniques entail specific things that researchers use to sample (for example, stratified random sampling), measure, collect (for example, telephone interviewing) and analyse information (for example, calculating the product moment correlation coefficient).

You will find that the scope of research methodology is wider than that of research methods (which in turn is wider than the scope of research techniques), which form a part of research methodology (where the logic behind the methods that are used is considered and explained).

This book as a whole, and this chapter in particular, is concerned with the scientific method of attaining knowledge of human behaviour in a business and administrative context. Knowledge that has been obtained in this manner differs in important respects from a naive, or lay, person's knowledge of human behaviour.

Lay people usually associate the concept *science* with the medical and natural sciences, and with the technological achievements, such as heart transplants, the Katse dam at the Lesotho Highlands Project, and so on, connected with these disciplines. This stereotype is further reinforced by advertisements in which a person, dressed in a white laboratory overcoat, claims the superiority of some well-known brand name of washing powder, toothpaste or motor oil over other brand names.

However, the concept *science* is not restricted to knowledge in certain fields of study so that only subjects such as physics, chemistry, surgery, and so on, may lay claim to being scientific.

Note

The value of SCIENTIFIC RESEARCH is shown in the following example of a method of investigation into the impact of public health policies on the spread of AIDS in Scotland (Pitts & Phillips, 1991).

The study investigated the patterns of sharing syringes and needles among drug addicts. This is believed to be a crucial factor in the spread of HIV, that is, the virus that is believed to cause AIDS by attacking the immune system.

In Glasgow and Edinburgh it was legal for pharmacists to sell syringes and needles to intravenous drug users. The Edinburgh police pursued a policy of arresting people found carrying injecting equipment, whereas in Glasgow no such policy existed. Despite this policing policy in Edinburgh, the rate of HIV infection among intravenous drug users grew more quickly (from 3% in 1983 to 50% in 1984) than in Glasgow, where the rate at the end of 1986 was around 5%. This is illustrated in Figure 1.2.

The researchers found that although it was common for drug users to share syringes and needles in both cities, they did so in very different ways. This difference seemed to relate directly to the policy adopted by the police force. In GLASGOW, sharing syringes and needles tended to occur in small local groups, between just a few known drug users. In EDINBURGH, however, the policing policy made it dangerous to carry syringes and needles. So drug users set up "safe houses", also known as "shooting galleries", where users could obtain both the drugs and the means of injecting them. This led to many more drug users sharing syringes and needles, which in turn led to a wider mixing of blood, and therefore a faster spread of HIV.

Edinburgh	**Glasgow**
BOTH CITIES	
Legal for pharmacists to sell syringes and needles to intravenous drug users	
Police policy to arrest people found carrying injecting equipment	No such police policy
BOTH CITIES	
Users share equipment, but the pattern of social organisation differs	
"Safe houses"	Small local groups
CITIES DIFFER	
Rate of HIV infection among intravenous drug users	
In 1983 = 3% In 1984 = 50%	At end of 1986 = ±5%

Figure 1.2 The impact of public health policies on the spread of AIDS in Scotland

1.2 Scientific as opposed to non-scientific knowledge

1.2.1 Sources of non-scientific knowledge

In this section, we will introduce different sources of lay people's knowledge and contrast these sources with the scientific manner of arriving at conclusions on research problems.

1.2.1.1 Authority

Scientific knowledge is not something that is merely accepted on the authority of some or other source.

> **Example**
>
> In 1610, with the aid of his newly invented telescope, the Italian physicist Galileo discovered that there were spots on the sun. His colleagues rejected this finding because it was not in accordance with the prevailing opinion that was based on the authority of Aristotle, a 4th century Greek philosopher, who said that the sun was spotless.

According to the scientific approach, we should check the way in which such findings are acquired and not accept them merely because they originate from a so-called expert. This means that we must examine the evidence on which a claim is based.

1.2.1.2 Opinions of peers

Instead of calling on the opinions of experts, we may turn to our friends to obtain knowledge.

> **Example**
>
> First-line factory managers do not ask only personnel practitioners for advice when they want to promote some of their workers, but also ask their fellow first-line managers, who have already promoted their workers.

Similarly, students who have already completed a course may be consulted by their fellow students on whether it is better to prepare for the final examinations by studying regularly through the semester or studying shortly before the examinations.

1.2.1.3 **Traditions**

Another source of naive knowledge is that which is carried over from one generation to the next.

> **Example**
>
> Consider the commonly held beliefs that women are less capable of thinking logically than men, and that fat people are always happy.
>
> Such traditional beliefs are often reflected in idiomatic expressions such as the following:
>
> - Birds of a feather flock together.
> - Like father like son.
> - A leopard cannot change its spots.

1.2.1.4 **Debating**

The implication here is that people attempt to obtain knowledge and insight by arguing in a seemingly logical manner.

> **Example**
>
> Some students may argue that it is not worth the trouble to start revising early in the semester, because then there is more time before the examination in which to forget what they have learnt. Others, however, may argue with as much conviction that they should begin revising in good time so that there will be enough time for the learnt material to "sink in".

This method appeals to the intellect rather than to experience. Politicians often act as if they have access to such knowledge through debating.

Methods of "logical" reasoning

However, research (Feather, 1964) suggests that people are inclined to judge illogical arguments that correspond with their own attitudes and convictions, as logical, whereas they judge those that are logical but do not correspond with their own attitudes and convictions, as illogical. It is therefore not unusual for advocates and adversaries of one or other issue to reach diametrically opposed conclusions by means of their methods of reasoning. Often they reason logically, but from a false premise so that the ultimate conclusions are erroneous.

1.2.1.5 **Accidental observation**

If we notice something happening in one situation, but do not investigate the phenomenon in a systematic and planned manner, we may come to incorrect conclusions about what really happened.

> **Example**
>
> A supervisor may observe that trainees who started studying a week before the course examination the previous year, and were successful, used the correct learning method. Somebody else, however, might remember cases of trainees who prepared well in advance yet failed hopelessly.

Concerning the above example, in our everyday dealings we naturally come into contact with only a small group of people and therefore we cannot necessarily elevate our perceptions (such as in the above-mentioned example) to become generally accepted rules. The same bias that was apparent in the previous source of knowledge (debating) also applies here: we are inclined to observe that which fits in with our preconceptions or prejudices and to ignore that which differs. This is called SELECTIVE OBSERVATION.

1.2.2 Scientific knowledge

This entire book deals with the expansion of scientific knowledge, so it is impossible to fully describe the process at this early stage. For the time being it will suffice to describe THREE CORE FEATURES OF SCIENTIFIC KNOWLEDGE. Each of them reflects a critical predisposition towards claims generated by the aforementioned non-scientific sources, or any other source for that matter, and which, on the face of it, may even appear to be quite convincing.

1.2.2.1 Systematic observation

Firstly, we should obtain scientific knowledge by means of SYSTEMATIC OBSERVATION, which we should clearly distinguish from selective observation.

Accidental observations tend to be selective rather than systematic, so we tend only to see that which supports our presumptions and to turn a blind eye to the rest.

Furthermore: instead of merely debating which learning method should be the most effective, the scientific approach requires an investigation to be planned in which we use the results of two groups that have actually applied these methods strictly, as the final arbiter.

1.2.2.2 Control

Secondly, we should obtain scientific knowledge in a controlled manner. By control we mean that alternative explanations for the obtained results should be eliminated systematically.

For example, in RESEARCH EXAMPLE 1, scientific research would require the following explanations for the better performance of, say, the group that has studied regularly, to be ruled out:

- that they have studied a greater number of hours in total
- that they were more familiar with the study material from the start
- that they were more intelligent than the other group.

Obtaining knowledge in a controlled manner (eliminating alternatives systematically)

Research Example i: Distributed versus massed learning

The object is to obtain scientific knowledge about the relative effectiveness of distributed learning, that is, regularly mastering study material in more than one session, versus the practice of massed learning, that is, trying to learn all the study material in one session. This will require a study to be conducted in which we compare:

- the performance of one group of apprentices that has learned in a distributed fashion; with
- the performance of another, comparable, group that has studied the same material by means of massed learning.

1.2.2.3 Replication

Thirdly, the manner in which we obtain scientific knowledge must be replicable. We should place a great deal of emphasis on the replication of research results. By this we mean that comparable results should be obtained by other researchers, independent of the original/s, involving other research participants and other circumstances, yet still compatible with the same theory.

Therefore the expansion of scientific knowledge is not a private matter. Rather, the manner in which scientists reach their conclusions is put before the SCIENTIFIC COMMUNITY for thorough inspection. (Read Chapters 3 and 10 concerning the publication of a research report.) They are thus open to critical evaluation, and anybody who cares to do so, may replicate, or repeat, the procedures used to check whether comparable results are obtained.

The SCIENTIFIC COMMUNITY consists of people who, according to certain goals and rules, recognise the scientific way of creating knowledge. The products thereof should be rewarded by accepting such scientific information from scientists to be published in accepted credible and accredited academic journals (Chapter 3), and so on.

The development of scientific knowledge is thus a democratic process. The most humble student and the most famous scientist have equal access to arriving at scientific claims. At this stage we may formulate the following principle of public scrutiny that applies to the scientific expansion of knowledge:

The procedures (arguments, choice of data, collection and analysis of data, interpretation of results, conclusions, and so on, which will be addressed in the following chapters – see Figure 1.1) of scientific research should be submitted to the careful and critical evaluation of other members of the scientific community.

Self-evaluation questions

(Some answers appear in Appendix B on page 273.)

1.1 Suppose it occurs to a group of people travelling through South Africa that cars with Gauteng (GP) registration numbers are involved in most cases of reckless driving they encounter. They come to the conclusion that drivers with GP registration numbers are the most reckless drivers in the country. Are we dealing here with a source of:

a) non-scientific knowledge, or
b) scientific knowledge?

If (a), identify the particular source of non-scientific knowledge as one of the following:

- authority
- opinions of peers
- tradition
- debating
- accidental observation.

1.2 Suppose school children regularly eat apples because their teacher has taught them that this habit promotes healthy teeth. Are we dealing here with a source of:

a) non-scientific knowledge, or
b) scientific knowledge?

If (a), identify the particular source of non-scientific knowledge as one of the following:

- authority
- opinions of peers
- tradition
- debating
- accidental observation.

1.3 Qualitative and quantitative research cycles

In the introduction to this chapter we referred to the usefulness of the natural-scientific method in human behavioural research. If we apply the strict natural-scientific approach to the human behavioural sciences, it must be limited to what we can observe and measure objectively, that is, that which exists independently of the feelings and opinions of individuals.

- The philosophical approach underlying the NATURAL-SCIENTIFIC METHOD is known as LOGICAL POSITIVISM and the anti-positivists oppose this.
- Among the anti-positivists, we can distinguish different sub-groupings, such as the phenomenologists, but they all share a resistance to upholding the natural-scientific method as the norm in human behavioural research.

We can say that the NATURAL-SCIENTIFIC APPROACH strives to formulate laws that apply to populations (that is, are universally valid) and that explain the causes of objectively observable and measurable behaviour.

By "objective" we mean that people other than the researcher should agree on what is being observed, such as the score that the observation should register on a measuring instrument (See Chapter 7).

Example

Botanists must agree (be "objective" that mealies that have been planted in certain soil; have received a certain amount of a specific compost; and have been given a specific quantity of water, will grow to 1,45 m a certain number of days after planting.

According to the ANTI-POSITIVISTS, it is inappropriate to follow strict natural-scientific methods when collecting and interpreting data. They hold that the natural-scientific method is designed for studying molecules, organisms and other things and is therefore not applicable to the phenomena being studied in the human behavioural sciences.

In Chapter 8 you will see that according to the phenomenologists (a sub-group of the anti-positivists), for example, human experience, which is the object of behavioural research, is not to be separated from the person who is experiencing it.

The phenomenologists oppose the way in which, for example, researchers in the business and administrative science try to imitate the natural-science researchers by distancing themselves from the phenomena they are studying and, in a manner of speaking, attempt like a fly on the wall to objectively and detachedly research another fly (struggling along in, say, a plate of soup – see illustration on page 8).

The different points of view held by the POSITIVISTS and ANTI-POSITIVISTS are reflected in their definitions of their fields of study and their quantitative versus qualitative research aims.

The POSITIVISTS define their approach as the study of observable human behaviour, while according to some ANTI-POSITIVISTS, it must deal with the experiencing of human behaviour (that is, experience the phenomena "in their bones", so to speak).

While the positivists aim at uncovering general laws of relationships and/or causality that apply to all people and at all

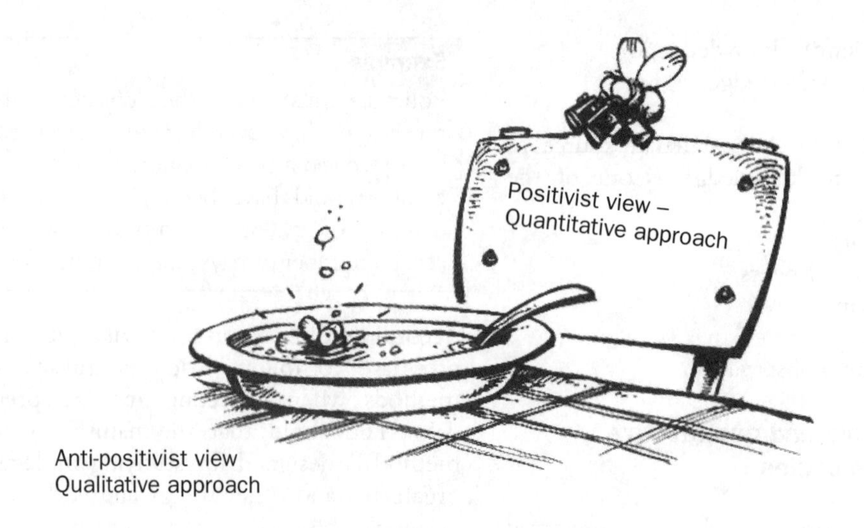

times, phenomenologists are concerned with understanding human behaviour from the perspectives of the people involved. Therefore, phenomenologists are not concerned with the description of phenomena, because these exist independently of the participants' experience of them, but with their experience of these phenomena.

Example

While the positivist researcher attempts to develop and test theories and models whereby, for example, leadership can be explained and predicted, the phenomenological researcher will attempt to understand how leaders in South Africa experience their transactional role as opposed to leaders in other countries.

Essentially, the anti-positivists claim that the positivists have absolutised the natural-scientific method in fields of study in which this method is lacking.

Although the approaches we deal with in Chapter 8 fit in better conceptually with the anti-positivist approach, it would be incorrect to maintain that, by definition, all such approaches are anti-positivist in nature. As a result, it does not mean that those considering using these methods should first make an anti-positivist confession.

Note

To view the so-called QUALITATIVE RESEARCH *approaches as easier substitutes for the so-called* QUANTITATIVE APPROACHES *would reflect a serious misjudgement. The quantitative methods have built up an extensive arsenal of checks and balances which may aid researchers in averting unjustified conclusions (Chapter 6).*

In the quantitative approach that we will describe in Chapters 5 and 7, by contrast, THE QUALITATIVE RESEARCHER (Chapter 8) *constitutes the primary research instrument. In a sense the researcher must take over the function of the control group to rule out counter explanations; observe without affecting that which is being observed; and keep his or her expectations under control.*

Example

A researcher wanting to determine the nature of prison gangs, and the reason for getting involved in them, would get little cooperation from the prisoners with regard to answering a questionnaire, for example. (They would probably tear it up and throw it away.)

In order to get close to his or her subjects, the researcher would have to try to be accepted as a member of one of the gangs. In this way, the researcher would be able to collect data concerning the reasons why prisoners form gangs. But there is also the danger of the researcher becoming involved to such an extent that the scientific community would question his or her objectivity.

It requires a seasoned and mature researcher with both a sound knowledge of these threats and complete self-insight to be so detached from, yet so involved with, his or her object of study. The reason for this is that in the final analysis *qualitative researchers*, to the same degree as quantitative researchers, have to defend their conclusions before the critically disposed scrutiny of their colleagues. If qualitative researchers believe that they have obtained new insights but those insights cannot withstand the test of scrutiny, such supposed knowledge is no different from everyday observation and idle speculation.

Summary

There are major steps in the process of doing scientific research (presented in Figure 1.1 on page 1). These steps are usually NOT followed by day-to-day enquiries about things that we experience and do not understand, and by NOT following these steps, our so-called "knowledge" contributes to the mystery of unexplained phenomena. Quantitative and qualitative research methodology allows us the means to explore all kinds of unexplained as well as the so-called previously explained but misunderstood phenomena. Through the use of methods and techniques that are scientifically defendable, we may come to conclusions that have a high probability of being justifiable in a court of law if so needed.

Multiple choice and true/false questions

Only *one* of the answers for each question is correct. Identify and mark the correct one. (Answers appear in Appendix E on page 285.)

1.1 Methodology can be described best as
   a) the logical step of science
   b) the science of knowing
   c) the discovery of reality through experience
   d) the discovery of the truth through scientific methods.

1.2 Scientific enquiry, in comparison to non-scientific inquiry,
   a) should guard against certain scientific errors
   b) does not view the ordinary citizen's opinion as valuable
   c) takes special precaution to avoid error
   d) is less concerned about making mistakes.

1.3 Something for helping us organise and interpret the world is referred to as a
   a) paradigm
   b) theory
   c) hypothesis
   d) concept.

1.4 The essential features of science are
   a) counter-intuitive and definite findings
   b) didactic rules of evidence and quantification
   c) intuition, inference and experimentation
   d) systematic observation, control and replication.

2 The research topic, project title and research problem

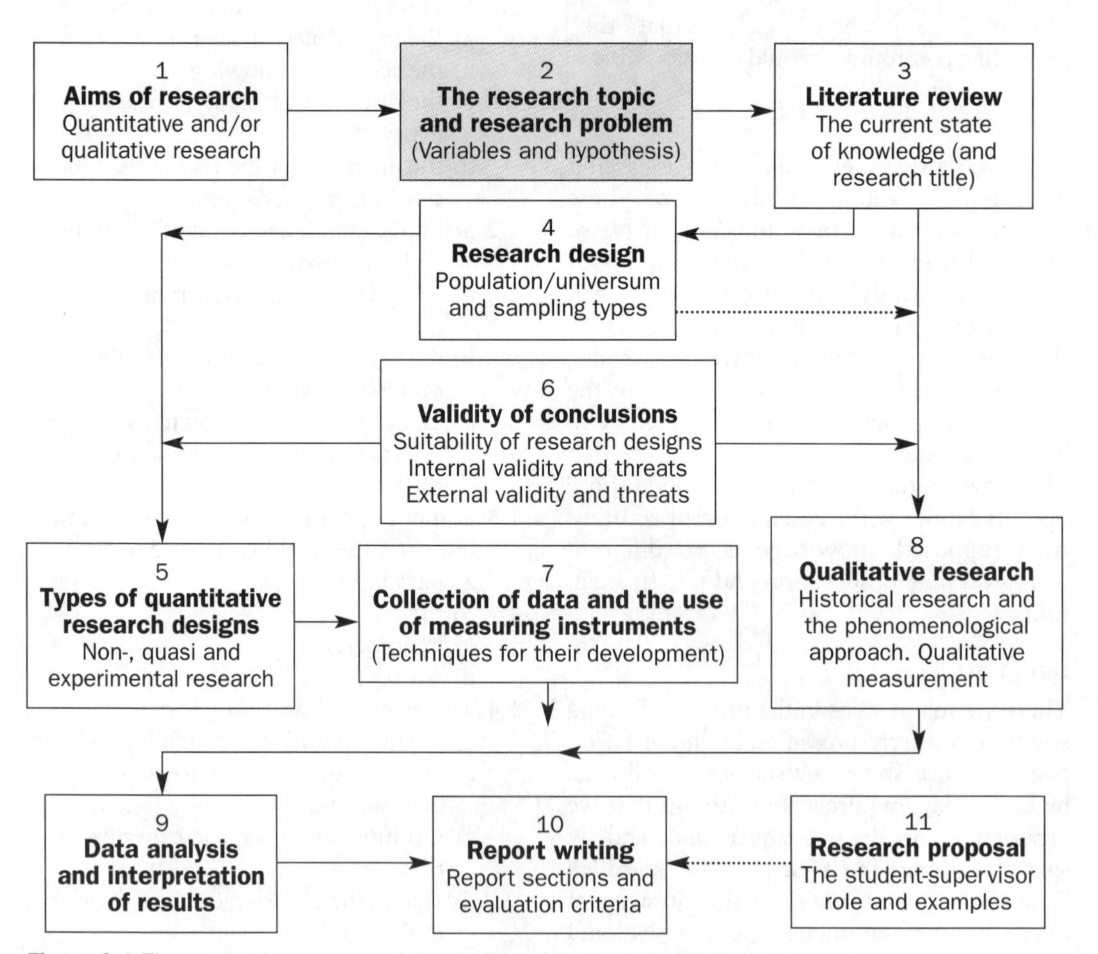

Figure 2.1 The research process and the outline of chapters in this book

Learning Outcomes

After studying this chapter, you should be able to:

1. list four typical examples of research topics appropriate to your field of study
2. explain the role of theory in scientific research
3. illustrate some basic purposes of doing research by means of an example
4. explain the importance of identifying the purpose of an investigation before starting the research
5. identify the most important variables concerned in Outcome 1 above and distinguish them in terms of dependent and independent variables
6. explain the function of a hypothesis in doing research
7. explain briefly why applied research instead of basic research will typically be done in industry and commerce, and describe two examples of applied research
8. explain briefly why action research will typically be done in industry and commerce.

2.1 Introduction

The first concrete step in the scientific research process is to clearly formulate the specific problem that is to be examined.

Say the objective of our research project is to test HYPOTHESES stemming from some THEORY. We should then state this theory, and indicate explicitly the manner in which the proposed hypotheses are implied by the theory.

Definitions

- A HYPOTHESIS is a tentative assumption or preliminary statement about the relationship between two or more things that needs to be examined. In other words, a hypothesis is a tentative solution or explanation of a research problem and the task of research is to investigate it.
- A THEORY is a group of logical, related statements that is presented as an explanation of a phenomenon. A theory therefore encompasses one or more hypotheses.

2.2 Statement of the research problem/question and its variables

In the process of scientifically investigating research problems, we may distinguish different, successive stadia, called the EMPIRICAL CYCLE, which is represented in Figure 2.2 below.

The first stage in any research project is to choose a research area or a general topic. This process (the statement of the research problem) requires the delineation of a problem area and the description of one or more research problems.

Consider the following RESEARCH PROBLEMS (RESEARCH QUESTIONS) that are relevant to the business and administrative sciences:

- Which factors play a role in the incidence of fraud?
- Does exposure to aggressive role model behaviour encourage aggressiveness among security company workers?
- Does the number of bystanders have an effect on the probability that assistance will be given to someone in distress?
- Why does poverty appear more often in some societies than in others?

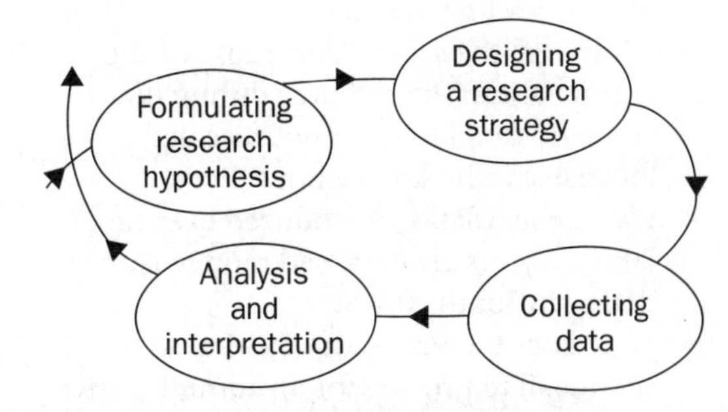

Figure 2.2 The deductive, empirical cycle in the scientific expansion of knowledge. (Adapted from Huysamen (1994, p. 10).)

- Which programmes are likely to promote socio-economic development?
- What are the causes of violence in so-called black townships?
- What steps can working South Africans take to supplement their pension plans to lessen the effect of the 25% tax increase on their retirement fund announced in the 1998 budget?
- How can our organisation system be made compatible for the year 2002 by using our existing computer technology?
- Is a police presence more necessary around household driveways than at shopping centres to prevent the hijacking of motor vehicles in suburban areas?
- What other means are there to deal with the payment and allocation of welfare pensions and/or taxation if the government's computers and programmes are not changed to automatically accommodate the year 2004?
- Will specialists familiar with computer languages such as COBOL be better equipped to make large mainframe computer programmes compliant with requirements than those specialists not familiar with COBOL?
- Does the publication of the expectations of major private employment organisations in South Africa regarding a decrease in employment levels decrease the level of union initiated strikes?
- Why were the secret "coverups" of the South African Police Force during the "total onslaught" years not revealed by journalists who knew about them?
- Has the legislation introduced over the last two years criminalised money laundering in South Africa?
- Why does the Proceeds of Crime Act (1996) fail to provide for an administrative framework for the confiscation of convicted criminals' assets?
- Will the mega-city idea combine the best elements of the existing system with the single-city model in Gauteng?
- Will the South African tax collection system be enhanced by requiring taxpayers to do their own assessment when they file their tax returns, as is the case in Namibia?
- How heavy should the penalties imposed by the Receiver of Revenue be for under-assessment by taxpayers filing their tax returns?
- What measures must be taken to advance the convergence of information technology and telecommunications in Southern Africa?
- Will a company's customer relationships be improved by providing "call centres" to ensure that requests are acted upon without the necessity for endless telephone calls?

To define a problem correctly, the researcher must know what a problem is.

A RESEARCH PROBLEM refers to some difficulty that the researcher experiences in the context of either a theoretical or practical situation and to which he/she wants to obtain a solution.

Note

EXPLORATORY RESEARCH does not start with a specific problem – the approach of such a study is to find a problem or a hypothesis to be tested (typical of qualitative research – see Section 1.3).

The researcher should rephrase a research problem to put it in terms that are as specific as possible to make it operationally viable (see Section 2.3.2) and able to help in developing hypotheses.

We can illustrate the technique of DEFINING A PROBLEM by taking the following example of a research problem, stated in broad general terms:

Why is productivity in Japan so much higher than in South Africa?

In this form the question or statement is much too general and there are several ambiguities such as:

- What sort of productivity is being referred to?
- Which industries are involved?
- What time period of productivity is being talked about?

We can narrow the research problem down to:

What factors were responsible for the higher labour productivity of Japan's manufacturing industries during the decade 1991 to 2000 in comparison to South Africa's manufacturing industries?

This version of the research problem is an improvement on the first one, but we can rethink it further and rephrase into an even better one:

To what extent did labour productivity from 1991 to 2000 in Japan exceed that of South Africa in respect of 15 selected manufacturing industries, and what factors were responsible for the productivity difference between the two countries?

Now we have a well-defined research problem that is meaningful from an operational point of view and may pave the way for the development of HYPOTHESES (Section 2.3) and for means of solving the problem itself.

Implicit in each research question (research problem) is the view that some VARIABLES are the causes of other variables and, vice versa, that the latter are the effects or consequences of the former.

For the time being, we will regard a VARIABLE as a characteristic or an attribute of the study object. The study object may be individuals, groups, organisations, human products and events, or the conditions to which they are exposed, which are not the same for all the study objects within the spectrum of the business and administrative sciences.

Example

The main aim of a diamond mining company such as Ocean Diamond Mining Holdings is to retrieve diamonds from the sea successfully and profitably. Therefore at least TWO VARIABLES are important, namely:

- diamond retrieving (which may be called diamond production); and
- the price the company is paid for its products (diamonds).

The price of diamonds VARIES (some diamonds may fetch a high price and others a low price on the diamond market), as does the number of diamonds retrieved (for example, one day only 100 diamonds may be retrieved and the next day 2 000). This is why they are called VARIABLES.

A variable such as weather conditions will most definitely play a major role in the achievement of the company's aim. Fortunately, variables such as "technological progress" and "improved ships" diminish the role of bad weather conditions in retrieving diamonds from the sea.

In the case of an experiment, our aim is to determine whether one or more specifically chosen variables, known as the INDEPENDENT VARIABLES, affect another variable, referred to as the DEPENDENT VARIABLE.

The dependent variable is the one that we eventually have to measure to determine whether the research participants (study objects) in the various levels of the independent variable differ in terms of it.

- The INDEPENDENT VARIABLE *(x)* is that factor which the researcher selects and manipulates in order to determine its effect on the observed phenomenon (the problem that is being investigated).

  This variable is considered to be independent because the researcher is interested in how it affects the other variable(s) being studied. In other words, the researcher seeks to find a cause and a resultant effect relationship, if it is present. By definition, the independent variable must have at least two levels in order to qualify as a variable.

- The DEPENDENT VARIABLE *(y)* is that factor which the researcher observes and measures to determine what effect the independent variable has on it, that is, that factor which appears, disappears, or varies as the researcher introduces, removes, or varies the levels of the independent variable. It is the dependent variable that will change as a result of variations in the independent variable.

  This variable is considered to be dependent because its value is assumed to depend upon the values of the levels of independent variable.

Example

In this example, we differentiate between the independent variable and the dependent variable.

Fire (independent) causes smoke (dependent) – the more a fire rages on a piece of land, the more smoke will occur. It can be illustrated as follows:

Fire independent variable *(x)* ──────▶ smoke dependent variable *(y)*

In RESEARCH EXAMPLE II, the independent variable is the management style, or role model behaviour, of the supervisors. It has two levels, namely an iron-fisted style and an approachable style. The dependent variable is the management style of the trainee supervisors. The independent variable is the level that the researcher purposefully chooses and in terms of which he or she divides the research participants into groups.

Research Example II: The transmission of management style

In 1999, researchers working for a big company randomly assigned (Section 6.2.6) 48 male and 48 female trainee supervisors working for the company to two main groups of 24 males and 24 females each. Half of the first group (12 males and 12 females) individually watched a video of a female supervisor's rude behaviour towards one of her subordinates, called Bobo. Bobo had interrupted the supervisor by calling her while she had been taking her tea-break. The supervisor's iron-fisted management style was relatively unique. For example, she pointed her finger and said rude things such as, "I will punch you in the nose" and "I will kick you". The remainder of the first group watched the same behaviour, but performed by a male supervisor.

Half of the second group (also 12 males and 12 females) watched the same female supervisor as the first group. This time the female supervisor showed an approachable management style, being friendly and willing to listen to her subordinate. The remainder of the second group watched the same male supervisor as before, but this time showing a friendly willingness to listen to the subordinate who had called him during his tea-break.

After watching the behaviour of the supervisors, the trainee supervisors were allowed individually to participate in recreational activities during their teabreak. Once they were engrossed in these activities (typically within two minutes), they were impolitely called on by the subordinate (Bobo) to rouse their frustration.

The number of times (called a tally – see Section 7.7.6 and Chapter 9) a trainee supervisor repeated the behaviour of one of the supervisors was recorded. The groups who had watched the iron-fisted supervisors displayed a management style significantly more similar to that manifested by the supervisor than did the other group. The males exhibited more iron-fisted responses than did the females.

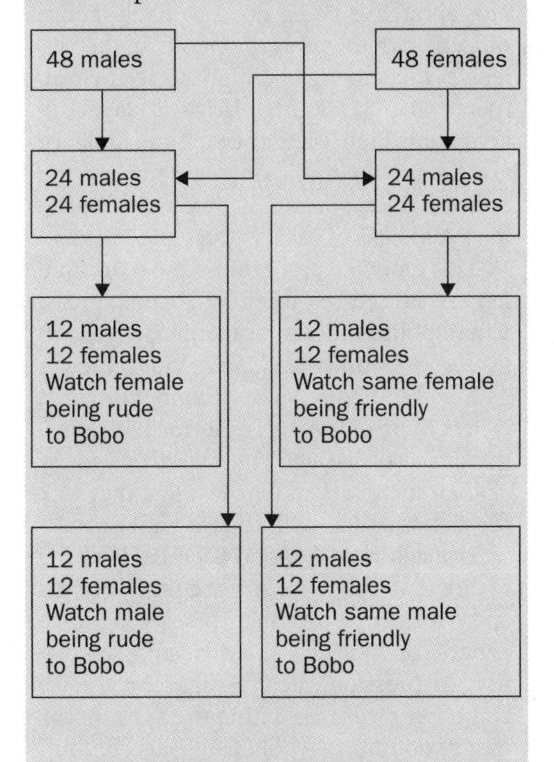

See illustration "Exposure to an iron-fisted role model ..." on page 131.

Activity 2.1

Read the following problem statement and answer the question. Compare your answer with the one given.

Problem statement

A manager believes that good supervision and training will increase the production level of the workers.

Question

What are the dependent and independent variables in this case? Give brief reasons for your answer.

Answer

Independent variable: Supervision
Independent variable: Training
Dependent variable: Output (production)

Reason

The manager wants to ascribe the differences in output (also called production levels) to, or explain them according to, the influence of the level of supervision (for example, strict control versus the absence of control) and the level of training (for example, memory learning versus knowledge of application).

If the manager regards strict control and knowledge of application as aspects of good supervision and training respectively, he/she would want to prove through research that the output level of the workers was increased by these factors rather than, for example, poor control and rote learning.

Next, read Case Study F in Appendix D on page 284.

Question

Write down the two most important variables in the case study and say whether they are so-called *dependent* or *independent variables*. Briefly give a reason for your answer.

Answer

BUSINESS PEOPLE (entrepreneurs/managers) is the *independent variable*, and INNOVATIVE PROBLEM-SOLVING STYLE is the *dependent variable*.

It appears from the literature in the introduction of the case study that people who are entrepreneurs or managers differ in terms of the extent (level) that they use innovative problem-solving. Using an innovative problem-solving *style* to a certain extent therefore seems to depend on whether a business person is an entrepreneur or a manager of a large business in South Africa.

Self-evaluation question

What are the variables (dependent and independent) in the list of research problems (questions) given in Section 2.2?

2.2.1 The origin of research problems

We could view the following as typical sources of research problems:

- practical problems;
- previous research; and
- theories.

2.2.1.1 Practical problems

Let us have a look at South African society with its wealth of practical problems, caused by rapid political, social and economical changes that are crying out for research. These include:

- the high population growth that is out of all proportion to what is economically sustainable
- the excessive culture of violence
- the increase in the incidence of AIDS and its effect on group life assurance policies
- the prejudices between different population groups that need each other so that South Africa can become internationally competitive
- the appointment of unqualified managers to provide for the increase in the numbers of vacant black advancement posts.

Only smaller aspects of these problems could, in fact, be examined in a single research project (a dissertation or thesis for academic degree purposes), for example, or even in a bigger project conducted by a national research organisation such as the NRF (National Research Foundation).

Example

NATIONAL CONFERENCE: POLICE OFFICIALS AS VICTIMS OF TRAUMA AND CRISIS.

MEDIA RELEASE 25 AND 26 FEBRUARY 1998 AT TECHNIKON SA: CONFERENCE CENTRE, JOHANNESBURG

Not enough is being done to equip police officers with the tools to operate in the violent, fast-changing and high-stress environment that is South Africa today. Unacceptably high levels of crime and violence are taking their toll on members of the police service, who are increasingly displaying symptoms of severe stress and trauma.

This emerged at a ground-breaking conference hosted last week by Technikon SA, where police officers, academics, psychologists, social workers and international experts gathered to find ways of dealing with what is becoming a growing crisis for the SAPS – the dangerously high stress levels of many of their members and the fact that they lack the necessary life skills to deal with them.

The failure to respond adequately to the reality that police too are victims of crime and violence is leading to growing incidences of suicide, absenteeism, resignation, depression, alcohol abuse, violence and other problems within the SAPS. In the past two years, 269 police officials committed suicide, with the rate escalating rapidly last year. High levels of stress and depression are reflected in absenteeism (as many as 10 000 police officers are absent on any given day), under-performance and resignations (an average of 450 members leave the SAPS each month).

Delegates adopted a resolution at the end of the two-day conference to elicit the support of top management in helping police to cope better with the psychological traumas of the job. A task team was also set up to "maintain the momentum of the conference" by organising follow-up skills-building workshops, identifying crucial areas of research and developing links between various people in the field.

2.2.1.2 **Previous research**

Significant research has usually already been conducted on most topics and new research proceeds from such existing research.

You will find the results of previous research projects in books, journal articles, congress papers and unpublished research reports. In the section of a research report (Section 10.1) in which you record your results, you usually have to point out the problems, gaps, and contradictions that have arisen from your research. It is not unusual for a research project to generate more new questions than it originally set out to answer. Especially when one study comes up with results that conflict with the results of another study or theory, the researcher may suggest ways in which this apparent contradiction may be solved.

2.2.1.3 **Theories**

You should preferably associate a research project with one or other theory. For the purposes of this discussion, we define a THEORY (see Section 2.1) as follows:

A THEORY is a statement or a collection of statements that specify the relationships between variables with a view to explaining phenomena such as human behaviour (for example, producing machines, organising an event, formulating a policy) in some or other POPULATION (universe).

This definition of a theory encompasses several concepts that we should first describe further in order to help you fully understand the complete definition, as well as the role of theory and other research problems in the generation of scientific knowledge.

- FIRSTLY, theories and research problems deal with the relationships between VARIABLES (as defined in Section 2.2).

Example

In RESEARCH EXAMPLE II (page 14), the two variables were *management style role model behaviour* and *management styles of trainee supervisors*.

Some, if not the majority, of the variables in human behavioural theories and research problems qualify as CONSTRUCTS.

A CONSTRUCT is an abstract concept that is deliberately created to represent a collection of concrete forms of behaviour. The concrete behaviours thus qualify as indicators of the construct.

Important constructs in the human behavioural sciences include attitudes, management style, problem solving, socio-economic status, and so on, to mention but a few.

Each of these constructs does not have a self-evident meaning as does *body height* or *eye colour*, but is deliberately conceived to represent a divergent collection of concrete behaviours.

Example

Under *management style* we may understand the ability to motivate people in organisations, such as schools, hospitals, churches, retail and manufacturing stores, security departments, local and state government agencies, to achieve goals; and the ability to devise solutions for practical problems, and so on.

- SECONDLY, theories and research problems are concerned with the *relationships* between variables.

Example

RESEARCH EXAMPLE II (page 14) involved an implication of a theory about the relationship between the exposure to management style role model behaviour and management styles among company trainee supervisors.

We will see in Section 5.2.2 that such relationships may be either CAUSAL or CORRELATIONAL in nature.

RELATIONSHIPS BETWEEN VARIABLES

- One variable is regarded as the direct CAUSE of another if the former precedes the latter in time and if changes in the latter can be related to changes to only the former (and not to any other variables).
- A CORRELATIONAL relationship means that changes to one variable are accompanied by, or associated with, changes to the other, but that the one is not necessarily the cause of the other.

A causal relationship between variables *X* and *Y* necessarily also implies a correlational relationship between them. However, a correlational relationship between variables *X* and *Y* is not necessarily an indication of a causal relationship between them.

Example

In RESEARCH EXAMPLE II (page 14), a causal relationship is suggested: the more iron-fisted the role model management style (*X*), the more iron-fisted the management style of the company trainee supervisors (*Y*) exposed to it tends to be.

- THIRDLY, theories and research problems are not concerned with the behaviour of *individual units* such as Lindiwe, Anna, Bongani or Johnny, as displayed in a few situations, but with the behaviour of a particular *population of individuals under a universe of settings* (see Section 4.1).

  A POPULATION (for example, all South African women, or all companies listed on the Johannesburg Stock Exchange) encompasses the entire collection of cases (or units) about which we wish to make conclusions. In RESEARCH EXAMPLE II (page 14), it involves company trainee supervisors.

  By definition, a theory cannot apply to a few individuals or organisations only (see Section 6.4.2). If a separate theory were to be applicable to each and every different individual person or company, the concept of a theory would lose its appeal and usefulness.

- FOURTHLY, a theory applies not only to specific situations (for example, the tax policy in one province) but to universes of circumstances (for example, South Africa as a whole) (see Section 6.4.3).

Example

A theory about role model behaviour as a factor contributing to aggressive reactions should be applicable to all role models rather than to a specific supervisor, and to behaviour in a variety of situations (for example, workplace, tea rooms and at home) rather than to, say, the workplace only.

2.2.2 The purpose of research

We can regard the purpose of research as mainly threefold:

- to DESCRIBE how things are, that is, define the nature of the study object;
- to EXPLAIN why things are the way they are. It may be so because one thing has caused another to change. We also like to explain what this relationship between things is; and
- to PREDICT phenomena, such as human behaviour in the workplace, with the aim of using this information, for example, to screen job applicants.

Note

The purpose of EXPLORATORY RESEARCH is to determine whether or not a phenomenon exists, and to gain familiarity with such a phenomenon; not to compare it with other phenomena (see Note on page 12).

So, we can say that the purpose of conducting research into theories and other research problems is to define, explain and, consequently, predict and even modify or control, human behaviour, its organisations, products and/or events.

Example

- To DESCRIBE, or define, the levels of production staff turnover figures and the average level of job satisfaction, a researcher undertakes a study to describe the major characteristics of a successful first-line manager in a manufacturing company in Gauteng. A successful manager may be found to have a certain leadership style.
- To EXPLAIN why production remains at a certain level, why employees resign, why they are dissatisfied, and so on: The researcher may state that "authoritarian individuals are successful leaders because the nature of the job requires the leader to tell the employee what to do and when to do it".
- To PREDICT which employees will be productive, who will be the most likely to resign, and who will be dissatisfied: The researcher may state that "authoritarian individuals in manufacturing companies in Gauteng will be successful leaders".

Note

It is quite possible that, due to the lack of knowledge of research methods, the purpose of your first research study will be to describe something. However, although descriptive research may appear to be less demanding than other types of research, this is often far from the case.

A census, such as the one conducted during 2001 in South Africa and that cost about 632 million rand (Pile, 2001) is a form of descriptive research. Here the purpose was to count and describe the characteristics of an entire population. By using descriptive methods we try to understand the way things are; while by using experimental methods we try to understand the way things could be if we changed and manipulated them.

There are two goals in defining, explaining phenomena such as and predicting behaviour:

- FIRSTLY, the goal of research is to explain phenomena such as human behaviour in the business and administrative sciences by indicating how variables (see Section 2.2) are related to one another and in what manner one variable affects another.

Example

- Research on crime is descriptive when it defines the kind of crime, when, where, by who, and how often it is committed. However, we would also want to explain why the crime rate is higher in Gauteng than in the Northern Province.
- Learning theory provides an explanation for the incidence of management style among trainee supervisors. By describing the relationship between two variables, we are actually defining the one variable in terms of the other. In RESEARCH EXAMPLE II (page 14), we defined the management style of trainee supervisors in terms of the management styles of role models.

- SECONDLY, the possibility of explaining and predicting human behaviour may enable us to change, or control it. (This, however, is not the same as prediction studies – see Section 5.4.4.)

Example

- On the basis of our findings we would like to predict what kind of crime will determine decisions by the police. This could include, for example, why drug-sniffing dogs will be deployed in

Gauteng where there is a problem with drug smuggling, but power vehicles, like 4x4 bakkies, will be bought to patrol the green hills in KwaZulu-Natal where there may be a problem with weapon smuggling.

- In RESEARCH EXAMPLE II (page 14), senior supervisors could be trained not to act in an iron-fisted manner. This would in turn prevent trainee supervisors from emulating or copying such a management style.

Activity 2.2

Read Case Study A; Case Study B; Case Study C, Case Study D and Case Study F in Appendix D on page 273.

Question

Describe the investigation in each case study in terms of whether it is a *descriptive, explanatory* or *predictive study*. Briefly explain your answers.

Answer

CASE STUDY A is a *descriptive study* because one variable, "attitudes towards AIDS", is defined in terms of the other variables, "knowledge of AIDS" and "attitudes towards prostitution". The purpose of the study was only to describe the phenomenon "attitudes towards AIDS" in the sample, indicating the state of affairs amongst the medical staff of that hospital at that moment.

CASE STUDY B is an *explanatory study* because, on the basis of the results of the investigation, the researcher hopes to explain why implementing the role induction procedure will help goldsmith apprentices to experience supervision as less stressful and so reduce their period of adaptation.

CASE STUDY C is a *predictive study* because the researcher wishes, on the basis of the (expected positive) results of the investigation, to predict that there will be a significant increase in the knowledge of management principles of all current first-line supervisors (as well as other newcomers) who will attend the training course.

CASE STUDY D is a *descriptive study* because speech quality is defined in terms of preparation time and anxiety. It is a description of the relationship between the variables at that time between the group of technikon students without trying to explain it.

CASE STUDY F entails a *descriptive study*, because the researcher only wants to establish whether or not a difference already exists between entrepreneurs and managers in terms of their innovative problem-solving styles. (The question "why" there may be a difference is not addressed by the study and therefore it is not an exploratory or predictive study.)

2.2.3 **The purpose of other forms of research** (See Chapter 8)

2.2.3.1 **Historical research (Records)**

The first step in historical research is the problem statement. This includes explanations or interpretations which are not tested as research hypotheses but may rather be described as the CENTRAL THESIS or MAIN THEME of such a study.

The CENTRAL THESIS or MAIN THEME of this type of research concerns the investigation of specific events that have taken place with the purpose of establishing a set of propositions about it and postulating that the phenomena may be occurring universally.

Note

Historical research (as part of analytical research) is not concerned so much with collecting new information, as with finding new explanations for, or interpretations of, existing information.

In historical research, the sources that have recorded past happenings or preserved them in some or other way are located and evaluated. The evaluated sources are then synthesised and interpreted with a view to suggesting causal explanations (Section 5.2.2) for events or practices. By "past" we do not mean only the distant past, but also the *more recent past as in the case of corporate law.*

Example

We cite Rhoodie's (1986) explanatory study (which may be classified as analytic research) of white-black conflict and the development of revolutionary movements in South Africa in terms of Galtung's theory about revolutionary aggression.

Galtung identifies eight social and political factors which, in markedly stratified societies, give rise to revolutionary movements. According to him, the impetus for revolution is relative deprivation that is introduced into a social system when all members of a particular stratum or segment of the population do not occupy either the top or the bottom in respect of all the various criteria of ranking (for example, income, educational level, political power, and so on.).

During the eighties, Rhoodie came to the conclusion that the South African situation met these conditions and that apartheid society was practically and structurally programmed for revolution.

2.2.3.2 Case study research

We have seen that hypothesis-testing research deals with the general and the regular. In CASE STUDIES (see Section 8.4.1) the opposite happens and research is directed at understanding the uniqueness and idiosyncrasy of a particular case in all its complexity. Usually its objective is to investigate the dynamics of some single bounded system, typically of a social nature, such as a family, group, community, participants in a project, practice (for example, the institution and testing of drugs).

2.2.3.3 Action research

ACTION RESEARCH (Section 8.4.4) is conducted with a view to finding a solution for a particular practical problem situation in a specific, applied setting. It therefore corresponds to case study research (see Section 8.4.1) in the sense that the case in question refers to a problem situation. Unlike the typical case study, however, it is not directed simply at describing the case involved, but also at searching for a solution (to the problem situation).

Example

Lazarus (1985) helped develop and evaluate an alternative educational programme supported by a church community organisation and in which pupils who had left the traditional school set-up ("Bantu education system") in the early eighties, participated.

Note

The purpose of ACTION RESEARCH *is* not *to test or develop a theory, but rather to find a solution to a practical problem.*

Thus there is no theory from which one or more hypotheses (see Section 2.3) have been inferred and which are to be subjected to empirical research and testing (see Section 2.4). A theory may indeed exist that suggests particular solutions for the problem situation, but the purpose of action research is not to test such a theory, but to provide a solution to a problem.

Note

APPLIED RESEARCH in industry has several features that distinguish it from basic research at a university:

- *FIRSTLY, the need for research in industry develops because of organisational problems. Problems arise, for example, with excessive absence of employees, staff turnover and job dissatisfaction, and this could be the beginning of a research study that is designed to reduce the seriousness of the problems. Research in industry is virtually never used simply "to test a theory" or to satisfy intellectual curiosity.*

- SECONDLY, *the goal of research in industry is to improve the effectiveness of an organisation. This usually means an increase in profitability. For example, research is used to determine consumers' preferences regarding new products and services, to identify methods of reducing waste material, or to utilise human talent better in an organisation.*
- THIRDLY, *the participants in research in industry are typically employees or job applicants.*
- FOURTHLY, *if the results of research in industry are positive and usable, the research unit of the organisation where the research is done will attempt to have the conclusions of the study accepted and implemented by the rest of the organisation.* FOR EXAMPLE, *if it is found that a brief, realistic overview of the organisation is given to job applicants for administrative posts, and this leads to reduced staff turnover, the researchers will try to convince the rest of the organisation to use such procedures during the recruitment of new employees in other divisions. If the results are negative, the organisation will attempt to use secondary, but valuable, ideas obtained from the study.*

2.3 Research hypotheses

We will have to test hypotheses (of which some are derived from THEORY) during the research process.

Example

THEORY: People will try to balance their input (work) and their output (payments). Employees will do only as much work as they think is justified for the remuneration they receive.

According to this theory, we can therefore predict that a worker who feels that he or she is underpaid according to a piecework system (for example, stitching the shirt collar in a shirt manufacturing factory), will increase the quality of each item produced, but will reduce the quantity of items produced.

The purpose of this research is to test whether a prediction (hypothesis) such as this holds true.

Note

We will address the following types of hypotheses in this book:

- *Research hypothesis (Sections 2.3; 5.2.2.3 6.3.2.3 – third variable problem; 9.3.1)*
- *Rival hypothesis (Sections 2.3; 5.2.2.3; 6.3.2.3 – third variable problem, 9.3.2.1)*
- *Statistical hypothesis (Section 9.3.1)*
- *Counter hypothesis (Section 9.3.1)*
- *Null hypothesis (Section 9.3.1)*
- *Alternative hypothesis (Section 9.3.1).*

2.3.1 Formulating the research hypothesis

Where possible, we should translate the research problem (see Section 2.2) into a research hypothesis that states:

- a relationship
- between two or more variables
- in one (or more) population(s) (see Chapter 4).

We can use the following approach to develop a hypothesis:

- Discuss with experts the problem, its origin and the objectives in seeking a solution (see Section 8.4.3).
- Examine data and records concerning the problem (this is called SECONDARY DATA COLLECTION) for possible trends and clues (see Section 3.3.2 and 8.2.2.1).
- Review similar studies (this is called LITERATURE REVIEW – see Chapter 3).
- Interview interested parties and individuals on a limited scale to get greater insight into the practical aspects of the problem (see Section 7.7.4.5).

Although a research hypothesis is normally formulated in accordance with an implication which is deduced from a theory, a COUNTER HYPOTHESIS, which amounts to the opposite of the research hypothesis, is usually subjected to testing.

Example

In RESEARCH EXAMPLE II (page 14), the counter hypothesis will be that there is no difference in management style between trainee supervisors who observed an iron-fisted management style role model and trainee supervisors who observed an approachable management style role model.

If we investigate an implication of some or other theory (see Section 2.2.1.3), we DEDUCTIVELY INFER the research hypothesis from the theory (see Section 2.4 – Figure 2.5).

To INFER DEDUCTIVELY means to begin with one (or more) statement(s) that are accepted as true and that may be used to conclude one logical true statement (from the broad and general to the specific). We may say that deduction means "testing theory" and has mainly to do with quantitative research (see Section 1.3).

Example

Deductive reasoning:

- All supervisors have an iron-fisted management style.
- All trainee supervisors are supervisors.
- All trainee supervisors have an iron-fisted management style.

Example

In RESEARCH EXAMPLE II (page 14), the research hypothesis may read as follows:

Trainee supervisors who are exposed to specific forms of role model management styles that go unpunished will imitate this behaviour in corresponding situations.

Furthermore, different hypotheses may usually be based on different aspects or implications of the same theory. In fact, a theory may be regarded as a collection of such different hypotheses.

Note

In the case of EXPLORATORY RESEARCH (Section 2.2 and Note in Section 2.2.2), that is, research in a relatively new area that lacks established theories or research findings, specific research hypotheses may not be feasible. In such instances a question about the relationship between variables may be posed.

If we want to investigate the research problem or question in the most economical manner, we must formulate it in the form of a research hypothesis that we can test on the basis of observable data, and reject, if necessary. To serve this purpose, we should formalise the research hypothesis in terms of OPERATIONALISED CONSTRUCTS (see also Section 2.2.1.3).

2.3.2 Formalising the research hypothesis in terms of operationalised constructs

An OPERATIONALISED CONSTRUCT represents an attempt to get a grip on an abstract construct by means of concrete variables.

Note

The meaning of concepts such as the freedom of the individual, indoctrination, affirmative action, and sexual harassment in the workplace, cannot be as readily defined as, say, the mass of an object – 80 kg.

The definition (conceptual or operational) of constructs and their relationships thus precedes their empirical testing. Consequently, CONCEPTUAL ANALYSIS comes into play before data are collected (Chapters 7 and 8) to test research hypotheses. It plays a role in the definition of constructs and in the deductive inference of hypotheses from a theory about such constructs.

CONCEPTUAL ANALYSIS involves the careful analysis of the constructs (concepts) and their relationships (as postulated by a theory). It requires the implications of these constructs to be clearly spelled out, possible inconsistencies between their definitions to be pointed out and modifications to them to be proposed.

We have to define such constructs in terms of concrete, observable behaviour or the products of human behaviour, so that others may understand exactly what we mean by such a definition. In this kind of definition, known as an OPERATIONAL DEFINITION, the procedures required for bringing about the construct are explicitly described.

Example

In RESEARCH EXAMPLE II (page 14), the exact manner in which the role model supervisors were to act to generate a management style in the trainees was clearly specified.

In a sense we can say that the operational definition of a food dish is its recipe. In other words, the construct validity (see Section 7.4.1) of the independent variable (Section 2.2) refers to the degree to which the independent variable as implemented represents the independent variable as conceptualised.

The first step we have to take to operationalise the independent variable is *to carefully define it in the light of the theory* in which it appears. This definition should provide clear guidelines about the concrete procedures and manipulations for producing/generating/developing the independent variable (see Section 2.2). However, we must be careful that we do not come up with an operational definition that bears little relation to the conceptual variable that it was supposed to create.

Usually we should first investigate how the independent variable has been generated in previous research (see Chapter 3) and consider whether such procedures will be adequate for operationalising the independent variable (see Section 6.3.3) in the proposed research project (see Chapter 11).

Often the experimental manipulations required for creating a treatment factor (see Section 5.2) are dictated to some degree by the RESEARCH HYPOTHESIS.

If the RESEARCH HYPOTHESIS states that one method for increasing achievement motivation is more effective than another, these two methods are already defined to a greater or lesser degree. An operational definition of these methods will then require the researcher to describe the materials and procedures for their application clearly. It is often difficult to operationalise independent variables, especially those in the social sciences.

Example

In RESEARCH EXAMPLE II (page 14), an iron-fisted role model management style was created by having a supervisor handle a subordinate in a verbally rough manner. The subordinate frustrated the trainee supervisors by calling them from their tea-break.

Operational definitions do not guarantee accuracy or "truth", but enable researchers to communicate with one another. By always clearly defining constructs operationally, other researchers are in a position to evaluate the appropriateness of these definitions. Moreover, such definitions enable them to repeat the procedures contained in such definitions to check whether they obtain comparable results. This requirement again focuses attention on the principle of public scrutiny in the scientific expansion of knowledge that we have mentioned (see Section 1.2.2.3).

The procedure and components involved in testing an implication of a theory in this manner may be represented diagrammatically as in Figure 2.3.

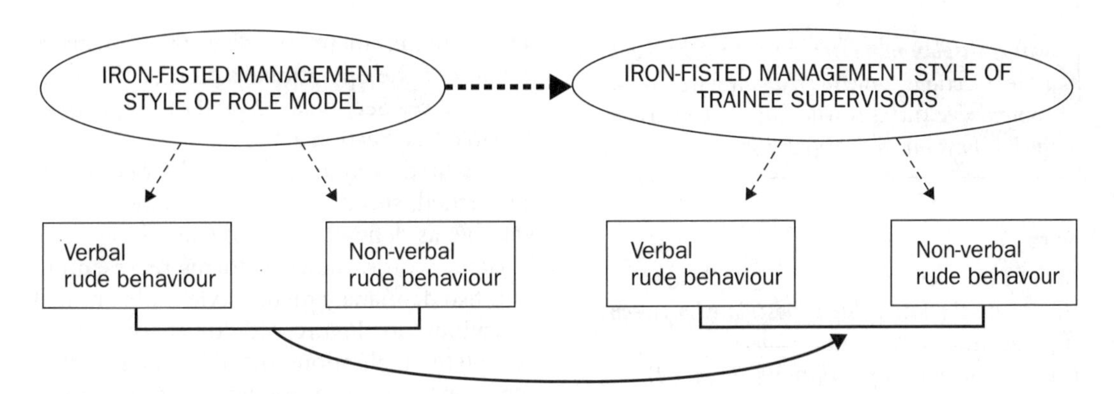

Figure 2.3 Testing the relationship between construct in terms of observable variables (Adapted from Huysamen [1994, p. 12].)

The cigar forms in Figure 2.3 represent CONSTRUCTS, such as "iron-fisted management style of role model" and "iron-fisted management style of trainee supervisors", while the rectangles symbolise indicators of these constructs. (Obviously, we can make the theory more complex by including constructs such as hereditary rude behaviour and socio-economic status.)

The dark, dotted line between the two constructs represents a constitutive definition, that is, a definition of management style displayed by trainee supervisors in terms of exposure to a role model's iron-fisted management style. Because this dotted line also constitutes a one-directional arrow, it implies a causal (instead of merely a correlational) relationship.

The light, dotted lines symbolise operational definitions. For example, in RESEARCH EXAMPLE II (page 14), a role model's "iron-fisted management style" is defined operationally in terms of verbal behaviour, such as uttering, "I will kick you" and "I will punch you in the nose".

The uninterrupted one-directional arrow between the rectangles at the bottom of Figure 2.3 (denoting the four observable variables) represents the relationship posed by the research hypothesis.

Thus, in practice, an implication from a theory or any research problem, which in Figure 2.3 is symbolised by the dark, dotted one-directional arrow at the top, is investigated by means of a RESEARCH HYPOTHESIS.

A RESEARCH HYPOTHESIS is a positive statement about the relationship between operationalised variables and is symbolised by the uninterrupted one-directional arrow at the bottom of Figure 2.3.

In a sense, the operational definitions (the light, dotted arrows in Figure 2.3) also represent hypotheses that may be investigated (in what is known as PSYCHOMETRIC RESEARCH), but typically the operational definitions are accepted as valid. If the results obtained support the research hypothesis, both the constitutive definition (the dark dotted-line arrow) and the operational definitions (light dotted lines) are provisionally confirmed.

Example

In RESEARCH EXAMPLE II (page 14), the research hypothesis may be formulated as follows:

Trainee supervisors who watch supervisors exhibiting an iron-fisted management style behaviour towards a subordinate, will after-

wards display more iron-fisted management style reactions towards subordinates than comparable trainees who have not watched such behaviour in the supervisor.

Note

In this example:
(i) a causal relationship is postulated between
(ii) operationally defined variables
(iii) in an identified population (Chapter 4).

As far as (ii) is concerned, the researchers working for the company described exactly how the role model should behave to give the appearance of iron-fisted management style behaviour and how the management styles of the trainee supervisors should be measured (RESEARCH EXAMPLE II, page 14).

2.3.3 The construct validity of the operationalisation of the independent variable and of the measurement of the dependent variable

Construct validity requirements mean that we do not wish merely to interpret a finding as applicable only to the x embodied in our dependent variable, and the y that we have measured, but that it should be applicable to X and Y, the constructs thought to underlie x and y.

Example

If the greater number of reactions (among the group that watched rude behaviour in RESEARCH EXAMPLE II – page 14), considered to be indices of iron-fisted management style, is to be attributed to the exposure to the simulated iron-fisted role model management style, we would like to interpret this finding as meaning that an iron-fisted role model management style promotes iron-fisted management style behaviour among trainee supervisors.

These requirements involve the construct validity of the operationalisation of the independent (see Section 6.3.3) and the dependent variable (see Section 7.4).

It is firstly required that x, the operations performed, should create X, the independent variable as defined (and not something else). In other words, the cigar forms representing iron-fisted management style role model behaviour in Figure 2.3 must provide a complete realisation of the square that represents the corresponding construct (iron-fistedness).

Example

In RESEARCH EXAMPLE II (page 14), if the trainee supervisors were to view the actions of the role model as being comical rather than iron-fisted, it would mean that the operationalisation of the independent variable did not bring about the intended level of the independent variable (that is, iron-fisted role model management style).

The *construct validity* of the operationalisation of the independent variable would then be unsatisfactory. This requirement is discussed further in Section 6.3.3.

By the same token, the square box on the right-hand side at the bottom of Figure 2.3 should represent the corresponding cigar on the right-hand side at the top. If y, the trainees' reactions that were recorded, did not reflect Y (iron-fistedness) but, say, excitement, it would mean that what was measured represented a different variable than the construct in which we were interested.

Note

This requirement is known as the construct validity of the measurement of the dependent variable and we will discuss it further in Section 7.1.1.

Activity 2.3

Read the following problem statement and answer the questions. Compare your answers with the given answers.

Problem statement

The manager of TABOK Company observes that the morale of her employees is low. She thinks that if the working conditions, the pay scales, and the leave benefits of the employees are improved, their morale will also improve. She doubts, however, that increasing the pay scales is going to raise the morale of all employees. Her guess is that those who have good side incomes (by doing other work in their own time) will not be motivated by higher pay.

Questions

1 State the problem definition of the researcher for the situation.
2 Develop FOUR different research hypotheses for the situation.

Answers

1 Will an improvement of the working conditions, pay scales and leave benefits improve the morale of all employees?
2 Combinations of these given research hypotheses are correct.
   a) When the working conditions improve, the morale of all employees will improve.
   b) Better leave benefits will improve the morale of all employees.
   c) An improvement of the working conditions and leave benefits will improve the morale of all employees.
   d) The morale of employees who do not have good side incomes will improve if their pay scales (and working conditions and leave benefits) improve.

Activity 2.4

Read Case Study A; Case Study B; Case Study C; Case Study D; Case Study E and Case Study F in Appendix D on page 276.

Questions

In your own words, formulate the research hypothesis (hypotheses) or research question(s) in each case study.

Answers

CASE STUDY A: Amongst a group of medical staff members at a specific hospital, there is a high correlation between their attitudes towards AIDS, their knowledge of AIDS, and their attitudes towards prostitution.

CASE STUDY B: Participation by goldsmith apprentices in a role induction procedure causes them to experience supervision more positively than before participation.

CASE STUDY C: The knowledge of management principles of first-line supervisors at a South African agricultural corporation will be significantly more after attending a training course than before, while there is no difference in the pre- and post-measurement of the knowledge of management principles of first-line supervisors who did not attend the course.

CASE STUDY D: There is a significantly high positive relation/correlation between the speech quality and the total preparation time of a group of technikon speech-making students at a technikon.

AND

There is a significantly high negative relation/correlation between the speech quality and the speech anxiety of a group of speech-making students at a technikon.

CASE STUDY E: Bankrupt small businesses have exceeded their bank overdraft limits with significantly greater amounts per month and experienced more cash flow problems than non-bankrupt small businesses during the past two years.

CASE STUDY F: Entrepreneurs will be significantly more innovative in their problem-solving style (obtain a significantly higher mean score on the KAI scale) than managers of big businesses.

2.4 The cyclic progress of the scientific expansion of knowledge

We have already referred to the important role that testing HYPOTHESES deduced from theories (see Section 2.3) plays in the scientific expansion of knowledge.

We have defined a THEORY as a general statement (see Section 2.1 & 2.2.1.3). From a satisfactory theory, which is supposed to apply to a POPULATION of individuals under a universe of circumstances (see Section 2.2.1.3), we can always DEDUCTIVELY infer conclusions or hypotheses as to what should be observed in certain circumstances (see Section 2.3.1). To derive an implication deductively from a theory, means to formulate a statement that must be valid if the theory is valid. The validity of the theory is then examined indirectly by testing whether these hypotheses hold good.

Example

In RESEARCH EXAMPLE II (page 14), this deductive order of thought (see Section 2.3.1) was approximately as follows:

Company trainee supervisor workers are inclined to imitate the behaviour of role models.

Therefore trainees who have been exposed to specific management styles (for example, pointing a finger at a subordinate) in their role models, will more often display similar iron-fisted management style behaviour when compared to trainees who observed an approachable management style in their role models.

A more complete rendering of the deductive thinking (see Section 2.3.1) involved would be as follows:

- Trainee supervisors are inclined to imitate the behaviour of their role models.
- Trainee supervisors are more inclined to imitate the behaviour of role models of their own sex than the behaviour of role models of the opposite sex.
- Iron-fisted management style is a highly masculine-typed behaviour.

Therefore, males will be more inclined than females to imitate iron-fisted management style behaviour and this tendency will be most pronounced in those who are exposed to an iron-fisted management style male role model.

Often the information that is collected in terms of a research design (see Chapter 5), eliminates beforehand any counter hypotheses ascribing the differences to factors other than those implied by the theory.

Example

In the research design in RESEARCH EXAMPLE II (page 14), we have taken the counter hypothesis (that the trainee supervisors who observed an iron-fisted role model management style were probably more inclined to show iron-fisted management style behaviour than those in the other group) into account from the very start.

Note

There is always the possibility that some or other smart guy may come up with other counter hypotheses or explanations (called rival hypotheses) that will explain our obtained results equally well, if not better. Although it is not possible to prove that a theory is correct, it may be falsified by failing to refute counter hypotheses. According to this FALSIFICATION PRINCIPLE, our confidence in a theory grows to the extent that implications and hypotheses in conflict with the theory are eliminated by research.

Our present confidence in the tenability of a theory is limited insofar as it has survived counter hypotheses suggesting alternative explanations for the obtained results, and no new ones are in sight.

If support is found for the counter hypotheses, we should consider possibly modifying the original theory. Next, hypotheses that are deduced from such a modified theory must be subjected to empirical testing afresh.

In Section 2.3 we assumed that a specific theory (for example, balance theory) must be examined. By starting with such a theory and by subjecting research hypotheses that have been deduced from it to testing, we are proceeding deductively (from the broad and general to the specific – see Section 2.3.1).

The explanation of the process of testing one or other implication of a theory represents one segment in the scientific expansion of knowledge. Often, however, we enter an area about which little knowledge and insight yet exist (for example, the issue of cloning mammals).

- In such circumstances, researchers should first observe and systematically describe the phenomenon being studied and attempt gradually to unravel relationships and patterns in order to eventually formulate a theory. In this connection, sociologists refer to *grounded theories*.
- Researchers into such areas proceed INDUCTIVELY, which means that they begin with an individual case or cases and then proceed to a general theory. These researchers are also more inclined to study an individual case carefully (also known as *ideographic research*) rather than study the average tendencies of large groups (as is the case in *nomothetic research*).

The INDUCTIVE PROCESS means to begin with an individual case or cases and then proceed to a general theory (in order to generalise to all cases based on the conclusions reached from observing one or more cases). We may say that induction has to do with building theory and the collection of qualitative data (see Section 1.3).

Example

Inductive reasoning:
- Trainee supervisor 1 (was observed to) have an iron-fisted management style.
- Trainee supervisor 2 (was observed to) have an iron-fisted management style.
- Trainee supervisor 3 (was observed to) have an iron-fisted management style.
- *All* trainee supervisors (was observed to) have an iron-fisted management style.

The inductive approach is concerned with generating theories and hypotheses on the basis of studying specific cases, the deductive course of action seeks to test hypotheses in terms of the data obtained. This process is illustrated in Figure 2.4.

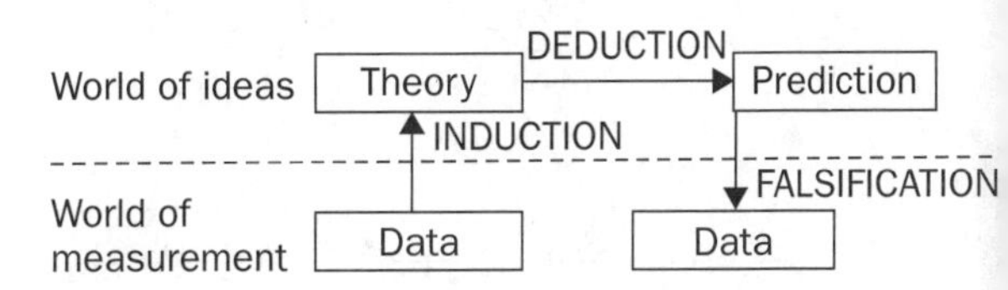

Figure 2.4 The three main steps in the research process

According to Figure 2.4, we should use facts and observations during induction to make a theoretical statement that explains the observations and facts. Through deduction, we can determine whether such a theory is a reliable version of reality. A prediction of a theory is made through logic to determine what can be expected in certain circumstances and specific conditions. The validity of the prediction is then determined through falsification – and the suitability of the basic theory is determined. This is done by collecting new data and checking whether the prediction(s) is/are thereby substantiated. If the prediction(s) is/are not supported, and it is assumed that the research methods and deductive logic are correct, we can assume that the theory on which the prediction was based must be adapted or changed. The process may be depicted in Figure 2.5.

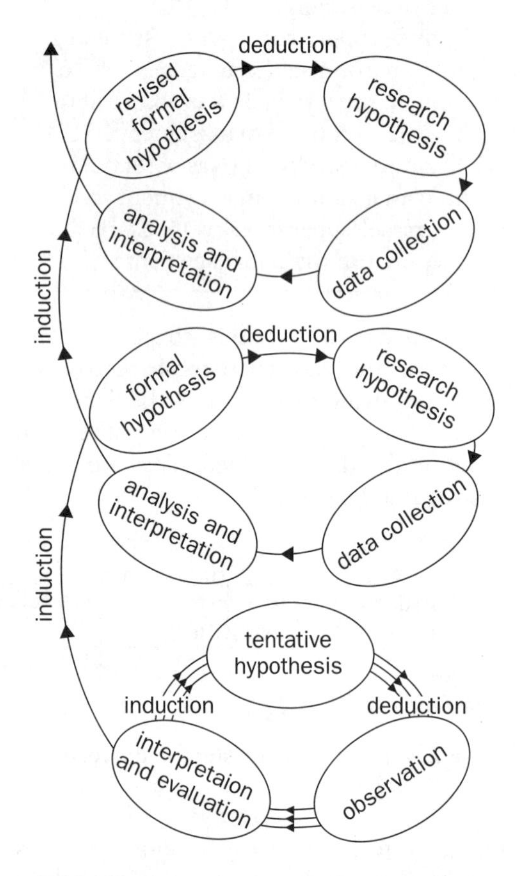

Figure 2.5 A sequence of qualitative and quantitative research cycles (Huysamen, 1997)

Self-evaluation questions

(Some answers appear in Appendix B on page 273.)

2.1 Provide some alternative explanations for the conclusion to which the researcher travelling through Gauteng arrived (see Chapter 1 – Self-evaluation questions 1.1 on page 6).

2.2 A few years ago, the principal of a South African university pointed out that the mean number of students per thousand of the population was 29,2 for whites; 19,8 for Asians; 4,7 for coloureds; and 2,2 for blacks in South Africa as compared to 7,5 in the United Kingdom and 11 in Australia.

On the basis of these figures he came to the conclusion that the whites in South Africa either must be much more intelligent than the citizens of other countries, or that they are occupying very favourable positions. Point out possible alternative explanations for the above statistics.

2.3 Identify and list the (a) the hypothesis, (b) the independent variable and (c) the dependent variable in RESEARCH EXAMPLE II (page 14).

2.4 A researcher sent false application forms of (fictitious) prospective students who differed in terms of sex, race and ability to each of 12 randomly assigned groups of 20 undergraduate universities. (Some applicants were male, white and highly intelligent, others were female, white and highly intelligent, and so on.) If an "applicant" was accepted with encouragement, it was scored 5; if he or she was merely accepted, it was scored 4; and so on down to those who were unsuccessful and obtained a score of 1.

Identify and list (a) the independent variables, and (b) the dependent variable.

Summary

A variable is the name for a characteristic of something (for example, the AGE of people, the PROFIT of a business in rands, the NUMBER of criminals convicted) that may differ from one thing to the next (called "unit of analysis" – see Chapter 4). One employee may be 18 years of age and the next employee that we study may be 47 years of age. Therefore, the variable "AGE" can be presented by various numbers.

Research hypotheses are statements about the relationship between variables. Research hypotheses arise from theory and/or findings from earlier research, from practical problems, or from accidental observation (for example, that married older females are more efficient secretaries than any other group of secretaries). A research hypothesis is similar to an expressed expectation of what the answer/solution/explanation for a problem is.

Multiple choice and true/false questions

Only *one* of the answers for each question is correct. Identify and mark the correct one. (Answers appear in Appendix E on page 285.)

2.1 Variables are empirical whereas concepts are abstract.
True False

2.2 Which of the following are variables?
a) female, Jewish, 21 years old
b) plumber, professor, dentist
c) occupation, age, type of risk
d) dishonest, violent, conservative.

2.3 The independent variable must occur later in time than the dependent variable.
True False

2.4 An independent variable is a
a) theoretical concept
b) variable influencing other variables
c) variable influenced by other variables
d) set of attributes.

2.5 The factors that a researcher controls (or manipulates) to establish their effect are called the
a) potential variables
b) dependent variables
c) intervening variables
d) independent variables.

2.6 A research report was entitled "Determinants of electrical power". The dependent variable was
a) determinants
b) electrical power
c) either (a) or (b), depending on the researcher's theory
d) there is no dependent variable.

2.7 If a researcher wanted to know why there was a noticeable increase in the number of electrical power failures in the Northern Cape during 1999, the researcher would design a(n)
a) descriptive study
b) explanatory study
c) panel study
d) exploratory study.

2.8 If a researcher makes systematic observations of a single dependent variable in circumstances at one point in time, it may be described as a scientific method of
a) explanation
b) prediction
c) exploration
d) description.

2.9 Scientific inquiry is a process involving an alternation of deduction and induction.
True False

2.10 In deduction we start from observed data and develop a generalisation that explains the relationship between the observed concepts.
True False

3 Literature review

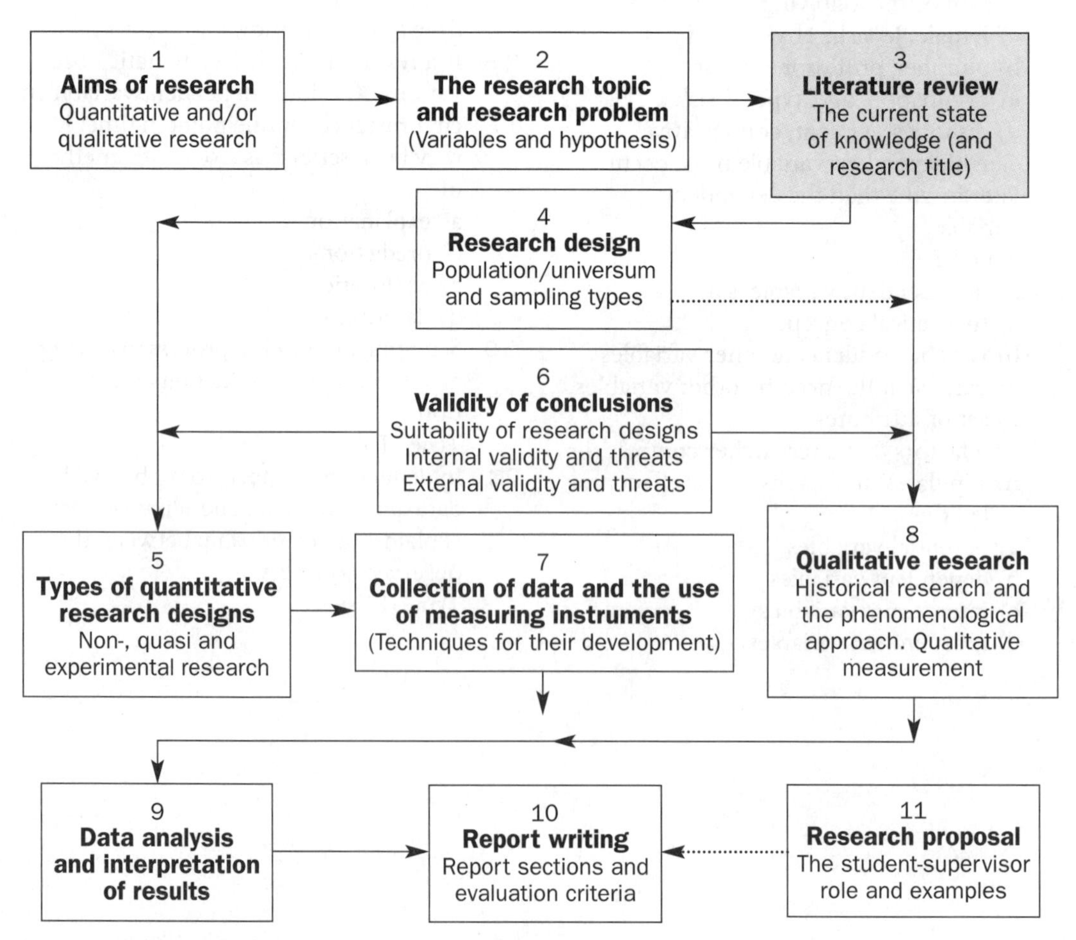

Figure 3.1 The research process and the outline of chapters in this book

Learning Outcomes

After studying this chapter, you should be able to:

1. use the necessary library facilities
2. do a literature search on a chosen topic
3. compile a literature review and reference system
4. advise a novice on the steps to be followed in preparing to write a review of literature relevant to a specific topic.

3.1 Introduction

To a great extent, in this chapter we focus on a few themes that we should attend to before we may start a particular project in earnest; whether for degree purposes or as an integral part of our daily activities.

The first concrete step in the scientific research process is the formulation, however incomplete or tentative, of the problem which should be investigated (see Section 2.2). Until we know what the problem is, we cannot begin to investigate it systematically. Consequently, finding a topic for a dissertation or thesis often represents one of the most frustrating problems (if not the most frustrating) for graduate students.

In Section 2.2.1, we briefly discussed theories, practical problems and previous research as sources of research problems. As far as the latter is concerned, we have pointed out that in discussing their findings (in their research reports), previous researchers may have suggested ways of eliminating inconsistencies between their findings and those of other studies or a theory. With this in mind, the appropriate starting-point for prospective graduate students in their search for a topic is probably to go through professional journals (see Literature Sources on page 42) to check what research has already been done and what still needs to be done.

We usually begin the literature review section by reviewing the literature dealing with our chosen topic. This will set the scene for a clear formulation of the research problem (research hypothesis or research question). The comprehensiveness of the literature review again depends on the kind of research report. Dissertations and theses require a more extensive review than a journal article in which only previous research directly related to the proposed research is referred to. If a literature survey on a particular topic has already been published in a review article, it may even be sufficient to reflect only its most relevant main points in a journal article.

3.2 Literature searches

3.2.1 Previous research

We have already stressed that prospective researchers should acquaint themselves with previous research (see Section 2.2.1.2) on a particular topic before they start planning research on it. Obviously, it will be of little use to research a topic on which more or less general consensus has been reached (unless, of course, the researcher intends to provide a new perspective on it).

By compiling a review of research findings on a particular topic that have already been published, researchers may become aware of inconsistencies and gaps that may justify further research. Such a review enables researchers to indicate exactly where their proposed research fits in. Considered on its own, someone's research may elicit little interest. However, if its relation to the body of knowledge is evident, it achieves greater importance and may even persuade other researchers to also do research on the particular topic.

3.2.2 Tracing and recording relevant literature

The first step to take in tracing relevant literature on a particular topic, is to list the headings or key words under which it may be classified in a library catalogue or in a computer retrieval system. Nowadays university libraries usually have staff available to assist researchers in conducting a computer search for references on relevant research on the basis of such a list of key words. If such key words are too specific, relevant references may possibly be excluded; if they are too general, you may be swamped by irrelevant references.

Until such time as the topic is delineated more clearly, it may be worthwhile for you to read too widely rather than too narrowly. You should preferably summarise any article, book, dissertation or other source that has a bearing on the topic and that may possibly be included in the literature survey. Pay particular attention to the most important conclusions and implications. It is not helpful to merely keep photocopies of these sources, because such a practice would require of you to re-read the same source repeatedly in order to determine its relevancy.

Not only should you summarise these sources, but also indicate any shortcomings in the reported research. Summarise each separate article or any other source of information on a separate index card (or as separate files in a directory on your computer) and indicate its complete reference as it should appear in the list of references (see Section 10.2.9). Remember to include page numbers if material is directly quoted. By following this approach, you can change the order of the index cards quite easily, for example, to group together those dealing with the same aspect. When you reach the stage where you must compile the list of references, you can readily rearrange the cards in alphabetical order. Of course, all these tasks become much easier if you have access to a personal computer.

Note

Libraries are no longer the only source of information. The development of the Internet and electronic publishing have had an enormous impact on research supervision, peer review of publications and general communications capabilities, and have changed the way researchers work.

Information from the Internet are considered less reliable than that of printed sources because web pages can be updated and changed on a daily basis. A printed hard copy of an Internet source should therefore be included with your research paper as an appendix. This will ensure that factual information used cannot later be contested.

Example

Researchers Networking Database is published with the Nexus Database System. It contains biographical profiles of individual researchers in South Africa, including their fields of interest and areas of specialisation in the social sciences and the humanities. If you have access to the Internet, visit the following websites. This will provide you with a list of expertise, and also let you view the TALK CONFERENCE database:

http: // www.hsrc.ac.za / nexus.html
EUROPEAN MONETARY *issues:*
www. cfp-pec.gc.ca / english / emu.htm
www.europe.ibm.com / euro / european_monetary_union_consultancy_bw.html

3.2.3 Planning the literature search

It is important to budget sufficient time for literature searches. Often some sources which you believe to be indispensable for an intended review will have to be ordered by interlibrary loan from another city or even from abroad. Nowadays, these could be faxed but the accompanying costs may prevent this from being done extensively. However, time is not only required to obtain and study the various sources, but also to reflect on them and to synthesise and integrate them into a meaningful entity. In Chapters 10 and 11 we make a few comments on how to write up literature surveys.

It is the researcher's responsibility to keep abreast of research reported on his or her topic up to at least the time that the research report is concluded. This practice will prevent the research from becoming outdated or irrelevant the moment it is published. In this sense, the literature search on a topic is a never-ending process.

3.3 Compiling a literature review

3.3.1 Integrating the studies

The literature review should not consist of a mere compilation of separate, isolated summaries of the individual studies of previous researchers. You should clearly show how these studies relate to one another and how the proposed research ties in with them. For example, group together those that are in agreement and refer to this agreement by using words like "similarly" when moving from the one to the next.

The most glaring blunder in this regard is to present the opinions or findings of different authors, who basically are in agreement but who have expressed themselves in different ways, as different contributions. If you cite contradictory findings, point out this discrepancy – even if you only do this by means of phrases such as "on the other hand" or "by contrast".

3.3.2 Primary and secondary sources

In Section 8.2.2.1 we will refer to the dangers associated with the excessive use of secondary sources. The most extreme example occurs when first-year textbooks or even explanatory dictionaries are consulted for the purpose of discussing concepts and theories. You should bear in mind that the author of a secondary source may be presenting the original source in such a manner that it gives credence to his or her particular biases. Doctoral students, especially, who are expected to thoroughly acquaint themselves with the background and the tiresome development of the theories underlying their research, should consult original sources (primary sources) as far as possible.

In this connection, let us distinguish between PRIMARY and SECONDARY SOURCES.

A PRIMARY SOURCE is the written or oral account of a direct witness of, or a participant in, an event, or an audiotape, videotape or photographic recording of it. It even may consist of household garbage (for example, in a study of the patterns of food consumption). This would then represent first-hand evidence of what happened.

Example

Hansard (the written report of what was said in parliament by politicians) may be regarded as a primary (documentary) source of events in parliament.

A SECONDARY SOURCE provides second-hand information about events. Such a source has not witnessed the events himself or herself, but has obtained the information either from someone else who did experience the event or who has himself or herself obtained the information from a person who had indeed experienced it first-hand.

Example

Whereas *Hansard* may serve as a primary source of parliamentary proceedings, newspaper reports of these proceedings based on interviews with members of parliament (who were indeed present) represent a secondary source.

The further the present source is removed from the primary source, the greater the possibility that biases and other inaccuracies have crept into the report about what happened originally.

The literature review also represents historical research (Section 2.2.3.1 and 8.2), and the excessive use of secondary sources in such reviews is equally undesirable, if not dangerous.

3.3.3 Quotations

With the exception of direct quotations, the entire research report should be presented in the author's own words, that is, without paraphrasing or patching together pieces from other sources.

Use direct quotations sparingly as they are actually only permitted when something is expressed so eloquently or in such an original way that you feel something will be lost in the process of reformulating it.

Here are *general guidelines* for using quotes in research reports:

- Incorporate quotations of up to (and not longer than) about 30 words into the text.
- Enclose the quoted material in double quotation marks.

> **Example**
>
> A quotation from Bem (1986, p. 430) relating to Section 10.1, likens the findings of a report to a jewel which is being cut and polished to get the very best out of it:
>
> *"Good report writing is largely a matter of good judgement; despite the standardized format, it is not a mechanical process."*

- Indent longer quotations as an independent block. This means the script should start about four spaces from the left of the page border, *without any quotation* marks.

> **Example**
>
> Kerlinger (1986, p. 11) eloquently expresses the effect of the principle of public scrutiny on report writing as follows:
>
> *Every scientist writing a research report has other scientists reading what he writes while he writes it. Though it is easy to err, to exaggerate, to overgeneralize when writing up one's own work, it is not easy to escape the feeling of scientific eyes constantly peering over one's shoulder.*
>
> This chapter deals with the sections of a research report, ...

- Apart from the surname of the author and the year of publication, all quotations should also be accompanied by the page number on which the material appears in the quoted source.

> **Example**
>
> According to the above two examples, Bem (1986, p. 430) and Kerlinger (1986, p. 11) ...

- If the first letter of a quotation is a *capital letter* that has to be changed to a small letter to incorporate the quotation into a sentence (in the report), put the modified letter between parentheses.

> **Example**
>
> B.F. Skinner (1904-1990), the famous psychological researcher, suggests as one of his "unformalized principles of science", that "(w)hen you run into something interesting, drop everything else and study it" (Bachrach, 1981, p. 6).

3.4 The reference system

In this section we will discuss the reference system required by the *South African Journal of Psychology* (SAJP). You should bear in mind that other reference systems such as the Harvard differ from the SAJP one in some aspects.

Our main concern regarding the use of a specific reference method is that it must enable the reader of our research report to locate the information sources we referred to if so needed. The reader may want to read more about the issue from the information source we referred to in our research paper.

There are minute differences between the method of referencing (according to the SAJP) described here and the more broadly used Harvard method. For example: REFERENCES IN THE TEXT of a research proposal/report are the same as indicated in Section 3.4.1, but also include specific pages as in "Strauss (1990: 34)" where the number "(...34)" is the page from where the researcher read about the reported issue even if no text was directly quoted (compare the previous guidelines mentioned in Section 3.3.3 "Quotations").

About the REFERENCE LIST: the Harvard method differs little from the following presented SAJP method. For more information, visit the Internet at: http://www.unisanet.unisa.edu.au/SubjectInforBooklet/06385/AppendixHarvardmethodofreferencing–9.htm

3.4.1 **References in the text**

- If you refer to theories, research findings or any other contribution previously reported, you should give the sources involved due credit. Give the surname(s) of the author(s), followed immediately by the year of publication between parentheses.

> **Example**
> In a well-designed experiment, Strauss (1990) found that ...

- You may not list a string of references that are not appropriate in the context in which you cite them. It is not permissible to cite sources without identifying their relevance. For example, it should be clear whether it is a finding or an opinion or whatever that has been obtained from the source.
- If you refer to the same source more than once in the same paragraph, the date should accompany only the first reference.
- If a source has more than two authors, you should list them all the first time it appears in the report.

> **Example**
> Plug, Meyer, Louw and Gouws (1987) ...

In all subsequent references, give only the surname of the first author, followed by "et al." (which is the Latin for "and others").

> **Example**
> Plug et al. (1987) ...

- If there is more than one source with several authors, and they have the first two authors and the same date in common, give the first three surnames plus "et al." (for the remaining authors) in further references to distinguish between them.

> **Example**
> The following references occurred in text:
> Smith, Jones, Botha and Tiffin (1990) ... and later also ... Smith, Jones, de Beer and Zwane (1990).
> Further references to the same authors must be made in the following way:
> Smith, Jones and Botha et al. (1990) ... and ... Smith, Jones and de Beer et al. (1990).

The above principle is extended in similar fashion to situations in which various sources have more than the first two authors and the same date in common: Give as many authors (plus "et al.") as may be necessary to distinguish between the different groups of authors.

- When more than one reference appears between brackets, put a comma between the author(s)' surname(s) and the date, and a semicolon (;) between the different references (source plus date). Note that when sources with two or more authors appear between brackets, the "and" between the last author and the author before the last is replaced by an "&".

> **Example**
> (Bachrach, 1981; Jordaan & Buthelezi, 1995; Plug, Meyer, Louw & Gouws, 1987) ...

Note that in a reference list (Section 10.2.9) the & appears as follows:

Plug, C., Meyer, W.F., Louw, D.A. & Gouws, L.A. (1987) ...

- To distinguish between *different publications of the same author* published in the same year, alphabetise them according to their titles and affix the letters a, b, c, and so on to these dates.

Example

When you refer to publications of the same author mentioned as follows in the reference list (Section 10.2.9), for example:

Kolb, D.A. (1976a). Management and the learning process. *California Management Review*, **18**(3), 21–31.

Kolb, D.A. (1976b). *Learning style inventory: Technical Manual.* Boston: McBer.

refer to them in the text as follows:

... Kolb (1976a) ... Kolb (1976b) ...

- Distinguish between different authors with the same surname by giving their respective initials together with their (common) surname.

Example

J.J. Zuma (1990) ... S.M. Zuma (1990) ...
instead of just
Zuma (1990) ... Zuma (1990) ...

3.4.2 Alphabetical order of sources in the reference list

Arrange references alphabetically in terms of the surname of the first author.

Example

Nel, T.J. appears before Nelson, A.M. even though **S** (in Nelson) alphabetically precedes **T** (in Nel, T.J.)

In addition:

Cronbach, L.J. (1980) appears before Cronbach, L.J. & Furby, L. (1970).

MacPherson precedes McArthur.

Arrange sources with the *same first author* but with different co-authors alphabetically *according to the surname of the second author*. The same principle applies when there is more than one collection of authors of which the first two, or first three, and so on are the same.

Example

Smith, J.C. & Erikson, M. (1989) ...
Smith, J.C. & Fromm, S. (1990) ...
Smith, J.C. & Green, S. (1980) ...

or

Smith, J.C., Jones, D. & Erikson, M. (1989) ...
Smith, J.C., Jones, D. & Fromm, S. (1990) ...
Smith, J.C., Jones, D. & Green, S. (1980) ...

If the same author or collection of authors has different publications, list them *chronologically according to the date of publication*.

Example

Khoza, R. & Mafumane, T. (1989). *The influence of ...*

Khoza, R. & Mafumane, T. (1990). *Woman in management ...*

Khoza, R. & Mafumane, T. (1995). *Affirmative action ...*

3.4.3 Language of reference

You should give all information in a list of references in the language of the source and not of the report being written. An English translation of a non-English title should be given in brackets immediately following the original title. Words appearing in the title should be presented as they appear. For example, the American spelling of "labor" and "center" should not be changed to the British spelling "labour" and "centre", respectively.

3.4.4 **Journal articles in the list of references**

To master any system of references, it is advisable to study examples in appropriate journals carefully. The following example gives a reference to a journal article with one author, followed by an example with more than one author.

> **Example**
>
> Eberhard, H. (1990). Induction guidance – what do the novices want? *South African Journal of Psychology*, **22**, 210–225.
>
> Nieuwoudt, J.M., Plug, C. & Mynhardt, J.C. (1997). White ethnic attitudes after Soweto: A field experiment. *South African Journal of Psychology*, **16**(2), 1–12.

Note

- *Above, the figures* **22** *and* **16** *that appear in the first and second references, respectively, are the volume numbers of the journal and appear in bold.*
- *Usually each year has a new number. For example, if the volume number of 1990 was 10, for 2001 it would be 21.*
- *If the numbering system of the pages of each edition of a journal starts with (page number) 1, the number of the edition should also appear between brackets immediately after the volume number.*
- *With regard to using capital letters in the titles of the article and the journal: Only the first letter of the article title (and, of course, proper names) but both the first letter and every important word in the journal title are capitalised.*
- *The name of the journal title appears in italics (or underlined).*

3.4.5 **Books and chapters in books**

Just as for journals, the name of a book appears in italics (or is underlined). Only the first letter of the first word of the book title (and of any proper names) is *capitalised.*

> **Example**
>
> Du Preez, P. (1991). *A science of mind: The quest for psychological reality.* London: Academic Press.

If you refer to a chapter in a book, the surname(s) of the author(s) of the book are followed by their initials.

> **Example**
>
> Valle, R.S., King, M. & Halling, S. (1989). An introduction to existential-phenomenological thought in psychology. In R.S. Valle & S. Halling (Eds), *Existential-phenomenological perspectives in psychology* (pp. 3–16). New York: Plenum.

Note

"Editor" is abbreviated to "Ed.", but "Editors" to "Eds" (that is, without a full stop because both end in the same letters).

When the author and the publisher of a book is the same organisation or body, the full name of the organisation, followed by its abbreviation, appears in the position of the author and only the abbreviation in the position of the publisher.

3.4.6 **Other sources**

The following are a few other kinds of references and the surname (of the author) that may be looked up in the list of references (see pp. 287–292) to check the corresponding kind of reference.

(a) Dissertation or thesis

Example

Botha, M.P. (1990). *Television exposure and aggressiveness among high-school pupils: A follow-up study over five years.* Unpublished doctoral thesis, University of the Free State. Bloemfontein.

(b) Book review

Example

Haertel, E.H. (1987). Review of "Foundations of behavioral research" (3rd ed.) by F.N. Kerlinger. *Contemporary Psychology*, **32**, 249–250.

(c) Unpublished paper delivered at a meeting

Example

Strümpfer, D.J.W. (1980, September). *One hundred and one years after Wundt*. Paper presented at the National Psychological Congress, Johannesburg.

(d) Article in a newspaper

Example

Botha, J. (1988, 1 Apr.). Worst USA TV series also broadcast here. *The Star*, p. 10.

(e) Article in a newspaper without any author indicated

Example

Too much beer leads to temporary impotence. (1991, 7 Jan.). *The Citizen*, p. 5.

(f) Letter to a newspaper editor

Example

Mathibela, J. (1996, 1 Apr.). The stars in black management [Letter to the editor]. *Sowetan*, p. 12.

(g) Reference to an Internet source

Example

Department of Labour. (2000). *Employment Equity Act*. http://www.labour.gov.za/docs/legislation/eea/forms/eea3-eng.htm (*date when document was accessed*)

(h) Reference to a CD-ROM

Example

20th World Conference on Open Learning and Distance Education. (2001). [CD-ROM] Fern Universität Hagen, Germany

Note

CHECKLIST FOR EVALUATING AND CRITICISING THE RELEVANCE OF REFERENCE LIST USED IN ONE'S RESEARCH REPORT:

- *How recent is the information from each referenced source?*
- *Does the information in each referred source to a large extent support and/or contradict your arguments? If yes (to either question), use the information source – it may add value to your study's external validity (see Chapter 6).*
- *Is this information source referred to by other well-known scientists in your field of study? If the answer to this question is yes, then one may assume that the information from the source is reliable.*

Activity 3.1

The aim of this exercise is for you to visit a library and to become familiar with the procedures (such as catalogue systems and library inter-loans) required to gather secondary sources (see Section 3.3.2). It is not meant to create extra work for the librarian at the library you visit.

Assignment

Compile a literature review (with references) on a topic relevant to your field of study for a research theme in which you consult most of the following sources of information and present them in a reference list, correctly according to a particular reference system (see Section 3.4).

- recent academic books (published during the past three years)
- academic journal articles (see the list on p. 42 for examples)
- research reports / studies of masters' / doctoral degrees
- practice-oriented (popular) journal articles (such as *People Dynamics* or *Servamus*)
- articles from newspapers and / or ordinary magazines.

Remember to first write down your literature research review topic (see Section 11.1) and underline it before you start the literature review.

Note

The three criteria taken as the basis for evaluating your literature review are as follows:

1. *Your answer should relate to your chosen topic and the information sources you listed in the list of references (see Section 3.4.4, 3.4.5, 3.4.6 and 10.2.9).*
2. *You have to start documenting the information obtained from the sources listed broadly and later narrow it down to make it more specific to your chosen topic (see Section 10.2.3, 10.2.4 and 10.2.5).*
3. *Your references to sources in your text must be correct and consistent according to a specific reference system, as described in Section 3.4.1, 3.4.2 and 3.4.3.*

The introductory paragraph on pp. 259–260 and the list of references on p. 252 of the article by Welman and Basson may serve as an example of what a literature review should look like.

Use the following GUIDE TO USING A LIBRARY to help you with this exercise:

1. Write down your chosen research topic (see Section 2.2).
2. Write down the key terms – the most important variables (see Section 2.2).
3. Use the library catalogue to find the sources containing information on your research topic. A library catalogue usually offers three ways of locating information, namely by authors, by titles, and by subjects.

   An example of a title may be this prescribed textbook for the subject "Research Methodology". So you will look in the title catalogue for "methodology" or "research".
4. Use the classification number given on the card or computer screen (for example 001.4) regarding the topic "research" according to the Dewey Decimal System. The Dewey Decimal System uses three-digit numbers ranging from 000 to 999. Each group of 100 numbers refers to a different broad academic discipline, for example, 300-399 is social sciences.
5. Use the group of numbers concerning your topic / subject to choose a specific information source. For example, for a book on assessment for learning in higher education, the specific classification number is: 378.1664 ASS
6. Now proceed to find the book you are looking for on the library shelves. For finding a specific article in a journal, do steps 1 and 2 and ask the librarian for a Journal Index. Then proceed with steps 3 to 6.

Note

If your library has limited resources on your chosen topic, write down the names of articles and important books relevant to your topic from the bibliographies and reference lists at the back of standard text books. Try to find these identified information sources through an inter-library loan.

Activity 3.2

Read Case Study F in Appendix D on page 276.

Question

Briefly criticise the *list of references* in the case study.

Answer

a) The names of the authors are not in ALPHABETICAL ORDER.
b) The source SWAYNE & TUCKER, 1973 is outdated.
c) Although there is reference to KIRTON, 1987 in the text, it is not mentioned in the reference list.

Literature sources

The following ACADEMIC JOURNALS contain mostly good articles that may be used as information sources for a LITERATURE REVIEW.

Academy of Management Review
Accounting and Business Research
Accounting Review
Acta Criminologica: SA Journal of Criminology
Administratia Publica
Administration & Society
Administrative Science Quarterly
Adult Education Quarterly
Africa Media Review
African Journal of Library, Archives & Information Science
African Studies
Annals of Tourism Research
Archives and Manuscripts
Assessment & Evaluation in Higher Education
Communicare: Journal of Communication Sciences
Comparative and International Law Journal of Southern Africa
Computer Integrated Manufacturing Systems
Computer Journal, The
Crime and Delinquency
Critical Perspectives on Accounting
De Jure
Development in Practice
Development Policy Review
Development Southern Africa
Discourse Processes
Distance Education
Ecquid Novi: Journal for Journalism in Southern Africa
Education + Training
Education Economics
Entrepreneurship Theory and Practice
European Management Journal
FM: Journal of The Financial Management Association
Frontiers of Entrepreneurship Research
Gender and Development
Homocide Studies
Industrial Law Journal
Information Processing & Management
Information Services & Use
Information Society
Internal Audit Review
International Information & Library Review
International Journal of Evidence & Proof
International Journal of Human Resource Management
International Journal of Purchasing and Materials Management
International Journal of The Society of Law
International Journal of Urban and Regional Research
International Journal of Vocational Education and Training
International Journal on Minority and Group Rights
International Review of Retail, Distribution and Consumer Research
Internet Research: Electronic Networking Applications and Policy
Journal for Juridical Science
Journal of Accounting Research
Journal of Accounting, Auditing & Finance
Journal of African Law
Journal of Business Venturing
Journal of Community Development
Journal of Criminal Justice
Journal of Direct Marketing
Journal of Education and Work
Journal of Financial Intermediation
Journal of General Management
Journal of Global Marketing

Journal of Hospitality & Tourism Education
Journal of Industrial Psychology
Journal of Information Science
Journal of Information Technology
Journal of International Marketing and Marketing Research
Journal of Management
Journal of Marketing Management
Journal of Offender Rehabilitation
Journal of Operations Management
Journal of Personal Selling & Sales Management
Journal of Policy Analysis and Management
Journal of Property Finance
Journal of Real Estate Finance and Economics
Journal of Real Estate Literature
Journal of Real Estate Portfolio Management
Journal of Real Estate Research
Journal of Research in Crime and Delinquency
Journal of Risk and Insurance
Journal of Security Administration
Journal of Small Business Management
Journal of Strategic Marketing
Journal of The American Society for Information Science
Labour Law Reports
Library & Information Science Research
Logistics & Transportation Review
Management Accounting Research
Management Dynamics: Contemporary Research
Negotiation Journal
New Zealand Valuers' Journal
Online & CDRom Review
Policing
Policing & Society
Politiko: South African Journal of Political Studies
Prison Service Journal
Property Management
Psychosocial Research and Practice
Public Administration and Development
Public money & Management
Real Estate Issues
Research in Education
S.E.E.: Studies in Economics and Econometrics
SA Journal for Entrepreneurship and Small Business
SA Journal of Accounting Research
SA Journal of Applied Language Studies
SA Journal of Business Management
SA Journal of Criminal Justice
SA Journal of Economic and Management Science
SA Journal of Higher Education
SA Journal of Labour Relations
SA Journal of Library and Information Sciences
SA Journal of Linguistics
SA Journal of Psychology
SA Mercantile Law Journal
SA Public Law
SAIPA: Journal of Public Administration
Security Journal
Social Work
Social Work Practitioner-Researcher
Software: Practice & Experience
South African Labour Bulletin
South African Law Journal
South African Statistics
South African Tax Cases Report
Strategic Management Journal
Tax Planning: Corporate & Personal
The Taxpayer
Transportation

Electronic sources

- The African Digital Library gives access to close to 8 000 full text on-line books to people living in Africa. Surf the Internet and go to *http://AfricaEducation.org/adl/*
- Sabinet Online provides access to a variety of high quality databases. Go to *http://www.sabinet.co.za* (contact *cll@tsa.ac.za* for a password)

Summary

In order to develop an understanding of, and insight into previous research findings that may be helpful to your own research question/problem, a critical review of the literature relating to your research topic is crucial. Such a literature review will help you to recognise and identify variables that may hamper or influence the results of your own study even before the empirical research starts.

By presenting the findings of other studies relating to your research topic broadly at the start of the literature review, you are familiarising the reader of the research report with the background of your investigation. As you progress with your literature review, you should narrow its focus to references relating as specifically as possible to your own situation and circumstances in which your empirical research is going to take place. In this way the reader of your report is prepared for the research hypothesis/es (usually presented in the next chapter of the research report).

Multiple choice and true/false questions

Only *one* of the answers at each question is correct. Identify and mark the correct one. (Answers appear in Appendix E on page 285.)

3.1 Documents in which one may get the most scientifically scrutinised findings or information on a specific topic is:
  a) recent academic books (published in the past three years)
  b) academic journal articles
  c) research reports/studies of masters'/doctoral degrees
  d) practice-oriented (popular) journal articles
  e) articles from newspapers and ordinary magazines.

3.2 Documenting large sections of another researcher's written work as your own, is called:
  a) misrepresentation
  b) illegal citation
  c) wrongful referencing
  d) plagiarism.

3.3 A published academic book that discusses work of another original academic book is called a(n)
  a) alternative source
  b) secondary source
  c) derived source
  d) primary source.

3.4 When making reference in a research paper to an original source that one has not read, one should:
  a) cite the original source
  b) mention that the original source was found in another source
  c) cite the secondary source in which the original source was found
  d) mention only the name of the author of the original source.

3.5 Which of the following evaluations may be used as criteria to determine whether a research report is scientifically unbiased?
  a) the reputation of the researcher writing the report
  b) the precision of the data that are reported
  c) verification of the scientific value by more than one peer researcher
  d) an accepted scientist that generally approves the scientific merits of the report.

4 Population and sampling types

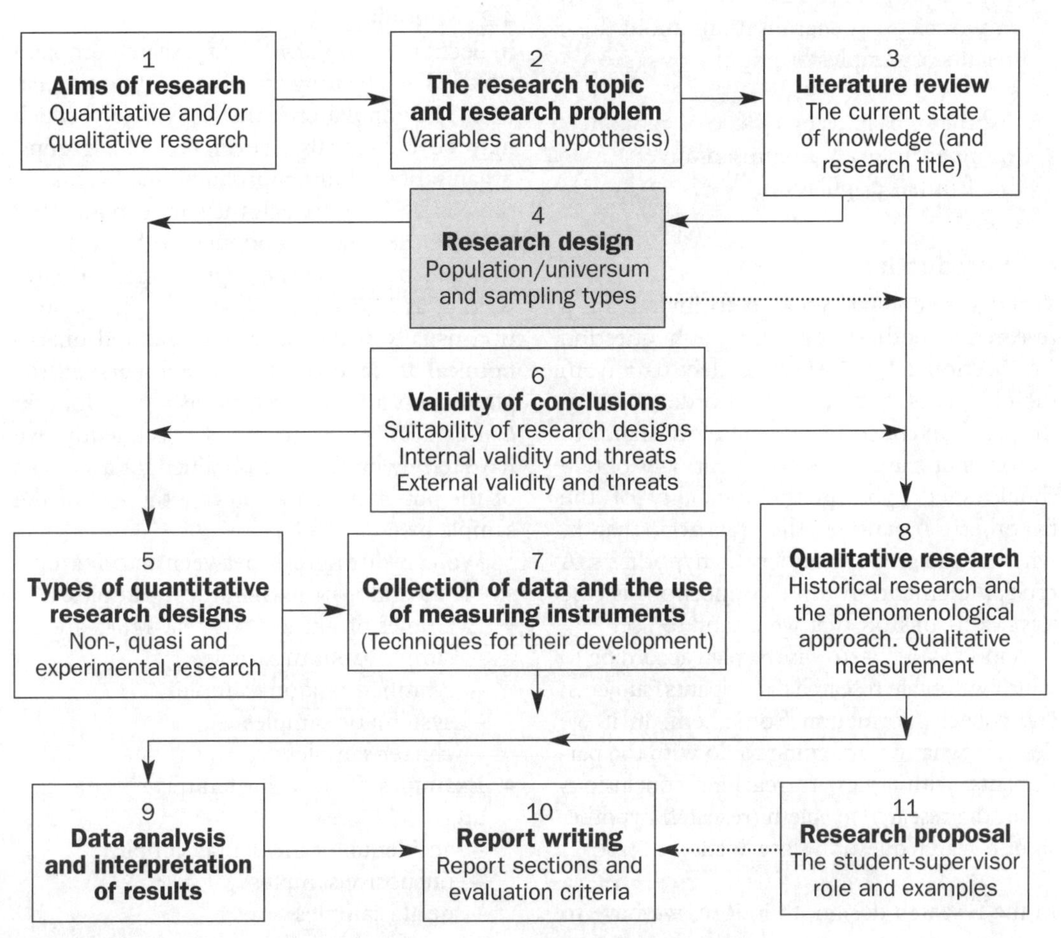

Figure 4.1 The research process and the outline of chapters in this book

Learning Outcomes

After studying this chapter, you should be able to:

1. differentiate between populations, universes, target populations, sampling frames and samples
2. list the five basic types of units of analysis found in the business and administrative sciences and illustrate them by way of examples
3. list the different types of sampling; their advantages and disadvantages in terms of their prediction power (see Section 1.2.5 & 2.2.2)
4. explain why we should be cautious when making generalisations about the results of samples of populations (see Section 2.3.3)
5. list the steps in using a table of random numbers to draw a representative sample from its population.

4.1 **Introduction**

When we conduct research to investigate a research hypothesis or a research question (see Section 2.2 & 2.3), we collect data from the objects of our enquiry in order to solve the problem concerned. It therefore stands to reason that the results we eventually obtain should shed light on the tenability of the hypothesis or answer the question, that is, whether to accept or reject the hypothesis. A crucial element in this connection is the RESEARCH DESIGN that we intend to use.

A RESEARCH DESIGN is the plan according to which we obtain research participants (subjects) and collect information from them. In it we describe what we are going to do with the participants, with a view to reaching conclusions about the research problem (research hypothesis or research question – see Section 2.3).

In the research design, therefore, we have to specify:

- the number of groups that should be used (this is necessary to decide which statistical technique to use – see Chapter 9)
- whether these groups are to be drawn randomly from the populations involved and whether they should be assigned randomly to groups (see Section 6.3.6)
- what exactly should be done with them in the case of experimental research (see Section 5.2.1).

In this chapter we deal with different facets of designs' sampling requirements. These requirements serve as criteria for the evaluation of research reports (see Section 10.4).

4.2 **Sampling**

In Section 2.2 we saw that a research problem usually has a bearing on some or other population. The population is the study object, which may be individuals (see Figure 4.2), groups, organisations, human products and events, or the conditions to which they are exposed. We indicate the size of a population by N. If, for example, the size of the population is 1 000, we write it as $N = 1\ 000$. The size of the population usually makes it impractical and uneconomical to involve all the members of the population in a research project (see Note on *Census 2001* on page 19). Consequently, we have to rely on the data obtained for a SAMPLE of the population. We indicate the size of the sample by n.

We can distinguish between PROBABILITY SAMPLES and NON-PROBABILITY samples.

- Examples of PROBABILITY SAMPLES are:
  - simple random samples
  - stratified random samples
  - systematic samples
  - cluster samples.
- Examples of NON-PROBABILITY SAMPLES are:
  - accidental or incidental samples
  - purposive samples
  - quota samples
  - snowball samples.

In the case of probability sampling, we can determine the probability that any element or member of the population will be included in the sample. In non-probability sampling, by contrast, we cannot specify this probability, insofar as it does exceed zero. Some elements have no chance (that is, a probability of zero) of being included in some examples of non-probability samples.

The advantage of probability sampling is that it enables us to indicate the probability with which sample results (for example, sample means) deviate in differing degrees from the corresponding population values (for example, population means). Unlike non-probability sampling, probability sampling enables us to estimate SAMPLING ERROR (see Section 4.2.5). This is a statistical term that has a bearing on the unrepresentativeness of a sample (see Figure 4.4). Nevertheless, non-probability sampling is frequently used for reasons of convenience and economy.

Note

By REPRESENTATIVENESS *we imply that the sample has the exact properties in the exact same proportions as the population from which it was drawn, but in smaller numbers. Consequently, a representative sample is a miniature image, or likeness, of the population (see Figure 4.3).*

4.2.1 The sampling frame

Usually the populations that interest human behavioural scientists are so large that, from a practical point of view, it is simply impossible to conduct research on all of them. Consequently, such researchers have to obtain data from only a sample of these populations. Before they draw a sample of the population for analysis, researchers should obtain clarity about the population, or units of analysis, to which their research hypotheses apply.

- A SAMPLING FRAME is a complete list on which each unit of analysis is mentioned only once. Unless such a sampling frame

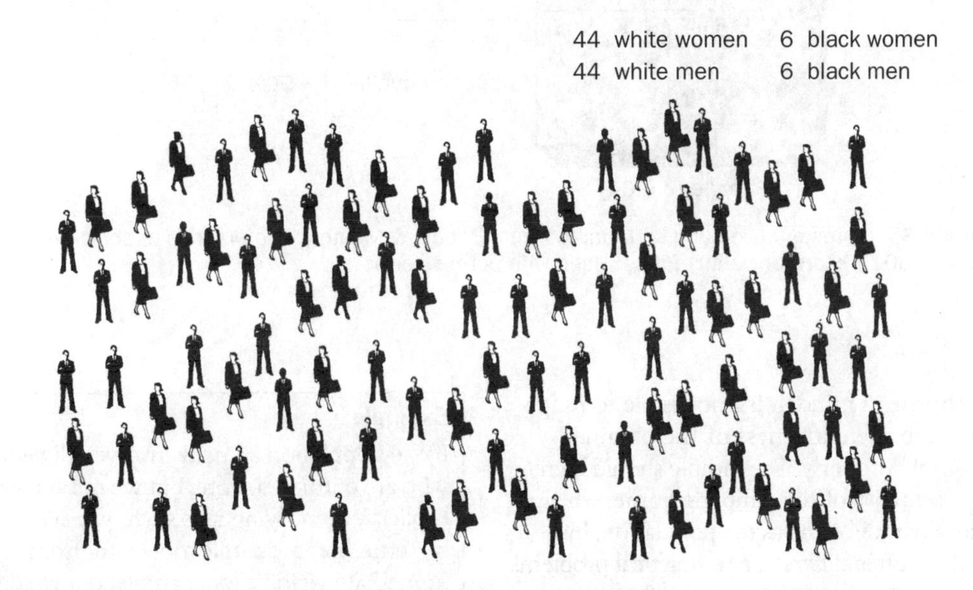

Figure 4.2 The population of 100 South African multi-millionaires ($N = 100$). (Adapted from Babbie & Mouton, *The practice of social research*, p. 169. 2001. Oxford University Press. Used with permission.)

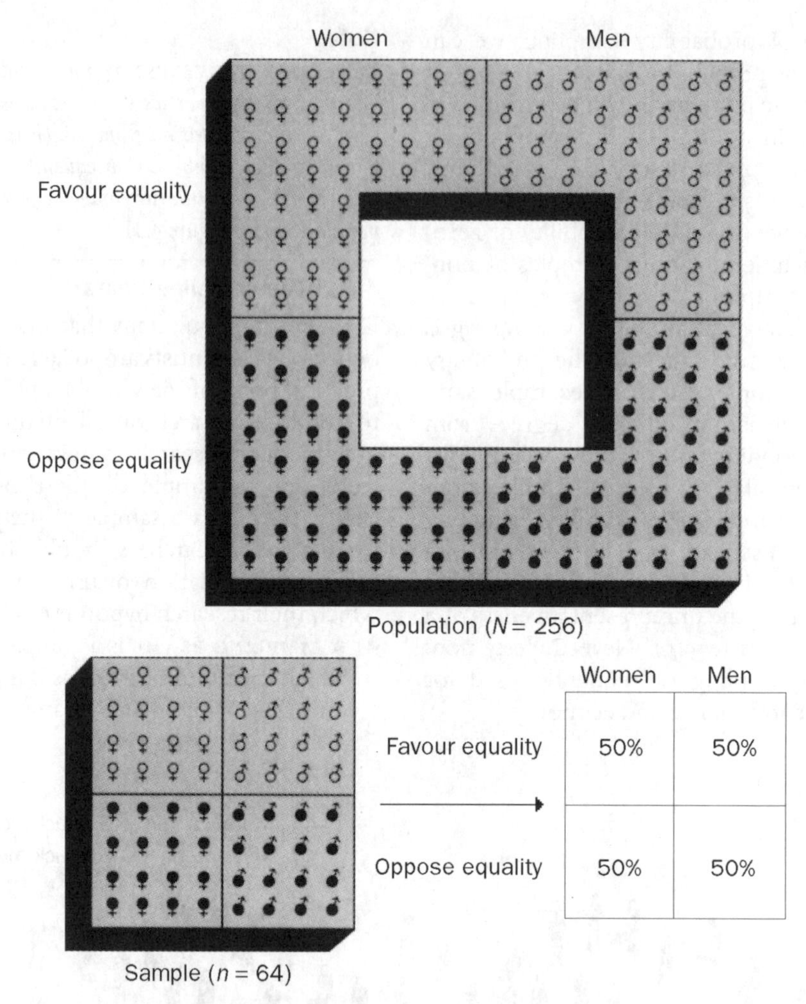

Figure 4.3 A representative sample. (Adapted from Babbie & Mouton, *The practice of social research*, p. 478. 2001. Oxford University Press. Used with permission.)

is borne in mind, it is impossible to judge the representativeness of the obtained sample properly. The sample should be representative of the sampling frame, which ideally is the same as the population, but which often differs due to practical problems relating to the availability of information.

- We refer to the MEMBERS or ELEMENTS of the population as the UNITS OF ANALYSIS (see Figure 4.5).

Example

If the population actually involves all people who are entitled to vote, but we refrain from explicitly identifying it as such, we may easily settle for a sample obtained from our immediate vicinity, for example, our residential area, hostel or workplace. An explicit specification of the sampling frame before commencing the research, may prevent us from regarding such a sample as being representative of the relevant population.

We have seen (see Section 2.3) that a research hypothesis postulates the relationship between variables in some or other population. The population encompasses the total collection of all units of analysis about which the researcher wishes to make conclusions.

Example

In RESEARCH EXAMPLE II (see Section 2.2, page 14), the research hypothesis deals with the (causal) relationship between the expo-

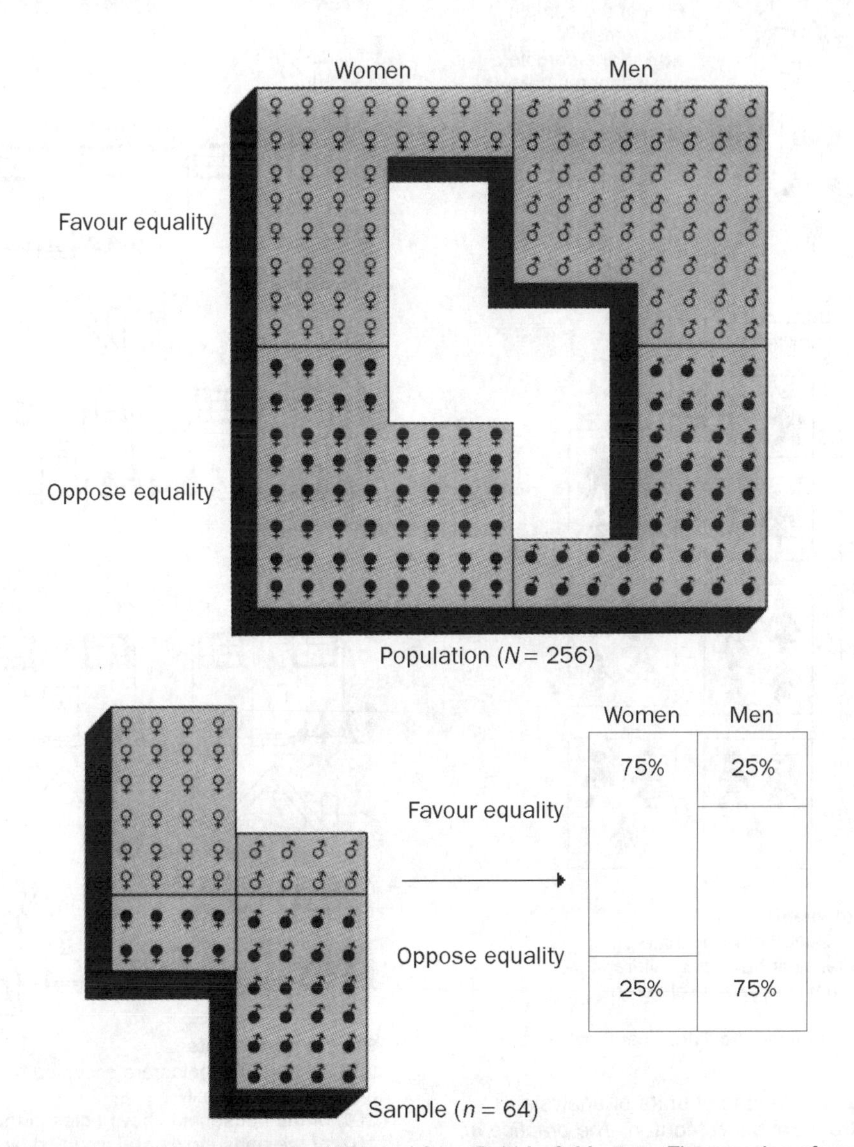

Figure 4.4 An unrepresentative sample. (Adapted from Babbie & Mouton, *The practice of social research*, p. 479. 2001. Oxford University Press. Used with permission.)

Units of analysis
Individuals ($n = 10$)

Sample statements
60% of the sample are women
10% of the sample are wearing a hat
10% of the sample are wearing a tie

Units of analysis
Families ($n = 10$)

Sample statements
20% of the families have a single parent
40% of the families have two children
20% of the families have no children

The average number of children per family is 1,2

Units of analysis
Households ($n = 10$)

Sample statements
20% of the households are occupied by more than one family
30% of the households have holes in their roofs
10% of the households are occupied by aliens from the planet Mars

Figure 4.5 Illustrations of units of analysis. (Adapted from Babbie & Mouton, *The practice of social research*, p. 91. 2001. Oxford University Press. Used with permission.)

sure of a population of trainee supervisors to an iron-fisted role model management style behaviour and these trainee supervisors' subsequent management style. Conceptually, each member of the population has a score on each of these two variables and the researcher wishes to draw conclusions about the relationship between these variables for the entire population (that is, all trainee supervisors). Here the units of analysis are the trainee supervisors.

Note

In the human behavioural sciences, units of analysis typically refer to:

- *humans*
- *groups (for example, couples married in a particular year; households in a particular geographic region; homosexual clubs; gangs; criminal syndicates; and so on)*
- *organisations or institutions (for example, schools; classes; congregations; hospitals; political parties; companies; and so on)*
- *human products or outputs (for example, houses; paintings; articles published in a particular journal in a particular period; dramas; and so on)*
- *events (for example, elections; riots; court cases; and so on). (See Section 7.7.6 for time sampling methods.)*

The compilation of a satisfactory sampling frame presents problems in large-scale survey research in particular (see Section 5.4.5). Frequently, a list that is comprehensive and accurate for a particular population at a specific point in time is simply not available. People daily relocate from one region to another, change from one population to another (for example, from being wealthy to bankrupt, and vice versa) and even die. Lists that we could possibly consider to be sampling frames in some instances include telephone directories, mailing lists of municipal ratepayers, lists of registered students at a university and lists of television licence holders.

If we use a list that does not contain all relevant units of analysis, and if the missing units differ in a systematic manner from those on the list, we could eventually draw incorrect conclusions.

Example

Suppose the population in question involves all voters in a city and we use the telephone directory for that city as our sampling frame. If a large proportion of the adults do not have telephones, and these people are exclusively from a particular socio-economic group, our sampling frame is deficient because it systematically excludes individuals who do not have telephones.

Under mentioned circumstances it is obviously impossible for a telephone survey (see Section 7.7.4) to yield a representative picture of the entire population of voters.

If we were to use the numbers listed in a telephone directory as a sampling frame for the population with telephones, the occurrence of unlisted numbers may present a problem. To overcome this problem, we could dial numbers randomly without using a telephone book (directory). A drawback of this procedure, again, is that we could dial business numbers or discontinued numbers instead of household numbers.

Note

To sample telephone numbers from a telephone directory "randomly" (see Section 4.2.2), one may decide arbitrarily on the length (let's say 4 cm measured with a ruler) to be used to identify the telephone number from the top (or bottom) of each page and, let's say, every second column of the following page in the telephone book. (See illustration on the next page.)

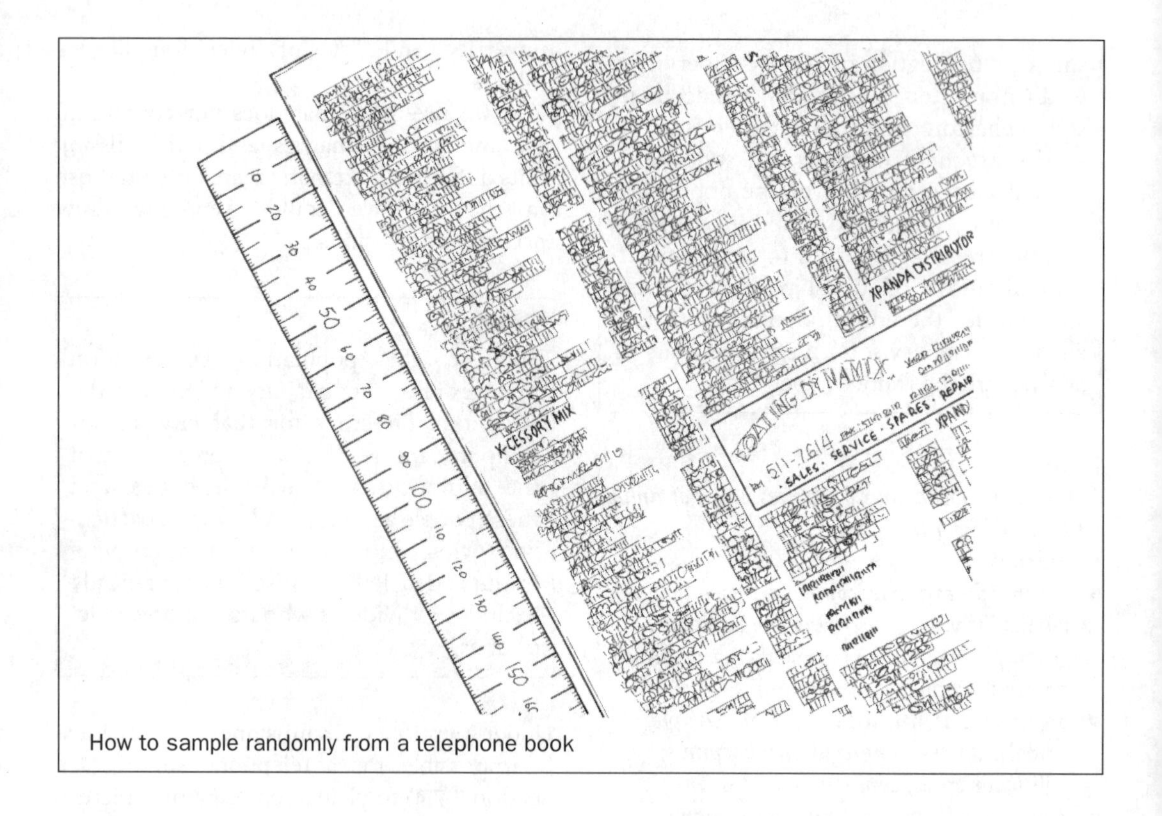

How to sample randomly from a telephone book

Activity 4.1

Read Case Study A; Case Study B; Case Study C; Case Study D; Case Study E and Case Study F in Appendix D on page 276.

Question

What is the unit of analysis for each case study? Explain your answer.

Answer

CASE STUDY A: The unit of analysis is individual people, that is, health care professionals, namely *nursing sisters and doctors* who serve mainly white and coloured population groups at a general hospital. These people completed the questionnaire used in the investigation.

CASE STUDY B: The unit of analysis is a group of people (not individuals), namely *goldsmith apprentices*, who all receive the same type of training and supervision and whose attitudes the intervention (role induction procedure) is intended to affect.

CASE STUDY C: The unit of analysis is people, namely *first-line supervisors*, employed at agricultural corporations in four of the provinces in South Africa. These are the people who attended the training course and had to write the three-hour test.

CASE STUDY D: The unit of analysis refers to a group of people at four technikons, namely *students in public speech-making* who all received the same type of training and whose speech preparation time, speech performance and speech anxiety were investigated.

CASE STUDY E: The unit of analysis refers to a *group of small businesses* in Pretoria, namely small businesses (between 40 and 60 employees) whose owners agreed to participate in the research project.

CASE STUDY F: The unit of analysis is *business people* (entrepreneurs and managers).

Self-evaluation questions

What is the unit of analysis in the research problems listed under Section 2.2?

4.2.2 Random sampling

We can say without a doubt that, conceptually, random sampling is the most attractive type of probability sampling. We must distinguish between simple random sampling and stratified random sampling.

4.2.2.1 Simple random sampling

In the simplest case of RANDOM SAMPLING, each member of the population has the same chance of being included in the sample and each sample of a particular size has the same probability of being chosen (see Figure 4.6).

> **Example**
>
> In a random sample of, say, 50 multi-millionaires from the population of all multi-millionaires in South Africa, each multi-millionaire, irrespective of sex, race, age, region, and so on, will have an equal chance of being included.

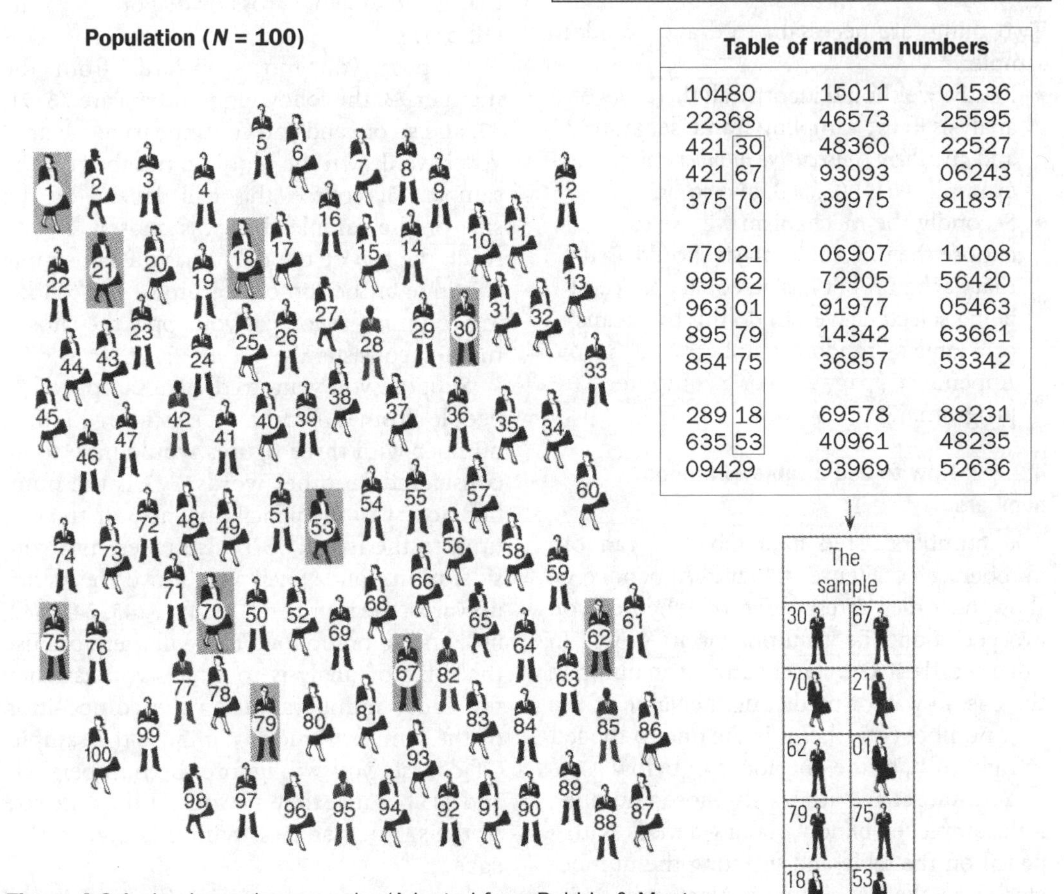

Figure 4.6 A simple random sample. (Adapted from Babbie & Mouton, *The practice of social research*, p. 189. 2001. Oxford University Press. Used with permission.)

Example

Suppose we wish to draw a random sample of three units of analysis ($n = 3$) from a population of five units of analysis ($N = 5$), A, B, C, D and E. In such a case each of the following 10 samples will have the same chance of being the randomly selected sample:

A, B and C	A, D and E
A, B and D	B, C and D
A, B and E	B, C and E
A, C and D	B, D and E
A, C and E	C, D and E.

Two things are necessary to draw a random sample:

- Firstly, we should identify all the units of analysis in the sampling frame separately and *give them consecutive numbers* (for example, 001, 002, 003, and so on).
- Secondly, the mechanism we use to choose the units of analysis should assure that each number has an equal chance of being selected. We can do this by means of a table of random numbers (see Appendix C, page 275) or a computer program.

4.2.2.2 How to use a table of random numbers

The numbers listed in a table of random numbers (see Figure 4.7 and Appendix C) show no order, irrespective of whether you proceed along its columns or its rows. In other words, if you start at any given number, there is no way of predicting the value of the next number (whether it is the one to the left or right of it, or the one above or below it).

You start at any arbitrarily chosen number, for example, by blindly making a mark with a pencil on the table and selecting the number closest to the pencil mark. Next, you write down the numbers assigned to the units of analysis that you encounter as you move along row by row or column by column from that point. If the same number appears for a second (or third, and so on) time, or a number that is greater than the highest number assigned to units of analysis in the sampling frame appears, you ignore it. Continue in this fashion until you have written down a collection (of numbers) equal to the size of the desired sample. This collection represents the numbers of the members of the randomly chosen sample.

In Figure 4.7, you can see that the pencil tip is placed randomly on the table and the number 73 is closest to the pencil tip. You can now move in any direction to the next number, that is, up, down, across or diagonally to the left or right.

Suppose you move upwards from the number 73; the following numbers are 26, 51, 43, and so on, and you continue to move until you have drawn the required number for the sample. Of course, this will depend on the size of the sample that was chosen. If you reach the top of the column, you can simply continue at the top or bottom of the following column – as long as you apply the chosen method consistently.

Suppose you want to draw a sample of 80 people from a SAMPLE FRAME OF 400; a number with three figures would have to be considered. In other words, 373 is the number closest to the pencil tip (the 3 of the column to the left of 73 is also taken into consideration), and when you move the pencil upwards, the numbers 326, 451, 243, 745, 342, 063, and so on, follow. You will therefore use the units of analysis to which you assigned the above numbers during the composition of the sample frame to compose the sample. Of course, you will ignore the numbers 451 and 745 because they are greater than the size of the SAMPLE FRAME, which is 400 in this case.

If any unit is chosen in this way, it will mean that each unit ultimately included in the sample has had the same chance of being selected.

Figure 4.7 An example of using a table of random numbers (see Appendix C)

The advantage of a simple random sample is that it is representative of the population in the sense that it does not favour one unit of analysis (individual or subpopulation) over another. The chances that the sample taken in Figure 4.6 will include only females, for example, is remote and the chance of this happening can be determined.

If large samples and populations are involved, access to computer facilities is required to draw random samples. As indicated, one of the prerequisites for drawing a random sample is the availability of a sampling frame, that is, a list of all the elements of which the population is composed. Especially if a very large population is involved, it may be very difficult, if not impossible (in terms of time and costs) to compile such a list.

4.2.2.3 **Stratified random sampling**

Suppose the population is composed of various clearly recognisable, non-overlapping subpopulations [which we may call strata (singular stratum)] that differ from one another mutually in terms of the variable (see Section 2.2) in question. The division into groups may be based on a single variable such as sex (so that there are two strata: men and women). It may also involve a combination of more than one variable, for example, sex and age (so that there are strata such as young adult males, young adult females, middle-aged males, middle-aged females, and so on).

The members of a particular stratum will thus be more alike or homogeneous than the population at large. Put differently, the variation within any particular or stratum will be smaller than the variation among the respective strata. It may be unwise to ignore the differences among such clearly discernible populations, so we have to include them when we draw a random sample

Example

Suppose heart attacks occur four times more frequently among men than women. If, in a single random sample of an equal number of men and women, the proportion of heart-attack patients is not separately determined for these two groups, the incidence of heart attacks will be seriously underestimated among men and seriously overestimated among women.

Two things are necessary to draw a stratified random sample:

- Firstly, we should identify the various strata according to one or more variables.
- Secondly, we should draw a random sample from each separate stratum.

In this manner, we can obtain a representative sample from a population with clearly distinguishable strata with a greater degree of certainty than is possible with simple random sampling. For example, in Figure 4.6, through simple random sampling we obtained a sample of five white male, three white female and two black female multi-millionaires. There was no black male in our sample, though we know from Figure 4.2 that they make up 6% of the population. Black multi-millionaires make up 12% of the population, and if we had drawn a random sample according to such strata, white versus black, there would have been a probability of 0,5 (50%) of a black male being included in our sample of 10 (see Sections 4.2.2.1 & 4.2.4 for an explanation).

4.2.2.4 **The advantages of a stratified random sample**

- In a random sample from a normal population that is stratified in terms of sex, the *probability* of a sample consisting of members of one sex only is zero. On the other hand, while there is a very small probability that a simple random sample from a small population of 50 cancer patients, for example, 25 men and 25 women, will be composed of men only, such a *possibility* does exist.
- A smaller sample (requiring less time and money) is required with stratified random sampling than with simple random sampling, to ensure that important strata are represented in the sample. The *probability* that a simple random sample will include, for example, men and women in the appropriate proportions, increases as the size of the sample increases.

Note

With a stratified random sample we are ensured of this representativeness, irrespective of sample size, because it has been built into the sampling strategy right from the very beginning (see Figure 4.8).

Naturally, in a stratified random sample approach, the researcher is required to be aware of the stratification variables, that is, the variables in terms of which the population may be divided into homogeneous strata, such as tax level; organisation authority level; industrial or commercial sector; crime type; technological generation order; and so on.

4.2.3 **Other types of probability sampling**

Systematic sampling and cluster sampling are simpler and more convenient than random

A. Some men and women who either favour (=) sexually equality or do not (≠) favour it.

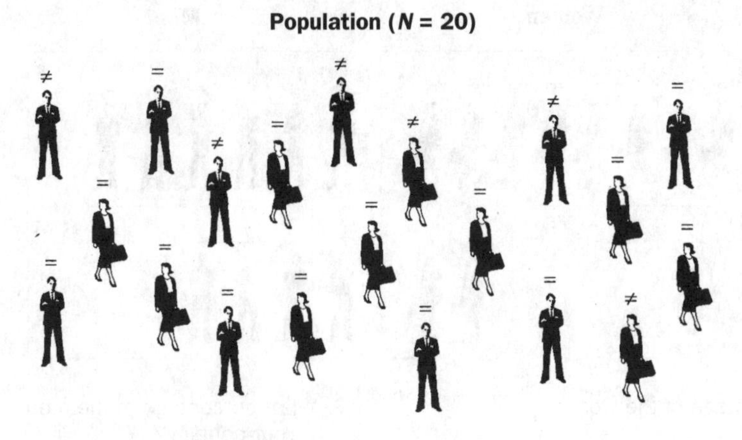

B. Separate the men and the women (the independent variable).

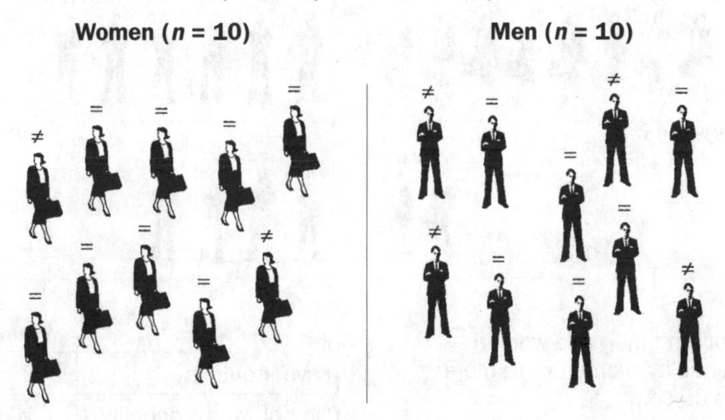

C. Within each gender group, separate those who favour equality from those who do not (the dependent variable).

Figure 4.8 Proportions and strata. (Adapted from Babbie & Mouton, *The practice of social research*, p. 432. 2001. Oxford University Press. Used with permission.)

D. Count the numbers in each cell of the table.

E. What percentage of the women favour equality?

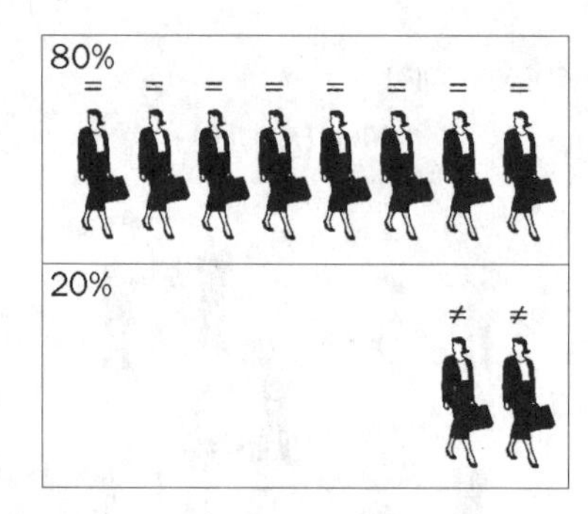

F. What percentage of the men favour equality?

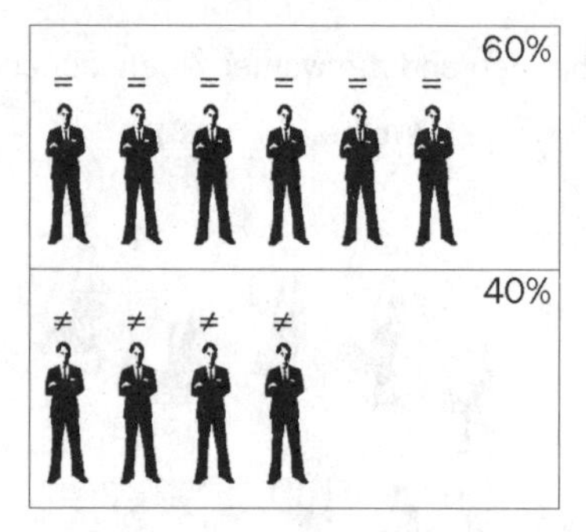

G. Conclusions.
While a majority of both men and women favoured sexual equality, women were more likely than men to do so.

Thus, sex appears to be one of the causes of attitudes toward sexual equality.

	Women	Men
Favour equality	80%	60%
Do not favour equality	20%	40%
Total	100%	100%

Figure 4.8 Proportions and strata (*continued*)

sampling, especially when we want to obtain a representative sample from the entire population, as in large-scale opinion polls (see Section 5.4.5). These sampling methods may be used in combination with each other or with simple or stratified random sampling.

4.2.3.1 **Systematic sampling**

Suppose we need to obtain a sample of n members from a population of N elements (units of analysis) that are numbered *1* through N. In systematic sampling, every N/nth element (where N/n is an integer, that is, a whole number) is included (see Figure 4.9).

Example (see Figure 4.9)

Suppose we need to select a systematic sample of 10 multi-millionaires from a total population of 100 in South Africa. In this instance, $N/n = \frac{100}{10} = 10$. To obtain a systematic sample, we first draw an element (multi-millionaire) randomly (see

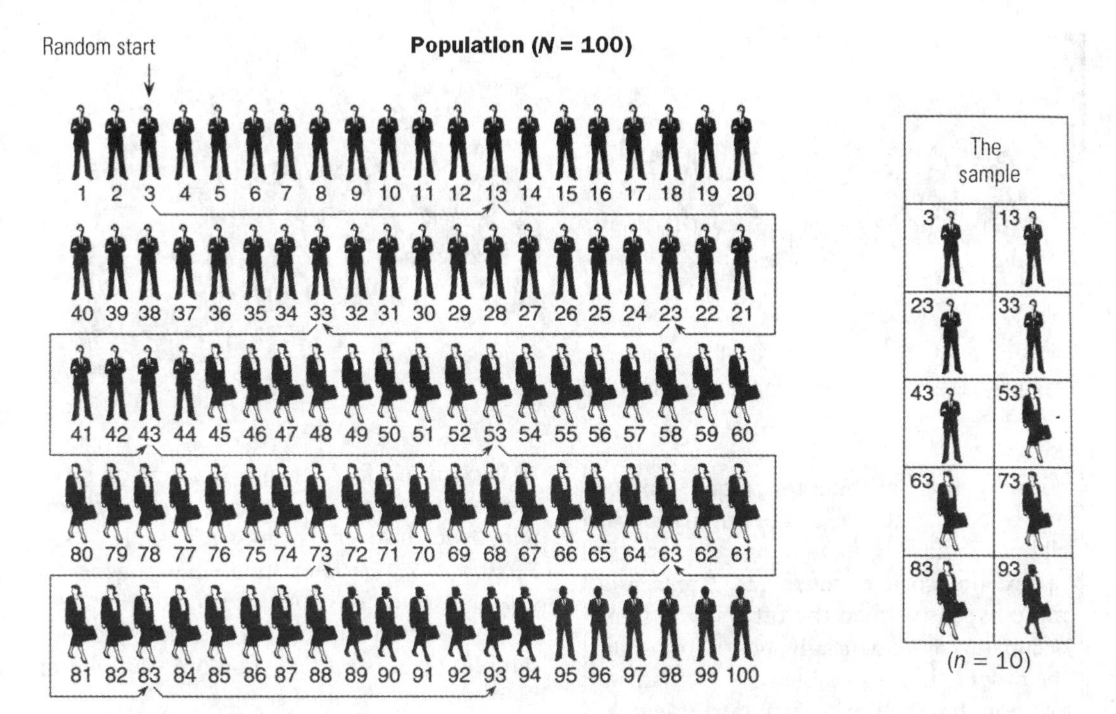

Figure 4.9 A stratified, systematic sample with a random start. (Adapted from Babbie & Mouton, *The practice of social research*, p. 198. 2001. Oxford University Press. Used with permission.)

Section 4.2.2.1) from the first 10 on the list. From there onwards we choose every 10th element of the residue of 100.

Suppose the number of the first element we draw is 3. The numbers of the elements that we subsequently select are 13 (obtained by 3 + 10), 23, 33, and so on, up to 93. Once we determine the number of the first element, the numbers of all *n* elements are fixed. Therefore, if we do not determine the first number randomly, the sample obtained is a non-probability sample (see Section 4.2.4).

Figure 4.9 illustrates the above example by combining systematic sampling and stratified sampling (where the different strata are grouped together – see Section 4.2.2.3).

In the case of systematic sampling, we should bear in mind the possibility of any cyclical order or regular pattern in the sampling frame (see Chapter 6) which is related to clearly distinguishable strata.

Example

Suppose a residential area is laid out in such a manner that each block contains eight stands, and the first and then every fourth and the next stand (on both sides of a side street) are corner stands (see illustration on page 60). If, in such a case, we select stands at intervals of eight, and the first stand number we choose randomly is two, there will be no corner stand included in our sample. In contrast, if we use the same interval (that is, four) and the number of the first stand is four, we will select corner stands only. Now, if the households of corner stands differ from the others in respect of a variable (see Section 2.2) that is related to our research (for example, financial

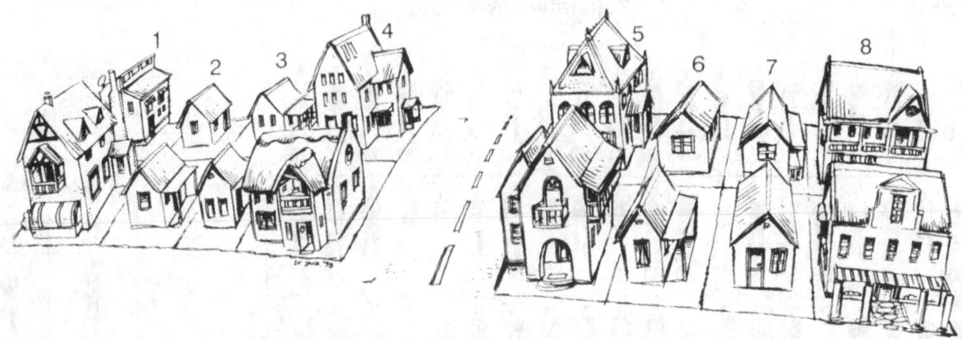

A regular pattern in the sampling frame related to financial strata.

position), none of these systematic samples will be representative of the population of all households.

Say the corner stands are larger and more expensive than the others, and their occupants are financially better off than the others, then a variable such as financial position has a bearing on our research; systematic sampling may very well affect our results.

Note

If there is such a systematic pattern in the numbers assigned to the members of the population, the most obvious solution is either to randomise the entire list prior to the assignment of numbers, or to rather use simple random sampling (see Section 4.2.2.1).

Because systematic sampling requires less time and is cheaper than simple random sampling, it is more practical. However, since simple random sampling ensures greater accuracy, we may consider systematic sampling to be more practical than, yet similar to, random sampling.

4.2.3.2 **Cluster sampling**

In large-scale surveys (see Sections 5.4.1, 5.4.5 & 7.7.3.1) it is usually difficult, if not impossible, to obtain lists of all the members (units of analysis – see Section 4.2.1) of the population as is required for drawing random or most systematic samples. In the case of cluster sampling, we draw (or stratify randomly – see Section 4.2.2) pre-existing, heterogeneous groups, called CLUSTERS, and all the members of the selected clusters (or a simple random sample or a stratified random sample of them) are the eventual sample.

Example

Suppose we have to draw a sample from the population of all the farm workers in South Africa. According to cluster sampling, we first draw a sample of, for example, all the farms in South Africa (for example, big and small; crop and cattle; and so on) and within each of these farms we obtain a random sample of farm workers.

We can perform cluster sampling in more than one phase.

Example

Suppose we wish to conduct an opinion survey on an issue such as reinstating the death penalty for the whole of South Africa. We can:

- first draw a sample from the nine provinces or regions within South Africa
- then draw a number of townships and cities within each region

- next, from a few street blocks within each of these townships and cities
- finally, draw a sample of individuals randomly within these street blocks.

Because we do cluster sampling in phases, we do not have to list all the members of the population initially (see Section 4.2.1 & 4.2.2), but only those who appear in the selected clusters. Even in cases in which a complete list of all members of the relevant population (units of analysis) is available, and a random sample of names or codes may readily be drawn (as is the case with simple random sampling – see Section 4.2.2.1), it may be impossible for practical reasons to reach all these individual units for research purposes.

Especially when the members of the relevant population are scattered throughout the length and breadth of the country, it may require a great deal of time and money to reach one or two individual units in remote areas that have been selected by a random sampling procedure. The greater the distance the selected individual units reside from one another, the higher the travelling expenses become, the more time is wasted criss-crossing the country, and the more difficult it becomes to collect the information (such as the opinions of people).

In contrast to simple random sampling, in cluster sampling fewer locations have to be visited but more than one or two individual units must be included at each such location.

The ADVANTAGE of cluster sampling is that there are considerable savings in time and costs when compared to simple random sampling.

However, when some clusters are homogeneous (similar) in terms of the variables of interest, cluster sampling may lead to BIASED samples. By BIASED samples, we mean samples that tend or lean towards a particular factor of the research topic.

Example

Say the relevant population (for example, personal computer users) includes about the same number of men and women. However, if several of the clusters drawn are composed of men only (for example, from the motor parts distributors sector), the eventual sample may include a disproportionately large number of men.

Thus, the DISADVANTAGE of cluster sampling is that there is a possibility of such *bias in each phase.* This means that in any phase we could draw a sample that is not representative (see Section 4.2) of the population. Even if all the clusters we draw during the first phase are representative of the population, the members we select during the second phase need not necessarily be representative of the various clusters. Consequently, we should be mindful of the sample size (see Section 4.2.5) and the accuracy of sampling during each phase in cluster sampling. Ultimately, to attain the desired *sample size*, there should also be a balance between the sample sizes in the successive phases so that the *initial samples* are not too large and the *eventual samples* too small, or vice versa.

4.2.4 **Non-probability sampling**

The probability that any element (unit of analysis) will be included in a non-probability sample cannot be specified. In some instances, certain members may have no chance at all of being included in such a sample (see Figure 4.10).

Example

If we use non-probability sampling to determine whether the majority (say 80%) of South African citizens are in favour of reinstating the death penalty, we may never be certain that the results we obtain are nearly as accurate as those we may have obtained with probability sampling. This means that we may not be as confident about our conclusions.

The ADVANTAGE of non-probability samples is that they are less complicated and more economical (in terms of time and financial expenses) than probability samples. Non-probability samples may be especially useful in pilot studies (see Section 7.6) in which a preliminary form of a questionnaire has to be tested.

4.2.4.1 **Accidental sampling (incidental sampling – see Figure 4.10)**

An accidental sample is the most convenient collection of members of the population (units of analysis) that are near and readily available for research purposes.

Example

Examples of accidental samples are the students who have registered for a particular course and show up at class on a particular day (this is also an example of what is referred to as a *captive audience*); the people who happen to be at a particular shopping centre at a particular time when the researcher is conducting interviews; the organisations that are close to the researcher's home.

Note

Researchers should consider using accidental samples only if they have no other option.

Insofar as the conclusions obtained inductively are based on accidental samples (see Section 4.2.4.1), they need not necessarily be typical of the relevant population of individuals and universe of circum-

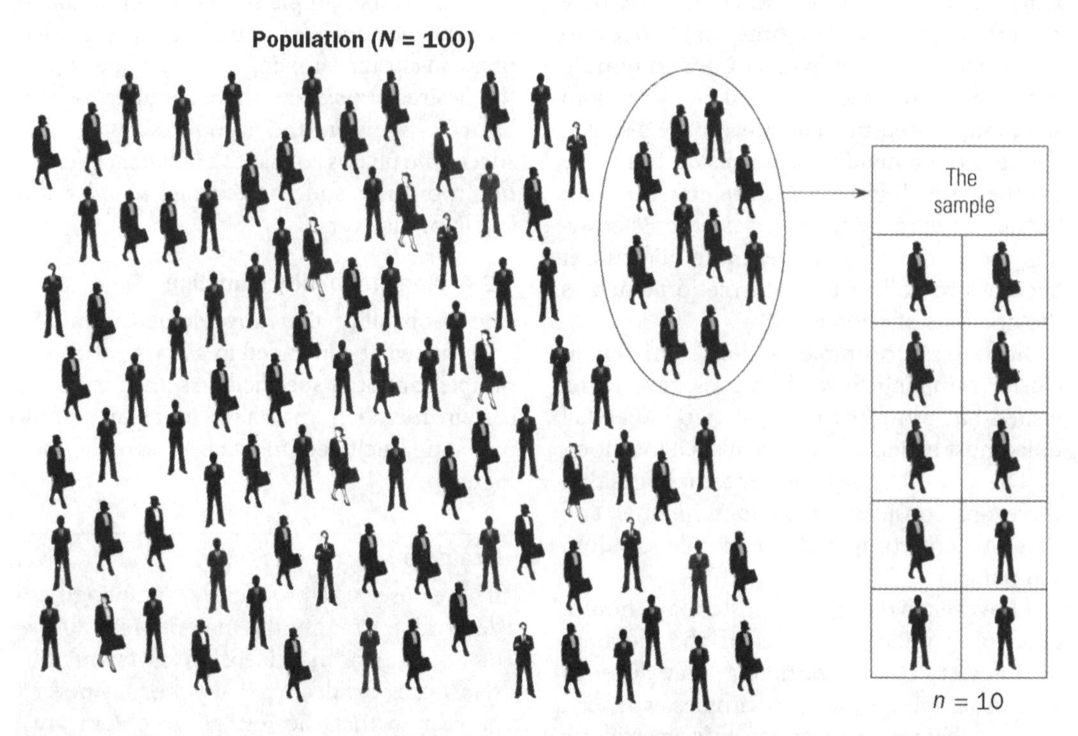

Figure 4.10 Accidental sample example. (Adapted from Babbie & Mouton, *The practice of social research*, p. 170. 2001. Oxford University Press. Used with permission.)

stances. Such conclusions could thus be seen as hypotheses that will have to be examined deductively according to the procedure in Section 2.3.1.

4.2.4.2 **Purposive sampling**

This is the most important kind of non-probability sampling. Researchers rely on their experience, ingenuity and/or previous research findings (see Section 3.3.2) to deliberately obtain units of analysis in such a manner that the sample they obtain may be regarded as being representative of the relevant population (see Section 4.2.1).

Example

If a minister of foreign affairs of another country wishes to assess the opinions of a broad spectrum of the South African public in 2001, he or she may decide to interview only a sample of opinion-makers. Such a sample, which may include, say, the state president and the leaders of the ANC, DP, IFP, PAC and UDM, would be an example of a purposive sample.

The problem with this kind of sampling is that different researchers may proceed in different ways to obtain such a sample and thus it is impossible to evaluate the extent to which such samples are representative of the relevant population.

4.2.4.3 **Quota sampling**

In the case of quota sampling, we make an effort to have the same proportions (see Figure 4.8) of units of analysis in important strata (see Section 4.2.2.3) such as sex, age, and so on as are in the population, but we obtain the units of analysis in any particular stratum accidentally.

Example

Suppose we know that of the population of top managers (N = 1 000) 80% are men (800) and 20% are women (200). In a quota sample (n = 100) of the population of top managers we will see to it that 80% are men (80) and 20% are women (20). However, we obtain both these groups in an accidental fashion as explained before.

We may find that a quota sample yields quite satisfactory results under certain circumstances.

- Firstly, we should know the important strata of which the population is composed and their respective proportions with a reasonable degree of accuracy, or be able to estimate them (see Figure 4.9).
- Secondly, we should include enough cases (at least 15, but preferably more than 25) of each stratum in the sample.

4.2.4.4 **Snowball sampling**

In the first phase of this kind of sampling, we approach a few individuals from the relevant population. These individuals then act as informants and identify other members (for example, acquaintances or friends) from the same population for inclusion in the sample. The latter may in turn identify a further set of relevant individuals so that the sample, like a rolling snowball, grows in size till saturated.

Example

An executive director of a well-known South African company, who obtained her academic qualifications during the sixties at Oxford University, may identify someone else with the same academic background, who in turn may put us on to another similar individual, and so on.

4.2.5 **Sample size (n)**

The issue of determining the desired sample size for a given research project falls outside the scope of this book. Only general principles and considerations will be pointed out (methods to determine the desirable sample size are discussed by Cohen (1988)). The previous sections of this chapter also contain information about sample size.

Note

As a general rule, we should not use any sample with less than 15 units of analysis, but preferably one with more than 25 units of analysis (Huysamen, 1991). If the population size is 500, then the sample size should be 200. It is not necessary to use a sample size bigger than 500 units of analysis, no matter what the size of the population may be if random sampling is done.

- Firstly, when we determine the size of the sample (*n*), we should bear in mind the size of the population (*N*). In general, it holds that the smaller the total population, the relatively larger the sample should be to ensure satisfactory results.

Example

If one population of 100 000 requires a sample of 1 000 (1%), it does not mean that a population of 1 000 may be equally satisfactorily represented by a sample of 10 people only (also 1%). As a matter of fact, if the population consists of only 10 cases (for example, the population of small business enterprises in a particular city that have doubled their taxable income within one year of establishing the business), it may be advisable to include them all in the sample.

The influence of absolute sample size (*n*) instead of proportion (*n*/*N*) to the size of the population (*N*) has to do with the standard error of the mean. So, the number of units (*n*) involved in our sample is more important than the percentage of the total population they represent. This is illustrated in Table 4.1.

This means that an increase in the sample size, in proportion to the size of the population from which the sample is drawn, results

Table 4.1
The effect of sample size on the standard error of the mean for a population of 10 000

Sample size (*n*)	Standard error
20	2,24
50	1,40
100	0,99
250	0,62
500	0,44
1 000	0,30
2 500	0,17
5 000	0,10

N = 10 000

in a decrease in the standard error. So, although we must try to draw as a big as possible a sample size, it becomes relatively unnecessary to draw a sample size bigger than 500 (because it has little effect in decreasing the standard error and margin of error).

- Secondly, the desired sample size does not depend on the size of the population only but also on the variance (heterogeneity) of the variable. As a general rule, the larger the variance of the variable, the larger the sample which is required. The sampling error may be estimated in the case of random samples. (Compare the formula in Chapter 7 of Babbie and Mouton [2001].)

Example

If, in a nationwide referendum, we expect the proportion of yes and no votes in one region to be closer to each other (say 45:55) than in another (so that the variance is larger in the former), we should draw a relatively larger sample from the former region than from the latter. On the other hand, if there were only a very few no votes in one region, it would be important to also represent this group in the sample.

- Thirdly, if each stratum of a highly heterogeneous population is relatively homogeneous, a relatively smaller stratified sample than that required for a random sample, may be sufficient. If the strata differ in size and heterogeneity, we should adjust the size of the respective samples we take from them accordingly – the smaller the stratum and/or the more heterogeneous it is, the relatively larger the sample that we should draw from it.

Example

If the 10 000 students at a particular technikon or university are composed of 8 000 undergraduate, 1 000 fourth year, 800 masters and 200 doctoral students, we should obviously select a much higher proportion of doctoral students than undergraduates. (Obviously, all students then would not have the same chance of being included in the sample.)

In large-scale surveys (see Section 5.4.1), such as opinion polls (see Section 5.4.5), in which we intend to assess the position of the entire population on a particular variable, much larger samples are normally used than in experimental research (see Section 5.2). Although these samples seldom exceed several thousand, samples of this magnitude may still yield quite accurate estimates of the responses of a population of several million.

Example

Almost two months prior to the referendum on a new constitutional dispensation in South Africa in 1983, *Mark- en Meningsopnames* (a survey research company) predicted, on the basis of a sample of fewer than 2 000 voters, that 67,4% would vote yes. Eventually 66,3% of the more than 2 million votes were recorded in this category (Perold, 1983).

- Fourthly, in determining sample size, we should also bear in mind that the number of units of analysis from which we eventually obtain usable data may be much smaller than the number that we drew originally. It may not be possible to trace some individuals, others may refuse to participate in the research, while still more may not provide all the necessary information or may not complete their questionnaires, so that their information will have to be discarded. Therefore, it is usually advisable to draw a larger sample than the one for which complete data is desired eventually.

Example

If we need a sample of 100 respondents' completed postal questionnaires, we would probably have to mail the questionnaire to 300 people or organisations (called response rate – see Section 7.7.3.1).

Activity 4.2

Read Case Study A; Case Study B; Case Study C; Case Study D; Case Study E and Case Study F in Appendix D on page 276.

Question

What *type of sampling* is used in the research in each case study? Briefly explain your answer.

Answer

CASE STUDY A: The sampling is a type of *non-probability sample* (because other nursing sisters and doctors who work with AIDS cases did not have the chance to serve as sample members), namely *an accidental sample*, because it was convenient to use the group of nursing sisters and doctors of just one general hospital, for which permission had been granted.

CASE STUDY B: The sampling is a type of *non-probability sample* (because goldsmith apprentices who do the same course with other jewellery firms did not have the chance to take part as sample members), *namely an accidental sample*, because it was convenient and economical to use the group of goldsmith apprentices at just one large jewellery firm.

CASE STUDY C: The type of sampling is a *simple random type* because each of the 60 first-line supervisors employed at agricultural corporations in South Africa had an equal chance of serving as subjects.

CASE STUDY D: The type of sampling is a *purposive non-probability type* because the data of students in public speech-making at only four technikons, but who had already completed seven assignments, were used.

CASE STUDY E: The type of sampling is an *accidental type* because the units of analysis firstly happen to be bankrupt small businesses in Pretoria whose owners were willing to participate in the project. Thus the units of analysis were not randomly sampled from all bankrupt small businesses in South Africa.

CASE STUDY F: The type of sampling is an *accidental sample* because the respondents (business people) were conveniently available from Gauteng and the Western Cape – those who agreed to participate in the project.

Self-evaluation questions

1 What is the main feature of probability sampling that distinguishes it from non-probability sampling?
2 Mention and briefly explain the two requirements that should be met for drawing a simple random sample from a particular population.
3 What should the researcher bear in mind when he or she considers drawing (a) systematic samples, and (b) cluster samples?
4 Indicate the similarity and the difference between stratified random sampling and quota sampling.
5 What type of sampling can you possibly use to personally interview at least 15 individuals from the same sampling frame on their opinion regarding the topic of your literature review done in Activity 3.1? Explain your answer briefly and state from which populaton the units of analysis will be drawn.

Summary

In each hypothesis one or more populations are implied (for example, all businesses in the Northern Province with fewer than 30 staff members). In this example, the population may be defined as the total collection of individual businesses who are potentially available for observation and who have the characteristic that the research hypothesis refers to ("fewer than 30 staff members"), in common. If it is not possible to involve all the members of the population, the researcher has to rely on a sample of the population, which is a relatively small subgroup of individual units from the population (for instance "males", instead of males as well as females. In such a case, "sex" can not be considered a variable – it is held constant – and "male" is the unit of analysis).

Multiple choice and true/false questions

Only *one* of the answers to each question is correct. Identify and mark the correct one. (Answers appear in Appendix E on page 285.)

4.1 The main purpose of sampling is to be able to select:
   a) a sample whose statistics will accurately portray a known population parameter
   b) a sample whose statistics will accurately portray an unknown population parameter
   c) a sample whose unknown statistics will accurately portray a known parameter
   d) simple random samples.

4.2 In a study where a researcher examined newspaper editorials from small South African towns that dealt with news on the topic of electrical power failures, the unit of analysis was:
a) electrical power failures
b) small towns
c) newspaper editorials
d) electricity.

4.3 In sampling, the complete list of the units of analysis of a population is called a:
a) population list
b) target list
c) sampling frame
d) sample list.

4.4 Generally, the more heterogeneous the population, the more beneficial it is to use stratified sampling.
True False

4.5 Cluster sampling is a useful sampling procedure for large populations that are geographically scattered.
True False

4.6 Cluster sampling requires a complete listing of all the primary sampling units.
True False

4.7 When the overriding factor used in selecting the units of analysis is mainly due to their availability, the resulting sample is called:
a) a cluster sample
b) a convenience sample
c) a snowball sample
d) an accidental sample.

4.8 To be able to generalise from a sample to the population depends on the following characteristic of the sample:
a) distinctiveness
b) power
c) representiveness
d) variability.

4.9 In general, as sample size increases:
a) the standard error fluctuates in size
b) the standard error is constant
c) the standard error decreases in size
d) the standard error increases in size.

4.10 We call the measure used to estimate the difference between the true population value and the results of the sample the:
a) sampling index
b) margin of error
c) discrepancy error
d) population equation.

5 Types of quantitative research designs

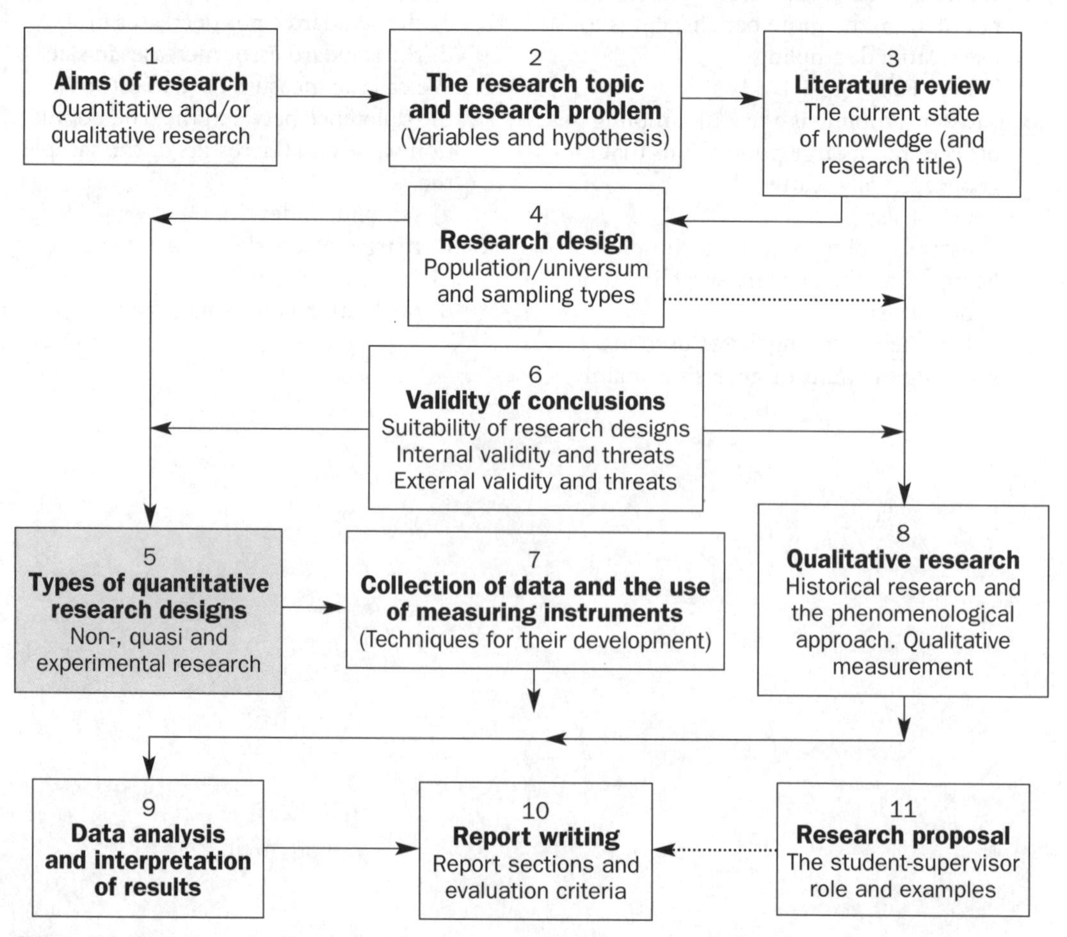

Figure 5.1 The research process and the outline of chapters in this book

Learning Outcomes

After studying this chapter, you should be able to:

1. illustrate with examples the three important components of the classical experiment
2. list and illustrate the prerequisites for establishing causality
3. explain why it is difficult to do random sampling in field research
4. explain the extent to which causality can be researched by the interrupted time-series design
5. explain briefly why mainly non-experimental research is done and non-random sampling is used in organisations, and explain what field investigations involve
6. explain why relationships (correlations), but not causality, can be researched by non-experimental research designs
7. compare cross-sectional and longitudinal designs
8. compare criterion-groups design with prediction studies
9. discuss the two major issues of any research design.

5.1 Introduction

We can distinguish between four different types of research design:

- experimental research
- quasi-experimental research
- non-experimental research
- qualitative research.

According to each "plan" (see Section 4.1), we will structure and execute our research in a different way.

In the following sections we will concentrate on quantitative research (which includes the first three types of research mentioned). We will address qualitative research in Chapter 8.

5.2 Experimental research

All types of experimental research have one thing in common, namely *intervention*. In other words, the participants (units of analysis – see Section 4.2.1) are exposed to something to which they otherwise would not have been subjected.

Figure 5.2 shows that the intervention (the independent variable – see Section 2.2) hopefully changes the dependent variable (see Section 2.2) of the units of analysis (See Section 4.2.1) considerably according to the statement made (the hypothesis – see Section 2.3).

We call measuring the dependent variable before the intervention PREMEASUREMENT, and measuring it after the intervention, POSTMEASUREMENT.

In such a research design where one group is involved, we speak about a premeasurement and a postmeasurement SINGLE-GROUP DESIGN (see Section 6.3.2).

If only one group receives the intervention, we have no way of knowing whether any considerable changes (in the dependent variable) would not have occurred in any case, that is, without the intervention (independent variable). What is required, therefore, is a CONTROL GROUP that is not exposed to the experimental intervention. (In Section 5.2.2,

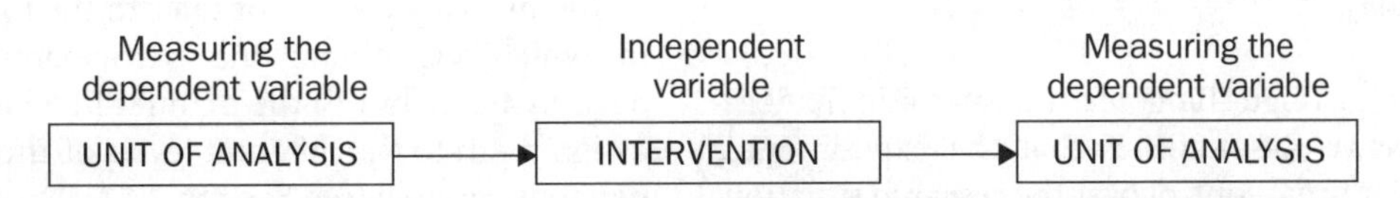

Figure 5.2 The effect of the independent variable (intervention) on the dependent variable

we deal with an important principle involved here, namely *causality.*)

A control group, as its name indicates, is a group that does not receive the intervention, but serves to exercise control over the nuisance variables (see Sections 5.2.1.3, 6.3.2.3, 6.3.7.2 & 9.3.2.3).

> **Example**
>
> Suppose we expose the trainee supervisors of one mine to aggressive supervisor behaviour towards a subordinate and expose the trainee supervisors of another company to neutral behaviour by the same supervisor.
>
> Subsequently, we measure the aggressive behaviour of both groups in the same manner. We want to attribute differences in the aggressiveness measurements of the two groups to the fact that the one group observed the aggressive supervisor behaviour (the experimental group) while the other group did not (the control group).

Note

This design is known as an intact-group design. Any intact groups (for example, the residents of two hostels, the students in two classes, the workers in two particular mining companies, and so on) may be self-selected in terms of the dependent variable or other variables related to it.

In terms of the way in which we decide which of the participants we should subject to which intervention, we may distinguish between:

- pre-experimental research (see Section 6.3.2)
- TRUE EXPERIMENTAL RESEARCH
- quasi-experimental research (see Section 5.3).

The distinguishing feature of TRUE EXPERIMENTAL RESEARCH is that the experimenter has optimal control over the research situation.

5.2.1 Characteristics of true experimental research

5.2.1.1 Control over the independent variable

There we have full control over the independent variable (see Section 2.2) in the sense that we may determine which levels of it we should use.

> **Example**
>
> If we wish to investigate the relative effectiveness of distributed learning and massed learning as in RESEARCH EXAMPLE I (see Section 1.2.2), we should determine how many hours of learning over what period of time qualifiy as distributed learning and how massed learning is defined. These will then serve as the two levels of the independent variable learning.

5.2.1.2 Random assignment of units of analysis to groups

Although all types of experimental research have some or other *intervention* in common, the distinguishing feature of true experimental research is that the different groups (exposed to the different levels of the independent variable) are formed by random assignment (see Section 6.3.6).

We can randomly assign individuals to groups by tossing a coin, or by using a table of random numbers (see Section 4.2.2.2, Appendix C and CD-ROM) and placing those with even numbers in one group and those with uneven numbers in the other. This assignment results in a 50/50 chance of any particular individual being assigned to Group 1 rather than Group 2.

By *randomly* we do not refer to the manner in which we obtain the participants (see Section 4.2.2), but to the manner in which we assign them to the different levels of the independent variable (see Section 2.2).

Example

In RESEARCH EXAMPLE II (see Section 2.2, page 14) a sample of trainee supervisors was randomly assigned to two main groups that subsequently observed iron-fisted and approachable role model management style behaviour, respectively.

Note

We call the design that is generated by assigning individuals randomly to groups in this manner, a RANDOMISED GROUPS DESIGN. *This design represents the simplest example of a true experimental design (see Section 9.3.2.3 for a more complex design, namely the* RANDOMISED-BLOCK DESIGN*).*

Figure 5.3 shows three types of randomised designs.

X_A	Y
X_B	Y

a) Randomised two-group design

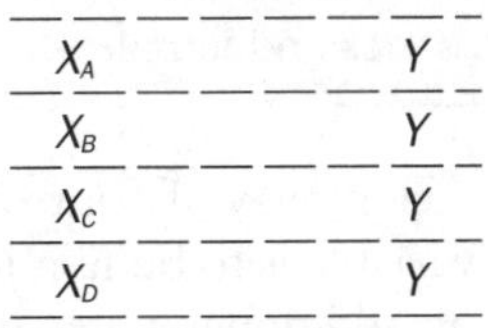

X_A	Y
X_B	Y
X_C	Y
X_D	Y

b) Randomised multigroup design

Y_1	X_A	Y_2
Y_1	X_B	Y_2

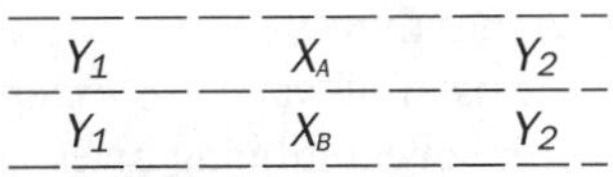

c) Randomised pre-test and post-test design

Figure 5.3 Diagrammatic representations of randomised groups designs (Huysamen, 1994 p. 58)

Note

Advice is that not less than 30 elements/individuals be assigned to a group. See Huysamen (1994, pp. 59–61) for an explanation of type (c), where Y_1 is a point in time before Y_2 (later).

(a) Randomised two-group design

In the simplest example of a randomised group design, participants are randomly assigned (see Section 6.3.6) to two groups that are subsequently subjected to two different levels of the independent variable (X_a and X_b). Therefore we may view the groups as being matched (see Sections 6.3.2 and 6.3.7).

Figure 5.3(a) is a diagrammatic representation of the randomised two-group design. THE DOTTED LINES, which represent the boundaries of the two groups, SYMBOLISE THAT INDIVIDUALS ARE RANDOMLY ASSIGNED TO THE DIFFERENT GROUPS and that the treatments are assigned randomly to these groups. The symbol X stands for the independent variable (see Section 2.2), and X_A and X_B for the different levels of this variable (see Section 2.2) (or groups A and B); while Y symbolises the measurement of the dependent variable (Y_1 is before Y_2). X appears in front of Y, meaning that the experimental intervention representing the independent variable takes place prior to (before) the measurement of the dependent variable (Y).

Example

X_A may represent government *loans* to small farmers, while X_B represents government *subsidies* with the aim of determining which type of these financial aids (intervention) has the largest positive effect on small farming practices (Y).

(b) Randomised multigroup design

If the treatment factor (independent variable) has more than two levels, the research participants (units of analysis – see Section

4.2.1) are randomly assigned (see Section 6.2.6) to as many groups as there are levels, *and* the levels are randomly assigned to these groups. The resulting design is simply an extension of the randomised two-group design described above.

Figure 5.3(b) gives a diagrammatic representation of such a design in which the independent variable X has four levels, namely, X_A, X_B, X_C and X_D The dependent variable is represented by Y.

5.2.1.3 Nuisance variables

In true experimental research, we have considerable control over irrelevant variables, also called NUISANCE VARIABLES (or third variable).

A NUISANCE VARIABLE is any variable that may influence the dependent variable (see Section 2.2) but that was not mentioned in the research hypothesis (see Section 2.3) and that the researcher must try to control (see Sections 6.3.2.3, 6.3.7.2 & 9.3.2.3).

Note

We can determine the speculated effect of nuisance variables by doing a proper literature review (see Section 3.2), and in so doing learn from previously documented research findings (see Section 3.2.1).

As a matter of fact, the basic purpose of experimental research is to control nuisance variables to such an extent that the various groups differ only in terms of the levels of the independent variable in question. (To the extent that the experimenter succeeds in achieving this, we may confidently attribute changes in the dependent variable (see Section 2.2), to the independent variable.)

How to exercise control over *nuisance variables*:

- In a few cases it may be possible to eliminate the effect of the nuisance variable completely.

Example

If noise constitutes the nuisance variable, we can perform the experiment in a noise-proof room.

If the nuisance variable refers to some or other attribute of the research participants, we can eliminate its effect by using only subjects who are as far as possible alike or homogeneous in terms of this characteristic. The disadvantage of this way of controlling nuisance variables is that the results we obtain will be applicable only to that level of the nuisance variable that we have used in the study.

Say sex (male or female) is the nuisance variable. We can eliminate its effect by using either only males or only females as research participants. For example, if males and females react differently to television violence, we could use only males in an investigation into the effects of television violence. If we then find that the most frequent viewers exhibit the most aggression, this relationship could not have been affected by the sex of the participants because only one sex (males) was involved. However, the relationship between television viewing and aggression would be applicable only to males and could not be generalised to all people of both sexes (males and females).

- A more efficient way of controlling such a nuisance variable is to build it into the design as an additional independent variable (see Section 9.3.2.3).
- Another way of controlling nuisance variables is to purposely form the various groups so that they are as far as possible alike in terms of all variables except the one of which the effect is being investigated. Instead of completely eliminating such nuisance variables, we attempt to keep their effects the same for all groups or, put differently, to hold them constant for all groups (see Section 6.3.7.2).

As we will indicate in Section 6.3.6, the most practically feasible way of holding nuisance variables constant for all groups is to randomly assign individuals to the groups that are to receive the various levels of the independent variable (the intervention to which the participants are exposed).

This control that researchers have over the assignment of subjects (to the various levels of the independent variable) in particular demonstrates their control over the experimental situation.

Example

In RESEARCH EXAMPLE I (see Section 1.2.2.2, page 6), to obtain scientific knowledge on the relative effectiveness of the practice of distributed learning (mastering study material in more than one session) versus massed learning (mastering all the study material in one session), we will have to conduct a study in which the performance of:

- one group of apprentices who have learned in a distributed fashion is compared with
- another, comparable, group that has studied the same material by means of the massed procedure.

By merely drawing lots, we may determine whether any particular apprentice (subject) will be assigned to the group that is to learn according to the distributed method rather than the massed one.

Say we then find differences in the dependent variable (examination results) between the two groups following these interventions (distributed and massed learning method). We might infer that these have to be the effect of the independent variable (distributed and massed learning method) rather than any other variable (because the groups were the same in terms of all other variables – possible nuisance variables).

5.2.2 Causality in the human behavioural sciences

The purpose of science is to explain phenomena and such explanation may consist of indicating their causes as far as possible (see Section 2.2.2). Philosophers of science have devoted much attention to the issue of causality, and this topic will be discussed very briefly in this section.

Any variable *X* may be regarded as a (sufficient or necessary and sufficient) cause of another variable *Y* if *each of the following three conditions* is met:

- there must be correlation between variables
- the cause must precede the effect
- the third variable must be controlled.

5.2.2.1 Correlation between variables

There should be a (correlational) association between *X* and *Y*, in other words, *Y* should tend to appear in association with *X*.

Example

If there is a correlation between the number of hours that mine workers spend watching violent films on television and their scores on a questionnaire of aggressiveness, the number of hours they spend watching violent films on television is not necessarily the cause of their scores on a questionnaire of aggressiveness.

The higher aggressiveness of some mine workers may make them more inclined to watch violent films, which may further reinforce their aggressiveness. This would be an example of a mutual relationship (between television watching and aggressiveness).

However, the existence of such a relationship only (even if it were perfect) would not necessarily be an indication that *X* causes *Y*. A correlation between variables *X* and *Y* may be the result of either a MUTUAL RELATIONSHIP between *X* and *Y*, or of a third variable *Z*, which may cause both *X* and *Y* (see Section 9.4.1.3).

A MUTUAL RELATIONSHIP means that one variable (*X*) plays a role in the occurrence of another (*Y*), which in its turn affects the former so that there is a mutual relationship between them.

Example

We may expect to find a high, positive correlation (see Section 9.4.1.3) between the number of churches (*Y*) in towns and cities and the incidence of crime (*X*). However, this correlation may be attributed to a third variable (see Section 6.3.2.3), namely the number of people (*Z*) living in the towns and cities. The size of the population of the towns and cities has an effect on both the number of churches and the incidence of crime (see illustration on page 75).

5.2.2.2 Cause must precede the effect

If we want to infer a causal relationship, it is necessary for the cause to precede the effect. In the human behavioural sciences it is often difficult, if not impossible, to meet this requirement. Often, causal factors are not events that take place and are concluded at some or other identifiable point in time because of a mutual relationship between the variables.

Example

Motivation plays a role in academic achievement, which subsequently raises motivation, which further promotes academic achievement. It is not clear what qualifies as the cause and what as the effect.

A distinction that is typically encountered in the discussion of causality is the one between necessary and sufficient causes.

A variable, or event *X* is considered to be a NECESSARY CAUSE of *Y* if *Y* cannot occur in the absence of *X* (see Figure 5.4).

Example

The irrigation of a lawn in a desert area requires a water supply (for example, a borehole or a reservoir somewhere in a neighbouring rainfall area). The water supply X is therefore a necessary cause of wetness on the lawn. However, the presence of such a water supply does not guarantee a wet lawn. Some or other functional irrigation system has to be connected to the water supply. The presence of a water supply is thus a *necessary*, but not a *sufficient*, condition or cause of a wet lawn.

A variable, or event, *X* is a SUFFICIENT CAUSE of *Y* if the presence of *X* necessarily results in the occurrence of *Y* (see Figure 5.5).

Example

We may regard the connection of a functional irrigation system to the water supply as a sufficient cause of a wet lawn. If such an irrigation system were to be switched on, it would necessarily lead to wetness on the lawn. However, the incidence of a wet lawn is not proof of the presence of a programmed irrigation system, because the lawn could also have been watered manually with a watering-can. The availability of an irrigation system would thus be a, but not a *necessary*, condition or cause of a wet lawn.

5.2.2.3 Control of the third variable

In the above example, a wet lawn was not necessarily evidence of one particular type of irrigation. *The existence of a correlation between X and Y, and X's precedence over Y in time, are not sufficient to conclude that X causes Y.* Therefore, there is a third condition for inferring causality, namely that there should be no third variable *Z* to which the effect in *X* could be attributed.

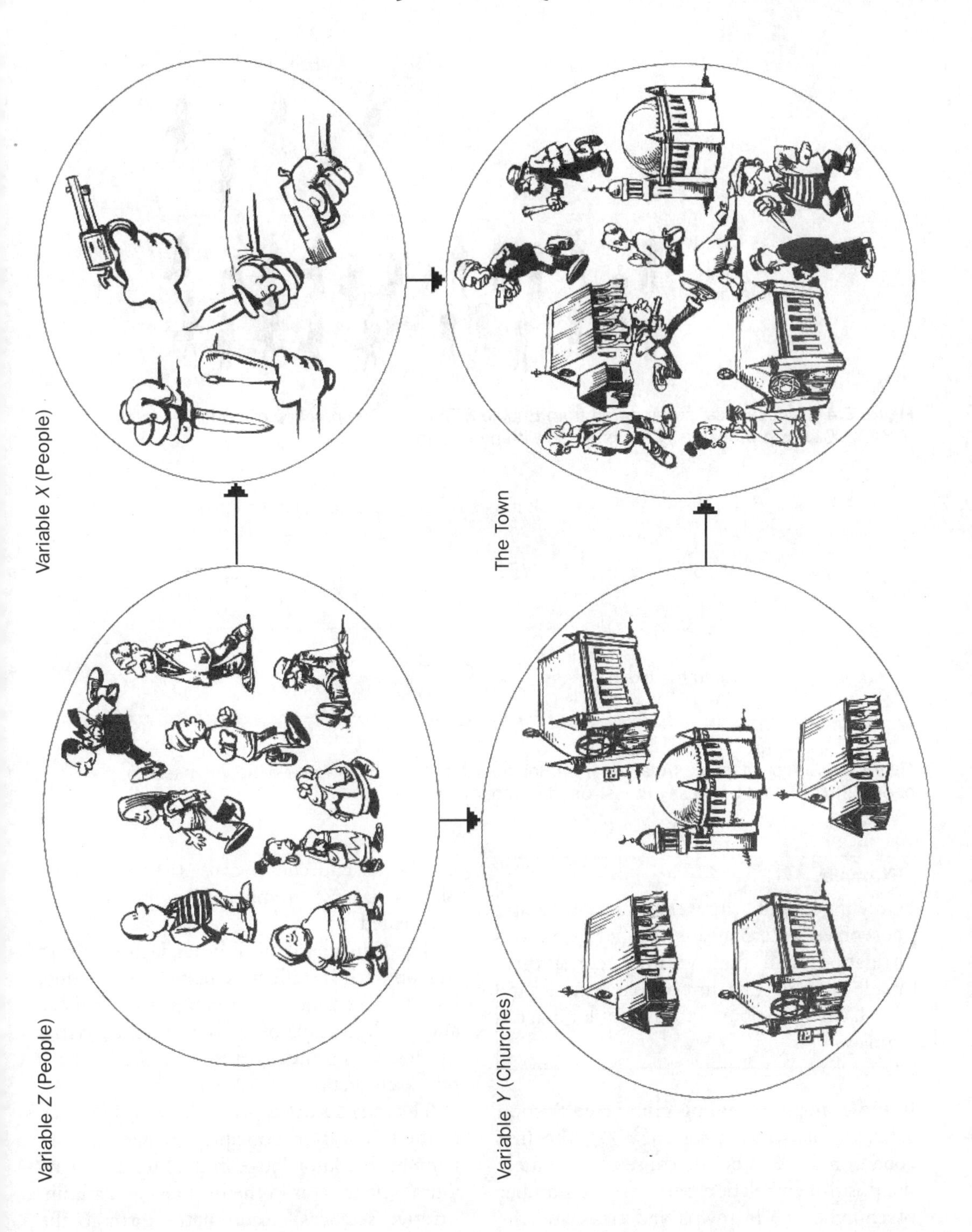

Causality and the role of a third variable

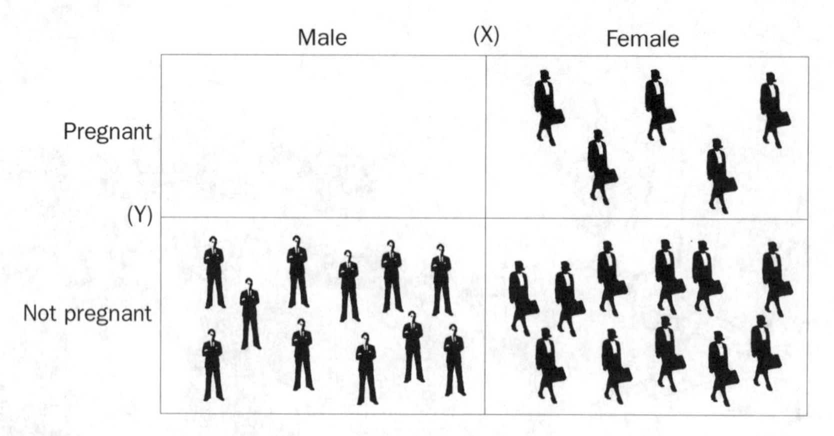

Figure 5.4 Necessary cause (Adapted from Babbie & Mouton, *The practice of social research*, p. 84. 2001. Oxford University Press. Used with permission.)

(Y) \ (X)	Took the exam	Did not take the exam
Failed the exam	F F F F	F F F F F F F F
Passed the exam	A A C A D A B C C B D B C A B C C B D D D A A C C A	

Figure 5.5 Sufficient cause (Adapted from Babbie & Mouton, *The practice of social research*, p. 84. 2001. Oxford University Press. Used with permission.)

> **Example**
>
> Only if we could show that there were no hosepipes, watering-cans or other means of irrigation, and that weather conditions made dew or rain impossible, could the wet lawn be attributed to a sprinkler irrigation system.

In the example regarding crime (see Section 5.2.2.1 & illustration on page 75), the first condition for *X* to be the cause of Y, namely the positive correlation between the number of churches (*Y*) in towns and cities and the incidence of crime (*X*), an increase in crime could not be ascribed to an increase in the number of churches because the role of population size (*Z*) (number of people) had not been ruled out.

The principle that all other factors except the one whose effect is being investigated, have to be excluded, is referred to in science and law by means of the Latin phrase *ceteris paribus*, which means *everything else being the same* (see Section 5.3 & 6.3.1).

The *ceteris paribus* principle brings us back to the falsification principle (see Section 2.4), namely, that knowledge in the human behavioural sciences (as in the business and administrative sciences) accumulates through the elimination of rival hypotheses or alternative explanations of behaviour.

Unfortunately, matters are not as simple in the human behavioural sciences as in the natural sciences, where the presence of a sufficient cause necessarily leads to a particular effect.

> **Example**
>
> In the above example regarding the irrigation of a lawn in a desert area, rain would always be followed by a wet lawn (provided that there is a lawn, of course).
>
> We could liken the situation in the human behavioural sciences to one in which the same amount of rain would wash away the lawn of one person and leave his neighbour's lawn bone-dry. The regularity notion about causality (which was addressed at the beginning of this section) thus presents an oversimplified construction of human behaviour.

What makes matters in the business and administrative sciences so complicated, is that there are seldom only one or two variables that we may identify as the causal factors. Any phenomenon tends to be dependent on a number of different factors. To investigate its effect with only one supposed *independent variable* would imply a negation of reality and an oversimplification of the problem.

> **Example**
>
> To perform well financially, not only a particular level of trading skill may be required, but also the necessary motivation, social support, physical facilities, practice, and so on, of the small business entrepreneur.

5.2.3 Laboratory versus field studies

Depending on whether we do research in a laboratory or under natural circumstances, we distinguish between LABORATORY and field studies. In the business and administrative sciences, a laboratory does not necessarily mean a room with burning gas cylinders, glass apparatus and people wearing white overcoats.

Any venue (place or even the environment) that is specially equipped for the purpose of studying a particular phenomenon, such as individual or group behaviour; the products of such behaviour; or the nature of a material, qualifies as a laboratory. To a greater or lesser extent such a LABORATORY may be characterised by artificiality to some degree in comparison with the real world.

RESEARCH EXAMPLE II (see Section 2.2, page 14) represents an instance in which experimental research was carried out in a laboratory situation. The training centre in which the trainee

The advantage of LABORATORY EXPERIMENTS is that they allow for maximum control over accidental nuisance variables by eliminating them or by equating them for all groups	FIELD SITUATIONS vary in the extent of control they allow, but usually they permit much less control. In a field situation there are many external factors that may operate as nuisance variables and that (as a result of the field situation) are much more difficult to control than in a laboratory situation.

supervisors' management styles could be observed, qualified as a laboratory because it was equipped with the necessary apparatus (video machines, recreation facilities and equipment to make tea) for the demonstration of their reaction to the subordinate Bobo and for observing such behaviour through one-way mirrors.

We could hardly study some problems (for example, taxi wars) in a laboratory situation. Even if this were possible, the *artificiality of the situation* would probably change the very behaviour that was being studied. Many research problems in the business and administrative sciences that could be investigated only with great difficulty in laboratory situations may lend themselves to *field studies*.

In a FIELD STUDY, we randomly assign subjects to the experimental and control groups, and the experimental intervention is effected in a natural, everyday environment.

The environment in which research is carried out actually constitutes a continuum, with laboratories at the one extreme and natural environments at the other.

Example

To investigate the research problem in RESEARCH EXAMPLE II (page 14) (see Section 2.2) in a field situation, we might be required to observe the management styles of the trainee supervisors at their work stations with their own recreational facilities. However, different trainee supervisors are exposed to different work situations at their stations and not all of them have a subordinate at a given time to show the behaviour of Bobo or that of the role model supervisor. Moreover, some visitor (for example, a company director) who has an inhibiting effect may pay an unscheduled visit so that an iron-fisted management style could possibly be impeded.

Although field researchers are careful to limit such nuisance variables (see Section 5.2.1.3) to a minimum, there is always the possibility that uncontrolled nuisance variables may put a spoke in their wheels. On the other hand, the chances that something similar may happen in a laboratory situation are relatively slim.

Activity 5.1

Read the following problem statement and answer the question. Compare your answer with the given answer.

Problem statement

A machine operator thinks that fumes emitted in the workshops play a role in the low efficiency of the operators. He would like to prove this to his supervisor by doing a research study.

Question

What would the study situation be: laboratory experiment or field experiment? Give brief reasons for your answer.

Answer

The study situation would be a field experiment, because: The research occurs in a natural, familiar environment (in a workshop) and not in a specially-designed environment (laboratory).

The investigation contains an experiment – where an attempt is made to control/check the amount or levels of fumes as opposed to pure air in a workshop.

Activity 5.2

Read Case Study B and Case Study C In Appendix D on page 276.

Question

Will the study situation in each case study involve a laboratory experiment or a field experiment? Give brief reasons for your answers.

Answer

CASE STUDY B: The investigation involves a field experiment rather than a laboratory experiment because the experiment (on the influence of the role induction procedure on attitudes) is carried out in the natural, everyday setting where the goldsmith apprentices receive their training – the ordinary scheduled practical meetings.

CASE STUDY C: The investigation involves a laboratory experiment rather than a field experiment because the experiment (the training course) was most probably carried out in a classroom situation where the hour long written test was written. The classroom situation functions artificially from the natural, everyday environment in which first-line supervisors at an agricultural corporation work.

5.3 Quasi-experimental research

We have indicated that the critical feature of true experimental research is the random assignment of subjects to different treatment groups (see Section 5.2.1.2). The purpose of such assignment is to equate such groups in terms of all known and unknown nuisance variables (see Section 5.1.2.3). To the extent that we have achieved this, we then have to attribute eventual differences (in the dependent variable – see Section 2.2) between the different groups to the different treatments (that is, the independent variable – see Section 2.2) rather than to any nuisance variables.

It may often be impossible or undesirable to assign subjects randomly to different groups and/or to bring about certain interventions and thus to effect the control that is characteristic of true experiments (see Section 5.2.1). The effect of earthquakes, the introduction of a new education system, and the repeal of influx control represent a few examples of problems that we cannot investigate along these lines.

Furthermore, it is often necessary for us to carry out research in NATURAL ENVIRONMENTS such as classrooms, workplaces or circumstances where the researcher does not have control over the intervention that takes place (by itself) nor over the particular intervention any particular individual may receive. True experimental research is therefore simply impossible in the case of several important problems in the business and administrative sciences. In many of these cases, however, QUASI-EXPERIMENTAL RESEARCH may be considered.

QUASI-EXPERIMENTAL RESEARCH differs from true experimental research in that the researcher cannot randomly assign subjects to the different groups (so that these groups may differ from one another in terms of nuisance variables too) (see also Section 5.2.1.2).

Although quasi-experimental research usually enables us to make conclusions about causal relationships (see Section 5.2.2) with less conviction than in true experimental research, it nonetheless allows us to draw conclusions about such relationships with much more confidence than in pre-experimental research (see Section 6.3.2).

To meet the *ceteris paribus* requirement (see Section 5.2.2), attempts are made to take known threats to internal validity (see Section 6.3) into consideration in several other ways. Quasi-experimental research then presents a second best alternative for eliminating known nuisance variables (see Section 5.1.2.3) as far as possible, and the corresponding rival hypotheses (see Section 2.3 & 9.3.2.1) on logical grounds.

5.3.1 The non-equivalent control group design

In the non-equivalent control group design, we use two pre-existing groups as an experimental and a control group, respectively (see Figure 5.6). Spector (1981) calls such a design *an ex post facto design*. The threat of group differences that may already have been present prior to the start of the experimental intervention (see Section 6.3.5) is taken into

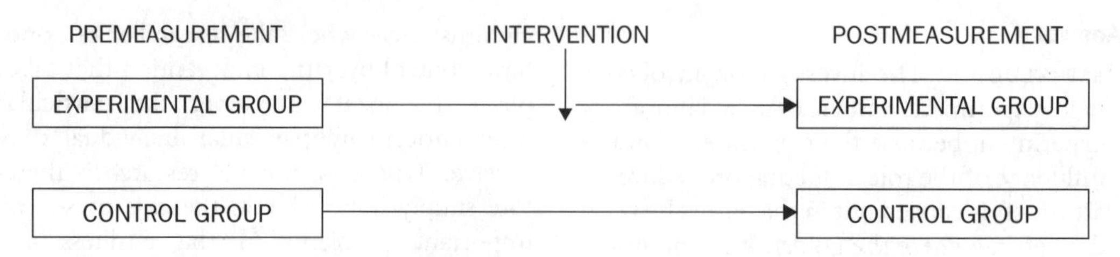

Figure 5.6 The non-equivalent control group design

account by measuring both groups on the dependent variable (see Section 2.2) prior to the experimental intervention. However, the groups may differ in respect of a variable that has not been detected by the premeasure but that does affect performance on the postmeasure (see Section 6.3.3).

If the experimental and control groups do not differ in terms of the premeasure, but do differ on the postmeasure, we can ascribe the difference in the postmeasure with some certainty to the difference in intervention that they have received (see Section 6.3.4), for example, threats such as historical events (see Section 6.3.2.1), spontaneous development (see Section 6.3.2.2) (in one or both groups), measurement reactivity (see Section 6.3.4.1), instrumentation (see Section 6.3.4.2) and statistical regression, may be in operation.

5.3.2 The interrupted time-series design

The interrupted time-series design represents an improvement on the premeasurement and postmeasurement design in that it keeps some of the above-mentioned threats at bay. In the interrupted time-series design more than one measure of the dependent variable is obtained, with equal intervals both before and after the intervention. Figure 5.7, Figure 5.8 and Figure 5.9 are schematic representations of this design.

Spector (1981) is of the opinion that there should preferably be an equal number of measurements before and after the intervention. The researcher may plan the intervention, or it may be an unplanned event (for example, an earthquake or the collapse of the stock market) in which case archival records (see Section 7.7.2.3) may be considered as measure of the dependent variable. The interrupted time-series design can be considered to be an expansion of the premeasurement and postmeasurement single-group design (see Section 5.2).

> **Example**
> Campbell and Ross (1968) analysed the traffic fatalities in the American state of Connecticut during the fifties and sixties. In reaction to a record number of traffic deaths of 324 in this state (or province in South Africa) in 1955, its governor (or premier in South Africa) introduced extremely severe penalties for speeding violations.

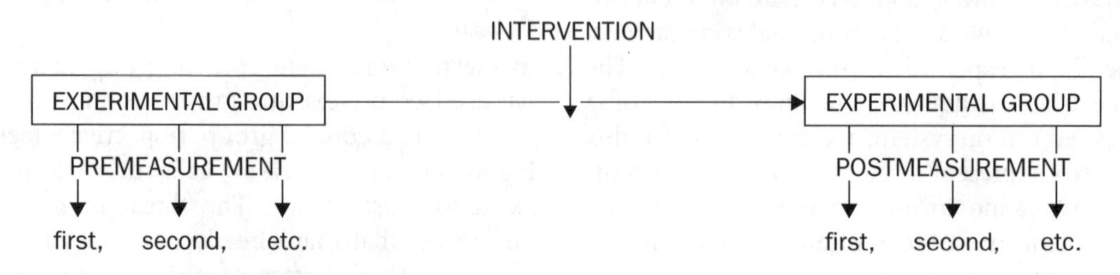

Figure 5.7 The interrupted time series design

When the number of traffic deaths declined by 12,3% (to 284) the following year, the governor took this reduction as evidence of the success of his crackdown on speeding (see Figure 5.8).

However, the mere comparison of the traffic deaths before and after the intervention corresponds to the use of a premeasurement and postmeasurement single group design (see Section 5.2). Such a design does not take into consideration the following factors (with which we will deal in Sections 6.3.2 & 6.3.5):

- historical events beyond the control of the researcher (more traffic accidents could have occurred because of the weather in 1955 than in 1956)
- spontaneous development (there could have been a gradual decline in traffic accidents countrywide as a result of the general realisation of its economic implications)
- statistical regression and accidental fluctuations (maybe traffic accidents fluctuate in any case from one year to the next)
- the interaction of selection and regression (maybe the decline in 1956 partially resulted from the shock of the high death figure for 1955).

Taking the factors (possible threats to internal validity) mentioned in the above example into account, Campbell and Ross (1968) traced the number of traffic deaths for the four years before, and the three years after, the speeding crackdown. They then produced an interrupted time-series design. (The data they obtained according to a premeasurement and postmeasurement single group design are indicated in the small block in Figure 5.8.)

In terms of this approach (interrupted time-series design) it would appear that this campaign did indeed have an effect on the number of traffic deaths. However, if we inspect the results of the interrupted time-series design, it is clear that we could not ignore the possible

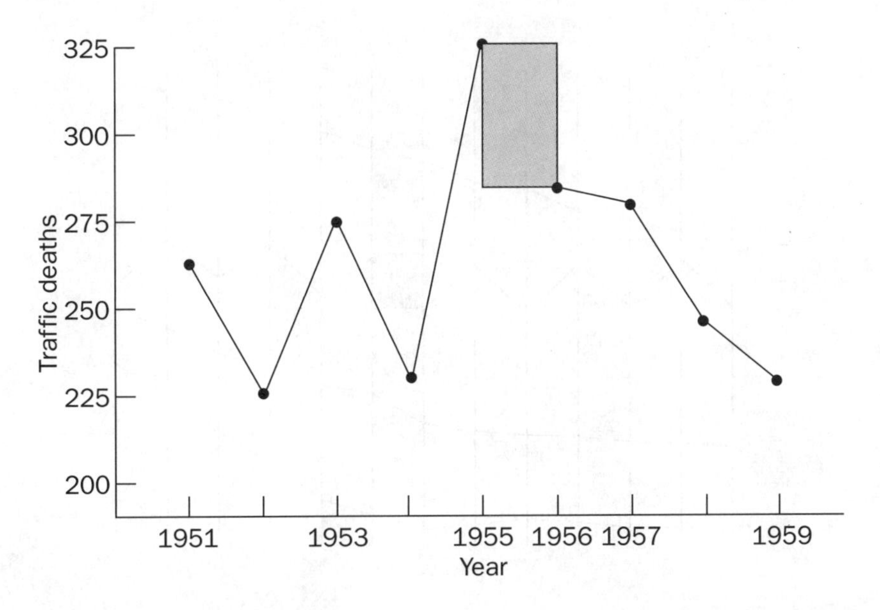

Figure 5.8 Traffic deaths in an interrupted time-series design. (From Huysamen (1994, p. 90).)

role of regression and accidental fluctuations (compare the drop in the number of traffic deaths from 1951 to 1952 and 1953 to 1954).

Note

Cook and Campbell (1979), and Glass, Willson and Gottman (1975) describe statistical procedures to analyse the data obtained in an interrupted time-series design.

Note

The time-series design enables us to determine whether changes taking place at the same time as the intervention represent a temporary fluctuation or the onset of a sustained change. In the case of graphs A and B in Figure 5.9, it appears as if the change at the time of the intervention would have occurred in any case as part of an established, ongoing pattern of change, while those in graphs C and D suggest a sustained, enduring effect.

If only a single measurement (premeasurement and postmeasurement single group design – see Section 5.2) was obtained both before and after the intervention, and the results resembled those in the shaded blocks in A and B in Figure 5.9, there would have been no way in which to distinguish between a real effect and the continuation of a tendency that had nothing to do with the intervention.

The interrupted time-series design eliminates the factor of spontaneous development (see Section 6.3.2.2), that is, that there could have been a gradual decline in traffic accidents countrywide as a result of the general realisation of its economic implications. However, it does not eliminate the factor of historical events (see Section 6.3.2.1) beyond the control of the experimenter, for example, more traffic accidents could have occurred because of the weather in 1955 than in 1956.

Example

If there had been fewer traffic deaths countrywide as a result of better weather conditions at the same time as the governor's crackdown on speeding, or because a drastic increase in the price of petrol kept motorists off the road, this design would possibly lead to incorrect conclusions.

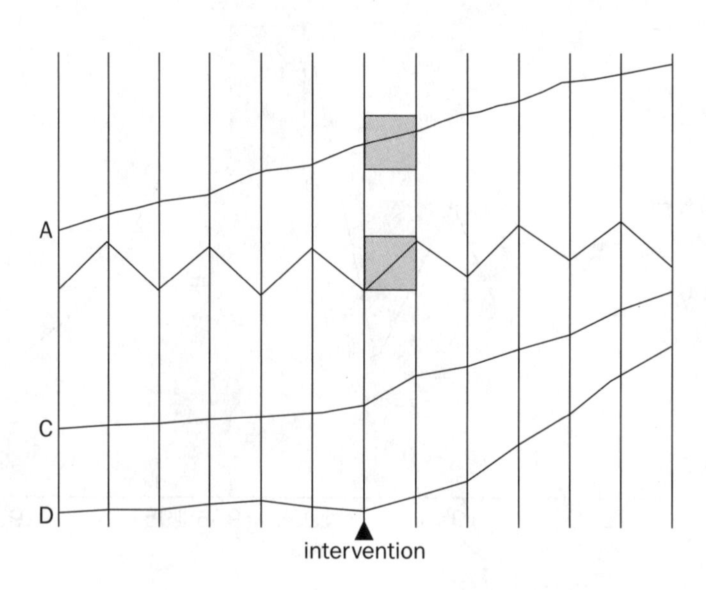

Figure 5.9 Possible results in an interrupted time-series design (From Huysamen (1994, p. 91).)

Note

The researcher may systematically check news reports of the particular period to determine whether any such events occurred at the same time as the intervention.

However, such threats are then eliminated by means of debating (see Section 1.2.1.4), that does not necessarily guarantee conclusions that are as foolproof as those that are possible with true experimental research (see Section 5.2.1). If someone else should convincingly argue that there were indeed historical events that might have led to the decline in traffic deaths, it would cast doubt on the researcher's conclusion.

Activity 5.3

Read CASE STUDY B in Appendix D on page 276.

Question

Does the research in Case Study B involve an interrupted time-series design? Give brief reasons for your answer.

Answer

The value of using a time-series design is that it enables the researchers to determine whether the change (in the case of Case Study B, this will be a change in the attitude of the apprentices towards supervision) that takes place during the intervention (participation in the role induction procedure) represents a temporary fluctuation or whether it is the start of a sustained change.

Viewed in this light, it appears that the research in Case Study B does indeed involve an interrupted time-series design, because the attitudes of the sample members were measured on three occasions (instead of two, as in the case of the pre-test/post-test, single-group design), namely, at the start of the training period, immediately before the role induction, and one week after the role induction. It would perhaps have been better for more measurements before and after the intervention (the role induction procedure) to have been made because, in the present case, a single angry outburst by one of the supervisors, for example, could easily have upset at least half (10) of the apprentices, bringing about negative scores on their attitude questionnaires and so having a substantial impact on the results of the study. If six measurements were taken, for example, such a solitary event would have a smaller influence (as third variable) on the results, and prevent the researchers from coming to the wrong conclusion. (This example also shows the negative effect that small sample sizes can have on results.)

5.4 Non-experimental research

Neither random assignment (see Section 5.2.1.2), nor any planned intervention occurs in non-experimental research. Because one or more variables (see Section 2.2), apart from the independent variable in question, could be the actual source of observed variation in the dependent variable(s), it is generally accepted that conclusions about causal relationships (see Section 5.2.2) may be made with greater confidence by means of true experimental research (see Section 5.2.1) rather than non-experimental research. This is because we cannot randomly assign subjects to the levels of the independent variable (and thereby equate them in terms of all other variables) (second characteristic of true experimental research – see Section 5.2.1).

It is important for us to be thoroughly familiar with the nature of the variables (see Section 2.2) in the field of research and the statistical methods (see Chapter 9) that are available in order to disentangle the relationships among them.

Note

If there is a great degree of regularity and orderliness in the phenomenon being studied, we may obtain highly satisfactory results by means of NON-EXPERIMENTAL RESEARCH.

Example

Almost all our modern knowledge about astronomy has been obtained by non-experimental means because we cannot manipulate the stars – not yet!

In experimental (see Section 5.2) and non-experimental research (see Section 5.4) we may make a further distinction in terms of whether data are collected in a *laboratory* or in a *natural environment* (see Section 5.2.3). The two types of research design, each of which may be executed in two different types of environment, thus result in a total of *four basic types of research design*:

- laboratory experiments
- field experiments
- laboratory surveys
- field studies (or field surveys).

Although we may collect data for non-experimental research in laboratory surveys, it is typically done in natural environments or field studies. RESEARCH EXAMPLE III falls into this category. Because there is no planned intervention and the data are collected in a field situation, these designs are supposed to show the greatest similarity to real life.

Research Example III: Preference for television programmes and aggressiveness of prisoners

A measure of both the level of violence of their favourite television programmes and their own aggressiveness (behaviour) was obtained for each of 644 males and 567 female prisoners. The prison warders were asked in individual interviews to list these prisoners' three most popular television programmes. Independent raters familiar with the contents of these programmes classified them as either violent or non-violent. At the same time, the aggressiveness (behaviour) of the prisoners was rated by their fellow prisoners. A strong relationship (statistically significant, positive correlation – see Section 9.4.1.3) was found between the violence ratings of the prisoners' favourite programmes and their aggressiveness ratings (see Section 5.4.2.1).

5.4.1 Survey designs (relationships between variables)

Although it is unsatisfactory to describe one type of research as being opposite to another, there does not appear to be a satisfactory umbrella term for non-experimental hypothesis-testing research at present. The most satisfactory candidate for this purpose appears to be survey research, but this terms tends to be associated mainly with opinion surveys. However, non-experimental hypothesis-testing research covers a wider spectrum than opinion polls (see Section 5.4.5) only. It includes such surveys as counting traffic at a road intersection or crossing; counting and searching a library collection; recording the repair activities and interaction between computer service stations and the computer users; and so on.

In non-experimental, hypothesis-testing research there is no planned intervention and no random assignment of research participants to groups (see Section 5.2.1.2) consisting of different levels of the independent variable(s) (see Section 2.2). In this type of research we only deal with the examination of relationships that occur between two or more variables (see Section 9.4.1.3) without any planned intervention.

Variables such as age, gender (or sex), socio-economic status, manufacturing sector, and so on, are of great importance, especially to non-experimental research in the business and administrative sciences, and it is impossible to randomly assign participants (see Section 5.2.1.2) who are already members of the various levels of such variables, to them.

There are often many variables that COVARY, in other words, walk hand in hand with each other, that mutually influence one another, so that it is actually not meaningful to talk about a *single independent variable* influencing a *single dependent variable* (see Section 2.2).

Example

When we examine the influence of a variable such as home language (independent variable) on the understanding (dependent variable) of work instructions being communicated in English only, the culture of the units of analysis (see Section 4.2.1) may also influence (thus COVARIES as an independent variable) the understanding of the work instruction.

Activity 5.4

Read Case Study A; Case Study D; Case Study E and Case Study F in Appendix D on page 276.

Question

Will the investigation in each case study involve an experimental research design or a survey research design? Give brief reasons for your answer.

Answer

CASE STUDY A: The investigation involves a survey research design because it investigates only whether there is a relationship between the variables. The influence (causality) of one variable on another (effect) is not investigated.

CASE STUDY C: The investigation involves a survey research design because it investigates only whether there is a relationship between the variables; the influence (causality) of one variable on another (result) which is typical of experimental research is not investigated.

CASE STUDY E: The investigation involves a survey research design rather than an experimental research design because the participants in the study are not randomly assigned as being bankrupt/non-bankrupt, nor is a group of small business owners told to exceed their bank overdraft limits and on purpose given a lot of cash flow problems in order to see what the effect would be – such manipulations are typical of experimental research.

CASE STUDY F: The participants in the study were not randomly assigned with regard to being an entrepreneur or a manager in order to see what the effect on their innovative problem-solving styles would be. The investigation thus involved a *generic survey research design* rather than experimental research. In other words, the researcher did not manipulate anything (did not have control) to see what such a change (an intervention) would bring about. Such manipulations are typical of experimental research to determine the influence of one variable on another (called causality). The study in question investigates only whether a difference already exists in the innovative problem-solving styles of entrepreneurs and managers.

5.4.2 Non-experimental research designs involving measurements at a single time

5.4.2.1 Correlational design

In the simplest non-experimental design, namely the CORRELATIONAL DESIGN, a single group of units of analysis (see Section 4.2.1) is obtained (preferably randomly – (see Section 4.2.2). Each individual is measured on two or more variables (see Section 2.2) at about more or less the same time; and the relationship (correlations) between these variables is analysed (see Section 9.4.1.3).

Example

In RESEARCH EXAMPLE III (page 84) the violence ratings (done by wardens) of prisoners' favourite television programmes were correlated with their ratings of aggressiveness by their fellow prisoners. This study thus concerns the relationship between two variables (see Section 2.2) in a single population (see Section 4.2.1).

Note

The name of this type of design does not necessarily identify the statistical technique (see Section 9.4.1.3) by which the data obtained are to be analysed because the data collected in such designs do not necessarily have to be analysed by means of correlational techniques (see Section 9.4.1.3).

5.4.2.2 The criterion-groups design

In the CRITERION-GROUPS DESIGN, samples (the criterion groups) are drawn randomly (see Section 4.2.2) from the populations representing the different levels of the independent variable (see Section 2.2) (which then qualifies as a *classification factor*). The intention then is to investigate whether these groups differ in terms of the dependent variable.

Note

Both the correlational (see Section 5.4.2.1) and the criterion-groups design concern the (correlational) relationship between variables.

Example

When we use the correlational design (see Section 5.4.2.1), we may draw a random sample of individuals who have been found guilty of shoplifting, then record each person's sex and his or her highest educational qualification, and examine the relationship between these two variables.

We could investigate the same problem in a criterion-groups design by first drawing a random sample of men and a random sample of women from the population of shoplifters and by recording each person's highest educational qualification. Suppose we find that women have, on average (see Section 9.4.1.2), a higher qualification than men. This finding also boils down to a relationship between the variables of sex and *educational qualification* of shoplifters.

5.4.2.3 Cross-sectional design

We may view the CROSS-SECTIONAL DESIGN as a special case of the above-mentioned criterion-groups design in which the different criterion groups typically comprise different age groups (such as technikon, university or organisational year groups), known as COHORTS, which are examined in terms of one or more variables (see Section 2.2) at approximately the *same time*.

Example

To investigate age-related changes in racial prejudice, 18-, 21-, 24- and 27-year olds may be measured in terms of this phenomenon at about the same time.

The problem with this type of analysis, however, is that the participants may differ in terms of other variables apart from age, which may have a greater relationship with racial prejudice. For example, we do not have any assurance that the racial prejudice of the present 18-year-old group was comparable three years ago (at the age of 15) with that of the present 15-year olds, or that in three years (when they will be 21) they will correspond with the present 21-year olds.

Furthermore, apart from various threats to internal validity (obviously history in the present example – see Section 6.3.2.1), any one of the groups may possibly not be sufficiently representative (see Section 4.2) of its age group.

5.4.3 Longitudinal designs

Instead of a cross-sectional design, a longitudinal design may be used in which the *same group* is examined at *different time intervals*. However, such designs are time-consuming and expensive undertakings.

Example

To investigate the above-mentioned problem longitudinally, the racial prejudice of the same group will have to be measured at the ages of 15, 18, 21 and 24 (that is, up to nine years after the initial measurement).

A LONGITUDINAL DESIGN is relevant when we want to investigate changes due to the passage of time. This time period may extend from weeks to years, and the accompanying events (such as the showing of television programmes) thus represent the independent variable (see Section 2.2).

Example

Say we want to investigate how the attitudes (see Section 7.7.3.3) of whites towards the ANC have changed in the late eighties and early nineties (that is, before, during and after the unbanning of this organisation), a longitudinal design is the proper one to consider.

Typically, the dependent variable (see Section 2.2) involves the attitudes towards some or other topic but it could be any other subject variable such as values, products, promotional methods, and so on.

For example, RESEARCH EXAMPLE IV deals with a LONGITUDINAL INVESTIGATION of the influence of the introduction of television in South Africa on the aggressiveness of teenagers.

Research Example IV: The effect of television viewing on the aggressiveness of teenagers

At the request of the SABC, the Human Sciences Research Council (HSRC) conducted a large-scale longitudinal investigation into the effects of television violence on mainly the aggressiveness of teenagers. A random sample of 1 000 white pupils who were stratified (see Section 4.2.2.3) in terms of sex, language of instruction, geographic area of origin (urban or rural) and province, was used.

These pupils completed a series of tests and questionnaires for the first time in 1974 (that is, before the introduction of television in South Africa) while some were in Standard 3 (Grade 5 nowadays) and others in Standard 6 (Grade 8). From then onwards these pupils annually completed the same test battery until they were in their matriculation year (1981 for the Grade 5 group; 1978 for the Grade 8 group).

The following measuring instruments were, inter alia, included in the test battery: the situations questionnaire (for assessing aggression) and a television questionnaire (which, among others, contained questions on the number of hours pupils watched television).

Several research reports were compiled on this project. In one (Botha, 1990) a strong relationship (see Section 9.4.1.3) was indeed reported between the number of hours of exposure to television and aggressiveness.

We may distinguish between at least *three types of longitudinal designs* (see Figure 5.10):

- panel designs
- cohort designs
- trend designs.

5.4.3.1 **Panel designs**

In a PANEL DESIGN, measurements are obtained at different points in time on one or more dependent variable(s) (see Section 2.2) for the *same sample* (see Section 4.2) that is more or less *representative of the relevant population* (see Section 4.2.1).

Example

We could obtain the telephone numbers of a random sample (see Section 4.2.2) of white Free Staters and telephonically (see Section 7.7.4) assessed their attitudes (see Section 7.7.3.3) towards the ANC in 1989, 1990, 1991 and 1992.

The merits of such a panel design are that it may indicate whether different subgroups exhibit different changes over time. For example, a panel design would be able to bring to light whether the attitude towards the ANC of people from the rural areas has become more negative, whereas that of individuals living in urban areas has become more positive or remained constant. Stated statistically, it could investigate whether there was an interaction between subgroups (see Section 4.2.2.2) and the passage of time. Other examples, such as an investigation into age-related changes in racial prejudice, may also be studied in this manner.

In a CROSS-LAGGED PANEL DESIGN, two or more variables (see Section 2.2) are measured at two or more different points in time (for the *same group of individuals*). Such a design enables us to investigate whether one variable at one point in time relates to another variable at a later point in time. However, there are statistical problems in analysing the data obtained in such a design (Cook & Campbell, 1979).

5.4.3.2 **Cohort designs**

The basic difference between a COHORT DESIGN and a panel design is that a cohort design does *not* involve a representative sample (see Section 4.2) from some or other population (such as members of a particular group).

Example

In a cohort design study, we use an *intact group* (see Section 5.2 – Note), such as the financial accountancy class that completed its studies in 1998 or the soldiers who began their military training at the Parachute Battalion at Tempe, Bloemfontein, in 1998. Such a group is then followed up over several years and measured in respect of the same dependent variable(s) (see Section 2.2).

5.4.3.3 **Trend designs**

In a TREND DESIGN, we measure *different samples* (see Section 4.2) from the same population (such as the voters who were born in a particular year), rather than the same sample (compare panel studies and cohort studies), at different times (see Figure 5.10).

The trend design does not necessarily have to involve people and historical studies (see Section 2.2.3.1 & 8.2) may utilise some or

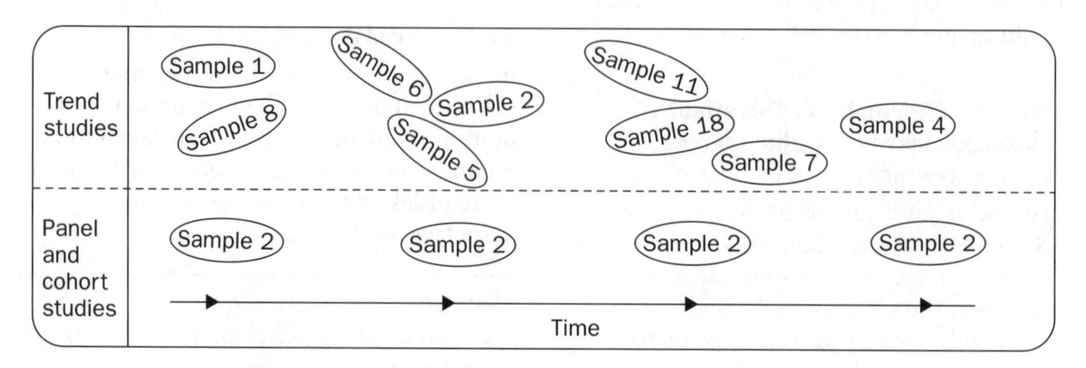

Figure 5.10 Trend designs and panel and cohort designs

other documentary record as measure of the dependent variable (see Section 2.2).

Example

- The number of registered business owners committing fraud (and trying to cheat the tax collection system) over different years (for example, before, during and after a new law to prevent fraud has been introduced) may serve as basis for a trend design.
- A content analysis (see Section 9.2) of editorials of newspapers may be examined with a view to determining whether any change in the form of addressing Mandela and Mbeki has taken place over time.
- Condom sales before, during and after the public denouncement of AIDS is another example.

Note

In the above examples, archival research, longitudinal designs (see Section 5.4.3) and quasi-experimental designs (see Section 5.3) overlap.

Activity 5.5

Read the following problem statement and answer the question. Compare your answer with the given answer.

Problem statement

A machine operator thinks that fumes emitted in the workshops play a role in the low efficiency of the operators. The operator would like to prove this to the supervisor through a scientific research study.

Question

Would the study be a cross-sectional or a longitudinal design? Briefly explain your answer.

Answer

This is a longitudinal design (panel study), because: The efficiency of the output of operators at a specific level (production level) is measured against/compared to a quantity/levels of the fumes measured; and the measurement of this phenomenon (producing information/data) has to occur more than once to confirm its effect.

5.4.4 Prediction studies

A PREDICTION STUDY has a time dimension (like a longitudinal study), but different variables are measured at different points in time (usually only two).

In a prediction study, we measure the units of analysis (see Section 4.2.1) in respect of one or more variables (see Section 2.2) at one point in time and (usually considerably) later the units of analysis (people or organisations) are measured in terms of another variable.

In addition, the independent variables (see Section 2.2) are biographical, psychological and other variables that apply to the units of analysis themselves at the initial point in time.

Note

These variables are also known as because they are intended to predict eventual behaviour (for example, heart attacks or juvenile delinquency, respectively) but it may also involve membership of different occupational groups or political parties or something similar.

Eventually subjects are thus divided into different *criterion groups* (those with heart disease and those without it; those who have become delinquent and those who have not; or different occupational groups).

5.4.4.1 The retrospective design

In a RETROSPECTIVE DESIGN, we know already in which criterion groups individuals are, and we wish to determine in terms of which (possible) predictor variables they have differed in the past.

The use of this design came from the obvious observation that already existing criterion groups may previously have differed in terms of one or more variables that possibly may be used as predictor variables (see Section 5.4.4) of current criterion status.

Example

It may appear that a great proportion of juvenile delinquents (such as cellular phone thieves) come from broken homes. This observation may lead to the following hypothesis (see Section 2.3):

A BROKEN HOME BACKGROUND WILL BE A CONTRIBUTORY CAUSE OF JUVENILE DELINQUENT BEHAVIOUR.

In true experimental research (see Section 5.2.1), we examine the effect of the independent variable (see Section 2.2) by making two or more groups the same, through random assignment (see Section 5.2.1.2), in terms of all variables except for the independent variable (see Section 2.2), and by examining the dependent variable for possible differences.

Because the supposed cause in the retrospective prediction design has taken place in the past, we have no control over it in the sense of exposing some individuals to it and withholding it from others. Instead, we begin with the observation that two or more groups differ (in terms of the dependent variable – one group is delinquent but not the other group; one is a heart attack group but not the other). Consequently, we obtain samples (see Section 4.2) that represent the levels of the criterion variable and examine them with a view to determining whether they differ in terms of one or more variables in their past which may possibly have contributed to the present difference.

Example

We may obtain:

- a sample of juvenile delinquents; and
- a sample without any delinquent behaviour and check whether there is a higher incidence of a broken home background in the sample of juvenile delinquents than in the sample without any delinquent behaviour.

The supposed predictor variable (social status) is a biographical variable and we may ascertain with a reasonable degree of certainty whether it has preceded delinquency or whether it has accompanied it.

Note

The main problem with the retrospective design is the same as for all non-experimental research, namely, the third-variable problem that we will discuss further in Section 6.3.2.3.

The meaningfulness of the retrospective design and the conclusions that we may reach in terms of it thus depend to a large extent on our knowledge of possible nuisance variables (see Section 5.2.1.3) that are active in a particular field of study and whether they may be controlled by matching (see Section 6.3.7) or not.

Example

Suppose social status is the main cause of juvenile delinquency, so that any sample of juvenile delinquents (such as cellular phone thieves) would tend to come from a lower socio-economic group than would a sample of non-delinquents.

If we measure variables, such as the motivation to be respected in the eyes of one's friends, rather than social status itself, the retrospective design may lead us to draw incorrect conclusions because we have overlooked the most important predictor variable.

Suppose we measure the motivation to earn the respect of one's friends of the two groups (delinquent and non-delinquent groups) and find a significant difference in favour of the non-delinquent group. Such a finding may lead us to conclude that *a high motivation to earn the respect of one's friends contributes to juvenile delinquency*, whereas it is actually social status that leads to both a high motivation to earn the respect of one's friends and juvenile delinquency.

On the other hand, suppose we suspect that social status rather than motivation to earn the respect of one's friends was the main cause of juvenile delinquency and decide to match subjects in terms of motivation to earn the respect of one's friends. For each person with a particular score (high or low) on motivation to earn the respect of one's friends in the group of delinquents we look for someone with the same score in the non-delinquent population for inclusion in the two groups, thus controlling the potential nuisance variable.

However, because of the correlation between social status and motivation to earn the respect of one's friends, we may end up with two groups with more or less the same social status, and thus fail to find a difference in this variable for the two groups.

5.4.4.2 The prospective design

In a PROSPECTIVE DESIGN, we initially measure units of analysis (see Section 4.1) in terms of the supposed predictor variables (see Section 5.4.4) and eventually their criterion-group membership is checked. This design is used to investigate the extent to which the future position of research participants on one or more variables, known as the CRITERION VARIABLES, may be predicted on the basis of the participants' original score on one or more predictor variable(s).

Thus, we measure the scores of individual units of analysis on the presumed predictor variables and some time later we measure their scores on the criterion variable.

Example

Suppose we test the attitudes (see Section 7.7.3.3) of all prisoners towards crime on their release from prison. After two years, we determine the criterion status of each, that is, whether he or she has broken the law in the meantime. We could then correlate (see Section 9.4.1.3) their original attitude scores with criterion status to determine whether the attitude tests may satisfactorily be applied to predict who will return to criminal behaviour.

Activity 5.6

Read Case Study E in Appendix D on page 276.

Question

Does the prediction study in Case Study E entail a retrospective or prospective design? Briefly give a reason for your answer.

Answer

Case Study E entails a RETROSPECTIVE DESIGN because when the research was begun, it was already known to which criterion groups the small businesses belonged (bankrupt or non-bankrupt), and the researcher now wishes to determine in terms of which predictor variables (concerning bank overdraft usage and cash flow problems) they differed in the past.

5.4.5 Opinion polls

In SURVEY RESEARCH (see Section 5.4.1) the proportions (or percentages) (see Figure 9.7) of a population falling into particular categories of some variable (see Section 2.2) are estimated on the basis of a sample drawn from the population (see Section 4.2). Typically, this variable relates to individuals' preference for various election candidates or for product brand names (such as Toyota, Volkswagen, and so on), or individuals' opinions, beliefs and convictions regarding some topic (such as reinstating the death penalty). An opinion poll is thus one example of survey research.

Example

We could conduct a survey to determine the popularity of different political candidates prior to a general election. This may involve merely the estimation of the proportions (or percentages) of supporters of the various candidates.

However, a survey is not restricted to predicting the percentages (frequencies – see Section 9.4.1) in the various categories of one variable. It may also be directed at the relationship between such preferences or opinions, beliefs and attitudes (see Section 7.7.3.3), on the one hand, and certain biographical variables (for example, sex, age, race, marital status, income, educational qualification and occupation), on the other (see Section 9.4.1.3). Questions such as the following may be investigated:

- Do the majority of men support candidate *X* whereas the majority of women support candidate *Y*?
- Are there differences in the expectations about the future of South Africa between unemployed male and female South African voters?

In RESEARCH EXAMPLE V we describe a survey of the opinions of various population groups about AIDS.

Research Example V: An opinion survey about AIDS

Between 13 and 16 May 1991, 54 interviewers conducted telephonic interviews (see Section 7.7.4) on behalf of the HSRC with 2 096 respondents. The samples (see Section 4.2) for whites, Asians, and coloureds were drawn country-wide from both rural and urban areas with the exclusion of the then TBVC states. The 919 blacks were drawn from the entire Republic of South Africa with the exception of Venda and Bophuthatswana.

At each residential telephone number one person was drawn randomly (see Section 4.2.2) from all persons of 18 years and older at that address. In the white residential areas the telephone numbers were drawn in such a manner that a geographically representative sample (see Section 4.2.2.3) could be obtained in terms of the 1985 census. As far as the other population groups were concerned, the samples were based on the estimated numbers of telephones per area.

Four questions were asked, concerning:

- whom the respondents regarded as responsible for the spreading of AIDS
- whether they regarded AIDS as a personal threat to their safety
- the use of precautionary measures
- the compulsory reporting of the incidence of AIDS to health authorities.

Whites and coloureds considered homosexual persons, blacks and immoral persons, in this order, to be the most guilty of spreading AIDS. Blacks blamed immoral persons, followed by whites and people from the then TBVC for this phenomenon; while 50% and 25% of the Asians viewed blacks and then immoral persons as responsible for this problem. Whereas three per cent of the blacks blamed their own population group for the spread of AIDS, less than one per cent of the whites and the coloureds blamed their own group.

Altogether 51% of the respondents were of the opinion that they would not get AIDS. Among blacks, 70% in the age group 16 to 24 years and 42% of those older than 25 years indicated that they had decided to use precautionary measures against infection by AIDS. Ninety-four per cent of the whites and Asians, 88% of the coloureds and 75% of the blacks favoured the compulsory reporting of AIDS cases to the health authorities.

Note

We should distinguish between a survey and a census. Whereas a survey is conducted on samples (see Section 4.2), in a census, each member of the population is supposed to be included and to be classified in terms of certain biographical variables (for example, sex, employment status).

The objective of a census is to determine the approximate number of people in the various categories of such variables for the entire population. A census focuses on questions that may vary from how many men and women there are in the population to the number of households that has no television set, one, or more than one television set.

We usually conduct a survey on a relatively small sample (see Section 4.2.5) from the total population, and it has certain advantages over a census:

- Firstly, it requires less time and financial expenses.

Example

Even if we were to take only a few minutes per person, a telephonic interview (see Section 7.7.4) conducted on the entire population of voters would require so much time and money that it would simply be impossible.

- Secondly, we may obtain data (information) of a higher quality through surveys. Because surveys usually involve fewer participants, fewer interviewers are required and, as a result, they may be trained better and their effectiveness could be better controlled. Consequently, more accurate information may be collected.
- Thirdly, it may measure the state of affairs at a specific time so that the opinions of all respondents are comparable. A corresponding census, on the other hand, will typically have to be conducted over a longer period of time.

Example

Suppose a research organisation wanted to investigate the attitude of South Africans towards reinstating the death penalty. It would be possible, at least theoretically, to complete a telephone survey within a week.

A census, on the other hand, would require at least several months. In the meantime, events such as a series of rape cases may affect opinions so that the information obtained at the final stages of the study may differ from that procured at the beginning. (The information obtained at the end may perhaps no longer reflect attitudes towards reinstating the death penalty only, but also attitudes towards the ensuing rapes.)

- Fourthly, a factor that promotes greater accuracy in the information obtained by surveys, is the greater co-operation and frankness that may be obtained from people willing to respond. This especially applies in the case of questions about sensitive issues, such as opinions about other races and about sexual practices.

Self-evaluation questions

(Some answers appear in Appendix B on page 273.)

5.1 A researcher sent false application forms of (fictitious) prospective students who differed in terms of sex, race and ability to 12 randomly assigned groups of 20 universities. (Some "applicants" were male, white and highly intelligent, other "applicants" were female, white and highly intelligent, and so on). If an "applicant" was accepted with encouragement, it was scored 5; if he or she was merely accepted, it was scored 4; and so on down to those who were unsuccessful and obtained a score of 1.

Identify the type of research and indicate whether it was a laboratory or a field study.

5.2 Suppose a researcher wants to investigate the effectiveness of a programme designed to increase the assertiveness of first-year students. All these students complete an assertiveness test at the beginning of the year. Those who appear to be in the greatest need of this programme, are enrolled in it. At the end of the semester their assertiveness is measured again.

Identify (a) the type of research, and (b) the design that is used here.

5.1 When in 1981 the film, *Death of a student*, in which a 19-year-old student jumped in front of an oncoming train, was shown on a German television channel, three times as many young adults committed suicide in this manner in the two-month period after the film was shown than before 1981. In terms of which quasi-experimental design were these data (the number of suicides before 1981 and in the two-month period following the show) collected?

5.2 Which quasi-experimental design would you recommend to investigate whether the lack of illegal immigrant influx control led to an increase in burglaries in urban areas in South Africa?

5.3 On the basis of the relationship between the size of the signature of borrowers of library books on the lending cards and their status (students and professors), Zweigenhaft (1970) came to the conclusion that the higher the book borrowers rate their status, the bigger their signatures tend to be.

Identify (a) the type of research, and (b) the research design involved in this example.

5.1 Explain the difference between a panel design, cohort design and trend design by describing how you would use these different designs to investigate the attitudes of young white adults towards the attitudinal object "the new South Africa" during 2000.

5.2 Explain the difference between retrospective and prospective designs by describing how you would use these two designs to investigate the role of family conditions during childhood in the development of drug dependency.

5.3 Does the longitudinal study in RESEARCH EXAMPLE IV (page 87) (see Section 5.4.3) qualify as a panel design, a cohort design or a trend design?

Summary

The design of a study concerns the plan to obtain appropriate data for investigating the research hypothesis and/or questions. In the simplest case, the experimental design, scores on one variable (for example, salary – the independent variable) are to be used to measure and sometimes to predict scores on another variable (for example, work productivity – the dependent variable) on one group of individuals (known as the experimental group). The control group does not receive the treatment (for example, a rise in salary).

Multiple choice and true/false questions

Only *one* of the answers to each question is correct. Identify and mark the correct one. (Answers appear in Appendix E on page 285.)

5.1 Experiments are especially appropriate for research projects involving all of the following *except*:

a) small-group interaction
b) hypothesis testing

c) descriptive research
d) explanatory research.

5.2 For a causal relationship to exist, there must be evidence:
a) of an empirical correlation between the variables
b) that one variable precedes the other in time
c) that a third variable did not cause the changes observed in the first two variables
d) all of the above.

5.3 Turning 18 years old is a NECESSARY cause (NOT sufficient cause) for voting in South Africa.
True False

5.4 The 100 km/h speed limit for buses was introduced in South Africa in 1999. Shortly thereafter the number of bus accidents declined. We can conclude that:
a) the reduced speed limit caused the decline in the number of bus accidents
b) the reduced speed limit had nothing to do with the decline in bus accidents
c) the reduced speed limit and the number of bus accidents are causally related
d) the reduced speed limit may have caused the decline in bus accidents.

5.5 An advantage of field research is:
a) it enables the researcher to draw conclusions about the population
b) the researcher can control the variables under study
c) the phenomenon can be studied in a natural setting
d) hypotheses can be rigorously tested.

5.6 *Ex post facto* hypothesising refers to the development of hypotheses "predicting" relationships that have already been observed in the data.
True False

5.7 The 100 km/h speed limit for buses was introduced in South Africa in 1999. If this legislation was following after years of investigating the number of traffic fatalities on many of the major highways, it illustrates the use of:
a) pretest-posttest one group design
b) the interrupted time-series design
c) the non-equivalent control group design
d) the one-shot case study.

5.8 Let the assumption (hypothesis) be that one defective electrical transformer affected a second one, which in turn affected a third, and so on. This caused a fire to break out. To analyse the data one should use:
a) factor analysis
b) time-series analysis
c) two-way analysis of variance
d) curvilinear regression analysis.

5.9 When one manipulates one or more independent variables in order to determine their effect in a natural situation, the procedure is called:
a) naturalistic observation
b) a field experiment
c) controlled observation
d) a structured experiment.

6 Validity of conclusions

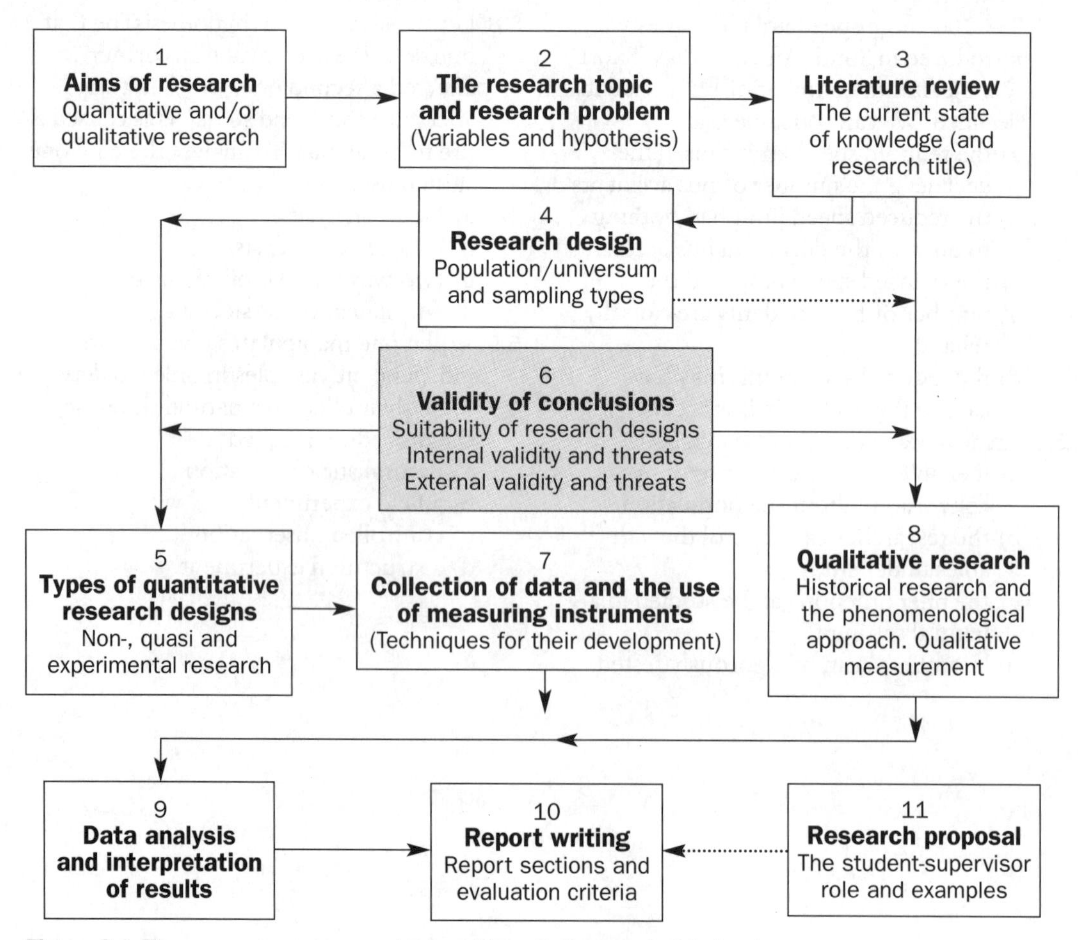

Figure 6.1 The research process and the outline of chapters in this book

Learning Outcomes

After studying this chapter, you should be able to:

1. illustrate the control of variables
2. distinguish independent variables from intervening, moderating, nuisance and third variables
3. identify the third variables in a research project that could influence the internal validity of the conclusions
4. evaluate the effect of a sample used in research on the external validity of the study
5. identify whether the conclusions of a research study are ecologically valid
6. explain how the following factors may threaten the internal validity of a research design and means of preventing it: history, spontaneous change, development and maturation, the third-variable problem, the subject effect, the experimenter effect, pretest sensitisation, selection of groups
7. show how true experimental designs take care of the above internal validity problems as well as the threats to external validity.

6.1 Introduction

We test research hypotheses (see Section 2.3) to help us to decide whether or not some or other implication inferred from a theory is tenable, or to provide an answer to a research question. To have confidence in these conclusions, they have to meet several requirements. In this chapter, we briefly define these requirements in terms of Cook and Campbell (1979) and Figure 6.2, which were also addressed in Section 2.3.2 (Figure 2.3).

If we explain these requirements in terms of Figure 6.2, they mean that the conclusion we reached about the relationship symbolised by the dark one-directional arrow at the bottom of the figure should be a true reflection of the relationship represented by the dark one-directional dotted arrow at the top of the figure.

Example

In RESEARCH EXAMPLE II (see Section 2.2, page 14), a greater number of reactions, such as finger pointing, or utterances such as "I will kick you" or "I will punch you", were observed among the group of trainee supervisors who had observed the corresponding behaviour by a supervisor.

The conclusion that iron-fisted role model management style behaviour leads to more iron-fisted management style behaviour among trainee supervisors should be warranted.

6.2 Suitability of research designs

A requirement that is so obvious that we tend to accept it as self-evident, is that the chosen design should be able to answer the research question (see Section 2.2) and thus serve the purpose for which the research was undertaken in the first place. The research plan as represented in the circle at the top right-hand side of Figure 2.2 (see Section 2.2.) must eventually provide feedback in connection with the formulated research hypothesis that is represented by the circle at the top left-hand side. For example, if we wish to investigate whether attitudes have changed over the course of time, a design that selects data at only one point in time would be inappropriate.

6.3 Internal validity and threats

6.3.1 Introduction

If a relationship between the independent and the dependent variables exists, the question arises as to whether this relationship may be interpreted as being of a CAUSAL NATURE (see Section 5.2.2). By the INTERNAL VALIDITY of a conclusion that ascribes changes in the dependent variable to the independent variable, we mean the degree to which these

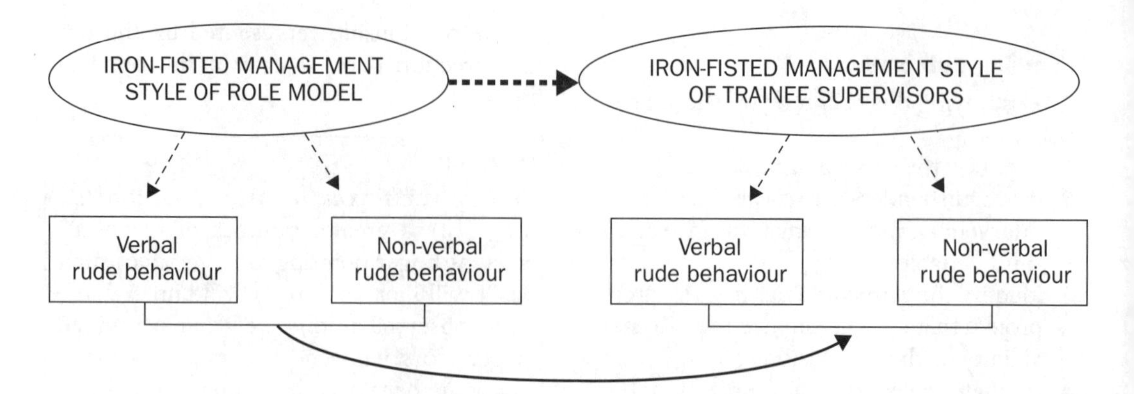

Figure 6.2 Testing the relationship between constructs in terms of observable variables

changes are indeed due to the independent variable rather than to something else.

The conclusion that changes in *Y*, the dependent variable as measured, may be attributed to *X*, the independent variable as operationalised, is *internally valid to the extent that y may unequivocally be attributed to* X rather than to Q, R or S.

> **Example**
>
> In RESEARCH EXAMPLE II (see Section 2.2, page 14), the researcher wished to ascribe the ways in which trainee supervisors managed the subordinate, Bobo, to the role model's (supervisor) management style that they had observed.
>
> However, if another researcher found support for the *rival hypothesis* (see Section 2.3), namely that the management style in the experimental group (trainee supervisors) was due to something other than exposure to the role model's particular style in managing the subordinate, the internal validity of the original conclusion would be questioned.

Note

In terms of Figure 6.2, the requirement of internal validity means that the two squares (boxes) at the bottom left-hand side should provide a complete explanation for the two squares (boxes) to the right.

As we have seen (see Section 5.2), the purpose of experimental research is to *identify causal relationships,* that is, to determine whether one or more independent variables are *responsible for changes* in the dependent variable. According to Section 6.3, the internal validity of a conclusion refers to the degree to which it correctly attributes changes in the dependent variable (as measured – see Section 2.2) to the independent variable (as operationalised – see Section 2.2), instead of to any irrelevant factors. Obviously, internal validity is therefore of *critical importance* in the case of experimental research (see Section 5.2). The distinguishing feature of experimental research designs indeed stems from their objective to promote internal validity.

When we wish to investigate the effect of an independent variable on the dependent variable, there are usually a host of other factors, apart from the independent variable under study, which may bring about changes in the dependent variable and which therefore may adversely affect internal validity. To meet the *ceteris paribus* principle (see Section 5.2.2 & 5.3), and thus to promote internal validity, it is necessary to eliminate such threats to internal validity. If we allow them to operate unchecked, we cannot unequivocally interpret observed changes in the dependent variable as the effect of the independent variable, and this will render the internal validity of our conclusions suspect. Should we succeed in controlling these threats, and should the groups still differ in respect of the dependent variable, we may attribute this difference with greater confidence to the independent variable than to any other factors.

In this section we will discuss the various threats to internal validity and measures for preventing them. We will show that the minimum requirement for internal validity regarding experimental research designs is some basis of comparison, which may be obtained by using:

- at least *two groups*
- that are *equal* in respect of both the dependent variable and all nuisance variables.

We will also discuss two ways in which to create such a basis of comparisons, namely:

- by *randomly assigning participants* to two or more groups; and
- by *matching participants* in respect of the relevant nuisance variables and randomly assigning the members of each matched pair or trio, and so on (see Section 4.2.2) to the groups.

To the extent that such a basis of comparison has been created, we can maintain with greater certainty that differences in the dependent variable may be attributed to the independent variable rather than to any nuisance variables. There is a group of designs, known as PRE-EXPERIMENTAL DESIGNS, which indeed include an experimental intervention, but which do not meet one or more of the requirements just mentioned.

Note

In terms of the way in which we decide which of the participants should be subjected to which intervention, we may distinguish between:

- *pre-experimental;*
- *true experimental (see Section 5.2); and*
- *quasi-experimental (see Section 5.3) research.*

As we will explain in Section 6.3.2, the internal validity of the conclusions reached by means of pre-experimental designs is suspect because they do not keep particular threats to internal validity in check.

6.3.2 Factors beyond the researcher's control

The two pre-experimental designs that we discuss in this section are both characterised by a *single sample* (see Section 4.2) of participants who are exposed to some or other treatment or experimental intervention (to which they would not have been subjected in the normal course of events). Although they involve some form of experimental intervention, these designs *do not qualify as true experimental designs* because they do not provide a sufficient basis of *comparison* to which we may unambiguously ascribe changes in the dependent variable to the independent variable. If such change is observed, we cannot determine whether it would not have occurred in any case, that is, without the experimental intervention.

Example

Say the research problem to be investigated is the effect of the exposure to iron-fisted role model management style behaviour on the management style of trainee supervisors that was at issue in RESEARCH EXAMPLE II (see Section 2.2, page 14).

- Suppose Researcher A arranges for a group of trainee supervisors to be exposed to the iron-fisted role model management style reaction towards a subordinate's behaviour (as was done to the experimental group in Research Example II) and that the management style of their reaction towards the same subordinate behaviour is observed afterwards. This design, in which a single group is subjected to an experimental intervention (see Section 5.2) and is subsequently measured on the dependent variable, is known as a ONE-SHOT CASE STUDY.

- Suppose Researcher B firstly obtains one or other measurement of the management style of a group of trainee supervisors, exposes them to the iron-fisted role model management style behaviour towards the subordinate, and then measures their management style again. Here we are dealing with a PRE-MEASUREMENT and POSTMEASUREMENT SINGLE-GROUP DESIGN (see Section 5.2).

It differs from the one-shot case study in that the dependent variable is measured both before and after the experimental intervention. The objective is to ascribe differences between the pre- and post-measurements to the experimental intervention.

As we will show, the internal validity of the conclusions reached by means of the preceding two single-group designs may be *extremely suspect* because it tends to be compromised by two factors beyond the researcher's control.

We will address the following factors that are beyond the researcher's control:

- history
- spontaneous change
- other third-variable problems.

Note

History and spontaneous change are third variables, which the researcher may eliminate statistically in order to have control over them.

It may be more appropriate to say that in experimental research rival explanations take the form of history or spontaneous change.

6.3.2.1 **History**

By the threat of history we mean events that take place concurrently with the experimental intervention and that may also affect the dependent variable. Usually participants are not under the direct control or supervision of the researcher for 24 hours per day. Consequently, there is a possibility that participants may be affected by events apart from the independent variable in which the researcher is interested, and which take place at the same time as his or her research. As a result, changes in the dependent variable cannot be attributed convincingly to the independent variable in question because the uncontrolled variables could also have played a role.

Example

This kind of threat is present in both the designs mentioned in the above example (comparing RESEARCH EXAMPLE II, page 14).

Suppose there was a general power failure during the hours immediately preceding the researcher's intervention, so that none of the mine workers had anything hot for breakfast that morning and are frustrated. The iron-fisted management style behaviour of the trainee supervisors of both researchers A and B could thus not be attributed exclusively to the researcher's intervention (the showing of the role model's management style on video).

The *rival hypothesis* may be that the iron-fisted management style behaviour was caused by the interruption in their eating habits, which made them irritable, rather than the researcher's intervention, and no convincing counter argument can be posed against this explanation.

6.3.2.2 **Spontaneous change (development, maturation, recovery or deterioration)**

If researchers A and B in the above example observed aggressive responses among the trainee supervisors, we cannot ignore the possibility that such responses would have occurred in any case at that stage of development or deterioration. The likelihood that this threat to internal validity may play a role increases as the duration of the experimental intervention lengthens.

Because changes may take place within relatively short periods of time among mine workers who are exposed to hazardous working conditions upon which they must act quickly, the possibility of spontaneous development (actually, deterioration of their control of frustration in this instance) should be borne in mind with the trainee supervisors.

The problem with one-shot case study and premeasurement and postmeasurement single-group designs is that they *lack a basis of comparison*. In other words, if we observe a change in the dependent variable, these designs provide no way for us to know whether it would not have occurred in any case, in other words, without intervention (non-equivalent control group design – see Section 5.3).

Internal validity does not depend on whether or not the experimental intervention has indeed had an effect, but on *our ability to draw a conclusion as to whether or not the experimental intervention caused the effect*. In the absence of a group that was not exposed to the intervention (control group – see Section 5.2), it is usually impossible to make such a conclusion with a reasonable degree of certainty.

Note

Although we may use a control group to draw a conclusion with a reasonable degree of certainty, our conclusion may still be susceptible because spontaneous change may also occur in the control group as in the experimental group (non-equivalent control group design – see Section 5.3.1).

Example

Suppose, in a NON-EQUIVALENT CONTROL GROUP DESIGN (see Section 5.3.1), full-time students, unlike distance education students, tend to start studying in earnest only after the first test. In such an instance, we could not ascribe a greater increase in the academic performance of the full-time students only to the intervention to which they have been exposed; we would also ascribe it to the spontaneous development that was present only in this group.

6.3.2.3 Other third-variable problems

Note

These problems occur in all research designs and it is therefore of major importance that they are recognised.

In Sections 5.2.2.3 and 5.4.1, we mentioned the MULTIVARIATE NATURE of human behavioural research. To compound matters, we are unable to keep all irrelevant variables constant (for example, by randomly assigning participants to the levels of the independent variable under study – see Section 5.2) as is possible in experiments.

We have already seen (characteristics of true experimental research – see Section 5.2) that we can eliminate the problem of *nuisance variables* by holding all variables constant except the one whose effect we are examining.

However, there are many research problems in the human behavioural sciences that cannot be investigated by means of such experimental research. In non-experimental research it is almost *impossible to exercise control over* variables in these disciplines as we can in experimental research.

Thus the "effect" of the socio-economic status of parents on the academic achievement of their children; the socio-economic "effects" of the repeal of influx control locally; and the "causes" of juvenile delinquency can hardly be investigated in true experiments, to mention but a few examples.

What makes matters so complicated in the human behavioural sciences is that there are seldom only a few independent variables that we can identify as causal factors (see Sections 2.2.1 & 5.2.2). There is usually a vast array of such variables that themselves *mutually influence and overlap one another.* There is always the possibility that a strong relationship (high correlation – Sections 2.2.1 & 9.3.1) between two variables may be explained by a third variable that relates strongly to the other two (both are highly correlated). We might direct our attention to the relationship between *X* and *Y* while, without our knowledge, variable *Z* is the real source of variation of both *X* and *Y*. This possibility is referred to as the THIRD-VARIABLE PROBLEM (see Sections 2.2.1 & 5.2.2).

Example

Here is an example of a typical third-variable problem in practice:

Television viewers observe more murders on television in one week than they or their entire family and circle of friends are likely to witness in their combined lifetimes.

With this in mind, Gerbner and Gross (1976) interviewed people about their television viewing habits with regard to how safe they felt and how likely they thought it would be that they would become victims of violence. Individuals who watched television for *more than four hours* per day were more distrustful than others, and rated their chances of becoming involved in some or other kind of violent incident higher than did those who watched television for *two hours or less* per day.

On the basis of these findings, Gerbner and Gross came to the conclusion that watching television leads to *fear of victimisation.*

Note

Understandably, these authors did not perform experimental research. They did not randomly assign people to groups that were forced to spend different numbers of hours watching television with a view to determining whether the more frequent viewers experienced more fear than the less frequent viewers.

Participants had already watched a certain number of hours prior to the beginning of the research. Consequently, this finding could not be interpreted as *showing unequivocally* that frequent television viewing *caused* fear of being victimised. It was impossible to equate participants on all variables, except for the number of hours of television viewing, with a view to investigating whether the number of hours of television viewing was a cause of the fear of victimisation.

However, previous research had suggested an (inverse) relationship between the number of hours of television viewing and *socio-economic status* (in the sense that people in the lower socio-economic groups tended to watch television more often than did those in the higher levels of this variable). Thus the variable *socio-economic status* may act as a third variable.

There is also evidence to the effect that the lower a person's socio-economic status, the more likely it is that they will be residing in an area with a high incidence of crime. Thus the variable *residential area* may also act as a third variable and in combination with the variable *socio-economic status*.

These two findings suggest the possibility that the most frequent television viewers have an increased fear of possible victimisation because they reside in high-crime areas. These considerations thus possibly bestow on viewers' residential area the status of a third variable in the relationship between watching television and fear of victimisation.

Consequently, Doob and MacDonald (1979) identified the 10 (out of 210) police patrol areas in Toronto, Canada, with the highest number of reported assaults and the 14 with the lowest number of such reports. Within each designated area they selected two geographic areas of approximately the same size. They visited altogether 204 households within each of these regions and selected one person from each household to respond to questions on his or her *television viewing habits* and his or her *perceived chances of becoming a victim of violence.*

Like Gerbner and Gross, Doob and MacDonald found that the more frequently individuals watched television, the more they tended to fear for their own safety. However, the people in the high-crime areas were also the most frequent television viewers.

Once the effect of the residential area had been controlled (by investigating separately the relationship for the two different socio-economic areas), they found *no relationship* between the number of hours of watching television and fear of crime.

Consequently, it could not have been watching television in itself that led to an increased fear of victimisation because, if that were the case, this relationship would have been present in *both areas.* The area in which individuals resided determined both their television viewing habits and their fear of victimisation. Those residing in high-crime areas were the *most frequent television viewers* (because obviously it was safer to watch television than to venture out on the streets) and they were also the *most fearful* (because of the reality of crime around them).

We say that the relationship observed between watching television and fear is an incorrect one because it is explained by these variables' *separate relationships with a third variable, namely socio-economic position of residential area.*

Doob and MacDonald (1979) investigated the relationship between watching television and fear by *holding constant the residential area* (the so-called third variable). They did this by examining the relationship between watching television and fear within the respective levels of the variable *residential area*, separately.

In this manner a distinction is made between two rival explanations, namely that *watching television promotes fear* and that *the socio-economic standing of a residential area influences both television-watching behaviour and fear.*

In general, the conclusions reached by means of non-experimental research tend to be less internally valid than those which are based on experimental and quasi-experimental research.

Note

On some occasions it is indeed possible to investigate a problem both experimentally and non-experimentally. More or less the same problem that was researched experimentally in RESEARCH EXAMPLE II *(see Section 2.2. page 14), was approached non-experimentally in* RESEARCH EXAMPLE III *(see Section 5.4, page 83).*

Instead of exposing one group of mine workers, but not the other, to aggressive behaviour shown by the supervisor (model), the level of violence of the prisoners' favourite television programmes was correlated with the prisoners' aggressiveness.

Consider the issue of the socio-economic status of parents as the cause of juvenile delinquency (retrospective designs – see Section 5.4.4). It is simply impossible to implement socio-economic status as a treatment factor (which implies that individuals are randomly assigned to the various levels of the independent variable), because participants already belong to some or other socio-economic grouping and cannot be randomly assigned to it.

If we do draw a random sample from each of the populations representing the respective levels of the independent variable, the latter is called a CLASSIFICATION FACTOR (criterion-groups design – see Section 5.4.2.2). By this we mean that the subjects already belong to the various levels of the independent variable prior to the research.

Example

Suppose we draw a random sample of adolescents from the population of adolescents whose parents have a *high socio-economic status*; draw another sample randomly from the population of adolescents with a *medium socio-economic background*, and do the same in respect of the *low socio-economic population*. Socio-economic status then qualifies as a *classification factor*.

As soon as we cannot randomly assign subjects to the levels of the independent variable (and thus equate them in terms of all other variables), they may possibly differ in respect of one or more variables other than the independent variable of interest. In such a case we say the participants are SELF-SELECTED in respect of *several other known and unknown variables*.

In the present example, such variables may have a greater effect than socio-economic status on the incidence of juvenile delinquency (criminal acts committed by adolescents).

Even if we found that there is a bigger proportion of juvenile delinquents in the low socio-economic group than in the other groups, it would be risky to identify socio-economic status as the cause of juvenile delinquency. It may be possible that the adolescents from the lower socio-economic level come predominantly from families in which the father is absent. The fathers' absence is then the principal cause that is related to both the socio-economic status of the parents and the incidence of juvenile delinquency among their children. Thus, it may be that the *absentee father* is the main cause of the incidence of juvenile delinquency.

Note

In the above example, we could have incorrectly directed the spotlight to the relationship between two variables, while the real "action" was taking place outside the spotlight (not to mention what was going on behind the curtains!). In other words, the ceteris paribus principle (see Sections 5.2.2, 5.3 & 6.1) is not met.

Although experimental research may thus be better equipped for isolating causal relationships, properly designed non-experimental studies and judiciously chosen multivariate statistical analyses (see Section 9.4) may go a long way to extending our knowledge about multivariate relationships, both correlational and causal.

However, we require a sound knowledge of the following:

- Firstly, which variables are *relevant in a particular research area* so that we can take these variables into consideration when planning research.
- Secondly, the necessary *multivariate statistical methodology*: Doob and MacDonald's (1979) research is a striking demonstration of the importance of knowledge of variables in a particular field for ruling out *rival hypotheses*. By eliminating rival hypotheses that state that third or fourth variables explain the relationships between the variables of concern (the independent and dependent variables), confidence in our knowledge of the relationships among variables grows.

Note

A rival hypothesis refers to a research hypothesis that is different from the research hypothesis under investigation (see Section 2.3) and to a different possible answer to the research problem that will have to be investigated in another study (research project). This means that the rival hypothesis refers to something (an independent variable) different from that of the research hypothesis under investigation.

> **Example**
>
> If our research hypothesis refers to the influence of a type of cure for AIDS, the rival hypothesis will state that it is something totally different (that may have been regarded as a third variable in the first mentioned study) that may cure AIDS.

Activity 6.1

Read the following problem statement and answer the questions. Compare your answers with those given.

Problem statement

The manager of TABOK Company observes that the morale of the employees in the company is low. She thinks that if the working conditions, the pay scales, and the leave benefits of the employees are improved, their morale will also improve. She doubts, however, that increasing the pay scales is going to raise the morale of all employees. Her guess is that those who have good side incomes (by doing other work in their own time) will not be motivated by higher pay.

Question

List the variables and label the third variable. Give brief reasons for your answers.

Answers

The variables are: *working conditions, pay scale, leave benefits and morale.*

The third variable is side incomes, because: If working conditions, pay scales and leave benefits are high in a work situation, then the employees' morale is high. But more pay does not result in higher morale of all employees – only of those who do not have a good side income. Therefore, "side income" interferes in the relationship between pay and morale.

Activity 6.2

Read Case Study A; Case Study B; Case Study C; Case Study D and Case Study E in Appendix D on page 276.

Question

Compile a list of the three most important variables in each case study and identify whether it is a so-called dependent, independent or third variable (in the case of the first three case studies and the last one). Briefly give reasons for your answer and explain the relationship(s) between the variables.

Answer

CASE STUDY A: The independent variable is *knowledge of AIDS*, the dependent variable is *attitude towards AIDS* and the third variable is *attitude towards prostitution.*

This is because, according to the introduction, previous research has suggested that effective education on AIDS (that is, an increased knowledge of AIDS) is sufficient to remove prejudices against AIDS sufferers (that is, to achieve a change in attitude towards AIDS). Further research indicates, however, that an attitude towards certain spreaders of AIDS, such as prostitutes, may also influence the attitude towards AIDS – not just the knowledge of AIDS.

For example: Suppose a doctor acquires more knowledge of AIDS (such as how it can be spread from one person to another by blood transfusions), we could expect the doctor's increased knowledge (influence of the independent variable) to make him or her more positive and sympathetic towards AIDS sufferers (as an expression of a more positive attitude towards AIDS – this is the effect or consequence on the dependent variable) when handling or treating such patients. But because this doctor has an antipathy to prostitution (prostitutes are often spreaders of AIDS, which is why the doctor has a negative attitude towards prostitution), his or her attitude towards AIDS cases in general (whether related to prostitution or not) may be negative (influence of the third variable), and he or she will deal with such patients less sensitively.

CASE STUDY B: The independent variable is *role induction,* the dependent variable is *attitude towards supervision,* and the third variable is *supervision of time.*

The researchers hope that the attitude of the people in the sample towards supervision will become positive, in other words, that their perception of the supervision procedure will change positively (this is the variable whose change depends on the influence of the independent variable). This would be as a result of the participation of the 20 sample members in the role induction procedure, that is, being informed by means of a videotape about the supervision process (the independent variable that the researcher can manipulate, for example, by allowing the sample members to view the videotape once, twice, or more often, thereby altering the level of the independent variable). But the supervision process itself surely has an influence over time on the attitudes of the 20 sample members towards supervision (that is, the third variable also influences the dependent variable).

CASE STUDY C: The independent variable is *training course*, the dependent variable is *knowledge of management principles*, and the third variable is *learned negative supervisory behaviour.*

The researcher hopes that the knowledge of management principles of first-line supervisors (in the experimental group) who attended the training course will increase significantly. The increase or decrease in knowledge of management principles is thus dependent on the attendance or non-attendance of the training course. Despite this it is possible that already learned negative supervisory behaviour may cause those who attend the course to distort or even reject the knowledge that they may acquire during the training.

CASE STUDY D: The independent variable is *speech preparation time*, the dependent variable is *speech quality*, and the third variable is *speech anxiety.*

CASE STUDY E: There are, in fact, two independent variables (predictor variables) involved, namely *bank overdraft usage* and *cash flow problems.* The dependent variable is *bankruptcy status*, and the third variable is *management skills.*

Seriously exceeding the bank overdraft limit combined with cash flow problems may have caused small businesses to become bankrupt. But as the reference to Levy (1998) in the introduction suggests, highly developed management skills such as coordination of enterprise functions may also influence bankruptcy status. Bankruptcy status is thus dependent on the bank overdraft usage and cash flow problems of the small businesses who participated in the research project.

6.3.3 **Factors that influence the researcher's control**

In human behavioural research the independent variable (see Section 2.2) is *typically a construct* (see Section 2.3) instead of a directly observable variable. To investigate the effect of such constructs, they have to be *operationalised in terms of observable variables.* When we consider ways in which to do this, we must bear the issue of the construct validity of the resulting variable in mind.

The CONSTRUCT VALIDITY of the operationalisation of an independent variable is the degree to which the procedures intended to produce the independent variable of interest indeed succeed in generating this variable rather than something else.

In practice, we seldom investigate the construct validity in itself. Usually, we clearly describe the way in which such a variable has been operationalised and leave it to the reader to judge whether these operations have succeeded in bringing about the desired independent variable. Just as in the case of the construct validity of the dependent variable (see Section 7.3.1), the eventual results provide feedback on both the tenability of the theory and the construct validity of the independent variable.

Example

Suppose our research hypothesis states that *anxiety causes a decrease in memory* and we operationalise an anxiety-provoking situation by locking up the experimental group (of fire fighters) in a room where smoke seeps in under the door. If this group later remembers fewer details, such as the colour of the walls and the contents of the paintings, than the control group (in a 'neutral' room), it provides provisional support for both the hypothesis being examined and for the construct validity of our operationalisation of anxiety-provoking conditions. If the *mean on a measure of anxiety* (for example, a questionnaire) is higher for the experimental group than for the control group, it may also support the construct validity of the operationalisation of the independent variable.

In addition, we require evidence that what we observed was not something other than was intended. It would be desirable to collect data suggesting that in the present example, anxiety was provoked and not anger (for example, towards the person who was held responsible for the locked door).

Note

Christensen (1985) describes some ways in which the construct validity of the independent variable in itself may be checked.

In this section, we deal mainly with ways in which we can deal with known THREATS TO CONSTRUCT VALIDITY, namely:

- the subject effect
- the experimenter effect
- pretest sensitisation.

6.3.3.1 The subject effect

Research participants do not approach experimental situations as passive, neutral beings. Research in the human behavioural sciences differs radically from research in the natural sciences in that, for example, its object of study does not simply react passively to stimuli, but also interprets them and attaches meaning to them.

Even the *reason* why individuals participate in a research project, for example, out of curiosity, to earn extra pocket money, or because they are required to do so as part of their course, may play a role in their subsequent behaviour in the experiment. The mere knowledge that they are guinea pigs in a research project may cause them to react differently than they would have done otherwise.

We often use the term REACTIVITY OF RESEARCH in this connection – by which we mean that the participants are affected by some or other aspect of the research setup apart from the treatment whose effect is being investigated. This may be compared to the reaction of spectators at a rugby match who behave quite differently the moment a television camera is aimed at them. This phenomenon may cause the implemented version of the independent variable to differ from the one the researcher has in mind. It creates the possibility that any effect observed in the dependent variable may be attributed to the independent variable, while it actually reflects a subject or reactivity effect.

In medical research the subject effect is called the PLACEBO EFFECT. A placebo is a tablet, capsule or injection that looks exactly like the drug whose effectiveness is to be investigated, but which has no medicinal value. In such investigations it is frequently found that the subjects to whom the placebo is administered also show improvements in the ailment for which the experimental drug is intended.

A term which we can regard as synonymous with the subject effect, is the Hawthorne effect. At the HAWTHORNE FACTORY of the Western Electric Company an experiment was conducted to determine which changes in the working environment (adjustments in temperature, working hours, and so on) would increase productivity. Interestingly enough, all these changes led to such an increase. After due consideration, it was decided that it was not the changes themselves that were responsible for this increase, but the *workers' awareness* that they were participating in an experiment designed to increase their productivity.

Participants' belief in the efficacy of a programme may cause them to indeed show an improvement in whatever the programme is supposed to improve.

If the research participants are familiar with the *research hypothesis* (see Section 2.3), they may consciously or unconsciously act in such a manner that their behaviour facilitates the confirmation of the hypothesis. In this connection, we often use the term DEMAND CHARACTERISTICS to refer to the real or supposed clues that participants infer from the task that confronts them in an experiment and to which they react so as to portray themselves in a particular light.

Example

If physically disabled (challenged) workers conclude that the purpose of an experiment is to raise their assertiveness, and if this kind of behaviour is viewed favourably, they may act in such a manner that their behaviour will confirm the hypothesis.

Often, subjects regard the researcher as an *expert* and they may tend to provide those responses which they suppose will *reflect positively* on them (for example, regarding their job satisfaction or organisation commitment).

On the other hand, subjects may deliberately try to *frustrate* the researcher by sabotaging his or her research project. This may occur especially when workers, as part of their training course, are required to participate in a research project.

Just as the Hawthorne effect may arise in the experimental group, so the so-called JOHN HENRY EFFECT may occur in the *control group*. The John Henry effect refers to the effect that appears when members of the control group, aware of the fact that their performance will eventually be compared with that of the experimental group, exert an *extra effort* and consequently perform better than expected.

This phenomenon is named after John Henry, a drill driver who, in response to the proposed replacement of human labour by a steel drill in building the railroad in the United States in the 19th century, over-exerted himself and beat the machine – but with fatal consequences.

Whether it be the Hawthorne or the John Henry effect, we should take care that, as far as possible, the demand characteristics are the *same for both* the experimental and control groups (see Section 5.2). This requires the following:

- Firstly, the control group should *match the definition* of such a group perfectly. In other words, the control group should differ from the experimental group only in that they receive a *different level of the independent variable*. In all other respects the two groups should be treated exactly the same.

Example

Say we wish to investigate the effectiveness of a programme that is intended to improve the self image of sexually harassed workers. Suppose we subject the experimental group to the programme but we do not give any attention to the control group. Strictly speaking, the control group does not qualify as a control group, because it *differs from the experimental group* in more respects than simply withholding the particular programme.

If, for example, the experimental group meets on a weekly basis to undergo the programme, the control group should also meet every week and be subjected to some or other control programme. It may very well be that merely attending any old programme, and not just that of the researcher, will have a beneficial effect.

- Secondly, an attempt should be made to *prevent the members* of either the experimental or the control groups *from knowing to which group they belong.* As soon as participants realise that they are members of either the experimental or the control group, there is the possibility that the subject effect, either the Hawthorne or the John Henry effect, may influence the results.

In *medical studies* the creation of a *placebo* to administer to the control group (while the experimental group receives the experimental treatment) usually does not present serious problems. In such studies it is therefore easy to prevent subjects from knowing whether they are members of the experimental or the control group.

However, in the *human behavioural sciences* the design of such a control treatment may require a great deal of ingenuity and creativity on the part of the researcher. When it is impossible to come up with such a control treatment, the control group should still *not differ* from the experimental group in terms of the impression that they are receiving a treatment designed to have a positive effect. The control group should not feel threatened by or consider themselves to be in competition with the experimental group, just as the experimental group should not be given the impression that they are something special.

Christensen (1985) discusses two additional ways in which we may attempt to counter the problem of the subject effect, namely, deception and disguised experiments.

- In the case of DECEPTION, all participants are deliberately misled as far as the purpose of the study is concerned. For example, in RESEARCH EXAMPLE VI (see below), participants were told that their personal problems as university students in an urban environment were to be discussed. In actual fact, their helping behaviour as a function of the supposed number of co-participants was investigated.

Christensen (1985) is of the opinion that it is apparently preferable to provide subjects with a false yet plausible hypothesis than to say nothing in this respect. If they are kept in the dark, participants may try to satisfy their curiosity by attempting to infer an hypothesis. Different participants may came to different conclusions, which could also create an unnecessary source of variation.

Research Example VI: A laboratory experiment on the number of bystanders and helping behaviour

Latané and Darley (1968) performed a series of laboratory and field experiments to investigate the conditions under which bystanders would help someone in distress.

In an example of a laboratory experiment, each research participant was seated in a cubicle at a table and provided with headphones and a microphone and instructed to listen to the instructions.

All participants were *led to believe* that they were to discuss personal problems in a stressful urban environment. Further, they were seated in the cubicles and would conduct the discussion over the intercom to prevent embarrassment and to maintain anonymity. Some were told that they were one of two such participants, others that they were one of three and still others, that there were another five such participants.

Furthermore, the subjects *were told (individually)* that to prevent their being inhibited by the presence of an outsider, the experimenter would not listen in to their discussion but would later obtain their reactions by means of a questionnaire.

In reality there were no other participants, but the *impression was created* that they were there, by playing tape recordings of people expressing ideas on the topic (personal problems in an urban environment).

The order in which the subjects were given an opportunity to talk was determined mechanically in that their microphones were switched on one after the other for about two minutes to signal their respective turns. The "co-participant" who first got his turn said that he was prone to seizures. During his next turn, the impression was created that he was in need of assistance because he was stuttering and indicating that he was in need of help and then became quiet. The participant was *actually listening to a tape recording* of a previously simulated emergency.

The dependent variable was the *time* it took from when the "co-participant" became silent and the subject left his cubicle to report the emergency to the experimenter. The most important independent variable was the *number of subjects* which the (only real) participant was informed were participating in the discussion.

In the case of only the participant and the supposed victim in the "group", 85% of the subjects reacted before the end of the "emergency". The corresponding percentages for the groups of two and five "other participants" were 62% and 31%, respectively.

- A DISGUISED EXPERIMENT is conducted in such a fashion that neither the experimental nor the control group *is aware* that they are participating in an experiment.

RESEARCH EXAMPLE VI also qualifies as an example of this approach. The participants were not aware of the fact that they were participating in an experiment in which the experimenter varied the number of co-participants.

The *ethical principle* (see Section 7.9) that participants should preferably be in a position to refuse participation in an experiment, is naturally disregarded in a disguised experiment.

In view of the important effect that DEMAND CHARACTERISTICS may have on the results of an experiment, and as a result of the difficulty of always anticipating them, it is frequently advisable to *interview participants after an experiment.* In such an interview, known as a DEBRIEFING INTERVIEW, the participants are asked about what they regarded the objectives of the experiment to be and to what degree these have affected their behaviour. If the information gained in this manner suggests that demand characteristics may have affected the results, this should be taken into consideration when the results obtained are interpreted or new research into the particular problem is planned.

6.3.3.2 **The experimenter effect**

The EXPERIMENTER EFFECT refers to the effect of the following on the obtained data:

- the *researcher's expectations* about the data to be collected, and
- certain of the *researcher's biographical attributes* (sex, culture, age, and so on).

- If such effects are present, it means that the participants are not exposed to the independent variable as intended, but to the independent variable as administered by the experimenter.

The fact that subjects who participate in an experiment have particular expectations is true to an even greater extent of researchers. The researchers (experimenters) are not merely neutral, detached observers of the experimental situation, because as designers of the experimental intervention they obviously have vested interests in the eventual results.

Example

A researcher who has developed a programme to improve the self-image of sexually harassed workers would obviously like to believe that it is a successful programme. It is not uncommon for researchers to become so involved in their research that their personal dignity is at stake. They are thus no longer concerned merely with the scientific ideal of the expansion of scientific knowledge as set out in Section 1.2.

The researcher's expectations may possibly play a role:

- when the independent variable is implemented; and
- when the dependent variable is measured.

Example

If the researcher himself or herself administers the programme designed to improve the self-image of sexually harassed workers, the thoroughness and enthusiasm with which this is done may possibly result in success, whereas if someone else implements it, it may make no difference.

Or else, the researcher's expectations may be conveyed to the participants in some or other manner that affects the eventual results. The researcher's expectations then become part of the demand characteristics of the experimental situation.

At the end of the programme the subjects may present those responses that they surmise will satisfy the experimenter. Improvements in self-image would then not be exclusively due to the effectiveness of the programme but also to the effect of both the experimenter and the research participant.

When we assess the dependent variable by means of *ratings* (see Section 7.7.3.4) or act as a rater, we may unintentionally rate the experimental group higher than the control group.

Just as subjects ideally should be unaware of which group, that is, experimental or control, they are members, so the test administrator or the rater or coder of subjects' behaviour should not be informed about this aspect. In the so-called DOUBLE-BLIND EXPERIMENT, neither the subjects nor the researchers (or their assistants) administering the levels of the independent variable or measuring the dependent variable, are aware of the group membership (experimental or control) of any particular individual. When this approach is followed, not only the subject, but also the experimenter is blind as far as the group membership of the former is concerned.

It stands to reason that the possible effect of the experimenter's expectations should be prevented in advance and that the researcher's biographical features (such as gender) should be taken into account as a way to deal with the possible threat to construct validity.

6.3.3.3 **Pretest sensitisation**

We have already indicated (see Section 5.2) that in a premeasurement and postmeasurement single-group design, a measurement of the dependent variable is obtained prior to, that is, before the experimental intervention. Apart from administering a pretest to investigate whether the experimental and control groups are comparable initially, or for the very reason of matching these groups in respect of this variable, there may be other reasons for pretesting. Pretesting may also be performed with a view to determining whether a ceiling effect exists.

Example

We could hardly demonstrate an improvement in attitude towards the donation of blood if individuals had already obtained pretest scores of 16 to 20 on a test with a maximum possible score of 20. These scores mean that the individuals are already as positive as possible towards donating blood, that is, their attitude has reached the ceiling. If a pretest had been administered it may have identified such a ceiling effect and would have alerted the researcher to consider another attitudinal measure.

Unfortunately it is possible that if the participants complete a pretest, they may react differently to the experimental intervention than they would have reacted had they not been exposed to the pretest. We refer to the phenomenon as PRETEST SENSITISATION.

What this phenomenon boils down to is that the pretest sensitises the individuals in the experimental group to the subsequent intervention and thereby affects their eventual scores on the dependent variable either negatively or positively.

As a result of pretest sensitisation, the independent variable as implemented does not correspond with the independent variable as conceptualised because the subjects are not subjected to the independent variable only, but also to the pretest.

6.3.4 Measurement problems

In this section, we describe two additional threats to internal validity that are the result of the very use of pretests (see Section 6.3.3), namely:

- measurement reactivity; and
- instrumentation.

Each threat offers another possible explanation for any observed change in the dependent-variable scores.

6.3.4.1 Measurement reactivity

Participants' awareness that they are completing a test (a measuring instrument such as a questionnaire – see Section 7.7.3.1) may affect their responses to the test or to their subsequent completion of the test without the experimental intervention having anything to do with it. We refer to this phenomenon as MEASUREMENT REACTIVITY.

Participants may remember the answers that they gave on one occasion and wittingly or unwittingly change them on subsequent occasions. On the subsequent testing occasion they may thus tend to respond differently from the way they would have if they had not been tested before.

Note

The potential effect of measurement reactivity is not something that can be determined by mere speculation but should be investigated empirically. Such an investigation falls outside the scope of this book.

6.3.4.2 Instrumentation

This threat refers to CHANGES IN THE MEASUREMENT of the dependent variable, rather than in the dependent variable itself.

Example

Suppose we modify the method in which a management training course is presented after the first test has been written. We now want to examine the effect of this modification by comparing the scores on the second test with those on the first test (for example, in a premeasurement and postmeasurement design).

> If these two tests were incomparable due to different levels of difficulty, it would constitute an example of the threat of instrumentation.

If we assess the dependent variable (see Section 2.2) by means of ratings (see Section 7.7.3.4), the raters may be more tired, or more experienced, or more bored when performing the ratings after the intervention than before it.

If we use official statistics (see Section 7.7.2) as a measure of the dependent variable, the accuracy in reporting the phenomenon in question may differ after the intervention from before it.

> **Example**
>
> Suppose a campaign is launched to combat sexual harassment of workers. The number of molestations which are reported to official bodies is taken as a measurement of the extent of this problem. The publicity given to the campaign on radio and television may lead to a heightened awareness among the general public, so that cases which previously would have gone unreported are now brought to the attention of the authorities.
>
> As a result there may be an increase in the number of reported cases of sexual harassment of workers that may conceal any decrease in the actual incidence of this problem.

6.3.5 Group differences

We have already indicated (see Section 5.2) that if only one group (which receives the experimental intervention) is used, we have no way of knowing whether any considerable changes in the dependent variable would not have occurred in any case, that is, without any such intervention. What is required, therefore, is a control group that does not receive the experimental intervention. Although the threats of history and spontaneous change (see Section 6.3.2) are thus controlled by making use of a control group, the internal validity of such a design is subject to threats that involve the composition of the groups used. This entails:

- selection; and
- interaction between selection and spontaneous change.

6.3.5.1 Selection

The threat to internal validity, called SELECTION, is concerned with initial or pre-existing differences between the experimental group and the control group.

Because the experimental group and the control group are not necessarily equal in respect of the dependent variable or all possible nuisance variables, such a design lacks an adequate basis of comparison.

If the one group (mentioned in the first example of Section 5.2), namely the workers of one mine, is more aggressive after exposure to the aggressive role model than the so-called control group, the workers of another mine, it cannot be attributed conclusively to that exposure, because this group possibly may have been more aggressive even before the beginning of the investigation.

6.3.5.2 Interaction between selection and spontaneous change

Even if initially the experimental and control groups were equal in terms of both the dependent variable and all nuisance variables, the one group may subsequently show a greater degree of spontaneous development, maturation, recovery or deterioration than the other. In such a case we are dealing with an interaction between the threats of selection and spontaneous change.

> **Example**
>
> Although trainee supervisors in both groups (RESEARCH EXAMPLE II – see

Section 2.2, page 14), may have exhibited the same degree of management style initially, the trainee supervisors at one regional company office may react differently to a particular intervention than the trainee supervisors at another regional office. This is because the one group is stationed in a particular geographical area where riots have started to take place.

For the same reason, it would be unwise to use teenage boys and teenage girls as two treatment groups in any research, even if they were equated in terms of their pretest scores on any variable that is susceptible to development. At that stage of development males and females tend to develop at different rates so that, without any intervention, these groups may reveal differences in their post-test scores.

6.3.6 **Random assignment to groups**

The purpose of RANDOM ASSIGNMENT is to equate the groups in terms of all known and unknown nuisance variables, that is, variables apart from the independent variable in terms of which groups may possibly differ and that may affect the dependent variable.

Example

Suppose the independent variable is *training method* and the dependent variable is *examination marks.* It is generally known that there is a substantial relationship (correlation – see Section 9.4) between intelligence and examination marks. If the group taught by the one method was on average more intelligent than the other, we would be at a loss to know to what extent an eventual difference in mean examination achievement would be attributable to the different training methods rather than to possible differences in intelligence.

By randomly assigning participants to the two treatment groups, we attempt to get more or less an equal number of highly intelligent participants, and an equal number of moderately intelligent participants, and so on, in the two groups.

If the one group still significantly outperforms the other group, we are in a position to ascribe this difference with greater confidence to the greater effectiveness of the method to which they were subjected rather than to their possibly higher intelligence. Of course, we do not necessarily succeed in equating the two groups in terms of all nuisance variables, but if a sufficiently large number of participants are randomly assigned, the chances are high that the resulting groups will meet this requirement.

Note

TRUE EXPERIMENTAL RESEARCH (such as the different randomised group designs – see Section 5.2.1.2) differs from PRE-EXPERIMENTAL research (see Section 6.3.2) in that all the groups being used have been randomly assigned.

6.3.7 **Matching**

We may consider MATCHING participants in terms of a nuisance variable in cases where we know that there is a very strong relationship (considerable correlation) between this nuisance variable and the dependent variable.

Example

We have already pointed out (see Section 6.3.6) that there is a relatively high correlation between intelligence and examination marks.

Intelligence thus operates as a systematic source of variation in this connection in that the more intelligent individuals consistently tend to outperform the less intelligent, irrespective of which training method they are subjected to.

6.3.7.1 **Precision control**

We may, however, equate groups that are to be subjected to different teaching methods by matching them in terms of the positively identified nuisance variable *intelligence*. In the case of precision control, we use the following method:

We administer an intelligence test to all participants and then rank them in terms of their intelligence-test scores. In other words, the person with the highest score is ranked first, the one with the second highest is placed second, and so on, until the one with the lowest score appears in the bottom position.

Beginning with the people in the first two positions, we subdivide participants into pairs so that the members of each pair have more or less the same intelligence-test score. Finally, the two members of each pair are randomly assigned to the two groups. In other words, for each person with an IQ of say 106 who is assigned to the one group, someone else with more or less the same IQ is allocated to the other group. The two groups formed in this manner will have more or less the same mean intelligence-test score. If one of these groups then performs better on average in the examination, this difference may be ascribed more readily to the greater effectiveness of the teaching method to which they were subjected rather than to a higher intelligence.

In this design (see Figure 4.2(d) – Section 5.2), we subdivide the participants into pairs so that the members of each pair are similar in respect of one or other nuisance variable whose effect we want to eliminate. We then randomly assign the members of each pair to the two levels of the independent variable. The interrupted double lines forming the boundaries of the adjacent rows indicate that the groups represented by these rows were matched and randomly assigned to the two levels. As in the case of the two-group design, the one level refers to the treatment whose effect is being investigated, and the other represents the control treatment. The two levels may also, for example, represent two methods.

6.3.7.2 **Nuisance variable**

Matching does not have to be limited to a single nuisance variable. If we want to match individuals in respect of both IQ and sex, it means that for each man with an IQ of, say, 106, who is assigned to the one group, a man with a similar IQ should be placed in the other group. For each woman with an IQ of 102 allocated to the one group, another woman with a similar IQ should be placed in the other group.

Each of the variables that are matched in this fashion should show a high correlation with the dependent variable, but a low correlation with the other variables in terms of which matching is done. If each nuisance variable does not separately show a high correlation with the dependent variable, it does not make sense to match participants on it. If there is not a low correlation between any two nuisance variables, it means that they partially overlap and that matching on both of them may be superfluous.

In practice, it is generally difficult to match individuals on more than two such variables, because it is usually difficult to find two (or more) individuals who are equal in respect of each of more than two such variables. For this reason, it becomes increasingly difficult to effect matching as the number of variables in terms of which groups are to be matched, increases.

Note

We equate groups only in terms of those variables in which they are matched specifically. The problem with matching as the only strategy of equating groups is that there may be several potential nuisance variables which are unknown to the researcher and in terms of which subjects thus cannot be matched. To equate the matched groups in terms of such variables, the individuals in each matched pair or trio, and so on, should still be randomly assigned to the various groups (which are to receive the different levels of the independent variable).

6.3.7.3 **Frequency distribution control**

In the case of the frequency distribution control method, we should ensure that the mean(s) on the nuisance variable(s) is/are the same for the different treatment groups.

Example

If age is the nuisance variable, the ages of the members of one group may be 15, 17, 19, 21 and 23, whereas those of the other are 17, 18, 19, 20 and 21. Each of these groups has a mean of 19 although there is, for example, no 15-year old in both groups.

Note

In the precision control method that we have discussed so far, individuals are matched in groups of two or more each so that all the members of such a group are the same in respect of the nuisance variable(s) (before they are randomly assigned to the respective treatment groups).

In the usual precision control method the researcher has to omit individuals for whom nobody with approximately the same status on the nuisance variable(s) can be found.

The ADVANTAGE of the frequency distribution method is that such an occurrence results in the elimination of fewer participants because there does not necessarily have to be a partner with approximately the same status on the nuisance variable(s) for each research participant.

A DISADVANTAGE of this type of matching becomes evident when there are two or more nuisance variables that have to be taken into account.

Example

Suppose we need to match two groups in terms of both sex and intelligence. The one group may then contain only men with high IQs and women with low IQs, and the other group only men with low IQs and women with high IQs, while the number of men and women in the two groups or the mean IQs for the two groups remains the same.

Note

If there is no considerable relationship (correlation – see Section 9.4) between the nuisance variable (see Section 5.2) and the dependent variable (see Section 2.2), it is better to use the regular randomised groups design (see Section 5.2) with the same number of participants, rather than the matched groups design.

Of course, this matching technique (matched groups design) need not be restricted to two groups. If, for example, there are four training methods, groups of four participants each, with more or less the same intelligence quotient (IQ), may be randomly assigned to four groups that are subsequently taught by the four training methods respectively. However, as the number of groups increases, it may become more difficult to obtain groups of the required size of which all the members are more or less the same in respect of the nuisance variable (on which they should be matched). For example, it would be more difficult to get six subjects with an IQ of more or less 140, than to get only two with this IQ.

6.3.8 **Unplanned developments within and between groups**

In this section we discuss threats to internal validity for which researchers should be on the lookout during the research project. This involves the following aspects (compare Section 9.3.1):

- communication between treatment groups; and
- differential attrition between participants.

Even if we initially equate all samples in terms of all possible variables, threats to internal validity may become apparent during the course of the research project. As researchers, we are to a great extent, if not exclusively, at the mercy of the co-operation of research participants. We are not in a position to keep participants imprisoned, as it were, until the end of a research project.

6.3.8.1 **Communication between treatment groups**

The entire purpose of using control groups is to treat them in exactly the same manner, except for the different level of the independent variable that they receive. This requirement is necessary to enable us to ascribe eventual between-group differences in the dependent variable exclusively to the independent variable.

If the groups are to share their respective experiences in the research project, the control group may be indirectly exposed to the same experience as the experimental group, or they may even compete with the experimental group.

> **Example**
>
> If the experimental group undergoes a relaxation programme, members of the control group may obtain details of this programme and may implement or simulate some aspects of it. Similarly, access to the programme to which the experimental group is exposed may cause the members of the control group to feel neglected, resentful and demoralised.
>
> All these contingencies represent threats to the internal validity of the eventual conclusions.

6.3.8.2 **Differential attrition of participants**

It is not uncommon for participants to "disappear" during the course of a research project. In this connection the term SUBJECT MORTALITY is often used as an analogy for biological studies in which organisms may literally die.

The problem of subjects who disappear during the course of a research project is not so much due to the decrease in the data that are obtained ultimately, but that their disappearance may be connected to the level of the independent variable to which they have been exposed. As a result, it is also referred to as the DIFFERENTIAL ATTRITION of subjects.

> **Example**
>
> Say we randomly assign students to two groups and subject the experimental group to a computer-assisted course in research methodology. We use the other group as a control group that is taught by means of the conventional lecture method.
>
> Suppose the students with poorer numerical skills tend to be the same ones who fare poorly in research methodology. The students from this group who land up in the experimental group terminate their course in greater numbers than those in the control group. The disappearance of subjects from the experimental group, therefore, is directly related to the nature of the level of the independent variable to which they have been exposed. Their numerical ability does not agree with the computer-assisted course, so to speak.

Although the two groups were initially equal in respect of the dependent variable (achievement in research methodology), eventually there was a difference in favour of the experimental group because the students with the weakest numerical skills had dropped out of this group. Consequently, the pretest scores of the individuals who remained in the experimental group have a higher mean on the dependent variable than both the original experimental group and the control group.

Now, if the former group eventually fares better on the dependent variable than the latter, we will be unable to attribute this difference convincingly to the greater effectiveness of the computer-assisted method.

Self-evaluation questions

See some of the answers in Appendix B on page 273.

6.1 Suppose Researcher A wishes to investigate the effectiveness of a programme designed to increase the assertiveness of disabled workers. All these workers complete an assertiveness test at the beginning of the year. Those who appear to be in the greatest need of this programme are enrolled in it. At the end of the year their assertiveness is measured again.

In terms of this example, explain what is meant by the internal validity of conclusions and evaluate this feature of this design by identifying possible threats to it.

6.2 Suppose Researcher B investigates the same problem as Researcher A in question 6.1. She selects the same group as Researcher A but randomly assigns them to two groups and subjects one group, but not the other to the programme.

Evaluate the internal validity of the conclusions made possible by this design by identifying possible threats to it.

6.3 On the basis of the relationship between the size of the signature of borrowers of library books on the lending cards and their status (students and professors), Zweigenhaft (1970) came to the conclusion that the higher borrowers rate their status, the larger their signature tends to be.

Offer another explanation for the observed relationship by referring to a possible third variable.

6.4 External validity and threats

6.4.1 Introduction

We have pointed out (see Section 2.2.1.3) that a theory always holds for some or other population of units of analysis (for example, individuals, organisations, and so on) and a universum of conditions. Any implication deduced from such a theory, and that is subjected to empirical testing, is similarly applicable to such a population and such a universum. These populations tend to be very large so that it may be practically impossible to involve all the members in a research project. Consequently, we must take a representative sample from the population. Typically, this sample comprises far less than 100 and at most 1 000 individuals, which is relatively small in comparison to the total population, which may amount to millions. The degree of population validity achieved thus depends exclusively on how representative the sample is of the population from which it has been obtained (see Section 4.2.5).

6.4.2 Population validity

As we have mentioned (see Section 2.3), research hypotheses are concerned with postulated relationships (between variables) in one or more populations. As a result of the size of the populations about which hypotheses in the human behavioural sciences are typically formulated, researchers in these disciplines have to rely on the data obtained for samples from such populations.

POPULATION VALIDITY refers to the degree to which the findings obtained for a sample may be generalised to the total population to which the research hypothesis applies.

Example

In RESEARCH EXAMPLE II (see Section 2.2, page 14) population validity refers to the degree to which the results obtained for a sample of trainee supervisors may be generalised to the total population of all trainee supervisors. If watching management style role model behaviour were to make the sample of trainee supervisors more inclined to imitate an iron-fisted management style, the researcher would like to conclude that watching such management style behaviour would have the same effect on the total population of trainee supervisors. To make such generalisations, researchers have to draw, as far as possible, a random sample from the population to which they would like their results to apply.

Kempthorne (in Bracht & Glass, 1968) makes the following distinction:

- The TARGET POPULATION is the population to which the researcher ideally would like to generalise his or her results.
- The EXPERIMENTALLY ACCESSIBLE POPULATION is the population that corresponds to the sampling frame from which a random sample is actually drawn.

Example

In RESEARCH EXAMPLE II (see Section 2.2, page 14), the *target population* may have consisted solely of trainee supervisors younger than 30 years, while only those in the specific company constituted the *experimentally accessible population*. Strictly speaking, the statistical model only permits generalisation to the (experimentally accessible) population from which a random sample (see Section 4.2.2) has actually been obtained. The generalisation from the experimentally accessible to the target population can only be made on extrastatistical grounds.

Say the researcher can convincingly argue that trainee supervisors younger than 30 years in a specific company are representative of all trainee supervisors younger than 30 years in South Africa as far as susceptibility to an iron-fisted management style is concerned. Then the results obtained for a random sample from the population of trainee supervisors younger than 30 years in the specific company may be extrapolated to the population of all trainee supervisors younger than 30 years in South Africa. However, convincing arguments to the contrary would restrict such generalisations.

Although there is nothing wrong with conducting research on subjects from an easily available population (whether it be mine workers, prisoners or hospital patients), we should be careful not to generalise the results obtained to the entire human race, but to restrict them to the experimentally accessible population. Knowledge of any population is valid as long as it is presented as knowledge of that population. Moreover, populations that are clearly distinguishable in terms of some variables may be expected to show a great degree of similarity in, for example, physiological-psychological investigations. However, when we are dealing with personality and social-psychological research, such similarities should be less readily assumed as fact. Researchers would do well to investigate relationships previously found in populations of white, university students, in new populations. Alternatively, the effect of both the independent variable and group differences and the interaction between these two variables may be investigated in randomised block designs (see Section 9.3.2.3).

The use of volunteers may similarly affect the population validity of results obtained. To the extent that volunteers differ from the remainder of the relevant population in respect of variables related to the dependent variable, biased results may be obtained.

Example

Suppose we wish to investigate the effectiveness of a computer-assisted system to teach research methodology to students in the human behavioural sciences.

Suppose we obtain a sample of volunteers and randomly assign them to two groups that subsequently undergo the computer-assisted and conventional methods, respectively.

Students interested in computer-assisted methods and who present themselves as volunteers for this kind of research, are likely to achieve different results from those of students in general. The results we obtain for the sample of volunteers interested in computer-assisted methods will thus be less readily generalised to the population of students.

Finally, we should point out that in experimental research (apart from programme evaluation), population validity is regarded as less important than in survey research. As we have already indicated (see Section 6.3), internal validity is of primary importance in experimental research where the purpose is to draw conclusions about causal relationships.

In non-experimental research, again, especially in attitude surveys, population validity is of extreme importance. The assumption, again implicit, is that subjects tend to exhibit great variation in respect of the variables that are usually studied in non-experimental research, and therefore biased results may be obtained if data are obtained for unrepresentative samples. Consequently, we should take great care to obtain representative samples if, for example, we want to predict the results of a forthcoming election.

Note

Whereas the random selection of participants is required for population validity, the random assignment of participants promotes internal validity (see Section 6.3.6).

6.4.3 Ecological validity

The ECOLOGICAL VALIDITY of the obtained results refers to the degree to which they may be generalised to all circumstances that are implied by the research hypothesis (see Section 2.3).

Example

We may wish to *generalise the results* obtained in a specific laboratory situation to all real-life situations where such behaviour is manifested.

If workers for a mining company, in response to aggressive role model behaviour, acted aggressively in a laboratory, we would like to conclude that they would act similarly in response to comparable behaviour by their supervisors in the work place.

This requirement relates to ecological validity (which we may also interpret as part of the construct validity of the independent variable) on which we have focused in Section 6.3.3.

Usually, we do not only obtain research data for a particular sample of subjects, but also in a particular research setting or set of conditions (experimenter, apparatus, venue, time of the day and year, and so on). Seldom, if ever, do we wish to restrict our findings to a particular group of individuals under a specific research setting.

Example

Suppose we investigate the effect of television violence on the aggressiveness of mine workers by showing a violent video to a group of mine workers during a regular training session. By ecological validity in this instance we mean the degree to which the results obtained are not restricted to the particular video shown in a training situation, but may be generalised to all (violent) videos, including those shown on television at home as part of scheduled television programmes or rented from video stores.

Here, the ecological validity would have been suspect if mine workers reacted differently to a violent video shown in a training situation than they would to videos that they watch alone at home or in the company of their families.

While *population validity* refers to the generalisation of the results obtained to the population to which the research hypothesis applies, *ecological validity* involves the generalisation to situations other than the one in which the experiment has been carried out. In other words, ecological validity refers to the generalisation to a relevant universe of conditions.

Obviously the presence of subject effects, experimenter effects and pretest sensitisation (see Section 6.3.2) may restrict the degree to which the results obtained can be generalised and thus adversely affect ecological validity. Typically, we would like to generalise our research findings to situations in which neither the subject effect, nor the experimenter effect, nor pretest sensitisation is of any consequence.

Findings obtained in a laboratory, for example, may be of little value if they do not tell us something of human behaviour in everyday life. According to some critics, the advantage of laboratory experiments as far as the control of nuisance variables (see Section 5.2) is concerned, also represents its greatest drawback. In an attempt to maximise internal validity, a laboratory experiment may be planned in which all possible nuisance variables (environmental noise, fluctuations in temperature, and so on) are eliminated. However, this approach may result in a highly artificial environment that yields trivial results that cannot be generalised to real-life situations, and that have an unsatisfactory ecological validity.

Consequently, research is frequently carried out in a field situation, not so much because it is impossible to do it in a laboratory but because the field situation is preferred on account of the greater degree of naturalness it affords. According to many authors (for example, Kerlinger, 1986), ecological validity increases in so far as the research situation becomes more realistic, in other words, the more it corresponds to real, everyday situations. According to the proponents of field research, generalisations to "real people in everyday, real life" may be made only on the basis of research conducted in natural surroundings. The advantage of field experiments in comparison to laboratory experiments is therefore said to be the greater ecological validity they afford.

Whether or not a laboratory environment as such is an obstacle in achieving ecological validity does not depend on its naturalness. The importance of the matter is the realism with which the independent variable is operationalised (see Sections 2.3, 6.1 & 6.3.3) irrespective of the environment in which this is done.

In the final analysis, whether findings obtained in a laboratory experiment can indeed be so generalised cannot be settled by means of speculation or debate, but should be investigated empirically. Thus, if we would like to know whether watching violent behaviour will be followed by aggressive behaviour in a field situation, as is the case in a laboratory situation, we should investigate this phenomenon in a field setting.

Activity 6.3

Read Case Study A; Case Study B; Case Study C; Case Study D; Case Study E and Case Study F in Appendix D on page 276.

Question

To what extent does the research design used in each case study make provision for threats to internal and external validity? Explain your answer in terms of the aim of each study and refer critically to sampling.

Answer

CASE STUDY A: Because there are many health professionals in South Africa who are involved with AIDS cases (the population in this case – also called the target population), it is advisable for the researcher to work with a sample instead of the total population. However, this sample should contain members who are representative of the total population concerned (that is, they should be selected randomly with regard to the relevant criteria such as age, population group, and so on) to increase the population validity of the study (as part of external validity). By doing so, the results obtained for the sample could be generalised to the whole population, namely all nursing sisters and doctors who work with AIDS cases in South Africa.

In this particular case study, the abovementioned threat to external validity (that the results may not be generalised) has not been avoided, because the sample of 74 people who work at a general hospital and serve mainly white and coloured population groups was obtained on the basis of convenience. If the study's external validity had been high, we could have said that the knowledge of, and attitude towards, AIDS and prostitution of all health professionals in South Africa who work with AIDS cases (the sample framework from which the sample had to be drawn) show a relation that matches that of the sample.

Because the study involved a correlational design (not an experimental design – where internal validity is important), there was no question of the influence of the independent variable on the dependent variable. Yet a moral question (such as attitude towards prostitution) could pertain to the relation between knowledge (of AIDS) and attitudes (towards AIDS), in that it could have an uncontrolled influence on both variables, and so negate the internal validity of the study.

CASE STUDY B: The threat to the internal validity of this investigation is that a change or lack of change in the apprentices' attitude to the supervision procedure may not be unambiguously attributable to their participation in the role induction procedure, but that other variables such as age also play a role. Because they are all young (19 to 20 years old) it could be, for example, that they are rebellious and negative towards any form of authority (and therefore also towards supervision). The socio-economic status of the households from which they come and/or their level of education could also have an influence.

It appears, therefore, that the study could have had a higher internal validity if the sample members were drawn randomly from various strata and subjected to the effect of the role induction procedure.

Regarding the external (population) validity of the study, the same arguments apply as those given above to Case Study A. The sample of apprentices in this investigation is not representative of all the members of the population of goldsmith apprentices. Only the 20 at one large jewellery firm were used, and therefore the results of the study cannot be generalised to all goldsmith apprentices. Because the role induction procedure took place during the apprentices' training in their natural, everyday setting (the time when and circumstances under which such a procedure is typically applied) the ecological validity of the study is not threatened.

CASE STUDY C: In the non-equivalent control group design that was used in the investigation, two existing groups were used respectively as an experimental and a control group. Provision is made, however, for the threat of group differences (these are differences that could have existed between the groups as a result of previous experience, acquired management skills, and so forth) by the non-equivalent control group design by measuring both parties before the experimental intervention (attendance of the training course) on the dependent variable. This was done when the researcher measured both groups' knowledge of management principles and ensured that the average was the same for both groups.

If the groups do not differ with regard to their knowledge of management principles before attending the course but indeed with regard to their knowledge after the course, the latter difference can certainly be ascribed to the influence of the training course. As a result of the presence of a control group, provision is therefore made for the threat of the internal validity of the investigation.

The threat of external validity (in terms of population validity) is rejected in that an equal sample of participants from the population of first-line supervisors is drawn, which ensures that the results of the investigation can be generalised to the population.

CASE STUDY D: The threat to the internal validity of this investigation is that not only anxiety but also variables such as gender, socio-economic status of the households from which the students come and their personalities (outgoing or inner-directed, and so forth) may play a role with regard to their speech quality. Should a student whose mother tongue is Zulu, for example, have to deliver a speech in Afrikaans it would, logically speaking, take such a student longer to prepare this speech than it would an Afrikaans-speaking student. It therefore appears that the study would have a higher internal validity if the subjects could be drawn equally from various strata (with regard to, for example, their home language, personality, age).

As far as the external (population) validity of the study is concerned, the same argument as in Case Study C applies. The sample of students in public speech-making in this investigation was not representative of all members of the relevant population of students because it was not a stratified random sample. If this had been done, the threat of external validity with regard to the population validity could have been rejected.

CASE STUDY E: In the research design in this investigation two existing groups were used. Factors such as business size (numbers of workers employed) and business sector (cafés, coffee shops, florists, and so on) could have acted as third variables if they had differentiated between the two groups by having an effect on the so-called dependent variables (which constitute the two criterion groups: bankrupt or not).

However, provision was made for these differences by ensuring that corresponding business size and comparable business sectors existed between the two groups. This eliminated most of the possible threats to the internal validity of the study. It cannot be assumed, however, that it was mainly the independent variables that predicted the dependent variable to differentiate between the two groups – management skills (indicated in the literature review – the introduction) may also have had an influence.

The threat to external validity (in terms of population validity) is not compensated for by the use of an accidental sample (see Section 4.2.4). Therefore the businesses involved in this study are not representative of the population of small businesses, and the results of the investigation cannot be generalised to the population of small businesses in South Africa as a whole.

CASE STUDY F: The threats to the internal validity of this investigation are mainly from the following third (nuisance) variables that could have an influence on the results of the study on the innovative problem-solving styles and therefore on the results of the study, in other words covary with the levels of the independent variable (entrepreneurs / managers):

- Age – because the average ages of the two groups differ significantly. (The average age of the entrepreneurs was 28 years while the average age of the managers was 42 years.)
- Sex (gender) – because proportionately more men were included in the entrepreneurial group (100 males to 12 females) than in the manager group (70 males to 40 females).
- Other variables such as "intelligence" or "motivation" could also have an influence on the level of innovative problem-solving styles of the respondents in the project.

With regard to external validity, in particular population validity, the sample of business people (entrepreneurs and managers of big businesses) was not representative of all members of the relevant target population of entrepreneurs/managers in Gauteng and the Western Cape because an accidental sample, and not a random sample, was used. If random sampling had been done, the threats to the external validity with regard to the population validity of this study could have been overcome.

But the ecological validity of the study is also under threat because only business people from the Western Cape and Gauteng were included. Businesses may differ in terms of their focuses depending on the different localities, for example wine making in the Western Cape, heavy industry in Gauteng and sugar cane production in KwaZulu-Natal.

Self-evaluation questions

See some of the answers in Appendix B, page 273.

6.4 Suppose a psychology lecturer develops a programme to modify the lifestyle of individuals with an unhealthy Type A behaviour pattern. All employees of an insurance company who obtain high scores on a Type A personality questionnaire are randomly assigned to either an experimental or a control group. The experimental group meets weekly for an hour to take part in the programme, which is presented by the lecturer's graduate students. At the conclusion of the project, the members of both groups are subjected to artificial situations supposed to elicit Type A behaviour, in a room equipped with facilities to record the participants' behaviour on videotape. Subsequently the researcher and his master's students rate the participants' behaviour in respect of the occurrence of Type A behaviour (from the videotapes) to investigate whether there is a difference (in this type of behaviour) between the two groups.

Comment on the population and/or ecological validity of the results obtained.

6.5 Evaluate the experimental realism of the research procedure in the Research Proposal in Appendix A and point out the possible consequences thereof on the ecological validity of the experiment.

6.6 It has been found in laboratory experiments that the sexual prowess of male rats of an age comparable to men in their twenties is adversely affected by drinking too much beer (*Te veel bier* [*Too much beer*], 1991). On the basis of this result, the conclusion has been made that drinking comparable amounts of beer in the corresponding period of time will cause temporary impotence in twenty-year-old men. Which kind of validity is involved in this conclusion and why?

Summary

Any study has to be valid in terms of the control of possible third variables. This concerns the internal validity of the study. It means that we have to be able to contribute a change in the dependent variable only to the effect/cause of the independent variable.

Although most scientific studies in business are concentrated on specific units of analysis and the circumstances of such cases (the ecological validity of the study), the results may benefit the broader community if the results can be generalised to them (the population validity of the study). It is therefore important to ensure that the cases and samples we use are representative of most South African circumstances and of a South African target population.

If our studies are not valid, we may come to incorrect conclusions.

Table 6.1 summarises the above-mentioned aspects. (Note that the table makes broad generalisations because the type of validity – be it high or low – depends on the specific research example's definition and empirical characteristics.)

Multiple choice and true/false questions

Only *one* of the answers to each question is correct. Identify and mark the correct one. (Answers appear in Appendix E on page 285.)

6.1 Internal validity refers to:
   a) generalisability
   b) whether the experimental stimulus (independent variable) really affected the dependent variable
   c) the comparison of the results obtained for the experimental group with those obtained for the control group
   d) the determination of the proper time to do the post-test.

6.2 The 100 km/h speed limit for buses was introduced in South Africa in 1999. Shortly thereafter the number of bus accidents declined. We can conclude that
   a) the reduced speed limit caused the decline in the number of bus accidents
   b) the reduced speed limit had nothing to do with the decline in bus accidents
   c) the reduced speed limit and the number of bus accidents are causally related
   d) the reduced speed limit may have caused the decline in bus accidents.

6.3 The problem of external validity refers to the generalisability of results.
   True False

6.4 If the findings of a research study can be generalised to different populations, circumstances, and conditions not included but represented in the original study, the findings are said to have:
   a) internal validity
   b) ecological validity
   c) transfer validity
   d) external validity.

6.5 Which of the following statements concerning the external validity of a scientifically conducted investigation is true?
   a) Neither laboratory nor field research will give externally valid results.
   b) Field research and laboratory research are equally likely to ensure valid results.
   c) Both field research and laboratory research are likely to ensure valid results.
   d) Field research is more likely than laboratory research to ensure externally valid results.

6.6 If the possibility exists that the participants of one's study are exposed to injury, it is essential for the researcher to obtain:
   a) conditional consent
   b) implied consent
   c) informed consent
   d) participation.

Table 6.1
Types of research and their correspondence to external and internal validity (Compare Chapters 5 and 8)

TYPE OF RESEARCH	TYPE OF VALIDITY
Experimental	INTERNAL validity is of PRIMARY IMPORTANCE whilst POPULATION validity is less important
Laboratory experiments	ECOLOGICAL validity is LOW
Field experiments	ECOLOGICAL validity is HIGH
Quasi-experimental	INTERNAL and EXTERNAL validity are important
Non-experimental	POPULATION validity is EXTREMELY IMPORTANT whilst INTERNAL validity is LESS IMPORTANT
Qualitative	ECOLOGICAL validity is much more important than other types of validity

7 Data-collecting methods and measuring instruments in quantitative research

Figure 7.1 The research process and the outline of chapters in this book

Learning Outcomes

After studying this chapter, you should be able to:

1. illustrate by means of examples how indicators may be used to define and help to measure nontangible things (for example, constructs such as values, opinions, expectations, and so on)
2. explain briefly the basic requirements for measuring instruments regarding validity and reliability
3. distinguish between the validity of a measuring instrument and the validity of the study in which it was used to collect data
4. briefly describe different data-collecting methods
5. distinguish between measurement and observation
6. describe how secondary data (obtained by means of computer simulations) may contribute to the understanding of certain phenomena
7. give four examples of secondary information sources and the benefits of using them instead of doing empirical research
8. list four steps regarding the follow-up of postal surveys in order to increase the response rate
9. describe why and how the semantic differential may be used to collect information
10. list six problems with telephone surveys and means to resolve them
11. distinguish between different measuring instruments
12. classify measuring instruments into four basic strategies for collecting data
13. use the guidelines for developing certain types of instruments to measure variables
14. explain why it is important to provide clear instructions to respondents on how to complete survey questionnaires
15. explain why ethical issues are important in measurement.

7.1 Introduction

Once we have decided on a particular research design (see Section 4.5), we have to obtain our research participants (subjects/units of analysis) according to our chosen sampling procedure (see Section 4.2.5) in order to carry out the research. Now we have to consider which data-collecting method is the most appropriate in the light of our research problem and the particular population in question. In this step we put the blueprint which we finalised in the preceding stage (see Chapters 4 & 5) into action.

Note

Each data-collecting method and the use of a measuring instrument has its advantages and drawbacks. Also, what counts as an advantage for one may qualify as a drawback for another, and vice versa.

Example

Employees who cannot read or write cannot complete questionnaires and thus we would have to observe their work behaviour directly. On the other hand, there are certain behaviours (which management style employees support, financial practices, and so on) that we can assess only by means of questionnaires and/or interviews.

In this chapter, we focus on measurement theory and various ways in which to use instruments to collect information, starting from where we, as researchers, are not in direct contact with the units of analysis (the objects and people we project will be involved with and by our study – Section 7.7.2) to

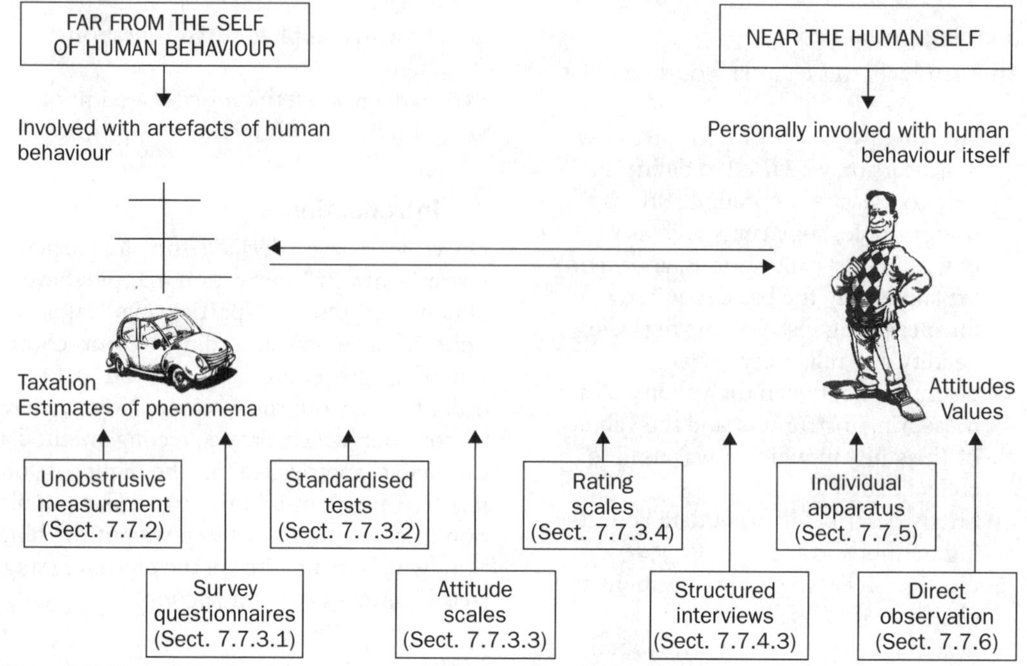

Figure 7.2 Means of using instruments to collect data

where we may be involved with groups of people, moving to be individually involved with our subjects/units of analysis, face-to-face. Figure 7.2 above illustrates this idea.

7.2 Systematic observation and quantitative measurement

In the final analysis, all measuring and data-collecting procedures are based on SYSTEMATIC (in contrast with everyday, accidental) OBSERVATION (see Section 1.2.2.1 & 2.2.2 and illustration on page 130).

By SYSTEMATIC OBSERVATION, we mean that it should be replicable, in other words, that independent observers other than ourselves should also be able to observe and report whatever we, as researchers, observe and report (requirements – see Section 1.2.2.3).

7.3 Measurement theory

In this section, we will focus on the NATURE OF MEASUREMENT and the REQUIREMENTS it should meet from a research perspective. Measurement theory is a highly technical field of study that we will discuss only synoptically and somewhat superficially.

If we wish to investigate the accuracy or "truth" of the research hypothesis (see Section 2.3) of our study, we need to measure the (dependent) variables (see Section 2.2, page 14) appearing in it.

Consider the test of the hypothesis in RESEARCH EXAMPLE II (see Section 2.2), which reads that exposure to the iron-fisted role model management style behaviour results in an increase in the iron-fisted management style behaviour of trainee supervisors. To test this hypothesis, the management styles of the trainee supervisors had to be assessed (measured and evaluated).

Measuring variables, such as the length or mass of things/people (subjects), does not present many problems. However, when it comes to measuring constructs (see Section

Systematic observation: Two researchers observing the behaviour of two animals

2.4) such as liquidation, paying TV licences, attitude towards affirmative action, entrepreneurship, the regional council, helping behaviour (see RESEARCH EXAMPLE VI, (page 106) Section 6.3.3), and so on, it becomes more problematic. We usually have to measure these constructs indirectly.

We may define any CONSTRUCT in the human behavioural sciences in terms of a UNIVERSE OF INDICATORS that collectively define that construct (see Section 2.2.1).

Example

The variable *socio-economic status* is an example of a construct because there is *no single indicator* that perfectly encapsulates it. To measure someone's socio-economic status we may use, for example, his or her income, his or her occupation, the area in which he or she resides, his or her educational level, and so on as indicators. Each of these variables (indicators), therefore, is only a partial and indirect indicator of the construct *socio-economic status*.

Constructs such as *attitude towards affirmative action* or *entrepreneurship* are even less directly observable than *socio-economic status*. In these examples, the constructs have to be *indirectly inferred* from supposed indicators of the construct involved.

We measure particular CHARACTERISTICS of individuals/things/events (rather than the individuals themselves). The characteristics that are of interest to the human behavioural sciences are seldom observable variables such as mass, length and the colour of someone's eyes. Instead, the variables we wish to measure (such as attitude towards affirmative action, socio-economic status, entrepreneurship, and so on) are constructs. By this we mean that they may be measured only indirectly by using so-called indicators (see Section 2.2.1).

Conceptually it should be possible, for example, to compile a catalogue or inventory of all things/behaviours which may be regarded as INDICATORS OF SUCCESS among small businesses, such as turnover, number of employees, taxable profit, and so on.

7.3.1 The nature of measurement

According to Stevens (1951), measurement involves the assignment of numbers, in terms of fixed rules, to individuals (or objects) to reflect differences between them in some or other characteristic or attribute.

Example

We measure length by noticing to which figure on a ruler the object alongside it compares. Certain requirements must be met, such as that the ruler should be straight and not bent. The rules in terms of which numbers are assigned, are nothing else but an operational definition (see Section 2.3) of the variable *length* (in this example) being measured.

In RESEARCH EXAMPLE VI (see Section 6.3.3.1, page 109), helping behaviour was operationalised in terms of the time that elapsed from the occurrence of the 'emergency' until the participant left the cubicle (to summon assistance). The numbers assigned were the number of seconds the various participants took to summon assistance.

Note

Naturally, the adequacy of the scores obtained depends on the adequacy of the rules according to which these numbers are assigned.

7.3.2 The levels of measurement

In measurement, we distinguish between different levels of measurement on the basis of the following four characteristics of numbers assigned in the process:

- distinguishability (the number 2 is different from the number 1)
- order of rank (2 has a higher rank than 1)
- equal intervals between successively higher numbers (0… 1… 2… 3…) and
- absolute size. (0 – 1 = –1 = 1 – 0 = 1).

These characteristics form a hierarchy in the sense that the fourth characteristic presupposes the third one, the third one presumes that the second one applies, and so on. If the numbers exhibit the feature of equal intervals, there has to be a rank order among them and they have to be distinguishable from each other. Corresponding to each of these four characteristics, a different level of measurement may be distinguished. These levels of measurement are (compare Figure 7.3):

- nominal measurement
- ordinal measurement
- interval measurement
- ratio measurement.

Exposure to an iron-fisted role model and its effect on a trainee on a trainee supervisor's behaviour towards a subordinate (called Bobo) (See **Research Example II** on page 14–15.)

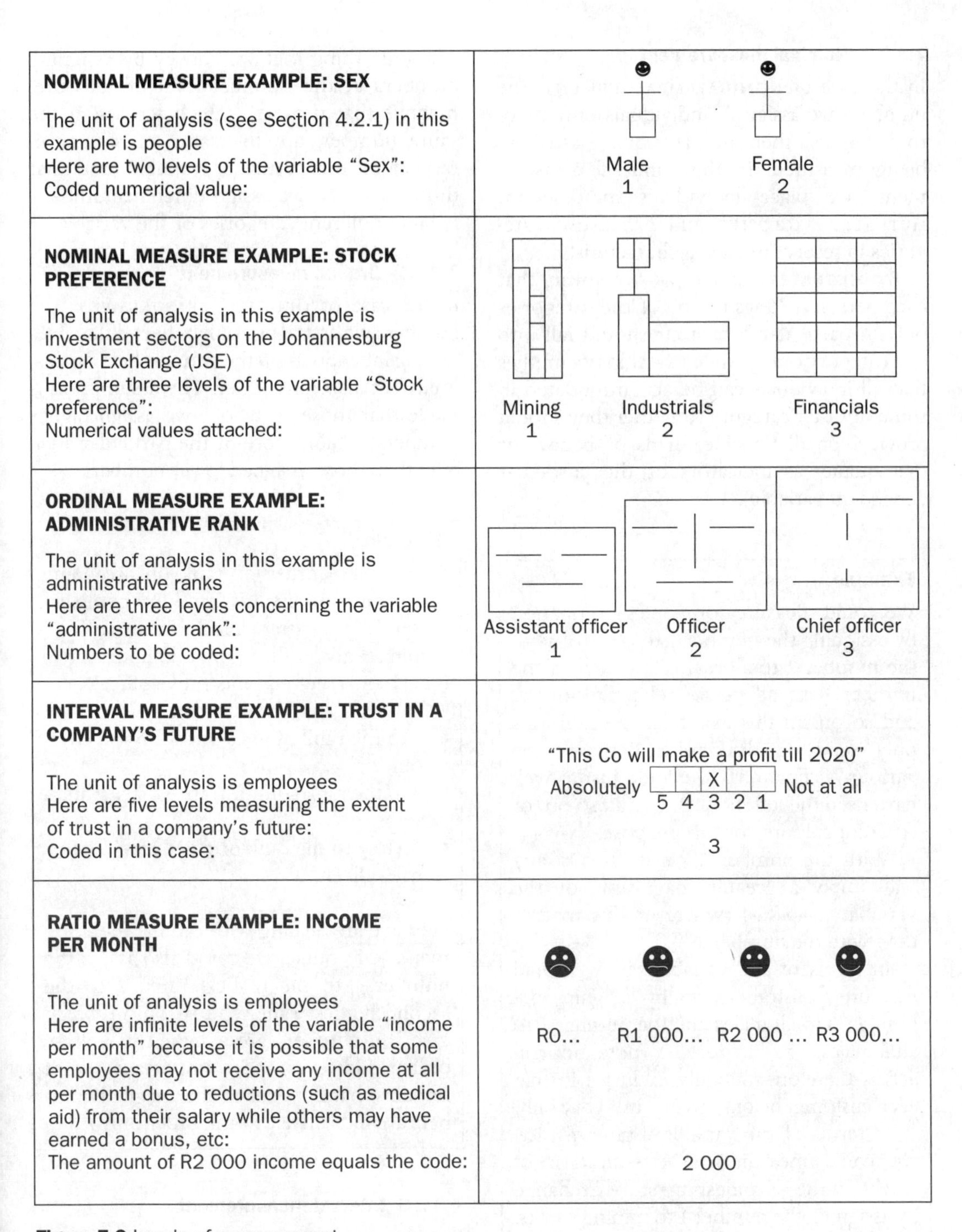

NOMINAL MEASURE EXAMPLE: SEX The unit of analysis (see Section 4.2.1) in this example is people Here are two levels of the variable "Sex": Coded numerical value:	Male 1 Female 2
NOMINAL MEASURE EXAMPLE: STOCK PREFERENCE The unit of analysis in this example is investment sectors on the Johannesburg Stock Exchange (JSE) Here are three levels of the variable "Stock preference": Numerical values attached:	Mining 1 Industrials 2 Financials 3
ORDINAL MEASURE EXAMPLE: ADMINISTRATIVE RANK The unit of analysis in this example is administrative ranks Here are three levels concerning the variable "administrative rank": Numbers to be coded:	Assistant officer 1 Officer 2 Chief officer 3
INTERVAL MEASURE EXAMPLE: TRUST IN A COMPANY'S FUTURE The unit of analysis is employees Here are five levels measuring the extent of trust in a company's future: Coded in this case:	"This Co will make a profit till 2020" Absolutely [ ][ ][X][ ][ ] Not at all 5 4 3 2 1 3
RATIO MEASURE EXAMPLE: INCOME PER MONTH The unit of analysis is employees Here are infinite levels of the variable "income per month" because it is possible that some employees may not receive any income at all per month due to reductions (such as medical aid) from their salary while others may have earned a bonus, etc: The amount of R2 000 income equals the code:	R0... R1 000... R2 000 ... R3 000... 2 000

Figure 7.3 Levels of measurement

7.3.2.1 **Nominal measurement**

In the case of NOMINAL MEASUREMENT, the numbers we assign to individuals only serve to distinguish them in terms of the attribute being measured. In this kind of measurement, we place individuals in different, MUTUALLY EXCLUSIVE and exhaustive categories in respect of such a characteristic.

By MUTUALLY EXCLUSIVE we mean that each person belongs to one of the categories only (a particular behaviour should fall into one category only), while EXHAUSTIVE implies that all individuals can be accommodated in some or other category (together they should provide for all possible forms of behaviour that qualify as indicators of the particular dependent variable).

Example

We could measure someone's occupation by assigning the number 1 to all attorneys, the number 2 to all real estate agents, the number 3 to all personnel practitioners, and so on. In this example, the numbers only serve to distinguish between the various occupations. We could just as well have used the letters A, B, C, and so on, or different colours, for this purpose.

With the number 2 we do not in any way imply a greater magnitude of the variable *occupation* (whatever this means) than with the number 1.

In terms of the variable *sex*, we could measure a customer's sex by assigning the number 0 to all males and the number 1 to all females. The category *sex* (note, not *gender*) is therefore mutually exclusive in that each customer belongs to one category only.

In terms of the variable *stock preference*, we could measure the classification of stocks on the Johannesburg stock exchange by assigning the number 1 to mining stocks, the number 2 to industrials, 3 to financials, and so on.

The only thing that we convey by assigning numbers at the nominal level of measurement is that those to which we assign the same number, are the same or similar in respect of the particular variable, and that those to which we assign different numbers, fall into different categories of the variable.

7.3.2.2 **Ordinal measurement**

In the case of ORDINAL MEASUREMENT, the numbers we assign not only reflect differences among individuals (in the variable being measured) but also rank order. The assumption is made that those to whom we assign higher numbers, exhibit more of the particular attribute than those assigned lower numbers.

Example

Suppose the order of rank (in ascending order) for administrative staff in a company is as follows: assistant administrative officer, administrative officer, first administrative officer and chief administrative officer.

Say we assign the number:

- 1 to the rank of assistant administrative officer;
- 2 to the rank administrative officer; and so on
- up to 4 to the rank of chief administrative officer.

Now we are dealing with ordinal measurement. (Of course, we could also assign the number 1 to the highest rank; 2 to the second highest rank, and so on, in which case the numbers are assigned in inverse order. However, the important point remains that the sizes of the assigned numbers are indicative of rank order only.)

7.3.2.3 **Interval measurement**

In interval measurement, we use the property of equal differences between consecutively higher numbers.

Example

The classical example in this connection is the measurement of temperature. The difference between 10 °C and 20 °C is just as big as that between 30 °C and 40 °C, and twice as big as that between 20 °C and 25 °C.

However, note that 20 °C does not indicate a temperature that is as twice as hot as 10 °C. This statement would only make sense if 0 °C meant the complete absence of temperature. However, the zero point on both the Centigrade and Fahrenheit scales has been chosen arbitrarily – a reading of zero on the former corresponds to one of 32 on the latter (see Figure 7.3).

7.3.2.4 **Ratio measurement**

Only in ratio measurement is there a fixed and absolute zero point, and it further corresponds to the property of equal differences between consecutively higher numbers as used in interval measurement.

Example

A reaction time (for example, the time it takes to switch on a machine when a light flashes a warning) of 0 seconds implies the complete absence of reaction time. Consequently it makes sense to say that a reaction time of 1,60 seconds is twice as long as one of 0,80 seconds. The ratios between numbers assigned at this level of measurement can therefore be interpreted meaningfully.

The same properties apply to the example of the number of cigarettes a person smokes per day (see Figure 7.3).

Note

Strictly speaking, most measuring instruments in the human behavioural sciences yield measurements at the nominal and ordinal levels. For practical purposes, though, the scores on, for example, standardised tests, attitude scales and self-constructed questionnaires (see Section 7.8) may probably be regarded as satisfactory approximations of interval measurement (Kerlinger, 1986).

Example

Although we probably could not maintain with much conviction that the difference in intelligence as expressed by an intelligence quotient (IQ) score between 100 and 105 is just as large as one between 120 and 125, few experts would deny that the difference between, for example, 100 and 110 is greater than that between 110 and 115. (Someone who maintains that IQs merely represent ordinal measurement would have to deny the latter statement and insist that no significance should be attached to the size of the differences between successive IQs.) (Compare CD-ROM manual.)

Activity 7.1

Questions

1 Name two variables that would be naturally considered for nominal scales. Set up mutually exclusive and exhaustive categories for each of the variables mentioned above.
2 Develop an ordinal scale (with instructions to the research subjects) for consumer preferences for three different brands of cold drink.
3 Name three variables that could be measured on an interval scale.

Answers

1 Gender and language group.

Male	Female	and

English	Zulu	Sotho	Afrikaans

2 Arrange the following brands of cold drinks according to your preferences. Write 1 in the block next to your favourite brand, 2 in the block of your next

favourite brand, and continue until every brand is numbered. Tick (✓) the last block if you do not drink cold drink at all.

☐ Coke ☐ Iron Brew
☐ Sprite ☐ Ginger Ale
☐ Do not drink cold drink

3 Morale, satisfaction and experience.

Activity 7.2

Read Case Study A; Case Study B; Case Study C; Case Study D; Case Study E and Case Study F in Appendix D on page 276.

Question

What type of measurement level (nominal, ordinal, interval or ratio measurement) is involved in the dependent and independent variables (consult answers to Activity 2.1 and 6.2)? Explain your answer briefly.

Answer

CASE STUDY A: The dependent variable "attitude towards AIDS" is measured with the aid of a five-point Likert scale, and therefore an *interval measurement* is involved: point 5 (agree fully) is more positive than, for example, point 4 (agree) or point 1 (do not agree at all). A feature of an attitude scale such as the Likert scale is the equal differences between progressively higher numbers, which is characteristic of an interval measurement.

CASE STUDY B: The dependent variable "attitude towards supervision" is measured with the aid of a semantic differential (a seven-point scale), and therefore it involves an *interval measurement*: point 7 represents a specific attitude towards supervision (for example, positive), and point 1 represents the opposite attitude (negative). The feature of equal differences between progressively higher numbers (characteristic of an interval measurement) is involved in an attitude scale such as a semantic differential.

CASE STUDY C: The dependent variable "knowledge of management principles" is measured with the help of a one-hour written test and therefore a *ratio measurement* is involved – the first-line supervisor who, for example, scored 80% in the test, has twice as much knowledge (it is generally believed) as one who scored 40% and there is an absolute zero mark involved seen in terms of the learning objectives of the training course.

CASE STUDY D: Although time (measured in seconds, minutes, and so forth) can be classified as a *ratio measurement*, it can be argued that total preparation time involves an *interval measurement*. This is because speech preparation includes various aspects and it therefore can not be proven that the student who took 30 minutes to prepare prepared twice as well as someone who took 15 minutes.

The two other variables also involve *interval measurement* because the characteristics that are measured involve equal differences between consecutively higher amounts as is typically the case with judgement scales (five- or four-point scales).

CASE STUDY E: The independent variables "bank overdraft usage" and "cash flow problems" are measured in terms of the average amount exceeding the bank overdraft limit per month and by means of a four-point scale respectively.

Thus the variable "bank overdraft usage" concerns *ratio measurement* because a small business that exceeded the bank overdraft limit by, for example, R20 000,00 per month used twice the amount of one that exceeded the limit by R10 000,00, and there is an absolute zero involved for businesses that did not exceed their bank overdraft limits.

The other variable, "cash flow problems", involves *interval measurement* because the characteristics that are measured involve equal differences between consecutively higher degrees of experiencing cash flow problems than is typically the case with rating scales (four-point scales). No absolute zero is involved because any business at some time could have cash flow problems.

CASE STUDY F: In the case of the dependent variable "innovative problem-solving style", *ordinal* (or at most *interval*) measurement is involved because, according to the KAI scale, there are five levels of the style (the KAI scale consists of 32 five-point items: 5 x 32 = 160) and there are equal differences between consecutive higher numbers.

The independent variable "business people" has two levels (entrepreneurs and managers) with no successive rank between them and therefore *nominal* measurement is involved. (In other words, we could have mentioned the managers first and then the entrepreneurs, or vice versa.)

7.4 Validity (construct validity of the dependent variable)

In this section, we will discuss two kinds of validity, namely:

- construct validity; and
- criterion-related validity.

Note

Other forms of validity such as content and face validity are not addressed in this book.

Any given measuring instrument measures three components, namely:

- the construct (see Sections 2.2.1 & 7.4) intended;
- irrelevant constructs; and
- random measurement error (reliability – see Section 7.5).

The first two components represent systematic sources of variation because they remain constant for any given individual. The latter, again, is an unsystematic source of variation (reliability – see Section 7.5) because it refers to accidental factors that may vary from one measuring occasion to the next, and from one individual to the next in a completely haphazard fashion.

Example

A paper-and-pencil measurement/test of mechanical aptitude may possibly measure the following:

- mechanical aptitude (the construct intended);
- the ability to read and comprehend the instructions of the measurement/test (an irrelevant construct, because if the person cannot read or write, it is impossible to measure his/her mechanical aptitude); and
- measurement error (the third component – see Section 7.5 & 9.3.1).

7.4.1 Construct validity

When we measure something, for example, a variable, with an instrument, the instrument we use to measure the variable must measure that which it is supposed to measure. We refer to this requirement as the CONSTRUCT VALIDITY of the scores obtained on a measuring instrument.

Example

If the general level of communication skills of the trainee supervisors had been measured in RESEARCH EXAMPLE II (see Section 2.2, page 14) instead of their management style, it would obviously have led to incorrect conclusions.

We have pointed out (see Section 2.2.1) that there may be more than one operational definition or measuring instrument of the same construct and that these various indicators may *overlap* and *differ* to some extent.

Example

The importance of designated group (African black, Coloured, Indians, etc.), academic qualifications and relevant work experience may overlap in their importance to the operational definition of affirmative action in different company policies.

Furthermore, none of these individual measures or indicators completely succeeds in representing the construct because they also reflect other, irrelevant, constructs. (If any of these indicators did manage to perfectly represent the CONSTRUCT, we would no longer be dealing with a CONSTRUCT, but with a directly observable variable.)

The CONSTRUCT VALIDITY of a measuring instrument refers to the degree to which it measures the intended construct rather than irrelevant constructs or measurement error.

Note

Because any given measure of a construct also reflects irrelevant constructs, it is advisable to use more than one measure of the same construct. If this is not done, it is impossible to examine to what extent any given measuring instrument measures anything else but itself.

The more that two measures measure the same construct, the more they overlap and the higher the relationship (correlation – see Section 9.4) between them tends to be.

Example

There are various indicators of the construct "socio-economic status", for example, the person's income, his or her occupation, the area in which he or she resides, his/her educational level. Each of these indicators only partially represents it, and also partially overlaps with other indicators. However, collectively such indicators offer a more complete representation of the construct.

If we have to measure *extroversion* (that is, the tendency to be sociable, warm and active), it may be advisable to use questionnaires (see Section 7.7.3) as well as, say, ratings (see Section 7.7.3.4) on this construct.

Some authors compare this approach (that is, using *more than one measure of the same construct*) with *triangulation* in navigation. This is a procedure to determine the correct position of a ship or plane by comparing its position with those of two known navigation points.

Note

The construct validity of an instrument is not only supported by high relationships (correlation – see Section 9.4) with other measures of the same construct (so-called CONVERGENT VALIDITY), but also by low correlations with measures of different constructs (so-called DISCRIMINANT VALIDITY).

Measurement reactivity (see Section 6.3.4) especially represents a grave threat to the construct validity of questionnaire measurements of personality, interests and attitudes. The response sets of FAKING and SOCIAL DESIRABILITY and the response style of ACQUIESCENCE imply that individuals' responses are not true reflections of them.

In the worst case, FAKING may occur, which means that participants deliberately distort their responses in order to create a desired impression.

Example

To the question, *Do you easily lose your temper?*, a job applicant may answer negatively because he wishes to create a good impression; whereas a murderer may answer positively in an attempt to appear mentally disturbed.

In the case of SOCIALLY DESIRABLE RESPONSES, subjects deliberately or inadvertently provide the responses (answers or actions) that they believe to be SOCIALLY ACCEPTABLE.

Example

To the question, *Do you like everybody you know?*, individuals may answer positively because they believe that it would be socially unacceptable not to like some people.

ACQUIESCENCE refers to the phenomenon where research participants tend to consistents answer "yes" (to yes/no items) or "true" (rather than false), irrespective of the content of the question.

Example

An interviewee may reply "yes" to both of the following statements:

I prefer to spend a night out on the town with friends instead of staying at home reading a book, and *I prefer spending a quiet night at home reading a book instead of partying with friends*.

A "yes" answer to both questions is contradictory because on the one hand it appears that the subject likes to go out, whilst on the other hand the subject likes to stay home.

In personality questionnaires (see Section 7.7.3.2) we utilise various strategies to make provision for the possible effect of these response sets and response styles. Paper-and-pencil questionnaires of personality, interests and attitudes are susceptible to problems of distortion, social desirability and acquiescence as we have mentioned. However, most of these instruments have built-in precautionary measures to provide for these problems. Some personality questionnaires, for example, have lie or social desirability scales, the purpose of which is to identify individuals who provide such invalid responses.

7.4.2 Criterion-related validity

Note that construct validity is of special importance to research. There is another kind of validity that is essential to applied business and administrative practice, namely CRITERION-RELATED VALIDITY.

CRITERION-RELATED VALIDITY refers to the degree to which diagnostic and selection measurement/tests correctly predict the relevant criterion. The relevant criterion refers to the variable that is to be diagnosed or on which success is to be predicted, respectively.

Depending on whether the criterion is present at the time of testing, or whether it will only become available some time after the test is completed, we distinguish between CONCURRENT VALIDITY and PREDICTIVE VALIDITY.

Example

We may investigate the concurrent validity of a group intelligence measurement/test by correlating it with scores on an individual intelligence measurement/test (the criterion) that may be available at about the same time. (Individual measurement/tests typically require more administration time and it might be preferable to substitute them for the more economical group measurement/tests.) Both the group measurement/test and the individual measurement/test are administered to a large sample of individuals who are representative of the population (see Section 4.2) for which the intelligence measurement/test is intended, and the two sets of scores so obtained are correlated (see Section 9.4).

Similarly, if a measurement/test is considered for selecting junior managers, the intention is to predict which candidates will eventually become successful senior managers (the eventual criterion), or which of them will successfully complete the management training course (an intermediate criterion).

When we investigate the predictive validity of a selection measurement/test, all applicants from a large, representative sample from the population for which the measurement/test is intended must complete the measurement/test and be admitted to the course or job (or for whatever purpose selection is required). When the scores on an eventual or intermediate criterion (signifying success in the work or course, respectively) become available, these are correlated with the measurement/test scores obtained originally.

Example

The predictive validity of a selection measurement/test for junior managers may be investigated by correlating scores on the measurement/test (see Section 9.4) with the success criteria marks (for example, obtaining an MBA-degree or a number of management certificates) of all the original applicants obtained four or more years later.

Note

It is important to note that if this correlation is obtained only for those who have exceeded a particular cutoff score on the measurement/test, it will typically underestimate the actual measurement/test-criterion correlation (Huysamen, 1989b, Section 8.3).

A typical problem in criterion-related validation is trying to locate a measure of the criterion that has a sufficient reliability (see Section 7.5) and construct validity (see Section 7.4).

Example

Management success/achievement (as measured by means of a paper-and-pencil examination) in a management training course is not necessarily a construct valid indicator of successful managerial characteristics.

Note

For an instrument to be construct valid (for example, the paper-and-pencil management examination mentioned in the above example), it would have to involve items that form a representative sample (see Section 4.2) of all management success indicators (this actually entails the definition of content validity mentioned in Section 7.2).

Sometimes ratings (see Section 7.7.3.4) of the criterion variable are used, but the reliability (see Section 7.5) of such ratings may be just as suspect as that of the measurements whose criterion-related validity is to be examined.

7.5 Reliability

We can distinguish between (at least) three irrelevant sources of systematic variation in measurement (see Section 7.2), namely:

- measurement occasion
- measurement form
- measurement user.

It stands to reason that if we measure a construct (for example, small business or management success) (see Section 2.3 & 7.4) by means of a particular instrument (for example, taxable profit calculation formula or a management training course examination paper), comparable measurements should be obtained for the same individuals/things irrespective of, for example, when the instrument is administered, which particular version of it is used, and who is applying (administering and scoring) it.

Example

If the rank (first, second, third, and so on) of Bongani's score on a measurement/test of a stable construct depends on whether the measurement/test is administered on Monday or Tuesday so that, for example, he would earn more marks than Ann on Monday but do less well on Tuesday, the reliability of such a measurement/test is suspect.

In RESEARCH EXAMPLE I (page 6) (see Section 1.2.2.1) it would have been undesirable if the relative positions of the participants (trainees) depended on the particular sample of addition problems they had to solve.

In RESEARCH EXAMPLE II (page 14) (see Section 2.2) it would similarly have been unacceptable if the number of iron-fisted management style reactions recorded for any trainee was determined by the rater (researcher) who was recording the incidence of these reactions.

- The requirement of GENERALISATION relates to the reliability of the scores obtained. By generalisation we mean the consistency of the ranking (of the scores) that we assign to the individuals / things / and so on, irrespective of when the measuring instrument was applied, which form of it was used, and by whom it was administered or scored.
- RELIABILITY refers to the extent to which the obtained scores may be generalised to different measuring occasions, measurement / tests forms and measurement / test administrators. (As we will see later, there is actually a different kind of reliability for each of these irrelevant, systematic sources of variation, namely, measurement occasion, measurement form and measurement administrator.)

Note

An unreliable measurement cannot adequately measure what it is supposed to measure (in other words, it cannot be construct valid – see Section 7.4).

Apart from the intuitively obvious reason why a high reliability is desirable, there is also a statistical reason (see Section 9.4).

7.5.1 Estimating reliability

We have seen that we could make a distinction between (at least) three irrelevant sources of systematic variation in measurement, namely, measurement occasion, measurement form and measurement user. Each of these sources relates to different kinds of unsystematic sources of variation. Because reliability is affected by such unsystematic sources of variation, we may distinguish a different kind of reliability for each of the above systematic sources of variation, namely:

- test-retest reliability
- parallel-forms reliability
- internal consistency
- interrater / intercoder / tester / test or measurement-scorer reliability.

7.5.1.1 Test-retest reliability

TEST-RETEST RELIABILITY refers to the degree to which a measurement / test is immune, so to speak, to the particular measurement / test occasion on which it is administered, so that scores obtained on one occasion may be generalised to those that could potentially have been obtained on other comparable occasions.

Example

We have all had the experience of being, without any explanation (such as poor preparation), more measurement / test ready on some measurement / test occasions than on others. On one day we may feel on top of the world and the very next day we feel down in the dumps. The kind of reliability that pertains to such unsystematic sources of variation relating to measurement / test occasions, is known as TEST-RETEST (or simply, RETEST) RELIABILITY.

To determine the retest reliability of a measuring instrument, we must administer it on at least two occasions on the same large, representative sample (see Section 4.2) from the population for which the instrument is intended. We then correlate (see Section 9.4) the two sets of scores obtained in this way. The time interval between the two administrations should not be too long to prevent real and permanent changes from taking place in the attribute being measured. At the same time, it should not be too short so that participants may remember the responses given on the first administration (Huysamen, 1989b, see Section 2.2).

Note

Since ambiguous items and unclear instructions may cause subjects to interpret them differently on different occasions, such items and instructions may adversely affect reliability. The measurement/test compiler should therefore write unambiguous items and clear instructions.

7.5.1.2 Parallel-forms reliability

PARALLEL-FORMS RELIABILITY of a measurement/test is determined by interchangeable versions of a measurement/test that have been compiled to measure the same construct equally well but by means of different content.

Example

Standardised tests (see Section 7.7.3.2), such as the Parallel spelling tests, for example, are composed of different words (which are to be spelled), but are equally difficult.

Another example may be found in estimating the taxable value of individual citizens of South Africa. Two or more different formulae/equations/calculations of measuring the amount of money payable to the receiver of revenue may be used to determine the reliability of an existing form of taxation.

Thus, if there is reason to believe that someone's amount of money payable to the receiver of revenue, estimated by the existing form of taxation, provides an unrepresentative picture of his or her taxable value, a parallel measurement/formula/equation/calculation may be administered subsequently to his or her financial position.

Note

Concerning the measurement of human abilities (such as the ability to recognise depth or three-dimensional pictures), parallel measurement/test forms contain different items, because the individual then does not benefit from his or her memory of specific items (in the form already completed).

Just as individuals' measurement/test preparedness may be higher on one measurement/test occasion than on another, by mere accident they may be more familiar with specific items in one measurement/test than in a parallel form. (For instance, a primary school pupil may remember that London is the capital of the United Kingdom because some of her relatives happened to visit this city.) Just as retest reliability pertains to the degree to which the scores obtained on one occasion may be generalised to those that may be obtained on other measurement/test occasions, parallel-forms reliability deals with the generalisability over parallel measurement/test forms.

To determine the reliability of a measuring instrument by using the parallel-forms method, we administer such forms to the same, representative sample and correlate (see Section 9.4) the two sets of scores obtained.

7.5.1.3 Internal consistency

A high INTERNAL CONSISTENCY implies a high degree of generalisability across the items within the measurement/test.

In other words, if someone performs well on a few items in such a measurement/test, the chances are good that he or she will fare equally well on the remaining items in the measurement/test (compare Section 7.7.3.3(a) – last example).

Note

The longer a measurement/test is, in other words, the more appropriate content it covers, the higher its internal consistency should be.

However, this kind of reliability will be improved only if the measurement/test is lengthened by items that are similar to those in the original measurement/test.

Formulae (for example, Spearman-Brown) are available to estimate the number of such items by which a measurement/test with a given reliability should be lengthened to achieve a required degree of internal consistency (Huysamen, 1990b).

To determine the reliability of a measuring instrument by using the internal consistency method (Huysamen, 1989), we administer the measurement/test only once to a large, representative sample.

Cronbach's (1951) coefficient alpha is a measure of the internal consistency of a measurement/test. This index shows the degree to which all the items in a measurement/test measure the same attribute.

To compute coefficient alpha, both the variance (see Section 9.4) on the (total) measurement/test scores and the variances of the individual items are required. The reliability coefficient obtained may be interpreted as an estimation of the parallel-forms reliability of the measurement/test.

7.5.1.4 **Interrater/intercoder/tester/test or measurement-scorer reliability**

Unreliability due to accidental, inconsistent behaviour on the part of the individuals administering or scoring the measurement/test, falls into this category. In such cases it is frequently found that a particular tester consistently marks too strictly or too leniently.

Note

Especially in the case of ratings (see Section 7.7.3.4), it is advisable to investigate interrater reliability. This is done by having more than one rater rate the same individuals (on the relevant attribute) and correlating (see Section 9.4) the ratings obtained.

7.6 Pilot studies in the development of an instrument

When tackling their first research projects, novice researchers are often disillusioned to discover that the principles outlined in methodology textbooks are only encountered in an idealised research environment.

The purpose of a pilot study on a limited number of subjects from the same population (see Section 4.2) as that for which the eventual project is intended, is, inter alia:

- to detect possible flaws in the measurement procedures (such as ambiguous instructions, inadequate time limits, and so on) and in the operationalisation of the independent variable(s) (in experimental research);
- to identify unclear or ambiguously formulated items. Not only should the actual questions be put to the "participants", but they should also be asked to indicate how they have interpreted the formulated questions;
- at the same time, such a pilot study allows researchers or their assistants to notice non-verbal behaviour (on the part of the participants) that possibly may signify discomfort or embarrassment about the content or wording of the questions.

Such a pilot study is especially useful if the researcher has compiled the measuring instrument specifically for the purposes of the research project. It even may be necessary to investigate the validity (see Section 7.4) and reliability (see Section 7.5) of such instruments in an independent project (instead of in a pilot study intended as a dress rehearsal for another). (Compare Figure 7.4.)

Note

- *It is virtually mandatory to test survey questionnaires (see Section 7.7.3.1) on a small group of individuals who are representative of the populations for which they are intended. If the instrument is extensively revised in reaction to the results of the pilot study, the revised instrument should be subjected to a new round of testing.*
- *If a self-developed instrument is not tested in a pilot study, it is advisable to at least ask an experienced researcher/expert in the field to check the instrument with a view to spotting glaring flaws (determining, inter alia, its face validity).*
- *However, the development of a valid and reliable measuring instrument is such a comprehensive project that it should be avoided as far as possible as part of a typical dissertation or thesis.*

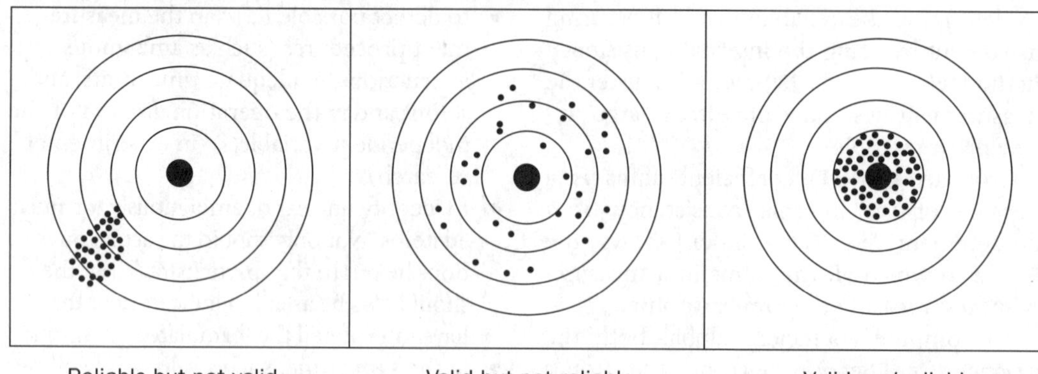

Figure 7.4 An analogy to validity and reliability (measuring the large dot-research question, with small tries-methods and measuring instruments)

7.7 Measuring instruments

7.7.1 Introduction

Because the constructs in the human behavioural sciences often involve human attributes, actions and artifacts, it may appear to lay people that these can be appropriately measured by merely asking research participants directly about them. Thus, in the case of the construct *dominance*, lay people might argue that participants should simply be asked whether or not they are dominant by nature. However, for several reasons the reliability and validity of the measurements obtained in this fashion would be highly suspect.

On the one hand, participants may have insufficient knowledge about themselves, or they may be unable to verbalise their innermost feelings. On the other hand, participants may deliberately provide incorrect answers with a view to putting themselves in a positive or negative light. Moreover, the reliability of a measure (of a construct such as *dominance*) that consists of a single question, would tend to be highly unsatisfactory.

In this chapter, we deal with various types of measuring instruments and provide guidelines for constructing some of them.

- By means of survey questionnaires (see Section 7.7.3.1), standardised measuring instruments (see Section 7.7.3.2) and attitude scales (see Section 7.7.3.3), we do not observe the behaviour of subjects directly, but we ask individuals to report on it (in terms of questions put to them). Therefore, these measuring instruments are susceptible to measurement reactivity (see Section 6.3.4), the consequences of which may vary from the withholding of co-operation to deliberate deception.
- Rating scales (see Section 7.7.3.4) require raters to assess the behaviour of participants, which again allows for the possibility of bias on the part of the raters.
- We can distinguish between secondary and primary data sources (see Section 3.3.2). SECONDARY DATA are information collected by individuals or agencies and institutions other than the researcher him- or herself. Primary data are original data collected by the researcher for the purposes of his or her own study at hand.
- INDICATORS such as the inflation rate, consumer price index, retail sales, building plans passed, registered unemployed, and so on, are compiled and calculated by people such as actuaries in government offices, including the Statistics South Africa (Stats SA), the Board on Tariffs &

Trade (BTT), university bureaux, chambers of commerce, portfolio managers, and so on. These people collect information on different enterprises and companies regarding their size and market share, as well as their imports and exports, and so on.

This information (figures) is published, inter alia, in reports, state budgets, manuals and academic journals and includes the following:

- Corporate profit growth addressing ratios such as wages as a percentage of production and its relation to an index such as the Gross Domestic Product (GDP).
- Foreign direct investment (FDI) as a result of privatisation.
- Cuts in tariff rates according to the World Trade Organisation (WTO).
- Statistics from the South African Revenue Service (SARS).
- Performance tables of different unit trusts in the Unit Trusts Quarterly Survey.
- Databases by private companies such as EDS Small Business Database.

Some of this information is also available on the Internet. (See list of websites on page 292.)

7.7.2 **Unobtrusive measurement**

In this section, we deal with approaches in which the participant, and sometimes also the researcher, is unaware that measurement is taking place for research purposes. The simplest form of unobtrusive measurement occurs when a subject's behaviour is observed through one-way mirrors or photographed by concealed video cameras. There are all sorts of other ingenious ways in which researchers can behave like detectives to collect information that people routinely and even unwittingly generate for purposes other than research. Consequently, the problem of measurement reactivity (see Section 6.3.4) is completely eliminated. These procedures may often be used together with other measurement methods to check whether comparable results are obtained. However, because the researcher has to rely on the residue of past events, it may sometimes be difficult to rule out alternative explanations for the obtained results (as may be in the case of investigating a crime). The following methods can be used in unobtrusive measurement:

- physical traces
- personal documents and mass media material
- official statistics and archival sources.

7.7.2.1 **Physical traces**

Among measures that are based on physical changes that take place over time, we distinguish between MEASURES OF EROSION, which involve the wear and tear of materials, and MEASURES OF ACCRETION, which are based on the forming of deposits on materials.

Example

- Suppose we want to investigate which exhibits at a museum are the most popular. To conduct interviews with visitors to the museum, or to request them to complete questionnaires, may result in measurements that are susceptible to unconscious or deliberate faking (see Section 7.4.1). The presence of observers in a museum, again, may affect visitors' spontaneous inspection of the exhibits.

- However, by checking the wear and tear on the carpets (a measure of erosion) in front of the different exhibits, an unobtrusive measure of their relative popularity may be obtained, which is unaffected by the response styles of either the participants or the observers.

  However, the problem of ruling out alternative explanations is evident from this example. Suppose all visitors to the museum are obliged to use the same route through the museum. They also tend to spend more time at the initial stages of their visit but become more hurried as their time runs out. *The greater degree of wear on the carpets in front of the exhibits at the beginning of the route than on the tiles at the end (exit) would then not be attributable to the greater popularity of the former, but to their favourable position along the route through the museum.*
- In the United States the popularity of television programmes has been gauged by checking the decrease in water levels during the screening of commercials (under the assumption that people are glued to their television sets during popular programmes and limit their visits to the toilet to commercial breaks).
- Examining garbage dumps may be used as a technique of measures of accretion. By inspecting garbage bags, the eating and drinking habits of present-day people can be studied.

7.7.2.2 **Personal documents and mass media material**

This measuring method entails investigating the means of communication of:

- the mass media (for example, newspapers, magazines, films);
- organisations and associations (for example, minutes of their meetings); or
- of a more personal nature (for example, paintings, diaries, personal letters, and so on).

It provides products of human behaviour that may be investigated by means of content analysis (see Section 9.2).

7.7.2.3 **Official statistics and archival sources**

These data are originally typically collected for purposes other than their use in human behavioural research.

Example

- Statistics South Africa publishes information about birth registrations, deaths, marriages, divorces, unemployment and road accidents on a quarterly basis. It also takes a census every five years, although this period may be changed due to circumstances. (For example, the one scheduled for 1990 was conducted a year later and the next one took place during 1996.)
- Official statistics and archival data may be used in an interrupted time-series design (see Section 5.3.2), for example. In the investigation into the effect of the crackdown on speeding in the American state of Connecticut during the fifties and sixties, archival records were consulted to obtain the road fatalities over a numberof years.
- Locally, Naude (1990) used official statistics to compare the application of the death penalty in South Africa with that in the United States. He compared the sentencing in terms of the race of the offender and the race and gender of the victim, and he compared commuting of the sentence in terms of the race of the offender.
- To investigate the relationship between fertility rates as idealised in magazine

stories and actual fertility, Middleton (in Webb et al., 1966) recorded the size of families in stories in eight American magazines at three points in time (1916, 1936 and 1956), and official statistics on family size at the same dates. It appeared that the shift in the size of fictitious families in the stories was closely related to the corresponding shift in the actual levels of fertility. Carlsmith and Anderson (1979) correlated newspaper reports of the incidence of urban riots and daily temperature reports in the United States and found that the probability of such riots increased with higher temperatures. [However, Tyson & Turnbull (1990) failed to duplicate these results locally.] In these examples, mass media material and official statistics were used together.

Apart from the non-reactivity associated with the unobtrusive nature of official statistics and archival sources, their greatest advantage is the ease and low costs involved in obtaining them. They are especially useful in large-scale investigations on macro level (as in the above example of road fatalities over time) that cannot be researched in other ways. In addition, these sources may provide information about human reactions to events such as earthquakes, riots, and so on, which researchers cannot create for practical and ethical reasons (see Section 7.9).

Because this information is often collected at regular intervals (for example, census information), it makes trend analyses (see Section 5.4.3.3) possible. Although official statistics do not involve excessive time and costs to collect, the screening process and the search for evidence to rule out alternative explanations may indeed require a considerable effort. Often it requires ingenuity to transform the available information into indicators of the appropriate constructs. Consequently, we may occasionally suspect the construct validity of the data obtained. Because the researcher is not in a position to ensure that the original collection of data took place systematically, there is also the possibility that the available sources may be incomplete.

Consequently, there may be doubts about how representative the data obtained are of the relevant universe.

Example

We could not compare the number of deaths at birth for different population groups if a greater percentage of births in one group took place at home instead of in hospitals and clinics, and if such deaths at home often went unreported.

7.7.3 Group contacts

The ADVANTAGES of group contacts as a method of collecting data are:

- Working with CAPTIVE AUDIENCES such as students or prisoners, the elderly in a home for the aged, and workers at a wine cellar or other factory. This procedure then corresponds to the administration of a group measurement/test. Since a single person (with possibly a few assistants) is required to give the instructions in one room or hall, the cost per questionnaire (in the case of surveys) is much lower than that of personal interviews.
- The RESEARCHER IS IN FULL CONTROL of the completion of the questionnaires. The session is arranged with the permission of the appropriate authorities (for example, school, university, and so on) so that no respondent has an excuse for not completing the questionnaire. Consequently, a response rate (the percentage of questionnaires handed back/returned/posted back) of close to 100% is the general rule.

Because the researcher and his or her assistants are present, queries about the completion of survey questionnaires may be answered immediately. (In the case of standardised group tests (see Section 7.7.3.2), the instructions are fixed and no deviations are actually allowed.)

- The group contact way of administering questionnaires corresponds to the personal interview (see Section 7.7.4) as far as the presence of the interviewer is concerned, but it allows for the same degree of anonymity as the typical postal survey (see Section 7.7.3.1). The personal interview does not allow this.

The only DRAWBACK to this method is that it is limited to a few populations. Associated with this drawback is the fact that such groups typically represent accidental samples (see Section 4.2.4.1), so that the population validity (see Section 6.4.2) of the obtained results becomes highly suspect.

7.7.3.1 **Survey questionnaires and postal dispatch**

We may use survey questionnaires to obtain the following types of information from respondents:

- biographical particulars (their age, educational qualifications, income, and so on)
- typical behaviour (which brand of toothpaste they use or which television programmes they favour, and so on)
- opinions, beliefs and convictions (about any topic or issue, for example, the present state of the economy)
- attitudes (for example, towards affirmative action).

Example

Mark your choice in one of the boxes. "The leadership in my organisation at the present time is":

Hard working | 1 | 2 | 3 | 4 | 5 | Lazy

Note

Attitudes should preferably be assessed by means of attitude scales (see Section 7.7.3.3) rather than survey questionnaires.

Whereas attitude scales (see Section 7.7.3.3) are completed by the respondents (typically under the supervision of research staff), we can obtain information about biographical particulars, typical behaviour, opinions and beliefs in person, by telephone (see Section 7.7.4), by mail or by e-mail.

In order to conduct a typical postal or mail survey:

- we first assemble the questions (asking for information about biographical particulars, typical behaviour, opinions and beliefs) that we want to put to the respondents in a structured questionnaire;
- then we post the questionnaires to respondents with the request that they be completed and returned by mail or be faxed back.

We should take the eyesight and the literacy level (see Section 7.8) of the intended respondents into consideration. Not only should the intended respondents be able to read and write, but they should also be able to follow the instructions.

Ignorant respondents may find complicated FILTER QUESTIONS (see Section 7.8), which involve different routes for different responses, confusing. Unlike personal interviews or telephonic interviews (see Section 7.7.4), the respondents cannot fall back on anybody else but themselves since the interviewer is not available to direct them around irrelevant questions.

The purpose of FILTER QUESTIONS is to determine whether respondents should answer all subsequent questions, or whether they can skip some of them (see Section 7.8).

Note

Dillman (1978) provides useful guidelines for the execution of postal surveys.

Although data collection by mail is associated with surveys (see Section 5.4.1), it is not restricted to this kind of non-experimental research (see Section 5.4).

The ADVANTAGES and DISADVANTAGES of postal surveys are:

- *Cost and ease of application.* The most important advantage of postal surveys is their relatively low cost. A postal survey is the least expensive of all survey methods. Irrespective of how far and wide respondents are scattered across the length and breadth of the country, they can all be reached by means of relatively equal postage stamps.
- *Anonymity.* Of all survey methods the postal survey provides the greatest possibility of anonymity, that is, no name or identification is given. As a matter of fact, in most cases the questionnaire may be returned without any indication of who has completed it. As a result, the chances are better that such questionnaires are completed honestly, even though socially acceptable responses may be given at times.
- *Control over responding.* The researcher has the least control over the conditions under which postal questionnaires are completed. The respondent's family may show little consideration when, for example, their mother or father sits down to complete a questionnaire in silence and privacy. The chances are great that some questions may be omitted or not be responded to in the order presented, or even that someone else may complete or censor some of the questions. (When a respondent leaves a single question unanswered, it may mean that the remainder of his or her responses cannot be used for purposes of analysis.)

  Of course, this lack of control could also hold a potential advantage in the sense that respondents are allowed to complete the questionnaires at their own convenience. For example, they are under no obligation to complete the questionnaire in a single session.
- *Response rate.* The researcher's lack of control over the completion of the questionnaires may result not only in poorly completed questionnaires, but also a poor response rate (the percentage of questionnaires handed back/returned/posted back). Postal surveys accordingly tend to have the lowest response rate of all survey methods. This rate frequently falls below 50% of the target population if the population involves the general public. Bluen and Goodman (1984) report response rates of 36% in South African postal surveys conducted on registered personnel practitioners.

As we can infer (see Section 6.4.2), a low response rate restricts the usefulness of a survey because we do not know to what extent a biased and consequently unrepresentative sample has been obtained. If those who have failed to respond systematically differ from those who have indeed responded, and the group who responded represents a minority (that is, a response rate of less than 50%), an entirely incorrect picture of the population may be obtained.

Example

Suppose we conduct a postal survey to assess the attitudes of nurses towards their working conditions. If only those who are highly dissatisfied were to react (possibly in the hope that something would be done about their situation), and if this group constituted a minority, a totally incorrect impression would be obtained of the opinion of the population of nurses.

Note

If the majority of the target population fails to respond, it may be advisable to conduct personal interviews (see Section 7.7.4.1, 7.7.4.2 & 8.4.3) with a random sample (see Section 4.2.5) of the non-respondents. The purpose of this exercise would be to check whether their reason for failing to respond also distinguished them in terms of the relevant variable (for example, attitude towards attitudinal object) from those who did indeed respond.

Respondents do not necessarily keep back questionnaires because they deliberately refuse to respond. Questionnaires may get lost in the post or the intended respondents may have moved or have been out of town for an extended period of time.

Note

More satisfactory response rates are usually obtained from special target populations (purposive samples – see Section 4.2.4.2), especially when they have some loyalty towards the organisation undertaking the survey, such as the alumni of a university who are also donors of the university.

> **Example**
>
> Strümpfer (1989) managed to realise a response rate of about 65% in a survey among business and industrial managers in Johannesburg and part-time MBA students of the University of the Witwatersrand.
>
> Of course, a high response rate in itself is not of much value if the population (for which the response rate has been obtained) is not representative of the target population (see Section 6.4.2).

Note

- *In order to improve the response rate of postal surveys, the questionnaires may be:*
  - *delivered in person to the respondents' addresses with a request that they be posted back on completion;*
  - *posted and collected personally; or*
  - *both delivered and collected personally.*

  (Of course, as the region in which the survey is conducted increases in size, the economic advantages of postal surveys may disappear if questionnaires are to be delivered and/or collected in person.)
- *Questionnaires can also be followed up by letters or postcards reminding the respondents to complete and return the questionnaires. Although such additional dispatches raise the costs, this still should not place the total expenses of the postal survey in the same category as that of personal interviews.*

  Bailey (1987) provides an extensive discussion on the role of the following factors on the obtained response rate of postal surveys: sponsorship; format, length and colour of the questionnaire; covering letter; ease of completing and returning the questionnaire; inducements to respond; nature of the respondents; type of dispatch (for example, airmail or regular mail); day, week or month of dispatch; and reminders.

Activity 7.3

Read the following questions on achievement motivation and develop an interval scale (that includes a graphical scale) to measure these questions. You may re-phrase the questions if you wish, without changing their meaning.

These questions were developed so that the answers from respondents would be indicative of their level of achievement motivation (those low on achievement motivation would perhaps choose the more routine jobs and/or not seek any feedback from any fellow worker at any time).

Questions

1 To what extent would you prefer a job that is difficult but challenging to one that is easy and routine?

2 To what extent would it frustrate you if people did not give you feedback on how you were progressing in your job?

Answers

1 Would you prefer a difficult, challenging job to an easy, routine job?

☐ Not at all
☐ Perhaps
☐ To some extent

☐ Definitely
☐ Most definitely

2 Would it frustrate you if people did not give you feedback on how you were progressing in your job?
☐ Not at all
☐ Perhaps
☐ To some extent
☐ Definitely
☐ Most definitely

7.7.3.2 **Standardised tests**

A STANDARDISED TEST is a collection of tasks in which:

- the content;
- the administration (giving the instructions and so on); and
- the scoring of the obtained responses are the same, irrespective of who is administering it, whom it is administered and by to whom it is scored.

Note

At present the Human Sciences Research Council (HSRC) is the most important local publisher of standardised tests. Primarily these tests are intended for educational, counselling and clinical use and not necessarily for research.

However, there are also other publishers and distributors of psychological assessment instruments. If you have access to the Internet, you can visit the following website to get more information on the Psychological Assessment Initiative (PAI):

http://sunsite.wits.ac.za/conferen/psychology/pai/pai.html

Standardised tests can take on a variety of forms. Some of them, which may only be administered individually (in other words, a test administrator can administer it to only one testee at a time), are known as individual tests (see Section 7.7.5). On the other hand, group tests may be administered to more than one individual in one session at the same time. All students are familiar with paper-and-pencil measurements/tests. In the case of apparatus measurements/tests (see Section 7.7.5), testees normally do not indicate their responses with a pencil on an answer sheet, but have to manually manipulate some or other object to make the end result meet certain requirements.

Because a certain degree of expertise is required to administer and interpret standardised tests, they are only made available to suitably qualified persons.

Note

In South Africa, the release and distribution of tests is controlled by the Health Professions Council of South Africa (HPCSA) in terms of specific legislation. For this purpose, standardised tests are divided into three categories. For example:

- *tests in Category C may be administered only by registered psychologists (or intern psychologists, registered psychometrists and intern psychometrists under supervision of a registered psychologist), whereas*
- *tests in Category A may be administered by psycho-technicians as well, but again under supervision of a registered psychologist.*

In terms of the characteristics (attributes) that standardised tests measure, we can distinguish between the following types of tests: aptitude tests (which include intelligence tests), academic achievement tests, personality tests and interest tests.

Whereas aptitude tests are aimed at the capacity of individuals to acquire skills in particular areas with the necessary training, achievement tests are focused on the knowledge and skills individuals have already learnt in a particular course.

7.7.3.3 **Attitude scales**

An ATTITUDE is a disposition towards a particular issue, the so-called attitudinal object, which may be influenced by individuals and events and is less permanent than personality traits. The attitudinal object may refer to:

Example (compare the CD-ROM manual)

This is an attitude scale to test the efficiency of a local bus service:
The typical service user (passenger) is asked to indicate his or her choice of answer to the question/item by marking his or her preferred box.

	Agree strongly	Agree	Agree in some cases	Do not agree	Strongly disagree
Buses are on time	1	2	3	4	5
Drivers are reckless	1	2	3	4	5
Fares are too high	1	2	3	4	5
Service is regular	1	2	3	4	5

- a political, economical or social issue (for example, abortion, tax on wealth creation, the death penalty);
- a custom (for example, greeting by kissing on the mouth or the slaughtering of animals at a wedding feast);
- a group (for example, COSATU); or
- a single person.

Note

There are only a few attitude scales available commercially, so that researchers as a rule have to compile their own attitude scales to measure the attitudes relevant to their research. (See list of websites on page 292.)

There are four different types of attitude scales, all of which comprise sets of items thta are supposed to measure different degrees of attitudes towards the attitudinal object, namely:

- the summated or Likert scale
- Semantic Differential
- the Guttman scale
- the Thurstone scale.

These attitude scales are based on different assumptions about the relationship between individuals; their attitudes and their responses to the items. We will address the first two types of scales.

(a) The summated or Likert scale

The summated or Likert scale was introduced by Likert (1903 – 1981). It is at present the most popular type of scale in the social sciences (Kidder & Judd, 1986). Its popularity stems from the fact that it is easier to compile than any of the other attitude scales (more particularly, those of Guttman and Thurstone, which we do not discuss here). The Likert scale may be used for multi-dimensional attitudes, which is not possible with the other attitude scales.

A summated attitude scale consists of a COLLECTION OF STATEMENTS ABOUT THE ATTITUDINAL OBJECT. In respect of each statement, subjects have to indicate the degree to which they agree or disagree with its content on, say, a five-point scale (for example, strongly differ, differ, undecided, agree, strongly agree).

Some statements represent a positive attitude, whereas others reflect a negative attitude (towards the attitudinal object).

Example

A negatively formulated item on a scale to measure attitude towards taxation, for example, in a study to determine preference for indirect taxation (VAT) rather then direct taxation (on one's salary – PAYE) could read:

Taxation on bread is nothing else but murder.

An example of a positively formulated item might be:

Taxation on bread is essential for government income.

Respondents have to indicate the degree to which they agree with such a statement by encircling, for example, the number 1 if they totally disagree with it, and 5 (on a five-point scale) if they totally agree with it.

An attitude scale should contain approximately the same number of positively and negatively formulated items to counteract the acquiescent response style (see Section 7.4).

We regard all positive items as being equal in attitudinal intensity, and the same applies to all negative items. In other words, a score of 5 on one positive item is interpreted as being just as positive as a score of 5 on any other (positive) item.

- If there are 20 such statements and the respondent encircles a 5 on each item, a total score of $20 \times 5 = 100$ would be obtained, which would indicate a highly positive attitude towards the attitudinal object.
- A score of $20 \times 1 = 20$, by contrast, would signify a highly negative attitude.
- A score of 60, for example, could be obtained in different ways, and they would all be supposed to reflect the same attitudinal intensity.

Example

Suppose one person obtains a score of 60 by encircling a 5 on the first ten items and (plus) a 1 on the remaining ten items; while another obtains the same score by encircling a score of 1 on the first ten items and (plus) a 5 on the remaining items.

Such a result could indicate that all the items in the scale do not measure attitude towards the same object; put differently, that the scale is MULTI-DIMENSIONAL rather than UNI-DIMENSIONAL. Unless all the items measure attitude towards exactly the same object, and to the same extent, two such scores of 60 will not reflect the same attitudinal intensity.

Note

If attitude towards some object is multi-dimensional, it is advisable to compile a separate subscale for each dimension (compare Section 7.5.1.3).

(b) The semantic differential

The semantic differential, which was developed by Osgood and his colleagues (Osgood, Suci & Jannenbaum, 1957) follows a rather different approach from that of the Likert scale. Each item in a semantic differential scale consists mostly of a seven-point scale, of which the two end-points are two opposite adjectives (words that describe the attributes/characteristics of an object such as "a strong leader").

Example

If we want to measure attitude towards taxation on bread, we could use bipolar adjectives such as the following:

Good : . : : . : : . : : . : : . : : . : : . : Bad
Moral : . : : . : : . : : . : : . : : . : : . : Immoral

The seven scale points may be left open as in the above example, or the numbers 1 through 7 may appear in the corresponding sections, as follows:

Good : . : : . : : . : : . : : . : : . : : . : Bad
7 6 5 4 3 2 1

Moral : . : : . : : . : : . : : . : : . : : . : Immoral
7 6 5 4 3 2 1

In respect of each item, respondents have to indicate their attitude towards the particular attitudinal object by making a cross somewhere along the continuum (between the two endpoints).

- A respondent who thinks that taxation on bread is very bad, would make a cross in the section closest to "Bad", like this:

Good : . : : . : : . : : . : : . : : . : : X : Bad
7 6 5 4 3 2 1

- A respondent who regards taxation on bread as neutral in terms of this continuum, would indicate this by means of a cross in the middle section (the fourth one), like this:

Good : . : : . : : . : : X : : . : : . : : . : Bad
7 6 5 4 3 2 1

- A respondent who thinks that taxation on bread is very good, would make a cross in the section closest to "Good", like this:

Good : X : : . : : . : : . : : . : : . : : . : Bad
7 6 5 4 3 2 1

Actually, each pair (item) of bipolar adjectives represents a scale on its own. A respondent's total score on the scale is the sum of the chosen scale values of all the individual items (number of items necessary for reliable measurement – see Section 7.5.1.3).

Note

Osgood et al *(1957) published 50 such pairs of bipolar adjectives of which the factor structure (the dimensions represented by them) is known. Although this list may possibly be sufficient for most purposes, it does not include all possible pairs and nothing prevents researchers from including new pairs that they consider to be more relevant to their particular studies. If they do this, it is important that they elicit different ratings from different individuals, in other words, that they show variance (see Section 9.3.1). It is also recommended that they investigate the factor structure (see Section 9.2.1) of such new items.*

Activity 7.4

Read Case Study A and Case Study B in Appendix D on page 276.

Question

1 Is the type of scale used to measure the attitudes of the subjects in each article the most suitable? Give a brief reason for your answer.

2 Develop graphic examples (items) of any two attitude questions used in the questionnaire in each article.

Answer

CASE STUDY A

1 Yes, the type of scale used is the most suitable, because the other attitude scales (Guttman, Thurstone and semantic differential) cannot be used like the Likert scale to measure multi-dimensional attitudes (such as moral judgements on AIDS or the rights of prostitutes). The attitudes (towards AIDS and prostitution) were measured by way of 24 questions in random order.

2

	Agree fully	Agree	Uncertain	Do not agree	Do not agree at all
AIDS is a punishment for immoral activities	5	4	3	2	1
Prostitutes must have job opportunities	5	4	3	2	1

CASE STUDY B

1 Yes, the type of scale used (semantic differential) is the most suitable, because the attitude of the sample members towards supervision had to be measured on three occasions. By adding the scores of each sample member for the six items, a total score for each member could easily be obtained for each occasion – something that is not as easy to do with the other scales (Likert, Guttman and Thurstone).

The instrument's reliability could also be determined easily and compared with the test-retest correlation of 0,85 that Osgood calculated for the semantic differential. It was assumed that all the apprentices could read and write so as to complete the attitude scale.

2 Supervision is GOOD __ __ __ __ __ __ __ BAD
1 2 3 4 5 6 7

PUNCTUAL __ __ __ __ __ __ __ LATE
1 2 3 4 5 6 7

7.7.3.4 **Rating scales and situational tests**

In the measuring instruments that we have covered thus far, the research participants reported on their own behaviour by answering questions about it.

- In RATING SCALES, someone else, that is, the rater, assesses the behaviour of the participants. In some cases the raters are supposed to be familiar with the behaviour of the participants and therefore to base their ratings on their memory about such behaviour.
- In SITUATIONAL TESTS the participants have to respond to questions or execute certain commands in the rater's presence, and are then rated on the basis of their execution of these tasks.

Alternatively, we may make video recordings of the participants' performance, in which case the rater need not be present at the original execution of the tasks but may use these recordings for rating purposes.

> **Example**
>
> A workshop manager may be requested to rate each worker on a five-point scale in terms of the degree of compliance that they normally display in terms of workplace safety measures.

We may present such rating scales in different ways, but basically they consist of:

- a collection of items, each of which
- involves a continuum of between three and nine rank-ordered scale points (for example, from "very good" at one end to "very poor" at the other).

The rater's task is to place each subject in terms of each of these items so that this placement reflects the subject's position in terms of the item involved. The different scale points could be labelled by one or more words or even brief descriptions.

Example

How compliant (adhering to the rules) is the worker in terms of workplace safety?

- ☐ Not at all compliant
- ☐ Only slightly compliant
- ☐ Moderately compliant
- ☐ Very compliant
- ☐ Extremely compliant.

In the case of a so-called NUMERICAL RATING SCALE, the description that appears at each point is replaced by a number (1, 2, 3, and so on) and a description such as "good" or "poor" is affixed to the two end-points only.

Example

How compliant (adhere to the rules) is the worker in terms of workplace safety?

POOR [1] [2] [3] [4] [5] GOOD

In the case of a graphical rating scale, each item is represented by a horizontal line and the various scale points are indicated at equal intervals by short, vertical lines. The two end-points are accompanied by descriptions so that the rater may know which one is the positive end-point and which one the negative end-point.

Example

How does the worker get along with the other workers?

WELL ├─┼─┼─┼─┼─┤ BADLY

The rater's task is to indicate the subject's position in respect of the item by means of a cross somewhere along the horizontal line.

Example

How does the worker get along with the other workers?

WELL ├─┼X┼─┼─┼─┤ BADLY

We may increase the interrater reliability (see Section 7.5) of rating scales by identifying as clearly as possible the behaviour that is to be rated by each item. With this in mind, each of the scale points in a so-called behaviourally anchored rating scale is illustrated with concrete examples of behaviour.

Example

We can break down a construct such as aggression into different, clearly described components, such as:

- physical aggression; and
- verbal aggression.

In addition, we can give concrete examples of behaviour which qualifies as:

- "physically very aggressive";

Extremely aggressive

- "physically moderately aggressive", and so on, respectively.

For example, to pinch someone may count as an example of moderately aggressive behaviour, whereas to give somebody a well-aimed blow with the fist may qualify as one of extreme aggressiveness.

We assign a score to each scale point (for example, a score of 1 for "not aggressive at all", and a score of 5 for "extremely aggressive").

We obtain the total score for an individual by adding the scores of the scale points he or she has chosen over all items relating to the same attribute. Both the retest reliability and the interrater reliability (see Section 7.5) of such total scores depend on the number of scale points per item and the number of items that are summed:

> The greater the number of scale points, or the greater the number of items, the more reliable the total measurement/test scores tend to be.

Note

Naturally we will find that there is a limit to the number of scale points which could be used, for example, ten scale points are likely to require discriminations from the raters which are too difficult.

Apparently, most researchers agree that five scale points per item are the optimal minimum.

7.7.3.5 **Response styles and how to prevent them**

We cannot separate rating scales from the people (the raters) who are implementing them. The validity (see Section 7.4) of rating scales is usually negatively affected by the presence of certain response styles on the part of the raters, for example:

- the halo effect;
- the severity or stringency error and the leniency error;
- the error of central tendency;
- the logical error;
- the proximity error; and
- the contrast error.

(a) The halo effect

The notorious halo effect is characterised by the fact that the rater, because of the general impression created by either a favourable or an unfavourable attribute of an individual, tends to rate the latter favourably or unfavourably in terms of all other attributes – even those that have little to do with the attribute being rated.

Example

- A training course member with an attractive handwriting may obtain high marks on variables such as knowledge about the subject studied, which may have little to do with handwriting.
- An individual who is verbally fluent may be rated highly on anything ranging from good interpersonal skills to general intelligence.

Note

In an attempt to prevent the halo effect from occurring, we can do the following:

- *firstly, rate all participants in respect of one attribute (to permit a mutual comparison between them)*
- *secondly, do the same separately in respect of each of the other attributes (instead of rating*

each person on all attributes in one go and then doing the same with the next person).

Behaviourally anchored rating scales may also be useful in this connection.

(b) The severity or stringency error

The severity or stringency error means that a rater tends to rate all individuals rather too strictly, while the leniency error means exactly the opposite – the rater tends to rate all individuals rather positively.

Note

To counteract the biases of the severity or stringency error and the leniency error, the raters may be asked to place the subjects in a rank order in terms of the attribute in question.

(c) The error of central tendency

Raters who are hesitant to assign extreme ratings and consequently tend to place most individuals in the centre of the scale, commit the so-called error of central tendency.

Note

To prevent distortion by the error of central tendency, we should, at the compilation stage, avoid statements that reflect extreme positions (for example, by replacing "I am completely satisfied with my work" with "In general, I am satisfied with my work").

(d) The logical error

The logical error is the tendency to rate individuals similarly on attributes that are incorrectly considered to be logically related.

Note

To prevent the logical error from occurring, maximally different names with clear descriptions may be used for the various attributes.

(e) The proximity error

The proximity error refers to the tendency to rate those attributes that appear close to each other on the rating scale similarly.

Note

We can prevent the bias of the proximity error simply by having different raters rate the attributes in different order.

(f) The contrast error

The contrast error occurs when raters exaggerate the difference between themselves and the ratees in respect of the attribute in question.

Example

A rater who highly regards the correct use of language, may tend to rate incompetent users of language more strictly than is necessary.

Note

Research on ways and means to assess rating errors such as the contrast error, and to correct them, includes that done by Saal, Downey and Lahey (1980) and Murphy and Balzer (1989).

We have said (estimation of reliability – see Section 7.5.1.3) that we can increase the reliability of measurements/tests by lengthening them by similar items. Similarly, the reliability of rating scales (where each individual's score is equal to the sum of all raters' ratings) increases as the number of comparable raters increases.

- Raters should first be properly trained.
- Their ratings should preferably:
  - first be compared with one another, and
  - then discussed in a trial run in order to
  - eliminate misunderstandings in the conceptualisation of the attribute being rated and differences in stringency or leniency.
- In addition (see Section 6.3.3), audio or audiovisual recordings may be used to eliminate the possible effect of the researcher's expectations on the obtained results.

- Instead of just one observer, rater or coder, more than one who are not aware of the treatment groups to which the different subjects belong, may rate their behaviour from the audio or audiovisual tapes.
- The greater the number of raters or coders that are used, the smaller the possibility that they will all commit the same errors.
- Differences in the obtained ratings could be discussed and be ironed out individually by the raters.

However, video recordings frequently require rooms that are especially equipped for this purpose, which raises the question of the ecological validity (see Section 6.4.3) of the conclusions obtained. If participants behave differently in such a specially-equipped venue than they would behave otherwise, the ecological validity of the results may be adversely affected.

Activity 7.5

Read Case Study D and Case Study E in Appendix D on page 276.

Question

1 Is the type of scale used to measure the speech quality of the subjects in Case Study D and the type of scale used to measure the cash flow problems of the businesses in Case Study E the most suitable? Give a brief reason for your answer.
2 Develop one numerical example (item/question) that might have been used in the speech quality rating scale in Case Study D.
3 Develop one graphical evaluation scale (items/question) that might have been used in Case Study D, and one that might have been used in the cash flow problems in Case Study E.

Answer

CASE STUDY D

1 Yes, because the rating scale can be used to measure each of the eight elements as indicated on the video tape. By adding together each subject's score for the eight items, a total mark for each subject could easily be acquired, irrespective of which rater did the rating.
2 Eye contact of the student is

Not good at all __ __ __ __ __ Exceptionally good
1 2 3 4 5

3

	Almost never	Some-times	Often	Almost always
I get out of breath before I have to give a speech				

CASE STUDY E

1 Maybe not, because the owners of the businesses in the study may be very subjective on the rating scale reporting experiences of cash flow problems. It may have been more suitable to ask them to report directly the amount in rands that they needed per month to pay the expenses, cover their costs, and so on.
3 My business experienced more cash flow problems than most other businesses

F	f	t	T

Note

With each of the scales, there would naturally have been instructions on how to complete the questionnaires, for example: "Indicate your preference by making a cross your choice."

7.7.4 **Personal visits and communication by telephone**

7.7.4.1 **Personal visits**

When we collect data by means of personal interviews, interviewers visit the respondents at home or at their work place. In the case of opinion polls (see Section 5.4.5) they may also approach people at public venues where there is an influx of people, such as shopping centres, post offices, and so on.

As a data-collecting method, the interview may vary from methods that are completely unstructured (see Section 8.4.3), on the one hand, to those that are completely standardised and structured, such as those used in survey research (see Section 5.4.5), on the other hand. In all these cases the interview functions as a data-collecting method, and as such should be distinguished from therapeutic or counselling interviews in which the objective is to help clients.

Note

Here are some general rules and recommendations for interviewers:

- *They should dress in more or less the same way as the respondents. Obviously, there may be resistance among residents of a squatter camp if interviewers arrive there all dressed up. Likewise, business people consciously or unconsciously may be offended and tend to be less co-operative if interviewers arrive at their offices wearing jeans and worn-out takkies.*
- *They should at all costs avoid any indications of affiliation with some or other group or organisation, for example, a Blue Bulls rugby tie or a Cosatu emblem.*
- *Although interviewers may be dressed discreetly, factors over which they have no control, such as their sex, race, physical appearance and background, may affect the respondents' responses. Consequently, interviewers should be careful not to engender resistance (among the respondents) against them.*
- *There is often the danger that the respondents may view the interviewer as an intruder. Especially in the South African context, white interviewers should be mindful of the possibility that black respondents may regard them as intruders, and vice versa.*
- *All these factors may cause respondents to provide biased or even false information. Bailey (1987) offers useful hints regarding the training of interviewers and conducting of interviews.*

The ADVANTAGES and DISADVANTAGES of personal interviews are:

- *Cost and ease of application.* While we regard flexibility and adaptability as great advantages of a personal interview, its high costs as far as its preparation and application are concerned, are regarded as its greatest drawback. Apart from the time required to conduct interviews, there are the costs associated with the proper training of interviewers. In addition, interviewers have to be paid for conducting the interviews and their travelling costs have to be reimbursed. When interviews are conducted at respondents' homes or workplaces, interviewers are usually paid more than if they contact them telephonically. In the case of vast geographic regions, the travelling costs of the interviewers may also amount to considerable expenses. Finally, personal interviews may be time-consuming. Not only the time taken up by the interview itself, but also that used to arrange appointments that suit both the interviewer and the respondent may contribute to this. It may even happen that interviewers have to return to a respondent's address several times before the interview eventually takes place.
- *Control over responding.* Probably the biggest advantage of personal interviews is that the interviewers are in complete control of the interview situation. If respondents are evasive, interviewers can attempt to gain their confidence. Moreover, they can ensure that the respondent's first response as well as any

changes to it are recorded, that all questions are answered, and that someone else does not provide the responses on the respondent's behalf. The interviewer is in a position to notice and to clear up any misunderstanding (in the case of semi-structured interviews) on the part of the respondent, to explain any questions that may be unclear, and to follow up on incomplete and vague responses. Consequently, the responses obtained are of a high quality.

- *Anonymity.* Naturally, interviewers cannot always conduct personal interviews anonymously. When they approach strangers in public places, there is still the possibility of anonymity. However, when they locate respondents by means of their names and addresses, anonymity is obviously impossible. As a result, there is the possibility that in responding to questions on opinions and attitudes, respondents may give those responses that they think the interviewer expects of them rather than those that actually apply to them. Interviewers should be properly trained not to say anything that may be construed as a hint about what are regarded as desired responses.
- *Response rate.* Because the interviewer physically confronts the respondent, there is less chance of the respondent eluding the interview. Respondents who may be unwilling to complete a questionnaire may be entirely prepared to talk to the interviewer. Consequently, personal interviews tend to have a higher response rate than telephonic interviews and postal surveys (see Section 7.7.3.1).

7.7.4.2 **Telephonic interviews**

In the case of telephonic interviews, the interviewer asks the questions from the interview schedule over the telephone and records the respondent's responses.

When an interviewer poses the questions contained in structured questionnaires to the respondent, whether in a personal interview or over the telephone, such a previously compiled questionnaire is known as an INTERVIEW SCHEDULE.

Telephonic interviews are used mainly in survey research (see Section 5.4.1). Obviously, standardised tests (see Section 7.7.3.2) and attitude scales (see Section 7.7.3.3) cannot be administered telephonically. Because the respondents do not have the questions in front of them, telephonic interviews are less suited to complicated questions. Even the number of alternatives in multiple-choice questions may present problems in telephonic interviews. Respondents may find it difficult to remember all the alternatives with a view to comparing them and finding the most appropriate one.

Naturally, telephonic interviews will be shorter than personal interviews, with 10 to 15 minutes being the norm. Where computers are used to dial the respondents, the interviewer simply reads the questions as they appear on the screen or monitor and immediately keys in the respondent's responses. An advantage of such computer-assisted telephonic interviews is that, where appropriate, the questions may be put in different orders for different respondents with a view to preventing any sequence effects from occurring.

Note

- *Dillman (1978) provides useful guidelines for the execution of telephonic interviews.*
- *Computer-assisted telephone interviewing such as the CATI system or call-centres can be used.*

We have pointed out (see Section 4.2) the danger of unrepresentative samples arising from using the telephone for data-collecting purposes. If an appreciable percentage of the population on which a survey is to be conducted does not have access to a telephone, the list of names in the telephone directory may differ in important ways from the population in which we are actually interested.

The ADVANTAGES and DISADVANTAGES of telephonic interviews are:

- *Cost and ease of application*. One of the most important advantages of telephonic interviews is the speed with which they may be completed. Especially when respondents over a vast geographical area have to be contacted, telephonic interviews may be conducted much faster than personal interviews because the interviewer may execute the entire project from an office and does not have to travel around.
  - The speed factor is of special importance when respondents' reaction to something like a bomb explosion or a television programme, or an event of which the actuality may tend to dissipate quickly, is to be investigated.
  - Associated with the speed with which telephonic interviews may be carried out, is the lower cost. Even if long-distance calls have to be made, their costs still tend to be considerably lower than the travelling expenses required for personal interviews.
- *Control over responding*. Interviewers have less control over the interview situation than in (personal) interviews where they are physically present with the respondents. A potential drawback of telephonic interviews is that respondents may be suspicious of the interviewer's intentions. For example, they may suspect that the interviewer wants to sell something or may even be playing the fool with them. Although it is possible to overcome such reservations, it remains more difficult to get the whole-hearted co-operation of the respondent over the telephone than in a personal interview. Naturally, it is difficult to cover anything but rather simple, superficial questions in telephoneic interviews. It also is easier for the respondent to summarily terminate a telephonic interview than a personal one.
- *Anonymity*. The respondent has a greater impression of anonymity in telephonic interviews than in personal interviews and this may result in greater honesty and fewer false responses. Usually the quality of the obtained responses compares favourably with that of personal interviews (Kidder & Judd, 1986).

7.7.4.3 **Structured interviews**

In a structured interview, the interviewer puts a collection of questions from a previously compiled questionnaire, known as an interview schedule (telephonic interviews – see Section 7.7.4.2), to a respondent face to face and records the latter's responses. The interviewer is restricted to the questions, their wording and their order as they appear on the schedule, with relatively little freedom to deviate from it.

Note

- *If the respondent appears to be surprised or upset about a question, the interviewer may repeat the question, but without paraphrasing it. (If this precaution is not taken, the responses that different interviewers obtain from different interviewees may not be comparable.)*
- *Interviewers should be trained properly. They should be thoroughly familiar with the questions in the questionnaire so that they may read them fluently or even ask them from memory without deviating from the questions as they are formulated.*

7.7.4.4 **Unstructured interviews**

We usually employ unstructured interviews in explorative research to identify important variables in a particular area, to formulate penetrating questions on them and to generate hypotheses for further investigation. Because of the unfamiliarity of the area being entered, it is usually impossible to compile a schedule for interviews in such instances. (We will return to this kind of interview in Section 8.4.3.)

7.7.4.5 **Semi-structured interviews**

Between the completely structured interview on the one hand, and the completely unstructured interview on the other hand, various degrees of structuredness are possible. Interviews between these two extremes are usually called semi-structured interviews (see Figure 7.5).

We may consider semi-structured interviews when:

- the topics are of a very sensitive nature;
- the respondents come from divergent backgrounds; and
- experienced and expert interviewers are available for conducting the interviews.

Instead of an interview schedule (telephonic interviews – see Section 7.7.4.2), INTERVIEW GUIDES are used in semi-structured interviews.

An INTERVIEW GUIDE involves a list of topics and aspects of these topics (note, not specific questions) that have a bearing on the given theme and that the interviewer should raise during the course of the interview (that is, if the interviewee does not do so him- or herself).

Although all respondents are asked the same questions, the interviewer may adapt the formulation, including the terminology, to fit the background and educational level of the respondents.

The order in which the interviewer broaches these topics may vary from one person to the next, and depends on the way in which the interview develops.

Semi-structured interviews offer a versatile way of collecting data. We can use them with all age groups (for example, with young workers participating in ABET who are still unable to read, as well as with elderly people with poor eyesight). This method may often be used when no other one is available or appropriate.

Example

It would be highly insensitive to shove a questionnaire into the hands of victims immediately after an earthquake, or of the survivors of a sea disaster immediately after they had landed on dry soil, with a request to complete it.

Furthermore, in in-depth interviews we can ask questions about sensitive and highly emotional issues that we cannot do in telephonic interviews and postal surveys. (As a matter of fact, the terms *in-depth telephonic interview* and *in-depth postal interview* are self-contradictory.)

Unlike completely structured interviews (see Section 7.7.4.3), unstructured and semi-structured interviews (see Section 7.7.4.4 & 7.7.4.5) allow the interviewer to use probes with a view to clearing up vague responses, or to ask for elaboration of incomplete answers.

Such PROBES may vary from "Why?" to "Could you elaborate on this?". Even by remaining silent with the pencil poised to continue writing, the respondent may be given the necessary encouragement to proceed.

Note

Kahn and Cannel (1957) is a source that is several decades old, but that still contains valuable advice on interviewing. (A more recent reference is Cannel & Kahn, 1986.)

Figure 7.5 The structuredness of different types of interviews

7.7.5 **Individual apparatus (measurements/tests)**

In INDIVIDUAL APPARATUS MEASUREMENTS/TESTS, the measurement/test administrator presents the subject with tasks (contained in a measurement/test) that should be executed (for example, to complete a puzzle). The administrator assigns marks in terms of the manner in which the subject completes the task (for example, by using a stop-watch to determine how long the subject takes to complete the puzzle – see Figure 7.6).

The instructions given to the subject, as well as the way in which marks should be assigned, are fixed and measurement/test administrators are not permitted to deviate from them.

7.7.6 **Direct observation (checklists)**

Whereas the use of rating scales (see Section 7.7.3.4) involves rating participants in terms of the raters' recollection of the participants' behaviour, in direct observation, the participants are observed directly (by the observer). In the final analysis, the observer is the measuring instrument in direct, systematic observation. Sometimes mechanical aids (for example, audio- or videotape recordings) are used to record the relevant behaviour, but the recording obtained in this manner ultimately has to be observed and coded or evaluated. The reliability and validity of the measurements (see Section 7.4 & 7.5) thus obtained depend on the experience and skills of the observer(s).

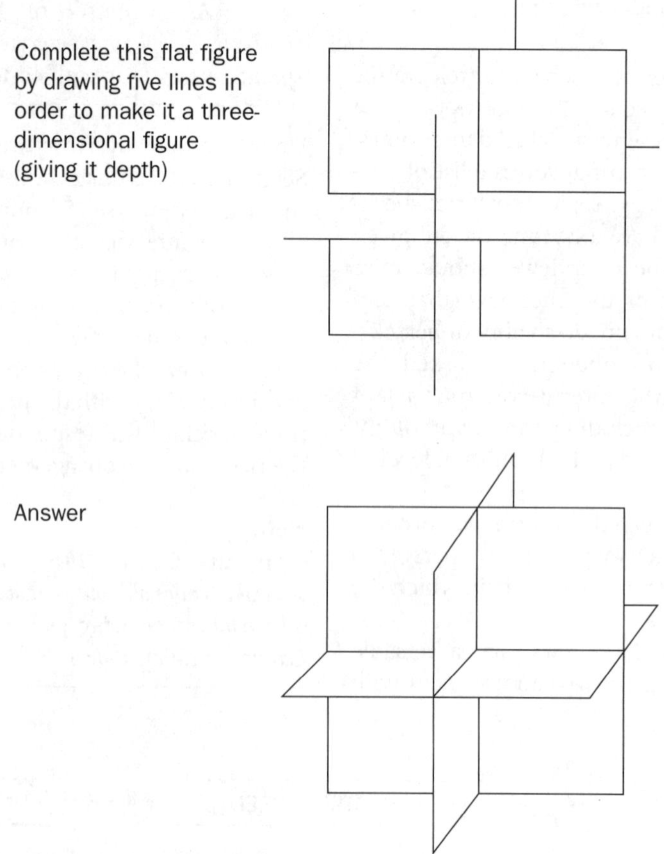

Figure 7.6 Example of a mental ability test item

The ADVANTAGES and DISADVANTAGES of direct observation are:

- The behaviour which is to be studied, is recorded first-hand, as compared to interviews and questionnaires in which information is presented as second-hand. Consequently, researchers do not have to depend on the participants' possibly misleading reports (either in interviews or on questionnaires) about the relevant behaviour, but instead observe it directly.
- However, this potential advantage also has two drawbacks:
  - Firstly, the presence of the observer, usually a stranger to the respondent, may influence the behaviour to be observed, resulting in reactive measurement (see Section 6.3.4.1).

Example

Say, after workers have experienced a violent clash in negotiations, a stranger (researcher) who intends recording evidence of aggressive behaviour, observes them on the shop floor. The workers may fool around to draw attention and thus exhibit behaviour that the researcher may interpret as being aggressive.

In some cases it is possible to eliminate the possibly undesirable side-effects of the observer's presence by means of one-way mirrors or concealed video-camera recordings. For example, in RESEARCH EXAMPLE II (page 14) (see Section 2.2) the behaviour of the trainee supervisors was watched through a one-way mirror from an adjacent room.

  - Secondly, the observers' prejudices may affect their observation and consequently the validity (see Section 7.4) of their ratings. (We indicated ways in which to deal with this in Section 7.7.3.4.)

In direct observation the observers are not expected to record all the behaviour (of the subjects) that they observe, but only those behaviours that are regarded as indicators (see Section 7.2) of the dependent variable (see Section 2.2) in question.

The following steps should be taken during systematic observation:

- Firstly, we must select all the behaviours that should be recorded. Sometimes a checklist is compiled that gives explicit descriptions of all the different concrete behaviours that should be regarded as indicators of the dependent variable.

Example

In RESEARCH EXAMPLE II (page 14) (see Section 2.2), the dependent variable (management style) was divided into subcategories, namely:

- non-verbal rude behaviour; and
- verbal rude behaviour.

Concrete examples of behaviours in each of these categories were listed, for example:

- To point a finger was listed as an example of non-verbal rude behaviour.
- To utter phrases such as "I will kick you" and "punch you", represented verbal rude behaviour.

Behaviours that did not fall into these clearly described categories were ignored.

- Secondly, we should make a decision concerning the recording or coding of the selected behaviours.

Example

The observer may make a tally RESEARCH EXAMPLE II (page 14) – see Section 2.2) opposite a category when he or she observes behaviour that falls into that category. In this manner, the observer determines the number of times he or she observes behaviour that is considered to be indicative of the dependent variable.

Thus, if aggressive reactions (say, of trainee supervisors who have observed an iron-fisted management style role model, namely, their supervisor) are to be studied, the number of times any of the trainees exhibits any of the iron-fisted management style behaviours listed (for example, pointing a finger at a subordinate) is established.

In continuous observation, each time the observer observes an example of the selected behaviour, he or she records it (by means of a tally – see Section 9.3). Alternatively, only samples (see Section 4.2) of the behaviour may be recorded.

- In *point time sampling*, the observer checks only at specific points in time (say, every ten seconds or every second minute) whether or not the subject exhibits the selected behaviour.
- In *interval time sampling*, the observer notices whether or not such behaviour occurs in a particular interval (say, every 60 seconds or every two minutes).

Note

These time sampling methods are especially appropriate when a large number of behaviours has to be recorded.

- *Event sampling* can be considered in the case of behaviour that does not occur as a matter of routine (for example, temper tantrums, riots, bank robberies) and that may therefore be missed by time samples. In this type of sampling, the researcher should be at the ready to observe such an event if it does occur, and to make the necessary recording.

Irrespective of how explicitly the checklist has been defined, observers act as raters of behaviour, because to a greater or lesser extent they have to decide whether or not a particular behaviour falls within a particular category.

Interrater reliability (estimation of reliability – see Section 7.5) may be improved in such instances by the following:

- carefully defining the dependent variable as explained above
- training observers properly in advance about the specific, concrete behaviours that should be regarded as indicators of the dependent variable
- warning observers about the danger of letting fatigue or over-confidence negatively influence the quality of their ratings
- letting any of the response styles that may be present in rating scales (see Section 7.7.3.4) have an effect on their ratings.

The less the observer is expected to *evaluate* or *interpret* whether or not a particular behaviour is indicative of the dependent variable, the better the chances of obtaining a SATISFACTORY interrater reliability (see Section 7.5). At the same time, there is the danger that such a precaution may negatively affect measurement validity because behaviours not listed (on the checklist) have to be ignored.

However, behaviour that does not appear on the previously compiled checklist, but that may possibly be appropriate (as indicators of the dependent variable), may be noted with a view to discussing its relevancy later. Preferably, however, all specific, concrete behaviours that qualify for inclusion should have been identified in a pilot study (see Section 7.6).

Of course, if the behaviour that is to be rated is available on videotape, different raters may rate the same behaviour, and their interrater reliability may be examined. The examination of the interrater reliability may be done by computing the percentage of agreement between assignments (to the different categories) of two or more independent observers.

Retest reliability (see Section 7.5) may also be investigated by having the same observers rate a video recording of the subjects' behaviour, say, two weeks apart.

Validity (see Section 7.4) may be investigated by comparing the rating results with the results obtained by other measuring instruments for the same construct.

7.8 Developing and constructing questionnaires, interview schedules and attitude items

When an interviewer poses the questions contained in a structured questionnaire to a respondent in a personal interview or a telephonic interview, such a previously compiled questionnaire is also known as an interview schedule.

Note

Schuman and Presser (1981) conducted valuable research on the formulation of questions in questionnaires and interview schedules.

In this section, several considerations that we should bear in mind when formulating questions for such instruments, are briefly mentioned. Some of these considerations are more important when opinions and beliefs are assessed than when information about biographical details and typical behaviour is to be collected. In the case of biographical details and typical behaviour, other considerations may be important. Minor adaptations may be required at times in the formulation of questions in view of the respective nature of personal visits and telephonic communication (see Section 7.7.4) or postal surveys (see Section 7.7.3.1).

Example

It is desirable to ask specific questions. Instead of asking:

Which brand of toothpaste do you usually use?

We should rather ask:

Which brand of toothpaste is in your bathroom right now? Do you normally use that brand?

CONSIDERATION 1: CHOOSE JUDICIOUSLY BETWEEN OPEN-ENDED AND CLOSED-ENDED (MULTIPLE-CHOICE VARIETY) QUESTIONS

We can make the questions in questionnaires or interview schedules open-ended so that respondents have to formulate their responses themselves. We can also present them as multiple-choice questions, where respondents have to select, from among two or more alternative responses, the one that best applies to them.

Example

An OPEN-ENDED QUESTION about smoking behaviour may read as follows:

Approximately how many cigarettes do you smoke per day? Answer ...

The corresponding MULTIPLE-CHOICE ITEM may list alternatives such as the following, from which the relevant response should be selected:

- [A] one per day
- [B] between two and five per day
- [C] between six and 10 per day
- [D] more than 10 per day

As with all nominal measurement (see Section 7.3.2), the categories reflected in the alternatives should be mutually exclusive and exhaustive (levels of measurement – see Section 7.3.2). This must be done in order to make provision for each and every possible response (alternative) but not simultaneously so in more than one category.

When it is difficult to anticipate all possible responses, or when there are too many possible responses to list, we may include the category "other" or use open-ended questions.

Example

If we ask the residents of a city what they regard as the most important problem in their city, there may be many possible responses. In such a case the category "other" or open-ended questions may be useful.

In fact, we can use OPEN-ENDED QUESTIONS in unstructured interviews (see Section 7.7.4.4) in pilot studies (see Section 7.6) with a view to determining which answers should be included (in a multiple-choice format) in later studies.

Note

Multiple-choice items in which only two alternatives such as "agree" and "disagree" appear, should be used with great caution. If such questions are indeed used, questions that suggest a positive and a negative attitude respectively towards the particular issue, should be alternated to counteract the possible effect of acquiescence (see Section 7.4).

In addition, a question to which the respondent has to choose between "agree" and "disagree" should preferably be reformulated to be more specific. For example, the question:

> *Ethnic differences are a greater cause of violence in South Africa than the police*

should preferably be reformulated to read:

> *Which, in your opinion, is the greater cause of violence in South Africa?:*
> *A ethnic differences*
> *B the police.*

What may count as an advantage of open-ended questions, may represent a drawback of multiple-choice items, and vice versa.

- Some respondents may feel irritated because multiple-choice items restrict them to particular responses that may not provide for their unique situation. As a result, they may prefer the freedom to express themselves that is allowed by open-ended questions.
- At the same time, this advantage of open-ended questions may be a drawback in that they require:
  - a better ability to express oneself; and
  - usually a higher level of education on the part of respondents than with multiple-choice items.
- Moreover, respondents who meet these requirements may be unwilling to exert the special effort required by open-ended items.
- Multiple-choice items:
  - do not rely on the ability of respondents to express themselves verbally, but, on the other hand,
  - tend to be superficial.
- The greater freedom afforded by open-ended questions results in the following:
  - the responses obtained are more difficult to score; and
  - more time is needed for scoring than with multiple-choice items.
- Furthermore, it is more difficult to compare different respondents' responses to open-ended questions than is the case with multiple-choice questions.
- The possibility of obtaining inappropriate responses is also greater in the case of open-ended questions than with multiple-choice questions.

Example

In response to the question on the approximate number of cigarettes smoked daily, someone may reply:

> *More than is good for my health.*

In this specific example, we could attempt to avoid an inappropriate response by formulating the open-ended question as follows:

> *What is the approximate number of cigarettes that you smoke every day?*

- However, inappropriate responses may also be obtained on multiple-choice items when respondents who:
  - are unfamiliar with the answers; or
  - do not have an opinion, respond to the question in a lackadaisical manner. (In fact, it is not uncommon to find that when alternatives containing incorrect or even fictitious information are

deliberately included, there are indeed individuals who select such alternatives.)

- There is nothing to prevent the researcher from using both open-ended and multiple-choice items in the same schedule.
  - Multiple-choice items may be compiled in connection with biographical details (sex, age, marital status, and so on).
  - Open-ended questions may be formulated on opinions that cannot be reduced to multiple alternatives.

Note

Even if a questionnaire consists exclusively of multiple-choice items, it may be a good idea to conclude it with an open-ended question with a view to determining whether anything of importance to the respondent has been omitted.

CONSIDERATION 2: TAKE THE RESPONDENTS' LITERACY LEVEL INTO CONSIDERATION

When we formulate the questions, we should use words and concepts with which we can expect the respondents to be familiar. The command of language of the group that is investigated should therefore be taken into account. Because we obviously want to obtain accurate information from the respondents, it stands to reason that they should know exactly what is being asked of them. With this in mind, technical terms should be avoided.

Example

Bachrach (1981, p. 166) tells of a question for small businessmen that a state department formulated as follows:

How many employees do you have, broken down by sex?

Now, "broken down" is standard jargon that means "divided in terms of". However, one businessman who was unfamiliar with this terminology replied:

None, our big problem is alcohol.

CONSIDERATION 3: BE CAREFUL NOT TO OFFEND

We should not only avoid technical terms, but also terms that might offend the respondents.

Example

- The interviewer should refrain from asking: *Is your boss an idiot?* Rather ask: *"Do you think your boss is an intelligent line manager?"*
- Similarly, the use of gang language in an attempt to gain the co-operation of gang members may be counterproductive because the gang members may tend to regard their language as their own and may resent it if outsiders (including the interviewers) use it too.

CONSIDERATION 4: BE BRIEF AND FOCUSSED

We should give preference to questions that are concise (brief and to the point) without being ambiguous (having more than one meaning). The longer a question, the longer it takes to read and the greater the possibility that it may create resistance in the respondents.

If the abstractness and/or complexity of the topic makes it difficult to cover in a single question, it should rather be dealt with in several simple, consecutive questions.

If we formulate a question ambiguously, different respondents may interpret it differently. They will then, in effect, respond to different questions. This consideration is especially important for questionnaires used in postal surveys (see Section 7.7.3.1), where the respondents, by definition, are left to their own resources to complete the questions. But this consideration is important even in a structured interview situation (see Section 7.7.4.3). If interviewers have to explain the questions, different interviewers may do it differently and the obtained responses may no longer be comparable.

- The following may give rise to ambiguity:
  - questions that are not formulated clearly
  - questions that are stated incompletely.

Example

To the question:

Do you approve of taxation on food?

a respondent may reply:

It depends on the type of food you are talking about.

- Beware of DOUBLE-BARRELLED QUESTIONS that actually contain more than one question but require a single response.

Example

Read the following question:

Do you disapprove of taxation on food and do you think people who are guilty of evading such tax should be fined?

A respondent may prefer to respond positively to the first part of the question but negatively to the second part.

The occurrence of words such as "and" (as in the present example) or "or" often, but not always, betrays the presence of a double-barrelled question.

Even when such words do no not occur in the question, it can still be double-barrelled. An example of this is when respondents are asked about their attitude towards the fringe benefits regarding their remuneration. A respondent may have a positive attitude towards the company's contribution to his/her medical aid fund, but a negative one towards the company's housing subsidy policy. A single response may therefore not be sufficient.

Obviously, the solution is to reformulate such questions as two (or even more) separate questions.

To prevent ambiguity, words such as "always", "regularly", "very often", "frequently", "seldom" and "never" should preferably be replaced with specific frequencies (numbers) such as in the example of the number of cigarettes being smoked.

Example

A question about smoking behaviour may read as follows:

Approximately how many cigarettes do you smoke per day? Answer: ...

Otherwise, alternatives such as the following may be listed, from among which the relevant response should be selected:

[A] one per day

[B] between two and five per day

[C] between six and 10 per day

[D] more than 10 per day

Note

We should bear in mind that in a multicultural society such as in South Africa, the same question could be interpreted differently in different cultures. Such questions should be avoided or be reformulated to prevent them from yielding confusing information. (Also, compare Preston-Whyte's [1982] evaluation of the applicability of the interview schedule in studies on poverty among rural blacks.)

CONSIDERATION 5: MAINTAIN NEUTRALITY

We should not formulate questions in such a way that we put certain responses into the respondent's mouth. Consider the following recommendations:

- Avoid leading questions: A leading question is one which is formulated in such a fashion that it suggests certain responses rather than others. It usually begins with:

Do you agree that ...? or Are you satisfied that ...?

> **Example**
> The following is a leading question:
>
> *Do you agree that affirmative action is necessary?*

- Avoid loaded questions. A loaded question is a leading question in which social acceptability or unacceptability may likewise influence the respondent to reply in a particular manner.

> **Example**
> The following is a loaded question:
>
> *It is your opinion towards affirmative action to compensate people for injustices that have been committed towards them in the past?*
>
> Irrespective of their opinion towards affirmative action, there would not be many people who would be against rectifying past injustices.

- Facilitate responses that may be regarded as indicative of socially unacceptable attitudes or habits.

> **Example**
> A questionnaire to be completed by visitors to a clinic for venereal diseases should ask:
>
> *How many sex partners have you had during the past three months?*
>
> rather than:
>
> *Have you had more than one sex partner during the past three months?*

- Do not suggest the range of acceptable responses.

> **Example**
> Respondents may give different responses (that do not include FREQUENCIES in order to prevent ambiguity) depending on whether the question reads:
>
> *Do you often tend to feel negative?*
>
> rather than:
>
> *Do you sometimes tend to feel negative?*
>
> This is because "often" is nearer to "always" in the range of response categories (and it is not socially acceptable to feel negative always), while "sometimes" is nearer to "never" (a socially more acceptable feeling).
> Even asking:
>
> *How long?*
>
> rather than:
>
> *How short?*
>
> the negative phases (a socially unacceptable feeling) tend to last, may have an affect on the responses obtained.

- Carefully consider questions about sensitive issues.

> **Example**
> Instead of asking respondents:
>
> *Have you completed your high-school training?*
>
> rather ask:

Indicate the highest school grade that you have passed.

Similarly, rather ask respondents for their dates of birth instead of their ages.

Questions about income should preferably not require an exact amount but rather provide broad categories (in a multiple-choice format). This may look like the following:

[A] No income

[B] R00,00 to R499,00 per month

[C] R500,00 to R1 000,00 per month

[D] More than R1 000,00 per month

CONSIDERATION 6: USE A JUSTIFIED SEQUENCE

We should carefully consider the order in which we put items because earlier items may affect responses to subsequent items. To put the respondent at ease, it is recommended that the questionnaire should begin with a few easy and non-threatening items (for example, multiple-choice questions with only a few alternatives) that are clearly related to the stated purpose.

Later on, more in-depth questions may follow. (Should the respondent offer resistance by that time, only the questions towards the end of the questionnaire will be affected.) Of course, what qualifies as a sensitive issue varies from time to time and from one context to the next, but may range from questions about:

- illegal behaviour (for example, tax evasion, illegal drugs, and so on);
- personal customs and practices (for example, of a sexual nature); and
- attitudes (for example, towards other races), to questions about
- age;
- income; and
- political affiliation.

In the final analysis we will find that the RAPPORT (A TRUSTING RELATIONSHIP) that the interviewer has built up with the respondent is of crucial importance in answering questions about sensitive issues. Consequently, telephone surveys (see Section 7.7.4) and postal surveys (see Section 7.7.3.1) are usually less suited for asking such questions.

WE SHOULD PREFERABLY GROUP TOGETHER QUESTIONS THAT ARE RELATED TO THE SAME ASPECT SO THAT RESPONDENTS DO NOT REPEATEDLY HAVE TO SWITCH THEIR FOCUS. The transition from one topic to the next should be clearly identified and should still be connected with the stated aim of the project.

Example

In a survey of attitudes towards the new war on terrorism, could be introduced by saying:

So far we have talked about the continued maintenance of Western standards. Now we get to the position of Islam.

Note

- *Sensitive topics should also be announced and their relationship with the overall topic should be clear. (The respondent should not get the impression that the other questions served merely as a cloak for the sensitive questions.)*
- *Within a particular topic, the so-called* FUNNEL ORDER *may be used. This means that we commence with a general question that is followed by increasingly specific questions. Not only is this practice in agreement with the preceding recommendation, but it is usually also easier to relate the general question rather than specific ones to the stated aim of the project.*

Because preceding questions may have an effect on the answers given to subsequent items, the order in which questions are set should be identical for all respondents. An exception to this rule is the use of FILTER QUESTIONS. The purpose of FILTER QUESTIONS is to determine whether all subsequent questions should be asked or whether some of them may be skipped.

CONSIDERATION 7: BE SURE THE QUESTION IS APPRECIABLE TO ALL RESPONDENTS

Questions to single respondents asking how long they have been married, or to unemployed persons about how long they have worked on their current jobs, are typical examples.

Sometimes the questions are applicable to all respondents, but the options in a structured item are not.

For example, consider the question in Figure 7.7. People working full-time from home might well object to this question. Sometimes people will respond to one of the options simply to oblige the questioner or to avoid embarrassment. This often occurs when they are asked their opinion on some topic they have not previously considered and on which they really have no opinion.

How would you describe your current employment status?

A Unemployed
B Part-time employed (less than 40 hours/week)
C Full-time employed (40 or more hours per week)

Figure 7.7 A question with an incomplete set of options

The necessary pretesting and planning for surveys using *branching* is worthwhile, as it makes it unnecessary to develop several sets of instruments for different types of respondents, and the identification of the respondent sub-samples that may be impossible prior to the administration or mailing of a survey.

One of the strengths of computer-administered surveys is that such branching is done automatically, as the respondents see only those questions that are relevant to them based on their prior answers. (Q 1 [Yes] [No]; if "yes", go to question 19.)

Example

If someone replied (for example, in a section A) in the negative to the question whether he or she is presently married, he or she does not have to respond to following questions about the age and occupation of his or her spouse (in section B) and may go directly (by skipping section B) to subsequent questions about attitudes towards affirmative action (in section C).

Similarly: In an opinion questionnaire about affirmative action, for example, it may be advisable to first ask whether respondents know what is meant by this concept and even to ask that it be defined to determine whether all subsequent questions should be asked or whether some of them may be skipped.

7.9 Ethical considerations

Ethical considerations come into play at three stages of a research project, namely:

- when participants are recruited;
- during the intervention and/or the measurement procedure to which they are subjected (see Section 6.3.3.1); and
- in the release of the results obtained.

Field experiments, field studies (see Section 5.2.3) and participant-observational studies (see Section 8.4.2), especially, often require that research participants be involved in a research project without their consent or knowledge.

Consider RESEARCH EXAMPLE VII, in which the effect of the number of bystanders on helping behaviour in an emergency situation is investigated.

Research Example VII: A field experiment on the number of bystanders and helping behaviour

In a field experiment by Piliavin, Rodin and Piliavin (1969), two male and two female student assistants boarded a New York subway train before it ran non-stop for about seven minutes. After 70 seconds one of the men, both of whom were standing, staggered forward and slumped to the floor. On some occasions the man who collapsed would be a white man, whereas on other occasions it would be a black man; in some trials he smelled of liquor and carried a liquor bottle wrapped in a paper bag, whereas in others he carried a black walking stick (pretending to be ill).

The two female students sat in the section next to the area where this "emergency" occurred and, as unobtrusively as possible, made notes about the sex, race and location of the passengers and how many of them were in the area where the "emergency" took place. They also made a note of the sex, race and location of each helper and how long it took before they rendered assistance.

If the "victim" was not assisted, the other male student helped him to his feet either about 70 seconds or about 150 seconds after the former had collapsed. All students disembarked at the next station and then proceeded to the other platform to board a train in the opposite direction for the next trial.

The major findings were that an apparently ill person was more likely to be assisted than one who appeared to be intoxicated; that the race of the victim had little effect on the race of the helper except when the former appeared to be drunk (in which case help was more likely to come from someone of the same race as the victim); that the longer the "emergency situation" continued without assistance being offered, the greater the probability was that someone would leave the emergency area; and that as the size of the group of passengers increased, the speed at which assistance was given, decreased.

If the passengers were first approached and requested to participate in a project in which they would be confronted by someone in distress, it would have made no sense to continue with the project. Obtaining their permission would have destroyed the internal and external validity of the results obtained, because individuals were likely to have reacted differently had they been aware of the nature of the study.

As a matter of fact, research suggests that if subjects are fully informed about the reasons for research, even if there is no possibility of physical pain of discomfort, they lose interest and highly unreliable results are obtained.

On the other hand, it is common practice to subject students, without their knowledge, to research procedures that require no deviation from their daily routine.

Example

To expose training course members to one training method rather than another, does not imply any change from their daily routine because they would have been exposed to some or other method in any case.

The same consideration applies when the effect of encouraging comments on subsequent academic achievement is investigated by writing such comments on the test papers of some training course members but not on those of other, comparable trainees.

The only ethical objections that we might level against the above practices relate to the withholding of a potentially beneficial treatment from some participants.

Activity 7.6

Read Case Study C and Case Study F in Appendix D on page 276.

Question

Briefly discuss possible shortcomings concerning the validity and reliability of the measuring instrument used in these case studies.

Answer

CASE STUDY C

Validity: The measuring instrument must measure what it is supposed to measure, namely knowledge of management principles and not something else, in order to avoid a shortcoming with regard to construct validity. In this respect, the validity of a written test to measure the knowledge could be questioned – would it not perhaps be more valid if the managers and subordinates of the first line supervisors were asked to judge the knowledge of the course attenders in the workplace?

If the questions (items) of the measuring instrument (the three-hour long written test) were not representative of the total spectrum of management principles that were offered during the training course, there would naturally be a shortcoming regarding the content validity thereof.

Reliability: If the marks of the course attenders remained the same irrespective of when they wrote the test, whether it was shorter or longer than an hour long test (form/version differs), and who might mark it, there would not be a threat with regard to the reliability of the measuring instrument.

The above-mentioned answers are, however, speculative because the researcher mentions nothing about the validity and reliability of the measuring instrument in the case study and also not whether its characteristics were ever investigated.

CASE STUDY F

Validity: The KAI scale may not be a valid instrument for measuring innovative problem-solving styles. This may be so because it is a printed questionnaire, while a large number of problems in real life have to be solved immediately without first being printed as questions. Also, if the 32 questions of the KAI scale are not a representative sample of typical problems to be solved, the scale cannot fully measure innovative problem-solving styles. There may also be other shortcomings because it is a self-reporting instrument – the managers and entrepreneurs may fake their answers and/or obtain the help of others while completing the questionnaire.

Reliability: The instrument may not be reliable if it measures different scores on different occasions.

Self-evaluation questions

Some answers are provided in Appendix B on page 273.

7.1 Identify the level of measurement in each of the following:
- a) the score on an attitude scale
- b) military rank (for example, corporal, sergeant, captain, and so on)
- c) blood group of a person
- d) marital status of a subject.

7.2 Suppose a finger *dexterity test* consists of round circles (on an answer sheet) that testees have to encircle as quickly as possible with a pencil. The test score is the number of circles that are so encircled within a given time limit.

Briefly describe how the retest reliability of such a *dexterity* test for trainees is to be investigated.

7.3 Suppose a researcher wants to investigate the attitudes of the same group of individuals towards three constitutional models simultaneously. According to which method could the researcher's attitude scale be compiled?

7.4 Explain the differences between the Likert and semantic differential approaches by using examples of possible items to measure the attitudes of white managers towards the concept of a new South Africa.

7.5 List the possible advantages and drawbacks of the various unobtrusive measurement procedures.

7.6 Which data-collecting method was used in RESEARCH EXAMPLE VII (page 172) (see Section 7.9)?

7.7 Compare personal interviews, telephonic interviews and postal questionnaires in terms of the following:
a) cost and ease of application
b) response rate
c) quality of obtained responses.

Assume that a researcher who wishes to conduct a survey of respondents' opinions on affirmative action has to select one of these data-collecting methods.

7.8 Suppose a researcher in a postal survey attempts to maintain the impression of anonymity as well as determine from whom a completed questionnaire has been returned (for example, to study the attitudes of the same person over time). Consequently, she affixes identification numbers in invisible ink to the questionnaires. Discuss the ethical implications of this strategy.

7.9 Suppose a psychology lecturer developed a programme to modify the lifestyle of individuals with an unhealthy Type A behaviour pattern. All employees of an insurance company who obtained high scores on a Type A personality questionnaire are assigned randomly to an experimental group and a control group. The experimental group meets weekly for an hour to take part in the programme that is presented by the lecturer's graduate students. At the conclusion of the project, the members of both groups are subjected to artificial situations supposed to elicit Type A behaviour, in a room equipped with facilities to record the participants' behaviour on videotape. Subsequently, the researcher and his master's students rate the participants' behaviour in respect of the occurrence of Type A behaviour (from the videotapes) to investigate whether there is a difference (in this type of behaviour) between the two groups. Comment on the construct validity of the measure of the dependent variable.

Summary

In order to determine whether the independent variable is related to the dependent variable, or caused a change in its levels, some form of measurement must be involved. The measurements of variables involve methods and techniques to obtain appropriate data for investigating the research hypothesis and/or question(s). By means of these methods and techniques, numbers are assigned to the characteristics of the units of analysis in order to reflect differences between them in the dependent variable.

Multiple choice and true/false questions

Only *one* of the answers at each question is correct. Identify and mark the correct one. (Answers appear in Appendix E on page 285.)

7.1 There is only one way to measure a variable.
True False

7.2 A particular variable can usually be measured in several ways using different sources of information and various observation techniques.
True False

7.3 Classifying an electrical stove as working or not working treats its functioning as:
a) a nominal variable
b) an ordinal variable
c) an interval variable
d) a ratio variable.

7.4 When the variable ELECTRICAL POWER source is classified as hydro, nuclear and coal-fire station, this variable has the important quality of being:
a) mutually exclusive
b) exhaustive

c) ratio scale
d) ordinal scale.

7.5 Which of the following dependent variables is most likely to represent a ratio scale of measurement?
a) ratings of intimacy of eye contact of a prospective customer with a promotional item
b) rank ordering of amount of eye contact of a prospective customer with a promotional item
c) duration of eye contact of a prospective customer with a promotional item
d) occurrence of eye contact of a prospective customer with a promotional item.

7.6 The lowest level of measurement that applies to physical as well as psychological measurement involves:
a) ordinal scale
b) ratio scale
c) interval scale
d) nominal scale.

7.7 When the research purpose is not clear, it is advisable to choose the highest level of measurement.
True False

7.8 Validity refers to the link between the operational and conceptual definitions.
True False

7.9 Predictive validity is another term for criterion-related validity.
True False

7.10 If a measurement is reliable, it must also be valid.
True False

7.11 The degree to which nine independent observers are in agreement is referred to as:
a) cross-observer reliability
b) replicated-observer reliability
c) paired-observer reliability
d) interrater reliability.

7.12 Which of the following is not illustrative of unobtrusive observations?
a) examining the floor tiles at a museum to determine which exhibits are the most popular
b) examining the number of beer cans in the garbage collections of a company's social club to determine beer consumption patterns amongst the workers
c) examining the wear on the tires of security bakkies to determine the extent of security patrols
d) examining the communication effectiveness of workers by walking around the shop floor and making notes of their behaviour.

7.13 Unobtrusive measures reduce the impact of the data collection on the phenomena being studied.
True False

7.14 For a scale or index to be considered unidimensional, its component items should be indicators of only one dimension.
True False

7.15 In contrast to interviews, self-administered questionnaires have the advantage(s) in survey research of:
a) being more effective in dealing with complicated issues
b) producing fewer incomplete questions
c) dealing with the context of work life
d) handling sensitive issues more effectively if the surveys are anonymous.

7.16 Assume that the following would be reasonable conversational questions based on an interviewee's previous statement. Which is the weakest probe / question?
a) "In what way is that a better job?"
b) "How is that a better job?"
c) "How do you mean that's a better job?"
d) "So you say *X* is a better job than *Y*?"

7.17 In survey research the interviewer should be a neutral medium through which questions and answers are transmitted.

True False

7.18 The best way to order items in an interview is to:

a) begin with the most interesting question
b) begin with the most threatening question
c) begin with demographic questions
d) randomise the questions.

7.19 The reliability of a measuring instrument is indicated by its:

a) coherence
b) precision
c) testability
d) consistency.

8 Qualitative research design

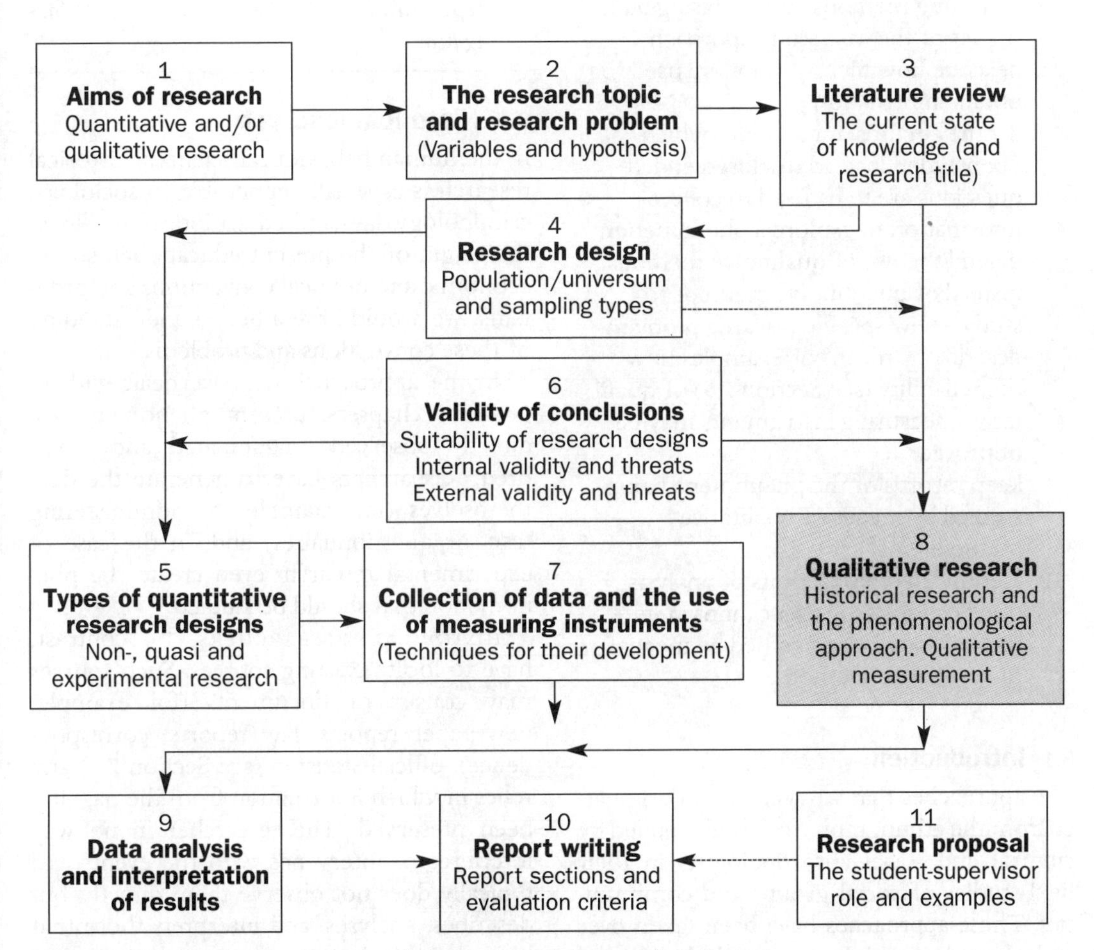

Figure 8.1 The research process and the outline of chapters in this book

Learning Outcomes

After studying this chapter, you should be able to:

1. distinguish and/or compare historical research from and/or with the unobtrusive design described in Chapter 7
2. discuss the role of historic research in the presiding judgement used in corporate law
3. explain why case study research approaches can be described as qualitative research and not as quantitative research
4. describe briefly participant observation and unstructured interviews as data-collecting methods and analysing techniques of the case study approach
5. describe how focus-groups are used to obtain information
6. list the circumstances under which open-ended instead of closed-ended questions are to be used to collect information to explore a phenomenon
7. defend the use of qualitative methods instead of quantitative methods to study a new specific research problem
8. describe by means of examples how the reliability (see Section 7.5) of qualitative measuring instruments may be improved
9. keep records of the phenomena being studied by means of qualitative methods
10. identify 20 types of units of analysis (see Section 4.2.1) that cannot in its natural state be researched by means of qualitative methods.

8.1 Introduction

The approaches that we will discuss originated from the ethnographic methods applied by cultural and social anthropologists in their field studies of social groups and communities. These approaches have been taken over and adapted by sociologists, psychologists and educationists, among others, and are often referred to as qualitative research approaches. Qualitative field studies can be used successfully in the description of groups, (small) communities and organisations. Whereas the so-called quantitative methods may be more useful in hypothesis-testing research, qualitative field studies, in turn, may lend themselves more aptly to studying cases that do not fit into particular theories.

Note

Visit the following Internet address for readings on qualitative and quantitative research: conjunctions and divergences:

http://qualitative-research.net/fqs/fqs-eng.htm

8.2 Historical research

In the human behavioural sciences, historical research is especially applicable to sociology, criminology, law and education. If we knew the origin of the present educational, social, economic and political conventions and problems, we would have a better understanding of these conventions and problems.

In the approaches we have dealt with in previous chapters, present phenomena are directly observed, manipulated and measured. Researchers have to generate the data themselves (for example, by administering tests or questionnaires) and, in the case of experimental research, even create the phenomenon that should be studied.

HISTORICAL RESEARCHERS, by contrast, have to locate existing sources. Such sources may consist of documents (for example, newspaper reports, law reports, correspondence), official statistics (see Section 7.7) and relics in which information from the past has been preserved. The researcher in no way interferes or intervenes with the events and typically does not observe them directly, but describes, analyses, and interprets those that have already taken place.

8.2.1 The principles of historical research

8.2.1.1 Primary versus secondary sources

The first basic principle of historical research is that, wherever possible, we should give preference to *primary* rather than *secondary* information sources (see Section 3.3.2). The reason for this preference is that with each transfer of information from one source to another, the information may be inadvertently or deliberately distorted.

> **Example**
>
> Zietsman (1990, p. 14) points out a literary-historical example of the dangers resulting from using secondary sources.
>
> A well-known literator used another author's English translation of a Dutch translation of an English letter of Milner's Director of Education during the Anglo-Boer War. In the original letter, the sentence reads:
>
> *Our military police has gathered the greater part of the child population into these camps ... and I feel that the opportunity during the next year of getting them all to speak English is golden.*
>
> The third-hand version reads as follows:
>
> *Our military operations have resulted in the greater part of the boys now remaining in the camps and I am convinced that we have no better opportunity than now to make them all English-speaking next year.*

If eyewitnesses to the event or practice being studied are available, we can collect their verbal evidence as primary sources. We can procure these people by means of purposive or snowball sampling (see Section 4.2.4.4) and then conduct unstructured, rather than structured, interviews with them.

8.2.1.2 Stringent criticism

Secondly, we should subject the information, irrespective of whether it is obtained by means of primary or secondary sources, to *stringent criticism*. In this connection, a distinction is made between external and internal criticism. Whereas external criticism is directed at the genuineness or authenticity of a source, internal criticism deals with the accuracy or credibility of the contents of the source. The question to be answered by external criticism, for example, is whether the supposed author of a document is really its author. Internal criticism, again, is concerned with the absence of bias in the evidence yielded by a source. It is not uncommon that under traumatic circumstances eyewitnesses tend to remember only certain aspects of an event. The eyewitness reports of people who have a vested interest in an event may also be coloured or distorted by suchinterest.

We should also check the developmental or educational level of the eyewitnesses. Documents that have passed muster as far as external criticism is concerned (that is, in terms of the authenticity of their author), may still fail the test of internal criticism (for example, if bias is suspected on the part of the author). The credibility of information may be enhanced if it can be corroborated by different, independent eyewitnesses and other sources.

According to Gottschalk (1969), internal and external criticism require researchers to be historically-minded, by which we mean that they should have an intimate knowledge of the milieu (individuals, conventions, practices, and so on) of the period in which the event being studied took place. If we are equipped with such knowledge, we may suspect inconsistencies and question the authenticity or the validity of sources.

8.2.1.3 Causal explanations

Thirdly, we must synthesise and interpret the information (so-called facts) that has stood the test of internal and external criticism, in an attempt to propose causal explanations (see Section 5.2.2). Basically, such explanations amount to interpretations of the evaluated information by means of inductive logic (see Section 2.4). Such explanations usually proceed from a particular point of view or frame of reference.

> **Example**
>
> Tyack (1976) and Rhoodie (1986) explained respectively the origin of compulsory education in the United States and revolutionary activities locally in terms of such frames of reference.
>
> It is not uncommon for studies operating from different points of view to present apparently contradictory explanations for the same historical event. Consider the contradictory explanations that people operating from different political frames of reference may put forward for the rise and demise of apartheid.

(a) Replicability

In historical research the scientific requirement of REPLICABILITY (see Section 1.2.2.3) does not refer to repeating the events or phenomena, but to the ability to duplicate the procedures, analyses and conclusions.

This means that another researcher should be able to come to a comparable conclusion after locating, evaluating, synthesising and interpreting the sources.

(b) Internal validity

In historical research, internal validity (see Section 6.3) is obtained to the extent that the available sources make it possible to rule out alternative explanations. External validity (see Section 6.4) which, in view of the uniqueness of historical events, does not enjoy a high-priority in historical research, refers to the effectiveness with which such research enables us to predict the course of events in other times and places.

(c) Sampling

Historical research is typically based on ACCIDENTAL SAMPLING (see Section 4.2.4.1) insofar as it depends on the accidental survival of documents. (The documents themselves are the products of unobtrusive measurement (see Section 7.7.2).)

As a result of accidental sampling, one of the most important drawbacks of historical research is that sufficient information to reach scientifically justified conclusions may often be lacking.

The DISADVANTAGES of historical sampling are:

- typical flaws of historical research, which include:
  - an excessive dependence on secondary information sources; and
  - succumbing to personal biases and favourite convictions. One researcher may convincingly argue the case for one explanation for a historical event, whereas someone else may equally convincingly put forward one with exactly the opposite drift.
- the inability to refute explanations of events that have taken place in the past, or even worse, the deliberate concealment of such explanations.
- the four key problems of which historical researchers should be mindful, as singled out by Kaestle (1988), namely:
  - *inferring causality* on the basis of correlational relationships
  - the *vague definition of key concepts* and the assumption that terms have had their present meanings in the past
  - the *failure to distinguish* between documented, official or professional prescriptions, on the one hand, and whether such prescriptions were indeed heeded by society, on the other hand
  - the *tendency to deduce the intentions* of historical figures from the conse-

> quences of their actions as if they could have foreseen such consequences as we can now observe them by hindsight.

8.3 The phenomenological approach

We can describe the different approaches of the positivist and the anti-positivist (see Section 1.3) proponents in terms of different themes. To illustrate these differences, we will contrast the most extreme positions of these approaches with each other. We will refer to some ways (methods) in which the PHENOMENOLOGICAL APPROACH may be applied.

8.3.1 The role of the researcher

While the POSITIVISTS claim to study a psychological or sociological reality independent of an individual's experience of it, the PHENOMENOLOGISTS question the possibility of studying such a reality with so-called objectivity.

According to the phenomenologists, what the researcher observes is not the reality as such, but an *interpreted reality*. We cannot detach ourselves from the presuppositions of our cultural inheritance, especially concerning the philosophical dualism (between the observable body and the intangible mind) and our glorification of technological achievements. As a result, the positivists and the anti-positivists interpret the researcher's role differently.

While natural scientists have nothing in common with their research objects (plants, gases, minerals, and so on), human behavioural scientists are in reality members of the group being studied. This enables direct *understanding* or, in German, *verstehen*, which implies that the researchers can understand the circumstances of the object of study because they can picture themselves in the latter's shoes – something that is naturally not possible with natural-scientific research.

While a positivist researcher *withdraws* as far as possible from the research situation to avoid being biased, the anti-positivist researcher becomes *absorbed* in the research situation. The anti-positivist approach is most clearly evident in *participant observation* (see Section 8.4.2 in which the researcher, by taking part in the activities of the group, strives to become part of the group.

8.3.2 The importance of the context of the study

Valle, King and Halling (1989, p. 7) express the unity between humans and their world as follows:

> In the truest sense, the person is viewed as having no existence apart from the world and the world as having no existence apart from persons. Each individual and his or her world are said to co-constitute one another.

Thus, a person derives his or her *true meaning* from his or her life world, and by existing he or she gives meaning to his or her world. By life world (from the German *lebenswelt*), a term which is peculiar to the phenomenologists, we mean the world as lived by a person and not some entity separate from or independent of him or her. The person is *dependent* on his or her world for his or her existence and vice versa. The philosopher Heidegger talks of "being-in-the-world". Because of the unity between the researcher and what is being researched, the phenomenologist believes that human behaviour cannot be understood without appreciating the context in which it takes place. Although the meaning of human existence is not equated with its context, it cannot be separated from it. Contrary to this, the positivists are searching for universal, context-free generalisations.

8.3.3 The aims of research

While the POSITIVISTS aim at uncovering general laws of relationships and/or causality (see Section 5.2.2) that apply to all people at all times, the PHENOMENOLOGISTS are concerned with understanding social and psychological phenomena from the perspectives of the people involved.

As a result, phenomenologists attempt *to experience* these phenomena as the people involved must have experienced them in their bones, in a manner of speaking.

Therefore, phenomenologists are not concerned with the description of phenomena, because these exist independently of the participants' experience of them, but with their experience of these phenomena.

8.3.4 Research design and methods

Whereas the POSITIVISTS require a research design to be decided on before data are collected, the ANTI-POSITIVISTS usually favour so-called EMERGENT DESIGNS.

> **Example**
>
> If a research participant (employee of an organisation) is described as being negative about the organisation's affirmative action policy, and the researcher is aware of this, the phenomenologist will attempt to understand how the participant experiences this feeling and attaches meaning to it. (See illustration below.)

This means that researchers may adapt their data-collecting procedures during the study to benefit from data of which they have only become aware during the research process itself.

Whereas phenomenological researchers aim at letting the phenomenon speak for itself, the danger exists that positivist researchers, by using interview schedules (see Section 7.7.4 & 7.8), checklists (see Section 7.7.6) for systematic observation, commercially available questionnaires (see Section 7.7.3.1), and so on, may force a possibly inappropriate structure on the phenomena being studied. (However, to some extent the possible inappropriate structure may be prevented by conducting appropriate pilot studies – See Section 7.6.)

8.4 Qualitative methods

8.4.1 Case study research

The term CASE STUDY pertains to the fact that a limited number of units of analysis (often only one) (see Section 4.2.1), such as an individual, a group or an institution, are studied

Symbolic experience of affirmative action

intensively. The term does not refer to some or other technique that is applied.

In hypothesis-testing research, we deal with the general and the regular deduction. In case studies, on the other hand, we are directed towards understanding the *uniqueness* and the *idiosyncrasy of a particular case* in all its complexity.

Example

Usually the objective of a case study is to investigate the dynamics of some single bounded system, typically of a social nature, for example, an organisation, a family, a group, a community, or participants in a project, a practice (for example, employing an accountant as personnel manager in rural financial bank branches) or an institution.

Although a case study may involve a single individual, we must distinguish it from *one-shot case studies* (see Section 6.3.2) because its purpose is not to examine the effect of some or other intervention.

Example

A female baby was incorrectly identified as a male at birth (because of an enlarged clitoris) and then raised accordingly. After being admitted to a hospital at the age of 16 because of the "passage of blood" (having periods), a medical examination revealed that the individual was a female. After minor genital surgery, "he" was re-registered as a female.

- On the one hand, if a *single individual* is studied in a case study, he or she should be highly *representative* of a particular population (see Section 4.2).
- On the other hand, such an individual should be extremely atypical of the phenomena being studied.

A case study cannot be both typical and atypical.

When we investigate a group or institution, we often conduct so-called FIELDWORK, conducting the investigation on the spot under natural circumstances of the specific case.

Example

Page (1976) investigated the reactions of the entire community of Tulbagh to the earthquake in 1969. In this study Page and his research team, equipped with notebooks and tape recorders, had to stay for some time in the area a few days after the earthquake occurred.

As far as the research procedure itself is concerned, participant observation (see Section 8.4.2) and unstructured interviews (see Section 8.4.3) are usually used to study the chosen case, but in some instances even descriptive statistics may be appropriate. An example of where *descriptive statistics may be appropriate* is a university principal's annual report (Stake, 1988) that describes the student community in terms of the numbers in the different faculties, and so on.

The unit of analysis (see Section 4.2.1) does not necessarily have to be human (for example, an individual, family, community, and so on), but may also involve *personal documents* (for example, diaries or letters) and *records* (indexes, ratios and calculation formulae).

Whereas the extent of mass media material (papers, journals, and so on) permits the application of *content analysis* (see Section 9.2), the small number of personal documents available for case studies may necessitate an analysis similar to that performed on the data obtained by means of *participant observation* (see Section 8.4.2).

Three aspects deserve special mention as far as conducting case studies is concerned.

- Firstly, the case should be *defined* or *demarcated*, in other words, its boundaries should be determined. In some instances (for example, if a single individual is involved) this decision is obvious. In other examples the researcher may, during the course of the study, find it necessary to adjust the boundaries that in any case have initially been determined arbitrarily.

> **Example**
> The study done by Page (1976) was at first supposed to be limited to only the white farmers and the coloured community in the vicinity of the Steinthal Mission. Later on it was extended to also include some of the coloured workers of the white farmers as well as residents of Newtown, a so-called coloured township.

- Secondly, whichever technique is used to collect data, the concern is not merely to describe what is being observed, but to search, in an inductive fashion, for recurring patterns and consistent regularities.

> **Example**
> Page (1976) encountered people who attributed the earthquake to a divine purpose as a recurring theme.

- Thirdly, triangulation (see Section 7.4.1) is frequently used to discern these patterns. Because the number of cases is limited, the very purpose of case studies is to intensively examine those cases that are indeed available. In view of the consideration that the researcher himself or herself is the research instrument, an attempt is usually made to corroborate findings according to at least three different approaches.

> **Example**
> Page (1976) used tape recordings of conversations, semi-structured interviews and newspaper reports to investigate the reactions of the entire community of Tulbagh to the earthquake in 1969.

8.4.2 **Participant observation**

PARTICIPANT OBSERVATION requires the researcher, for an extensive period of time, to take part in, and report on, the daily experiences of the members of a group, community or organisation, or the people involved in a process or event (or whatever is being studied).

In participant observation, we do not observe the experiences of the individuals involved as detached outsiders, but experience them first-hand as insiders. The participant observer thus becomes a member of the inner circle of the group or event that is being studied.

> **Example**
> To study the phenomenon of tramps by means of this approach would, strictly speaking, require us to live for a few days, weeks or longer with tramps and to participate in their daily activities.

As may be evident from this description, participant observation is mostly applied to study groups (for example, PAGAD, youth gangs), organisations (for example a police department, Anglo American's executive management), or communities (for example, the Jewish community in South Africa) in fields such as anthropology, sociology and criminology.

We (participant observers) have to assume the roles of the group members in order to personally:

- experience what the group members experience;
- understand their life-world;
- see things from their perspective; and
- unravel the meaning and significance that they attach to their life-world, including their own behaviour.

Instead of just discussing their activities with group members, complete participant observers strive to experience them viscerally, so to speak, as they are experiencing them. As indicated by their name, participant observers deliberately intend to distinguish themselves from detached observers.

The participant observer approaches the research situation with a minimum of preconceived ideas. Similarly, the flexibility of the participant-observation process allows room to follow up a host of clues that the researcher supposedly noticed.

8.4.2.1 **Degrees of participation**

The extent to which researchers participate in the activities of a group may vary from the situation in which the researcher, similar to systematic observation (see Section 7.2), maintains a distance from the phenomenon being studied, to that in which the researcher becomes a member of the inner circle of the group and gets fully absorbed in all group activities. However, it remains the task of the researcher to watch the activities and experiences of the group closely with a view to writing them down.

Researchers therefore have to perform a dual role: one of experiencing the activities of the group and the other of observing and recording his or her experiences. As researchers move away from the position of the detached observer and increasingly surrender themselves to the activities of the group, it may become increasingly difficult to report the events naturally. A possible dilemma between the roles of participant and observer cannot be ruled out.

The possibility that participant observers may become so engrossed in group activities that they abandon their role as observers in the process, represents a real danger in participant observation. Participant observers must decide which degree of participation may endanger their role as observer – a role that is indispensable from a research point of view.

8.4.2.2 **The process/course of participant observation**

- Once a researcher has decided to investigate some or other group, organisation or process by means of participant observation, the permission of the group members or of their representatives has to be obtained. (Such permission, of course, is unnecessary if the research is to be carried out in public venues – open spaces such as parks and beaches or closed spaces such as bars and public toilets.)
- The researcher should also disclose the objectives of his or her research to the group members. Although honesty is required in this connection, internal validity (see Section 6.3) is likely to be promoted by revealing too little rather than too much. It is especially important that the information divulged does not cause group members to react differently from their normal behaviour. On the other hand, it may harm the researcher's position of trust if group members should later discover that they had been misled.
- There should in any case be no doubt among the group members that their anonymity (that is, not disclosing their identity/name) would be ensured in future. It is usually preferable to gain access to participants by means of a mediator who has the confidence of both the participants and the researcher (see RESEARCH EXAMPLE VIII).

Research Example VIII: The experience of having fire bombs thrown at one's house

Cleaver (1988) conducted a study to gain an understanding of the experiences of individuals who had been victimised by having fire bombs thrown at their houses during the unrest situation in South Africa in 1988. With the help of an intermediary who was familiar to both the researcher and the participants, Cleaver came into contact with black adults whose houses in black townships in the former Transvaal had been burnt down in this manner.

Cleaver used unstructured interviews because she thought that, for example, a questionnaire "forces a subject into a particular mode and secondly, such a questionnaire can only be produced after the researcher has particularized the structure of the experience of the subject" (p. 77). To gain the confidence of the participants, Cleaver (being a white researcher from an Afrikaans-medium university) first talked with the participants for about an hour or longer before recording the actual interviews on audiotape. Participants were told that the information they provided would be used for the analysis of their experiences and that their identities would not be revealed. They were also told that their experiences, rather than their political beliefs, were of importance.

The actual interview commenced with the following instruction: "I would like you to tell me about the experience of having your house damaged. Tell me what happened, how it affected you and what you felt during and after the incident. Take your time. You can start wherever you like."

During the interview, Cleaver used phrases like: "Could you tell me more about that?" or "Could you explain that to me?". It was left up to the participants to determine how long the interviews would be.

According to Cleaver, the interviews provided rich descriptions of individuals' experiences of having their houses burnt down. She provides direct quotations from the way participants described their experience of the attacks before, during and after they took place. Here are a few examples:

Luke: "This happened to other people. I thought no man will ever think of committing such a crime to me."

John: "I only realised later that I could not build it up again. I just sat down and stared."

Paul: "I must go all over again for what I had. I felt I was half-way along the new road; now I am at the beginning and the road is too steep."

Next, Cleaver interpreted the participants' experiences in terms of the recommendations of previous authors. She suggests that the intentions of the victimisers were to intimidate the victims to change their socio-political views, but that they did not succeeded in achieving this. The attacks were seldom reported to the police because, among other reasons, the police were mistrusted and many blacks felt that they were not protected by the judicial system. Apart from the loss of material possessions, feelings of vulnerability and helplessness were experienced as an integral part of victimisation.

- The researcher should build up a position of trust with the group members. This is often easier said than done. Especially if the group follows practices and conventions with which the researcher is unfamiliar, he or she may unknowingly violate these practices and conventions, therby sabotaging the potential success of the study.
- As a result of the extensive periods of time that participant observers live together with the groups they study, they often develop firm friendships with the group members. On the one hand, such friendships have the advantage of allowing the participant observer to understand group members better. On the other hand, it poses the danger that the observer may get so involved with them that he or she fails to notice some developments that could have been picked up immediately by outsiders.
- The participant observer is the actual research instrument. The observer has to rely on his or her experience, expertise and intuition, and as such runs the risk of

arriving at highly idiosyncratic conclusions over which there may be no control.

- The researcher must write a report. Regardless of how comprehensive or how true to life the researcher's observations may be, the written report constitutes the final account thereof. When writing a report, the researcher should be careful not to simply summarise what is happening, because such summaries may involve premature interpretations. One should rather describe in detail who has done what to whom, and how, where and when this was done, in respect of each event. The report should include the verbal as well as non-verbal (by facial expressions, gestures, and tone of voice) expressions of group members' observations of their environment and experiences.
- These so-called observation notes should preferably be made while the group activities are taking place. This is, of course, impossible when the research is carried out in secret, or if note-taking is likely to interfere with the spontaneity of the group activities. If notes cannot be taken during the events, they should be written up as soon as possible thereafter (in secret, if necessary), so that as much as possible of the observations are preserved.
- The researcher may also consider taking along an audiotape recorder and to record his or her commentary on the activities while these are in progress. This can then be transcribed later. Naturally, such recordings will also be impossible if the research is carried out in secret, or will be undesirable if they interfere with the group activities.

As the group activities continue, the researcher makes inferences from, or interprets, what is taking place.

Note

The researcher should be on the lookout for themes or repeated patterns of behaviour that appear in the group activities, as well as for deviations from these themes or patterns. The notes of these inferences and interpretations are referred to as analytical notes, and should be made and kept separately from the observation notes.

- Finally, researchers can make methodological notes for their exclusive use. These notes serve to remind them of things to look out for during future occasions or to caution them against potential pitfalls. They may make notes of their own feelings and emotions so that they can check later whether these have affected their observations.

8.4.3 Unstructured and in-depth interviews (and focus groups)

Unstructured interviews are usually employed in explorative research (see Section 2.2) to identify important variables in a particular area; to formulate penetrating questions on them; and to generate hypotheses for further investigation. Because the area being entered is so unfamiliar, it is usually impossible to compile a schedule for interviews in such instances (see Section 7.7.4 & 7.8).

We have already dealt with the use of structured interviews (see Section 7.7.4.3). We stressed that in this kind of interview the interviewer should keep as much as possible to the previously formulated questions contained in the interview schedule to prevent different interviewers from collecting information that is not comparable. We also indicated (see Section 8.4.2) that participant observers purposefully deviate from the ideal of detached observation in order to experience the life-world of the group members in terms of the latter's perspective.

Just as observation may vary from detached observation on the one hand, to complete participation on the other hand, interviews may vary from completely structured to unstructured. To preclude questions that do not allow any room for revealing the feelings and beliefs of individuals, the latter kind of interview purposefully deviates from using an interview schedule, as used in structured interviews.

8.4.3.1 **Nature**

Unlike in structured interviews (see Section 7.7.4.3), in unstructured interviews the interviewer simply suggests the general theme of discussion and poses further questions as these come up in the *spontaneous development* of the interaction between interviewer and research participant.

> **Example**
>
> The theme of the unstructured interviews that Cleaver (1988) used in RESEARCH EXAMPLE VIII (page 185) (see Section 8.4.2.2) to better understand the experience of the owners of houses that have been burnt down (during political violence), was intimidation.

Not only do unstructured interviews differ from structured interviews in that they are not bound to a previously compiled list of questions, the interviewer also departs from his or her role as a detached interviewer and *interacts with the individual* with whom the interview is conducted.

In unstructured interviews an attempt is made to understand how individuals *experience their life-world* and how they make sense of what is happening to them. The interviewer's question should thus be directed at the participant's experiences, feelings, beliefs and convictions about the theme in question. Interviewers should be extremely careful not to suggest certain responses in the way in which they phrase their questions such as, for example, by asking *leading questions* (see Section 7.8). Compare the instructions that were given in RESEARCH EXAMPLE VIII (see Section 8.4.2.2) to the research participants.

In an unstructured interview, the interviewer focuses on the participants' FIRST-HAND EXPERIENCE of their life-world rather than on their interpretation or speculative explanations of it. Previously compiled questions, for example, such as those that suggest a particular theoretical point of view, should be restricted to a minimum if not avoided altogether. However, the interviewer is supposed to remain in control of the interview situation by, for example, encouraging the individual to continue undaunted if he or she is getting bogged down and to kindly yet firmly revert to the theme if he or she is straying from it.

Furthermore, questions about sensitive and highly emotional issues may be asked in *in-depth interviews* that cannot be done in telephonic interviews (see Section 7.7.4) and postal surveys (see Section 7.7.3.1), for example. (As a matter of fact, the term in-depth telephone interview and in-depth postal interview are self-contradictory terms.)

8.4.3.2 **Process/course of the interview(s)**

At the beginning, the interviewer explains the purpose of the study to the prospective participants and seeks their co-operation. Among other things, the researcher should give an indication of how long the interview or series of interviews is expected to take. As in participant observation, frankness and honesty are required from the interviewer to build up a position of trust with the prospective participants.

The prospective participants should not get the idea that they are among several who are going to be subjected to questioning, but rather that the interviewer is interested in them as individuals and respects their uniqueness.

Not only should the participants be assured of complete anonymity, but they should also feel completely free to express their true feelings and opinions without fear of disapproval (or condemnation) from the interviewer.

The interviewer should neither approve nor disapprove of the participants' actions, but be understanding. Even if a participant were to act (verbally) aggressively towards the interviewer or display signs of resistance, the interviewer should show understanding (instead of becoming aggressive or showing resistance, too).

Although this emphatic living through of experiences by the interviewer corresponds with the aim of the typical therapeutic interview, the purpose at present is to facilitate the revelation of information and not to provide therapy. Only when there is a relationship of mutual confidence and respect between the two parties, are the chances good that the participant will feel free to reveal his or her innermost feelings and beliefs to the interviewer. This is especially true when these feelings and beliefs are in conflict with the generally accepted norms of a community. Questions dealing with contentious issues should therefore be withheld until the middle or latter phases of the interview or series of interviews.

8.4.3.3 **Sampling**

The researcher usually obtains individuals with whom to conduct unstructured interviews by means of purposive or snowball sampling (see Section 4.2.4.4). Often, preference is given to key informants who, on account of their position or experience, have more information than regular group members and/or are better able to articulate this information.

Example

The leaders of gangs in prisons may be used as key informants when such gangs are studied by means of unstructured interviews.

Note

In the above-mentioned example, we may speak of focus groups where more than one individual is interviewed at a time. By doing so, the interviewees stimulate each other and share their ideas and thoughts. These focus groups are compiled by means of purposive or snowball sampling (See Section 4.2.4.2).

The phases in conducting focus groups are as follows:

- The researcher introduces the topic to the group.
- The researcher sets rules, for example that only one person should speak at a time.
- Each participant (in turn) makes an opening statement regarding their experience of the topic.
- The researcher guides the open group discussion by asking questions such as "Most people here mentioned Z, but how does that fit in with *A*?".
- The session ends with each person (in turn) giving a final statement that may not be challenged.

The data obtained from focus groups may be analysed by means of systematic coding through content analysis (see Section 9.2). Focus groups, in conjunction with participant observation (see Section 8.4.2), can be used as preliminary research, or follow-up research, or for the purpose of triangulation (see Section 7.4.1) and verifying data.

8.4.3.4 **Analysis**

Just as in the case of participant observation, the eventual analysis of the information obtained from unstructured interviews (and focus groups) is based on the *interviewer's records*. The interviewer may take notes of the participants' responses with a view to writing a more complete report afterwards. As an alternative, a *tape recording* may be made with a view to *transcribing* it later. In both cases the interviewer should still take notes of the participant's presumed non-verbal communication. Neither taking notes, nor recording on tape should, however, inhibit the participant's spontaneous behaviour.

8.4.3.5 **Reporting**

The interviewer should compile the complete report as soon as possible after the conclusion of the interview(s). At the same time, the interviewer should jot down reflective notes similar to the analytical and methodological notes in participant observation, with a view to using them in further interviews or in analysing the information obtained. On the basis of the descriptions of the individuals' experiences, the researcher must attempt to capture accurately the essence of the contents and of the recurring themes that bind them together.

8.4.4 **Participatory research**

Participatory research concerns the integration of elements such as the following:

- social investigation
- educational work
- action in an interrelated process.

We will therefore see that *action research* (see Section 8.4.4.1) is a form of participatory research in which action and research complement each other.

We can distinguish between participatory research and other conventional types of research on the basis of the *roles of the researcher* and *participants* as follows:

- The participants are *actively involved* in the planning and implementation of the research outcomes and are thus empowered.
- In bringing about social change, the researcher is *dependent on the participation* of the effected community members, state functionaries and political parties.

We mainly use in-depth interviews (see Section 8.4.3) and focus groups to collect data in participatory research.

8.4.4.1 **Action research**

Action research is *not a singular approach* and different people who profess to use this research may emphasise different aspects of it. The following concise summary captures the greatest common factor of these aspects.

(a) Versatile design

A distinguishing feature of action research is that it uses a versatile design that may continually be *changed* and *adapted* in reaction to information and results obtained during the research project.

In action research we do not finalise the research design in advance and consistently follow it up to the end of the research project – it evolves as the project progresses. A cyclical progression through phases of tentative planning, acting, observation, reflection on and evaluation of the preliminary results, may be distinguished. The evaluation of the preliminary results in turn provides feedback for the first phase of a following cycle.

In a certain sense, the empirical cycle of Figure 2.2 (see Section 2.2) is repeatedly executed in an informal manner in action research.

(b) Participant involvement

Action research places a high premium on *involving all participants* in each of the phases (tentative planning, acting, observation, reflection on and evaluation of the preliminary results).

Example

In an organisational training context, the trainers and course members will not be regarded as subjects who are going to be subjected to some treatment devised by an outsider. All interested parties, among others the administrators, employers, stakeholders, trainers and course members, will be jointly involved in the project.

This emphasis on the participation and the perspectives of the interested parties ties in with the qualitative researcher's preference for participant observation (see Section 8.4.2), for example. Insofar as these groups accept responsibility for the execution of the research and the implementation of its results, action research may be *characterised as democratic*.

The contribution of action research to social change is therefore met with approval in certain sociopolitical circles. In its purest form, action research is undertaken from *within an organisation*, for example, by the employees of an organisation, instead of by someone approaching from the outside and retaining the role of an outsider. It "allow(s) participants to influence, if not determine, the conditions of their own lives and work, and collaboratively to develop critiques of social conditions which sustain dependence, inequality, or exploitation in any research enterprise in particular, or in social life in general" (Kemmis, 1985, p. 36).

(c) External validity

Finally, we can conclude that *external validity* (see Section 6.4) *does not enjoy a high priority* in action research.

The programme of action that is developed and found successful by action research in one specific situation, is not necessarily held up as a solution for any other similar situation.

> **Example**
>
> A programme that was developed through action research to provide school training in *Soweto* for black youths who had become alienated from the prevailing educational system, need not necessarily be equally successful for similar black youths in the *Cape Peninsula*.

Activity 8.1

Read Case Study F in Appendix D on page 276.

Question

What type of *research design and measuring instruments*, other than the KAI scale, could the researchers possibly have used for the aim of this investigation? Explain your answer briefly.

Answer

The researchers could also have used a *qualitative design* instead of a quantitative design by making use of the following types of research and measuring techniques: In *historical research* the business documents and financial statements of businesses that are run by managers and entrepreneurs can be analysed. By comparing these indicators, the researchers could conclude the extent to which entrepreneurs are able to solve their problems more innovatively than managers (or vice versa).

The researchers could also make use of the *case study* method and *participant observation*, thereby studying the innovative problem-solving styles of two or more typical managers and entrepreneurs in the course of their day-to-day business activities. By conducting *in-depth interviews* and *focus groups*, the researchers could determine the styles of the business people.

Summary

Qualitative research is not concerned with the methods and techniques to obtain appropriate data for investigating the research hypothesis, as in the case of quantitative research. Qualitative data are based on meanings expressed through words and other symbols or metaphors. Qualitative studies can be used successfully in the description of groups, (small) communities and organisations by studying cases that do not fit into particular theories.

Multiple choice and true/false questions

Only *one* of the answers to each question is correct. Identify and mark the correct one. (Answers appear in Appendix E on page 285.)

8.1 There is only one way to measure a variable.
True False

8.2 The use of several different research methods to test the same finding is called triangulation.
True False

8.3 A particular variable can usually be measured in several ways, using different sources of information and various observation techniques.
True False

8.4 Eight focus groups were audiotaped to examine citizens' attitudes toward the building of an electric power station in their region. The advantage of using this approach to focus groups is:
a) interviewers need little skill
b) interviewers can easily control the focus group's discussion
c) the tapes are easily analysed
d) high face validity.

8.5 Assume that the following would be reasonable conversational questions based on an interviewee's previous statement. Which is the weakest probe/question?
a) "In what way is that a better job?"
b) "How is that a better job?"
c) "How do you mean that's a better job?"
d) "So you say *X* is a better job than *Y*?"

8.6 An advantage of field research is that:
a) it enables the researcher to draw conclusions about the population
b) the researcher can control the variables being studied
c) the phenomenon can be studied in a natural setting
d) hypotheses can be rigorously tested.

8.7 In field research the unstructured interview is used to:
a) minimise interviewer bias
b) gain in-depth understanding of respondents' views
c) obtain responses to close-ended questions
d) control factors that may affect the respondents' answers.

8.8 The basic tool of field research is:
a) a notebook and pencil
b) a tape recorder
c) a camera
d) a telephone.

8.9 Field research differs from other forms of observation in that it is both a data collecting and a theory-generating activity.
True False

Self-evaluation question

Conduct interviews with the individuals sampled according to your answer to the last self-evaluation question at the end of Chapter 4 about their opinion on your chosen topic. Record your questions and interviewees' answers on paper because you will have to analyse it later (see Chapter 9).

9 Data analysis and interpretation of results

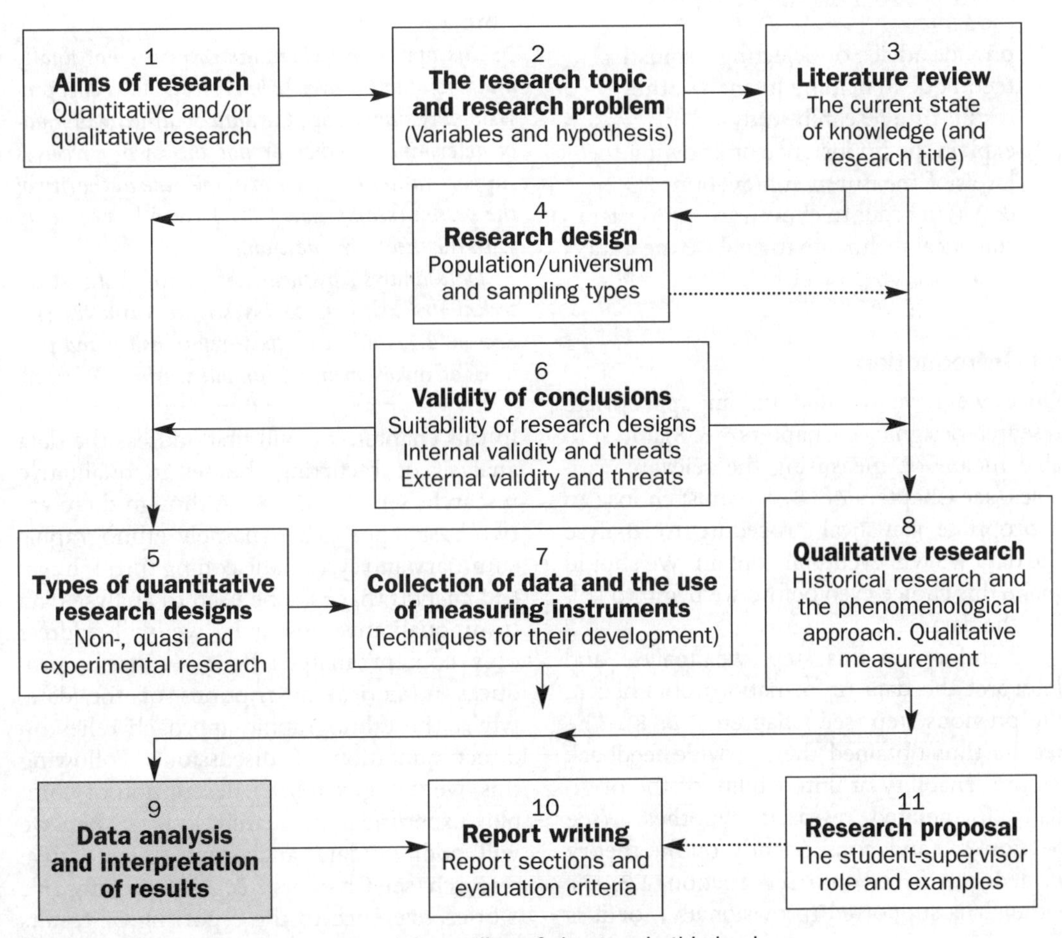

Figure 9.1 The research process and the outline of chapters in this book

Learning Outcomes

After studying this chapter, you should be able to:

1. describe how sampling influences the internal validity of a content analysis
2. describe the coding process and how it may be used to quantify information obtained by means of qualitative methods
3. explain the difference between descriptive and inferential statistics
4. list some of the assumptions underlying inferential statistics
5. group a collection of scores in tables and give a graphic representation of the scores
6. provide advice on selecting a statistical technique in helping to analyse the results of a research study
7. explain the importance of knowing the levels of measurement (Sections 7.3.2 & 9.4) in order to choose an appropriate statistical technique to analyse the data of a research project.

9.1 Introduction

Once we have decided on an appropriate research design (see Chapters 5 & 8) and suitable means of measuring the relevant variables (see Chapters 7 & 8), we must choose an appropriate statistical procedure to analyse the data we will eventually obtain. We should make this choice even before we begin to collect the data.

Therefore, in this step, we analyse and interpret the data (information) obtained in the previous step (see Chapters 7 & 8). The results thus obtained then provide feedback on the tenability or untenability of the originally formulated research hypothesis (see Section 2.3) and, consequently, on the theory if deduced from one (see Section 2.2.1.3): either it is supported (provisionally), or it is refuted.

If the results we obtained are in agreement with the hypothesis, we have not proven finally and irrefutably that the theory is correct, but it is only provisionally supported insofar as there is no other known theory that may explain the results obtained.

Example

Because the research in RESEARCH EXAMPLE II (page 14, see Section 2.2) supported the specific implication being investigated, it withstood an attempt to falsify (see Section 2.4) the learning theory, and as a result our confidence in this theory was strengthened.

Note

In this approach (where the theory is not finally and irrefutably proven to be correct, but is only provisionally supported), the data obtained will finally determine whether or not the theory receives support rather than, for example, the authority of the person (see Section 1.2.1.1) who has come up with the theory in question.

Data analysis by means of (mainly) statistical techniques helps us to investigate variables (see Section 2.2) and their effect, relationship and patterns of involvement within our world.

In this chapter, we will first address the data analysis of recurring themes in qualitative research (see Chapter 8). Although there are two basic approaches, namely ethnographic summary and systematic coding through *content analysis* that may be used to analyse data from qualitative research, we will address only content analysis here because it produces numerical descriptions of the data, whilst the ethnographic approach relies on direct quotation of discussions. Following this, we will give a brief description of complex experimental research designs; then we will address data analysis of quantitative research (see Chapters 5 & 7), and finally give a brief reference to the reporting of results (see Section 9.5).

9.2 Content analysis

A special application of systematic observation occurs in the content analysis of personal documents and mass media material (see Section 7.7.2.2). This may also be done with open-ended questions and the contents of unstructured interviews (see Section 8.4.3), and in order to report in a quantitative way in addition to making qualitative analysis of the essence of the contents of such an interview. This involves the contents of these sources being examined systematically to record the relative incidence (frequencies) of themes and of the ways in which these themes are portrayed.

In RESEARCH EXAMPLE IX below, we describe how Saling, Abrams and Chester (1983) performed a content analysis in South Africa of the photographic depiction of women cradling babies to determine whether there was any preference in terms of the side of the body (left or right) on which the babies were held.

Research Example IX: A content analysis of photos in respect of the lateral preference in cradling babies

Saling, Abrams and Chester (1983) performed a content analysis of magazine photos of black and white women who were cradling babies to investigate the lateral cradling preference of women in this behaviour.

An unspecified number of (unidentified) black- and white-oriented magazines published between 1977 and 1982 were scanned for photos of women who were holding babies on one side of the body (in the arm, over the shoulder or on the hip).

They classified the 196 photos thus obtained in terms of the race of the woman and the laterality of the position (left or right) in which she held the baby.

For each group the chi-square test (see Section 9.4.2.1) was statistically significant at the 1% level, which suggests a preference for the left side among both racial groups.

According to the authors, this finding was in agreement with previous observational studies and supported a biogenetic model of lateral preference in cradling babies.

9.2.1 Steps in performing a content analysis

The steps in performing a content analysis correspond to those of direct, systematic observation of behaviour (see Sections 7.2 & 7.7.6).

- Firstly, we should clearly define the phenomenon to be analysed. In RESEARCH EXAMPLE IX, this phenomenon was the lateral cradling preference of women. Of course, this decision is closely connected to the hypothesis or problem that is to be investigated.
- Secondly, we should define the universe of appropriate media/interviewees and choose the sampling methods (see Section 4.1) in terms of which the editions of the chosen media should be sampled. As in all research, the emphasis should be on the typical or the representative rather than on that which is likely to confirm the researcher's biases.

Example

Suppose we want to compare the editorials of pro-government and pro-opposition newspapers during the eighties in respect of the democratic values they emphasised. For practical reasons, it may be impossible to include the entire universe of editorials of all government and opposition newspapers that appeared during that period.

Consequently, we have to decide on which papers we should select – something that is easier said than done, because a daily provincial paper obviously would have a greater influence than a weekly regional paper.

Concerning the above example, after we have made a selection of the newspapers, we have to decide whether to select all editorials over a couple of months or at different times of the year over a few years.

Example

In RESEARCH EXAMPLE IX, an unknown number of editions of (unidentified) magazines published between 1977 and 1982 were systematically paged through in search of photos of women cradling babies.

- Thirdly, we should give a description of the way in which the units of analysis (see Section 4.1.1; photos in RESEARCH EXAMPLE IX) should be coded. This CODING PROCESS may require that the number of times (frequencies) that visible content (words or sentences in the notes or transcribed tape recording of the interview or open-ended question answers) considered as indicative of some construct (measuring theory – see Sections 2.3.2 & 7.3) occurs, be recorded.

On other occasions, the latent meaning or intention reflected in units of analysis (for example, newspapers) or the responses of individuals should be coded.

Example

The coder must infer whether a particular television commercial uses sex, humour, utility value, and so on to catch the viewer's attention.

The use of visible content may result in a high intercoder reliability (estimation of reliability – see Section 7.5.1.4), but construct validity (see Section 7.4.1) may suffer because such content may not be the only indicator that has a bearing on the construct.

Example

The democratic flavour of newspaper editorials may not be gauged properly by the number of times words such as "democracy", "general franchise", and so on are used.

Note

According to Viney (1983), there are sufficiently valid and reliable coding systems available for a variety of psychological conditions (such as anxiety and hostility).

- Fourthly, we must train the coders (raters) properly. This is especially important if ratings are required not only at a nominal (levels of measurement – see Section 7.3.2) but also at an ordinal level (for example, if the degree of preference or disapproval of what is depicted should also be rated – something looks extremely, to some extent, or not at all, acceptable). The objective of such training is to ensure high interrater reliability (estimation of reliability see Sections 7.5.1 & 7.5.1.4), a property that naturally has to be examined.

Typically, the statistical analysis of the data obtained consists of determining the frequencies or percentages of occurrence of the chosen content (for example, the word "democracy" in the above example may have occurred 300 times, or the there may have been an 87% occurrence of black women holding babies on their left side in RESEARCH EXAMPLE IX). The frequencies may be illustrated in a figure (such as a bar diagram or histogram – see Section 9.4.1.1).

Note

The phenomena of judicial behaviour and similar applications in the political and administrative sciences can be studied by means of the so-called Q-METHODOLOGY *and* Q-TECHNIQUE, *which rely on the factor analysis technique to help interpret individuals' self-concepts (Brown, 1980).*

Weitzman and Miles (1995) describe computer programs *that can be used* in qualitative research. *For computer-aided qualitative data analysis the software* ATLASTI *and* NUD-1ST *can be used. Zelger (1991) describes GABEK (Ganzheitliche Bewaltigung Sprachlich Erfasster Komplexität), a compter-aided methodology that can be used for the analysis of unstructured textual qualitative data analysis from open-ended instructions. Manual qualitative data analysis can be done with the help of N-Vivo, a tool for qualitative research data analysis.*

9.3 Statistical validity and techniques

A satisfactory research design (see Chapters 4, 5 & 8) also suggests the methods in terms of which we should eventually statistically analyse the data we obtain.

Note

If we postpone the decision on which statistical analysis method(s) to use until after the data have been collected, we may discover, much to our displeasure, that either there is no appropriate statistical method available for analysing the data, or that another method would have been more appropriate if the data had been collected in terms of another design.

9.3.1 Statistical validity

If we indeed find a relationship between the variables appearing in a research hypothesis (see Section 2.3), we expect our research hypothesis and our statistical methods to bring this relationship to light, in other words, we wish to make statistically valid conclusions.

If we want to investigate a research hypothesis by means of inferential-statistical methods, we must first transform it into a statistical hypothesis. Such a statistical hypothesis consists of two complementary statements, known as:

- a null hypothesis; and
- a complementary, alternative hypothesis (Hays, 1988; Huysamen, 1988).

Typically, the alternative hypothesis reflects the research hypothesis, so that the null hypothesis plays the role of devil's advocate.

Consequently, the research hypothesis will be supported by the rejection of the null hypothesis. In this manner the falsification principle (see Section 2.4) is implemented by statistical hypothesis testing (an implication inferred from a theory and represented by a research hypothesis being strengthened by falsifying a counter-hypothesis cast in the form of a null hypothesis).

In experimental research (see Section 5.2) the null hypothesis usually implies that there is no difference between the levels of an independent variable.

Example

From Case Study D (see Appendix D on page 276 we may recall that the research hypothesis (see Section 2.3) (which we can call the alternative hypothesis) was:

There is a significantly high positive relation/correlation between the speech quality and the total preparation time of a group of speech-making technikon students.

The null hypothesis in this case would be:

There is no relation/correlation between the speech quality and the total preparation time of a group of speech-making technikon students.

For Case Study E the research/alternative hypothesis was:

Bankrupt small businesses have exceeded their bank overdraft limits with significantly greater amounts per month and experienced cash flow problems to a greater extent than non-bankrupt small businesses during the past two years.

The null hypothesis would be:

There will be no differences concerning the amount of exceeded bank overdraft limits per month and the extent of cash flow problems experienced by bankrupt and non-bankrupt small businesses during the past two years.

Usually, the research hypothesis and the implication of the theory from which it is deduced are reflected by the alternative hypothesis. As a result, such an implication is thus partially supported or strengthened by the rejection of the null hypothesis.

To test such a null hypothesis, a *t*- or *F*-test statistic (see Section 9.4.2) is often used. This is basically made up of the following ratio:

$$\frac{\text{Between-group variation (numerator)}}{\text{Within-group variation (denominator)}}$$

The numerator (between-group variation) of this ratio reflects variance (in the dependent variable), which is due to the independent variable in question. The denominator (within-group variation) represents so-called error variance, which is caused by other variables.

Part of the denominator (within-group variation) source of variation is systematic in the sense that it affects the scores of all subjects in a predictable manner.

Example

If the dependent variable is *academic achievement* (as measured by way of a paper-and-pencil examination), intelligence would act as a systematic source of variation because the more intelligent managers always tend to obtain higher academic achievement scores than those who are less intelligent.

Unsystematic sources of variation, by contrast, affect individuals' scores in an entirely accidental and unpredictable manner.

Example

The pencil points of some managers may break purely by chance so that their academic performance is affected. In the long run such events should affect all individuals' scores (irrespective of the level of the independent variable to which they belong – more or less intelligent) to the same extent.

Measurement error is one of the sources of within-group variation (denominator). To the extent that the dependent variable (academic achievement) is unreliably measured (pencil points break), some portion of individuals' scores on the dependent variable will consist of measurement error.

The measurement error will increase the denominator (within-group variation) of the test statistic (a *t*- or *F*-test statistic – see Section 9.4.2), which, in turn, will decrease the value of the test statistic itself. The smaller the value of the test statistic, the smaller the probability that it will exceed the critical value signifying a *statistically significant* result (Huysamen, 1984).

Note

It is possible that two variables (such as academic achievement and intelligence) are indeed correlated in a particular population (such as managers) but that the denominator (within-group variation – within the less and more intelligent group of managers) of the test statistic is increased and thus the value of the test statistic (a t- or F-test statistic – see Section 9.4.2) (reflected by the ratio) is decreased to such an extent on account of unreliable measurement (of these variables – for example, the pencil points broke) that statistical significance is not achieved.

The higher the ratio (in other words, between-group variation is greater than within-group variation), the greater the power of the statistical test, that is, the probability that the null hypothesis will be rejected.

Example

The academic achievement (scores in the examination) of the different intelligence groups of managers (those who are less or more intelligent) will not be the same. Therefore the null hypothesis will be rejected and the alternative hypothesis will be accepted.

As in the case of any ratio, this ratio will be increased by (compare Section 6.3.8):

- anything which increases the numerator (between-group variance); and
- anything which decreases the denominator (within-group variance).

To the extent that the two groups of managers (low and highly intelligent) differ increasingly in respect of the dependent variable (academic achievement), the between-group variance increases in relation to the within-group variance. Thus the ratio itself increases so that the probability to reject the null hypotheses increases.

Usually the objective is to optimally increase the between-group variance so that the resulting ratio will lead to the rejection of the null hypothesis. By the same token, the within-group variance should preferably be reduced maximally because such a reduction leads to a maximal increase in the ratio.

9.3.2 The sensitivity of a research design

The sensitivity of a design (see Chapters 5 & 8) refers to the degree to which it reduces the within-group variance, thereby optimally increasing the ratio between the numerator (between-group variance) and the denominator (within-group variance), and consequently also the probability that the null hypothesis will be rejected (which is the researcher's aim).

In some research designs that are not too sensitive, as in the case of most non-experimental designs, the conclusions reached to reject the null hypothesis may obviously be invalid (the example of the correlation between the number of churches in cities and towns and the incidence of crime – see Section 5.2.2.1), whereas in others it may be less so.

9.3.2.1 Eliminating rival hypotheses

However, there are statistical procedures by means of which we can eliminate rival hypotheses (see Section 2.3) concerning third variables (see Section 6.3.2.3), under certain conditions, and we can thus enhance the internal validity (see Section 6.3) of conclusions in non-experimental research. One such statistical technique is partial correlation (see Section 9.4.2.3), by means of which we can determine the correlation between two variables by holding the effect of a third variable constant.

Note

Multiple regression, path analysis and structural equation modelling (Pedhazur, 1982) are additional methods which we can use in this connection.

The situations which may be investigated by means of these methods are much more complicated than the one depicted in Figure 1.2 on page 3.

9.3.2.2 **Eliminating the variance**

One method to eliminate the variance (in the dependent variable which is attributable to nuisance variables) is matching (see Section 6.3.7). In this manner the denominator (within-group variance) of the test statistic (a *t*- or *F*-test statistic – see Section 9.4.2) is reduced and a more sensitive design and a more powerful statistical test are thus obtained.

However, if there is not a considerable correlation (of at least 0,50 in absolute value – see Figure 9.6) between the nuisance variable (see Section 5.2.1.3) and the dependent variable (see Section 2.2), the matched-groups design provides a less powerful statistical test than a regular randomised groups design (see Section 5.2.1.2) with the same number of participants.

In other words, if all other factors remain the same, we need more subjects in the matched design than in the independent-groups design to obtain statistical significance. Thus, unless there is a rather high correlation between the nuisance variable and the dependent variable, it may not pay to match individuals in terms of the nuisance variable.

9.3.2.3 **Complex experimental research designs**

There are two reasons why we may consider including two or more independent variables in the same design.

- Firstly, we may wish to study the effects of more than one such variable simultaneously. In other words, our research hypotheses may dictate that a more complex design than a single-factor design be used (as addressed in the preceding chapters).

In the more complex designs, usually one of the independent variables is a treatment factor and the other one may either be a treatment factor or a classification factor (third variable problem – see Section 5.2.2). A classification factor may be included as another independent variable, either because we are interested in investigating its effect in its own right, or because we are aware that it is a nuisance variable and we want to eliminate its effect.

- The second reason why more complicated designs are often used, is to increase the sensitivity of our research designs. In the preceding paragraphs it was explained that some test statistics are made up of a ratio that increases in value if its denominator, which is based on the within-group variance, decreases.

By building a nuisance variable into a design as an additional variable, we eliminate that portion of the within-group variance which is due to this variable. As a result, the test statistic increases in value and there is a greater chance of obtaining a statistically significant result.

Note

This approach represents the fourth manner in which NUISANCE VARIABLES *may be controlled. (The other three were mentioned in Section 5.2.1.3).*

The following are examples of complex experimental research designs:

- the completely-crossed two-factor design (Solomon four-group design);
- the nested design;
- the randomised-block design (see Section 5.2.1.2);
- the repeated measures design (between-subjects design or intergroup design, within-subjects design or intragroup design, split-plot design); and
- the multi-factor design.

9.4 **Statistical techniques (and coding)**

Once we have collected data, we have to make sense of it. In order to do this, we must organise and CODE it so that we can analyse it (of course this does not apply to data obtained from psychological tests – see Section 7.7.3.2).

CODING means that we have to identify the variable that we want to analyse statistically and decide on the different code values such a variable level presents (see Table 9.1).

Example

If we interview 100 registered voters concerning their opinions on the re-introduction of the death penalty, we would at least be interested to know if there are differences between males and females and between different age groups regarding the issue. There may also be differences in this regard concerning their residential area. We could therefore use the codes in Table 9.1 to indicate the different values of certain variables.

Note that the variable *age* will need three spaces in the computer file because if someone is 102 years old, it would occupy three digits. If a respondent's age is nine years, then we will have to code it as 009.

Table 9.1
Coding the values of different variables

Width of computer column (in memory)	Variable	Code name	Code values	Levels
one space	Sex	Sex	1 2	Male Female
three spaces	Age	Age	?	18 yrs. to eldest voter
one space	Residential area	Rera	1 2 3	Rural Urban Metropolitan

Once we have coded all the data, it can be read into a computer and the analysis proceeds. We must now do one or more of the following:

- count, for example, the number of employees that "strongly disagree" on a 7-point questionnaire item concerning the right of management to make unilateral decisions;
- describe, for example, the inner experience of prisoners who were assaulted by gang members inside prison;
- compare, for example, the responses of taxpayers in different income-groups to the government's new proposed taxation system;
- categorise, for example, identified patterns of themes through the use of statistics (such as the preference averages towards different residential areas).

We also have to determine the *level of measurement* (see Section 7.2.3) pertaining to our study. This is necessary in order to determine the statistics available for different types of data and to select an appropriate statistical test (Huysamen, 1981; 1984). (See the following NOTE boxes.)

- The distinction between discrete and continuous variables refers to the nature of the numerical values that these variables can assume potentially. A DISCRETE VARIABLE may be defined as a variable that can potentially assume only certain values. For the purposes of the topics discussed in this book it would be sufficient to know that a variable that can assume only whole-number values is an example of a discrete variable. The number of books in a library is an example of a discrete variable because it does not make sense to talk about, say, 743,92 books. The number of books in a library can assume only certain numerical values – more precisely, integer values and not fractions.

A CONTINUOUS VARIABLE may be defined as a variable that can potentially assume any value, including fractional values, within a certain range. This means that a continuous variable can theoretically assume an infinite number of different values between any two points. An example of a continuous variable is height, because even between 181,54 cm and 181,55 cm an unlimited number of fractional values is possible. The nearest fraction of a centimetre to which length can be measured is limited only by the capacity of the measuring equipment used and not by the nature of the variable itself.

It should be noted that although some of the variables dealt with in social and behavioural research are continuous, the values obtained by measuring them are invariably discrete. For example, although IQ may be regarded conceptually as a continuous variable, IQ test scores can usually assume whole numbers only and thus constitute a discrete variable. Even for a variable such as time, which conceptually is a continuous variable, the measurements obtained are in practice discrete. Regardless of these practical restrictions in obtaining continuous measurements, the concept of a continuous variable is useful, as will become clearer later. Usually, variables that conceptually qualify as continuous are treated as such even though their measurement yields scores that are not strictly continuous.

- NOMINAL MEASUREMENT

In nominal measurement, people are classified into a set of mutually exclusive categories so that:

i) all of those in a particular category are alike (or nearly alike) with respect to the attribute being measured, and
ii) those in different categories are different with respect to that attribute.

For example, if people are classified with respect to the attribute sex, then all of those classified as male are alike with respect to their sex. The same applies to people classified in the female category. People fall into different categories and are then different with respect to the sex variable. These two categories are said to be *mutually exclusive* and *exhaustive* because it is assumed that no person can be classified as both male and female and that all people can be classified into one of these categories.

For identification purposes, different numbers may be assigned to people in such different categories. For example, the numbers *1* and *2* may be assigned to the people in the categories *male* and *female*, respectively. The one and only purpose of such numbers is to serve as *names* or *labels* to distinguish between different categories of the variable. Consequently, the particular numbers assigned are arbitrary as only the property of the distinguishability of numbers is used. The properties of rank order, equal units and absolute magnitude are immaterial in nominal measurement. For example, if the numbers *1* and *2* are assigned to males and females, respectively, a score of *1* in no way implies a higher rank than a score of *2*. It would also be meaningless to perform any numerical calculation (addition, subtraction, multiplication, or division) on these numbers. Adding 1 and 1, for example, gives 2 but it does not make sense to translate this result in terms of the measurement procedure by concluding that a male plus a male equals female.

Other examples of nominal measurement are the classification of sources of division profits such as trading, manufacturing, assembly, and so on, and the classification of the electorate in terms of the various political parties that they support.

Note

Legitimate statistics available for NOMINAL *data types are (compare the CD-ROM):*

- *The* MODE *(the score achieved by the greatest number of units of analysis)*
- FREQUENCIES *(bar diagram or pie chart) (check if the distribution is even across categories)*
- CORRELATION COEFFICIENTS *(a statistic to measure the degree of association between two variables)*

  If both variables are nominal (as in the case of a dichotomy such as sex [male/female] and cell phone ownership [own a cell phone/do not own a cell phone]), use the PHI COEFFICIENT. *If one variable is nominal and the other ordinal/interval/ratio, use the* POINT-BISERIAL CORRELATION
- CHI-SQUARES (χ^2) *(check if the difference between statistically expected and actual scores are caused by chance/accident or are they statistically significant – not caused by chance)*

  If one group is involved use the CHI-SQUARE OF INDEPENDENCE. *If two groups are involved and they are dependent on each other (related in terms of matching by the researcher [see Section 6.3.7] or because of an already existing relationship or because of measuring the same group twice, use the* CHI-SQUARE OF MCNEMAR. *If two independent groups are involved (if they are not related as mentioned) use the* CHI-SQUARE OF HOMOGENEITY
- CHAID-ANALYSIS AND CORRESPONDENCE ANALYSIS *(to determine in terms of which predictor variables criterion groups differed in the past – see Section 5.4.4.1)*

- **ORDINAL MEASUREMENT**

  Ordinal measurement takes place when people are classified into a sequence of ordered categories such that:
  (i) all of those falling in a particular category are alike (or nearly alike) with respect to the attribute being measured, and
  (ii) the cases in successive categories possess progressively more (or less) of that attribute.

Numbers may now be assigned to these categories so that the categories possessing progressively more of the attribute receive increasingly higher numbers. These numbers

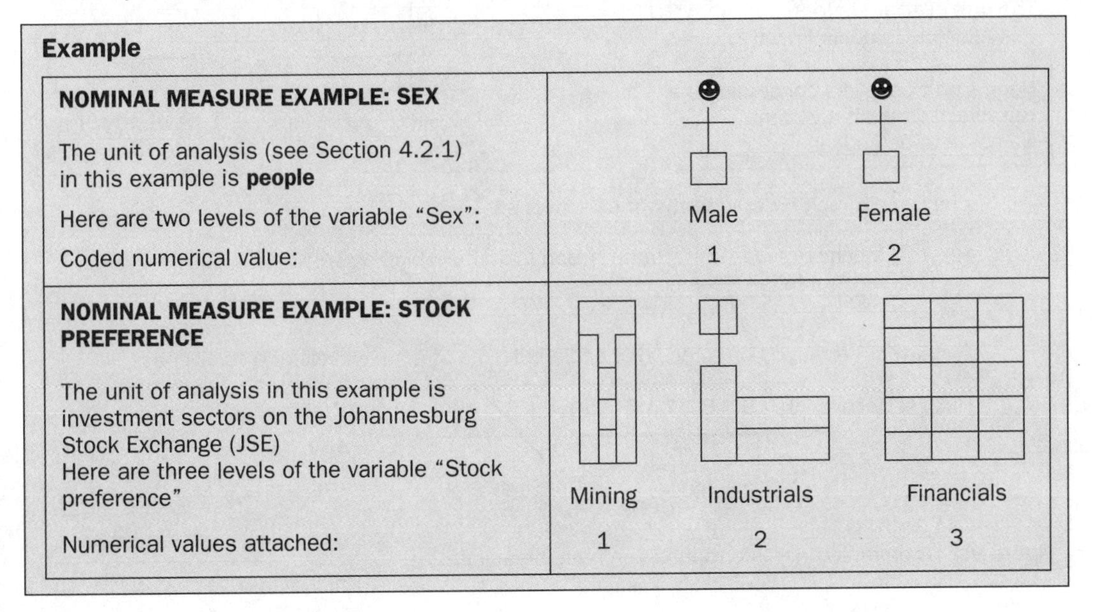

are then used not only to distinguish between the various categories but also to indicate the *rank order* of the various categories.

Suppose the teaching staff of a university is classified into junior lecturers, lecturers, senior lecturers, and professors. Suppose that a rank of *1* is assigned to junior lecturers, and rank of *2* to lecturers, a rank of 3 to senior lecturers, and a rank of 4 to professors. Thus, the number *3* would convey more seniority than *2*. This shows that the property of the distinguishability of numbers, as well as the property of the rank order, is used in ordinal measurement The properties of equal intervals and a fixed zero-point are not used in ordinal measurement. Thus, for indicating the order of the cases with respect to the attribute being measured, any set of numbers, say 11, 17, 19, 103, might have been used as long as the rank order of the numbers agrees with the rank order of the cases.

In ordinal measurement no meaning is attached to the size of the difference between successive numbers. Neither is the absolute-magnitude property of numbers used here. Because the size of the difference between numbers is not utilised in ordinal measurement, the results of numerical operations such as addition, subtraction, multiplication, or division cannot be interpreted meaningfully. For example, in terms of the numbers assigned to academic ranks it is not meaningful to say that because $3 - 2 = 1$, the difference in seniority between a senior lecturer and a lecturer is a junior lecturer. Neither is it meaningful to say that since $\frac{4}{2} = 2$, a professor is twice as senior as a lecturer.

Any rank ordering of individuals (such as in a beauty contest, for example) represents ordinal measurement. Classifying individuals into one of several socio-economic classes on the basis of occupation is another instance of ordinal measurement.

Figure 9.2 shows a situation where a decision to promote the top two candidates based

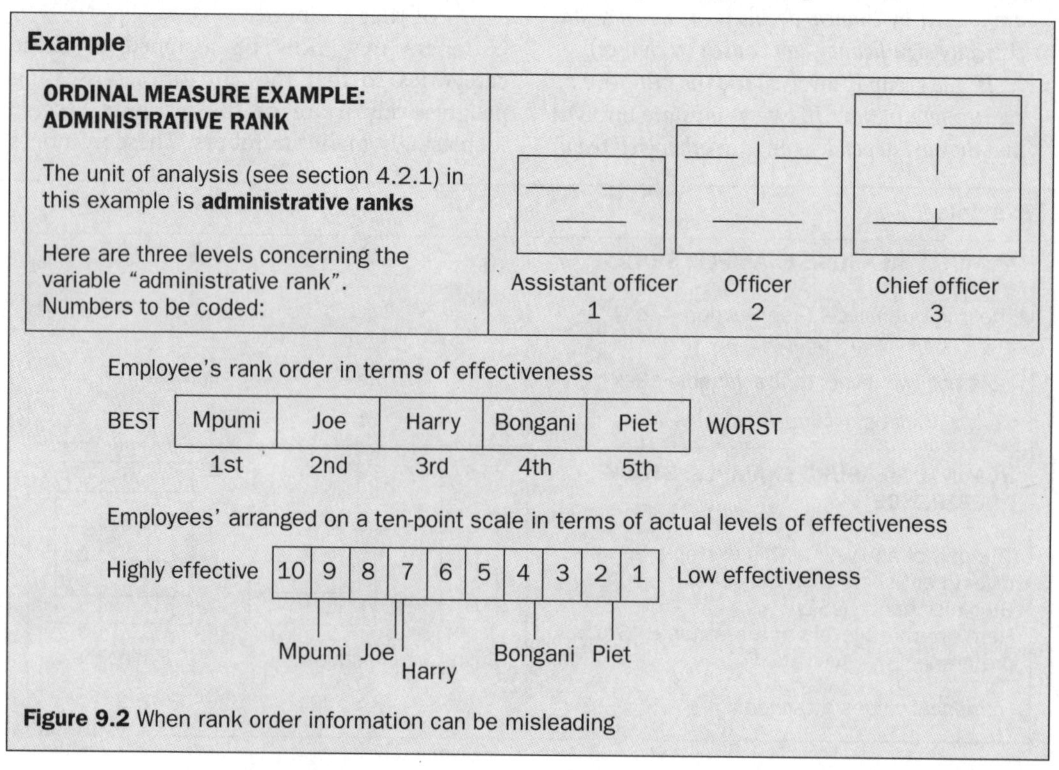

Figure 9.2 When rank order information can be misleading

only on rank information would unfairly disenfranchise the next runner up (Harry) who is, in fact, barely distinguishable from one who would be chosen (Joe).

Note

Legitimate statistics available for ORDINAL *data types are (compare the CD ROM):*

- *The* MEDIAN *(the score in the middle of the list of ranked scores).*
- FREQUENCIES *(bar diagram or pie chart) (check if the distribution is even across categories or if they cluster around one or two categories).*
- CORRELATION COEFFICIENT *(a statistic to measure if the scores of one variable correlate with the rank order positions for another variable).*

  If both variables are ordinal, use the SPEARMAN RANK-ORDER CORRELATION *(also called Spearman's rho). If one variable is not ordinal but on an interval/ration scale, the data should first be converted into ranks in order to compute Spearman's rho.*
- CHI-SQUARES *(χ^2) (check if the frequencies on a nominal variable (for example, sex) are statistically significantly related to an ordinal variable – that they are not caused by chance).*

  If one group is involved, use the CHI-SQUARE OF INDEPENDENCE. *If two groups are involved and they are dependent of each other (related in terms of matching by the researcher (see Section 6.3.7) or because of an already existing relationship or because of measuring the same group twice, use the* CHI-SQUARE OF MCNEMAR. *If two independent groups are involved (if they are not related as mentioned), use the* CHI-SQUARE OF HOMOGENEITY.
- *Tests of difference between distributions (statistics to measure any statistical significant difference between samples – the null hypothesis [see Section 9.3.1] tested by these tests is that the distributions of the concerned populations are identical).*

  If the two samples involved are dependent (related in terms of matching by the researcher [see Section 6.3.7] or because of an already existing relationship or because of measuring the same group twice), use the WILCOXON MATCHED PAIRS SIGNED RANK TEST *(which can be regarded as the nonparametric (parametric assumptions hold that populations are normally distributed [see Figure 9.3], or that their variances are the same) alternative to the t test for related groups – see Interval measurement). If the two samples are independent (in terms of the conditions mentioned), use the* MANN-WHITNEY U TEST *(which is the nonparametric counterpart of the t test for independent groups – see Interval measurement). For three or more independent samples, use the* KRUSKAL-WALLIS TEST *(which can be regarded as the nonparametric alternative to the regular one-factor analysis of variance).*
- DISCRIMINANT ANALYSIS *(to determine in terms of which predictor variables criterion groups differed in the past – see Section 5.4.4.1).*
- CHAID-ANALYSIS *and* CORRESPONDENCE ANALYSIS *(to determine in terms of which predictor variables criterion groups differed in the past – see Section 5.4.4.1).*

- **INTERVAL MEASUREMENT**

  In the case of interval measurement numbers are assigned in such a way that the size of the difference between any two of these numbers corresponds to the size of the difference in the attribute being measured. Furthermore, all differences of the same size correspond to equal differences in the attribute being measured regardless of the location of these differences on the scale. This means that the numbers assigned in interval measurement not only possess the properties of distinguishability and rank order, but also that of equal intervals between consecutive numbers. Consequently, it is meaningful to add two numbers or to subtract one number from another and to interpret the resulting sum or difference.

An obvious example of interval measurement is the measurement of temperature by means of the Centigrade or Fahrenheit scale. It does make sense to say that a rise (or difference) in temperature from 10° to 20° is a rise of 20° – 10° = 10° and to maintain that this difference is equal to a rise in temperature from 30 °C to 40 °C. This illustrates that the results of the numerical operations of addition and subtraction, performed on the numbers assigned in interval measurement, can be interpreted meaningfully.

Note, however, that the remaining property of numbers, namely, that of absolute magnitude, is not used in interval measurement. Upon dividing 30 by 15, it is not meaningful to say that a temperature of 30 °C is twice as hot as one of 15 °C. As is true of all interval scales, the Centigrade scale of temperature does not have a fixed zero-point. The chosen zero-point is arbitrary. For example, 32 °F corresponds to 0 °C, and neither of these indicates a complete absence of temperature. Consequently, if a number assigned in terms of the Centigrade scale is divided by another number obtained in the same manner, the resulting ratio is not meaningful.

Example

INTERVAL MEASURE: TRUST IN A COMPANY'S FUTURE

"This company will make a profit till 2020"

Absolutely			X			Not at all
Here are five levels measuring the extent of trust in a company's future.	5	4	3	2	1	

Coded in this case: 3

Note

The example above may be regarded as ordinal level measurement but for practical purposes may be regarded as satisfactory approximations of interval measurement – this may be the case for the scores on attitude scales and self-constructed questionnaires (Kerlinger, 1986).

The scores on IQ tests and various other standardised psychological and educational tests are usually considered to represent interval-scale measurement.

Note

Legitimate statistics available for INTERVAL data types are (compare the CD-ROM):

- *The MEAN: The average score for a group (also called the arithmetic mean) and which is equal to the total of individual scores divided by the number of scores.*
- *FREQUENCIES (histogram or box plot): Check if the distribution is even across the intervals or whether they cluster around one or two intervals. Are the responses skewed towards one end of the scale, for example, if respondents feel strongly about an issue?*
- *STANDARD DEVIATION: Check if the scores on a parametric test are evenly distributed and cluster closely around the mean (parametric assumptions hold that populations are normally distributed, or that their variances are the same).*
- *Z-SCORES (standard scores): A statistic used to convert scores from different scales (for example, one seven-point scale and the other a five-point scale) with different means and standard deviations, to a common scale in order to compare them fairly.*
- *PEARSON'S PRODUCT MOMENT CORRELATION: A statistic to measure the degree of association between two interval or ratio variables. (A scatter diagram may also be used.)*
- *CHI-SQUARES (χ^2): Check if the discrete classes into which an interval or ratio variable are grouped, are statistically significantly related to another variable, and that the relationship is not caused by chance.*

If one group is involved, use the CHI-SQUARE OF INDEPENDENCE. *If two groups are involved and they are dependent on each other (related in terms of matching by the researcher – see Section 6.3.7) or because of an already existing relationship or because of measuring the same group twice, use the* CHI-SQUARE OF MCNEMAR. *If two independent groups are involved (if they are not related as mentioned), use the* CHI-SQUARE OF HOMOGENEITY.

- *TESTS OF DIFFERENCE BETWEEN DISTRIBUTIONS: t-test statistics and analysis of variance to measure any statistical significant difference between the means and distributions of samples. The null hypothesis (see Section 9.3.1) tested by these tests is that the means and distributions of the concerned populations are identical. If parametric assumptions hold (that populations are normally distributed [see Figure 9.2], or that their variances are the same) and the two samples involved are dependent (related in terms of matching by the researcher [see Section 6.3.7] or because of an already existing relationship or because of measuring the same group twice), use the t-test for related groups. If the two samples are independent (in terms of the conditions mentioned), use the t test for independent groups. For three or more independent samples, use the F-test (also called the overall F-test of analysis of variance).*
- *Discriminant analysis: To determine in terms of which predictor variables criterion groups differed in the past – see Section 5.4.4.1.*

- **RATIO MEASUREMENT**
  In ratio measurement numbers are assigned to people in such a manner that the size of these numbers is proportionate to the amount of the attribute being recorded. Consequently, in addition to the properties of numbers that are used in interval measurement, the property of absolute magnitude or of a fixed zero-point, becomes effective in ratio measurement. If the number zero is assigned to an object in ratio measurement, that object completely lacks the attribute being measured. As a result of this property the numbers assigned in ratio measurement can be meaningfully multiplied or divided (to form *ratios* – hence ratio measurement).

  The measurement of height and mass are examples of ratio measurement. It does make sense to talk about zero height and to say, for example, that a height of 10 metres is twice that of 5 metres. The making of such ratio statements presupposes the existence of an absolute zero-point. This means that the magnitude of the numbers themselves is proportionate to the amount of the attribute being measured.

  Note that in interval measurement, the *differences* between numbers constitute a ratio scale, because these differences have a fixed zero-point (of zero), but that the numbers themselves do not represent ratio measurement. For example, it is meaningful to talk about a *zero difference* between two temperatures, and to say, for example, that a rise from 10 °C to 20 °C is twice as much as a rise from 25 °C to 30 °C. It does not make sense, however, to say that 20 °C is twice as hot as 10 °C.

  Measurements forming either an interval or a ratio scale are sometimes referred to as *metric* or *numerical* data.

Example

RATIO MEASURE: INCOME PER MONTH

The unit of analysis is employees	R0… R1 000… R2 000… R3 000…

Here are infinite levels of the variable "income per month" because it is possible that some employees may not receive any income at all per month due to deductions (such as medical aid) from their salary, while others may have earned a bonus, etc.

The code 5000 equals the amount of income in rand = R5 000

Note

Legitimate statistics available for RATIO *data types are the same as for interval data types mentioned before (compare the CD-ROM).*

Statistical techniques cannot select themselves, or interpret the results that they have obtained, or make conclusions on behalf of the person applying them. The choice of the appropriate statistical techniques and the interpretation of the results obtained remain the exclusive responsibility of the researcher using them. In this regard, we cannot emphasise strongly enough that statistical techniques merely serve as aids in assisting the researcher to come to a justifiable decision on the question of whether or not the data obtained support the hypothesis originally formulated. Consequently, those techniques that would be most helpful in making this conclusion should be favoured.

We can broadly divide statistical techniques into *descriptive* and *inferential* categories. If the scores of the units of analysis (see Section 4.2.1) of an entire population are available, the use of descriptive statistics would suffice. However, sometimes population numbers may be very large and therefore samples (see Section 4.2) must be used to make inferences about the corresponding population properties. In such cases, inferential statistics may be used.

9.4.1 Descriptive statistics

Descriptive statistics is concerned with the description and/or summarisation of the data obtained for a group of individual units of analysis. If one variable (see Section 2.2) is involved in our study, we call it UNIVARIATE ANALYSIS; if two variables are involved, it is called BIVARIATE ANALYSIS and if more than two variables are involved, it is called MULTIVARIATE ANALYSIS.

In this section, we will address grouping the data and presenting it in the form of tables and graphical distribution, and also describe means (averages) and variance as well as correlations.

9.4.1.1 Histograms/bar diagrams

A histogram, in the case of interval data (levels of measurement – see Section 9.4), and a bar diagram, in the case of nominal data (biographical variables), is a diagram in which columns represent frequencies of the various ranges of scores or values of a quantity. This provides an overall image of the description of the units of analysis as a whole group.

9.4.1.2 Mean/average and variability

The mean is the arithmetical average (denoted by $\overline{X}$ of a set of scores and we compute it by adding a list of scores and then dividing the total by the number of scores.

Variability refers to the range of the distribution of scores around the mean and we refer to it as the standard deviation (denoted by s).

The standard deviation is a measure of the spread of scores about the mean. The larger the spread, the larger the spread of the scores. Approximately 68% of scores that are normally distributed fall between one standard deviation to both sides of the mean.

A normal distribution is a distribution which:

- is perfectly symmetrical about its mean; and
- has a bell shape (see Figure 9.3).

In analysing and interpreting the results of surveys (see Section 7.7.3. 1), comparisons of basic descriptive data are usually conducted and are necessary to make the results meaningful and to use them to initiate appropriate policy changes.

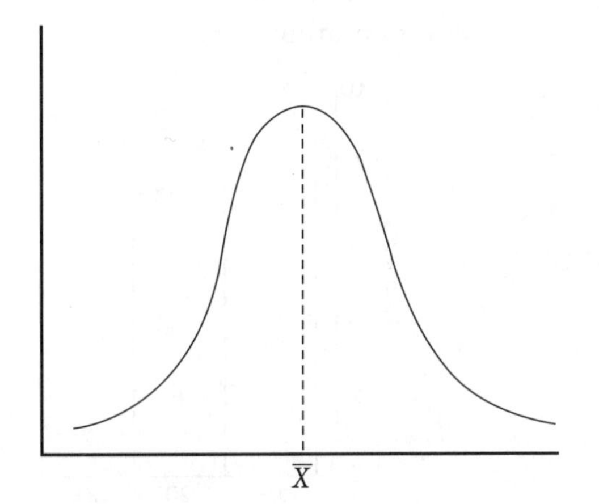

Figure 9.3 A normal distribution

At least four types of comparative data are possible, namely:

a) comparisons of different departments, locations, occupational groups, and so on, within an organisation
b) comparisons with similar groups in other organisations
c) comparisons of the responses of similar groups across time
d) comparisons of the same group to different aspects of some content area, such as a training programme or a work situation.

Without such comparative data, the survey is of little or no use.

When the responses of people in different divisions in an organisation are compared, one question that presents itself is whether the mean differences and percentile differences are meaningful. Statistical tests of significance can address the question of whether large differences could be attributable to chance, but equally important (especially when *N*'s are very large) is the practical significance of the difference. This is a more difficult determination to make and it probably always involves a value judgment. In such a case, it may be a judgment as to whether, for example, the relatively low job satisfaction in manufacturing and maintenance is a significant problem for an organisation. Are these groups characterised by abnormally high rates of turnover, product sabotage, absenteeism, or grievances? If so, then the organisation would want to further explore the reasons for low job satisfaction. Or perhaps there is no evidence that this low job satisfaction is being translated into unproductive behaviour, but the organisation is interested in positive work reactions among its employees.

These questions of practicality can be better answered when other types of comparative data are also available. For example, comparative data for the research and development and manufacturing units in similar organisations. The figures from the research and development unit in organisation A may not look very good in comparison with figures from the manufacturing area that do not appear to be very negative. Both groups may appear relatively average compared to similar groups in organisations B, C, and D.

Activity 9.1

Read Case Study A; Case Study B; Case Study C; Case Study D and Case Study F in Appendix D on page 276.

Question

Construct suitable graphical representations of a characteristic of the unit of analysis (see Section 4.2.1) in each case study.

9.4.1.3 **Correlations and cross-tabulation**

We use correlations to describe relationships between variables (see Figure 9.4) such as income, age and so on. For example, the relationship between the size of a city and its crime rate may be described with correlational analyses (see illustration in Section 5.2.2.1). Correlations estimate the extent to which the changes in one variable are associated with changes in the other variable. Essentially, a correlation coefficient is a number that summarises what we can observe from a scatter-

Answers

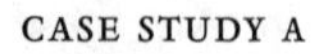

CASE STUDY A

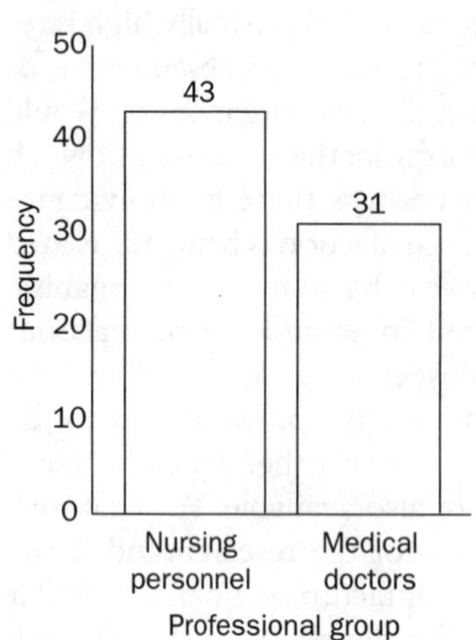

CASE STUDY B

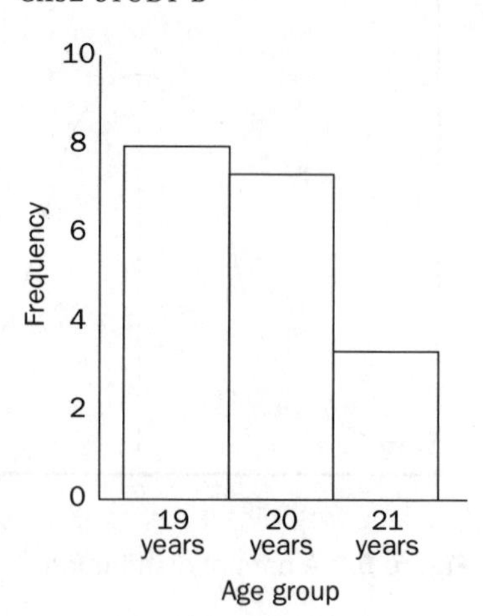

CASE STUDY C

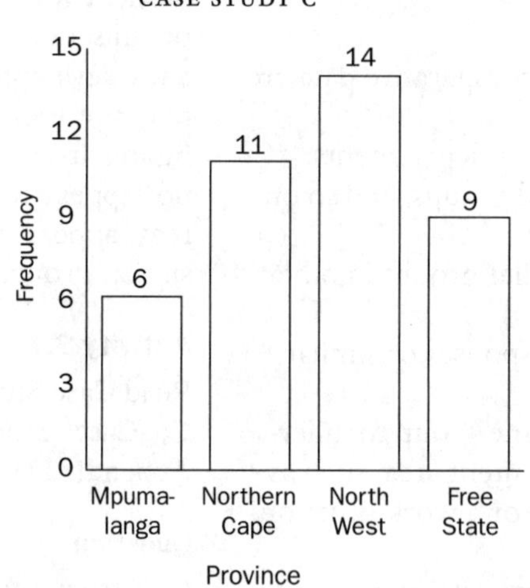

CASE STUDY D

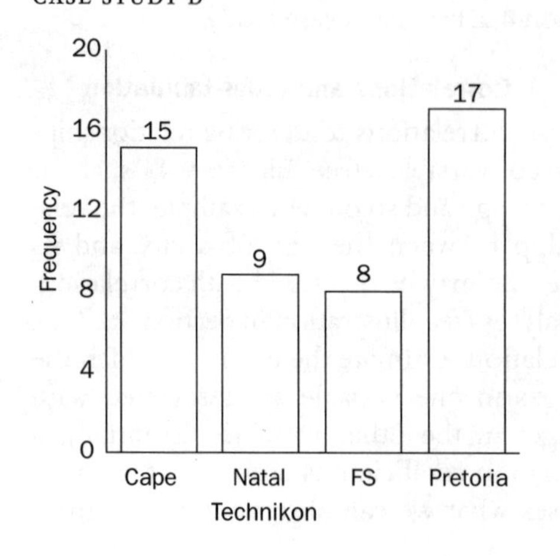

CASE STUDY F

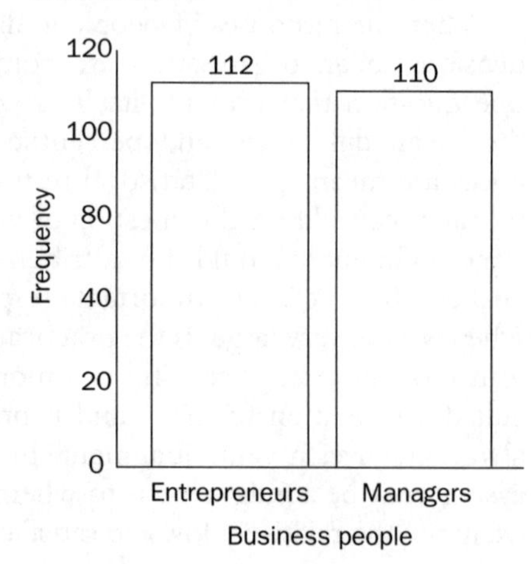

plot (see Figure 9.5). A positive correlation reflects a direct relationship – one in which an increase in one variable corresponds to an increase in the other variable. Two variables that are indirectly or inversely related would produce a negative correlation – indicating that an increase in one variable is associated with a decrease in the other.

We can see that there was a 100% comparison. This means that the variable *sex* (male or female) corresponds completely in terms of its relationship with the variable *road sign knowledge*. In other words, there is a perfect relationship (a correlation coefficient of 1,00) between the variables (see Section 2.2) *sex* and *road sign knowledge*.

A coefficient *r* of –1,00 represents a perfect, inverse relationship. A coefficient of +1,00 indicates a perfect, direct relationship. A coefficient close to zero indicates no relationship at all.

We cannot consider correlational relationships to be causal. This means that we are usually not able to infer that one event is caused by another.

Figure 9.4 The relationship between two variables or possibilities. (Adapted from Earl Babbie, *The Practice of Social Research*, 8th ed., p. 32. 1998. Wadsworth Publishing Co. Used with permission.)

Example

Say we take two people as our sample test (see Section 4.2), that is, one male and one female, and we ask them to complete a questionnaire (see Section 7.7.3.1) consisting of 10 items (questions) to do with road signs. The respondents (the male and female in our case) can score 10 out of 10 marks for each item (question) if they answer a question correctly.

We can tabulate their scores on the questionnaire as in Table 9.2 (called a spreadsheet).

Table 9.2 *Questions and the scores obtained*

Question	1	2	3	4	5	6	7	8	9	10
Male	6	3	0	9	0	3	0	4	0	2
Female	6	3	0	9	0	3	0	4	0	2

CROSS-TABULATION, or CONTINGENCY TABLES, requires a table of rows (horizontal from left to right) and columns (vertical from top to bottom), each representing a variable and its level) see Figure 9.6 G. It is customary to represent the scores of the so-called dependent variable (see Section 2.2) in the rows (compare the CD-ROM).

9.4.2 Inferential statistics

Broadly speaking, inferential statistics is concerned with inferences that we can make about population indices on the basis of the corresponding indices obtained from samples drawn randomly from the populations.

In this section, we will refer briefly to the use of the Chi-square test, and the *t*- and *F*-test

Example

Suppose a researcher investigated the extent of correlation between a measurement of subjects' *Attitude towards AIDS* and the following two variables *Knowledge of AIDS* and *Attitude towards prostitution.*

The results could be as follows:

- The correlation coefficient for the correlation between *Attitude towards AIDS* and *Knowledge of AIDS* is 0,22.
- The correlation coefficient for the correlation between *Attitude towards AIDS* and *Attitude towards prostitution* is 0,60.
- The correlation coefficient for the correlation between *Knowledge of AIDS* and *Attitude towards prostitution* is 0,03.

These correlations could be tabled as in Table 9.3 and illustrated in Figure 9.5.

Table 9.3 *Correlative findings*

	Attitude towards AIDS	Attitude towards prostitution
Knowledge of AIDS	0,22	0,03
Attitude towards AIDS		0,60

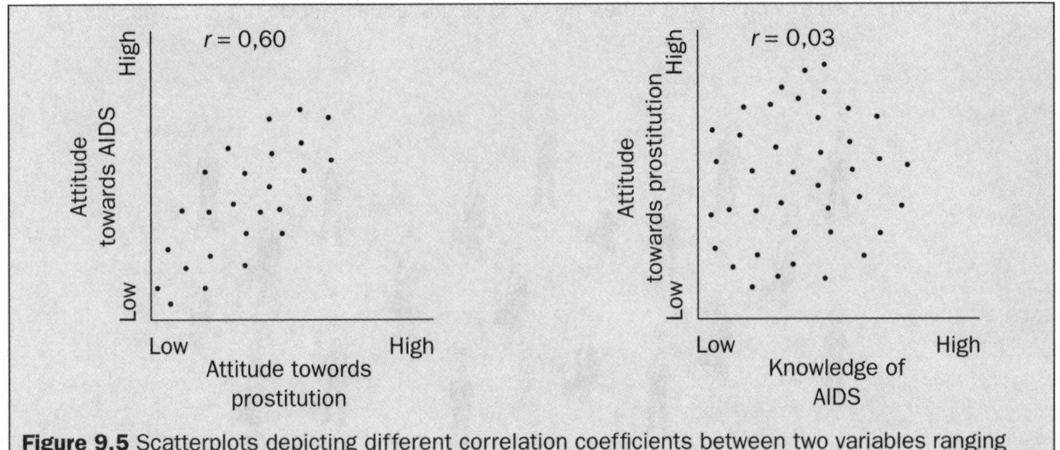

Figure 9.5 Scatterplots depicting different correlation coefficients between two variables ranging from $r = 1,00$ to $r = 0,00$

statistics. We will not deal with more complex statistical analysis techniques in this book.

9.4.2.1 **Chi-square (χ^2) analysis**

We generally use Chi-square analysis to make inferences when the data can be divided into different categories. A Chi-square analysis involves measuring participants in terms of categories such as male-female, voter-nonvoter, and so on. By using the Chi-square test, we can determine if, for example, consumers (males versus females) have a preference for a particular product (compare the CD-ROM).

9.4.2.2 ***t*-tests**

The *t*-tests and analysis of variance enable us to determine whether two groups have equivalent or different mean scores. Descriptive research involves comparing the mean of one group with the mean of another. *t*-tests (for two groups) and analysis of variance (for more than two groups) are the appropriate statistics to use (compare the CD-ROM).

A *t*-test determines whether an observed difference in the means of two groups is sufficiently large to be attributed to a change in some variable or if it merely could have taken place according to chance. The principle underlying *t*-tests and analysis of variance is the assumption that both groups represent samples from a normal CD-ROM.

9.4.3 **Using computers in statistical analysis (use the CD-ROM)**

The greater availability of computers makes the execution of some statistical procedures a matter of routine. Not only can we use the computer to perform time-consuming and complicated computations, but also to compile tables and to draw graphs and figures, to mention just a few functions. Moreover, computers accurately execute these highly complicated and time-consuming manipulations in a matter of seconds at a relatively low cost.

The notion that computers are able to make sense of any nonsense fed into them is a delusion. In the final instance, the computer is like a robot that executes with dog-like devotion any command on any data submitted to it. Among computer staff there is the saying "Garbage-in, garbage-out".

When we use a computer, we should do the following:

- preferably keep the research hypotheses in mind

A. Some men or women who either favour (=) sexual equality or do not (≠) favour it.

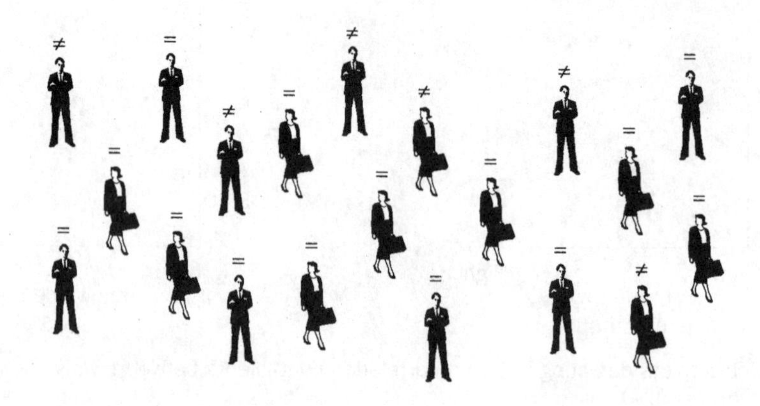

B. Separate the men and the women (the independent variable).

C. Within each gender group, separate those who favour equality from those who do not (the dependent variable).

Figure 9.6 Percentaging a table. (Adapted from Babbie & Mouton, *The Practice of Social Research*, 8th ed., p. 432. 2001. Oxford University Press. Used with permission.)

D. Count the numbers in each cell of the table.

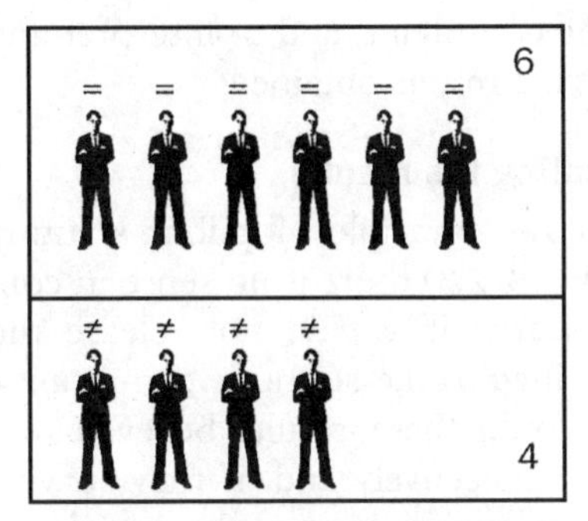

E. What percentage of the women favour equality?

F. What percentage of the men favour equality?

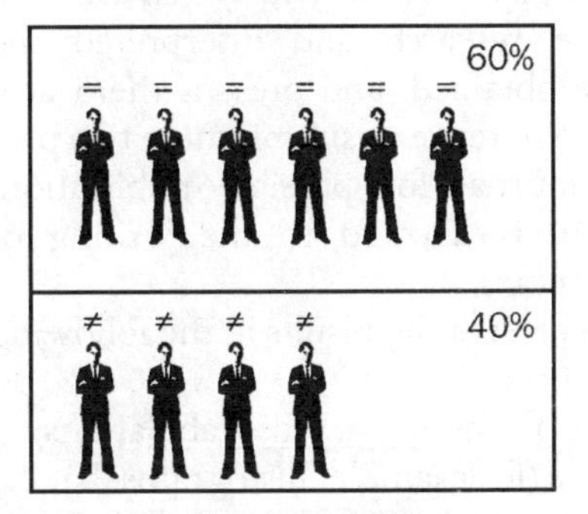

G. Conclusion
While a majority of both men and women favoured sexual equality, women were more likely than men to do so.

Thus, gender appears to be one of the causes of attitudes towards sexual equality.

	Women	Men
Favour equality	80%	60%
Do not favour equality	20%	40%
Total	100%	100%

Figure 9.6 *(Continued)*

- limit our statistical analyses:
  - firstly, to those that are required for investigating these hypotheses; and
  - secondly, to those with which the researcher is familiar.

It is preferable to use commercially available statistical analysis programs rather than to compile or have someone else compile a program specifically for a particular research project. Among these, the Statistical Package for the Social Sciences (SPSS), Biomedical Data Processing System (BMDP) and the Statistical Analysis System (SAS) are the best known (compare MoonStats on the CD-ROM).

Normally, the computer centres at universities and technikons have consultants who may assist researchers in processing their data. Such consultants serve as a link between the researcher and the computer. Even if their services are used, it remains the responsibility of the researcher to design the research, to select the statistical technique, to convey the latter to the consultant, and to interpret and to write up the results obtained.

9.5 **Presenting the results**

In view of the principle of public scrutiny (see Section 1.2.2.3) there is no sense in conducting research if we do not release the results obtained to the scientific community. How else could these results be evaluated critically yet objectively and, if they survive such criticism, become part of the discipline's body of knowledge? This is why we should commit to paper the way in which we conducted the research and interpreted the results we obtained, and present them at a scientific conference or submit them to a professional journal for possible publication. Chapter 10 is devoted to the writing of research reports.

We can present the results in the following ways:

- as tables (for example, cross-tabulations)
- as graphs (for example, histograms, bar diagrams, pie charts and scatter diagrams)
- as statistical summaries (for example, means, standard deviations, correlation coefficient, and so on)
- as selected quotations (for example, writing representative powerful statements from responses obtained from an interview).

> **Example**
>
> The academic performance results of students in public speech making may be presented as follows: the number of students involved (710), the mean (39,34), the standard deviation (13,40) and a frequency distribution (histogram) of the marks (see Figure 9.7).
>
> We can present the results (in the form of correlation coefficients) obtained from the study on public speech making in the form of a table (see Table 9.4), and we can give the distribution of the sample of participants in terms of the technikon from which they were drawn in a pie chart (see Figure 9.8).

Activity 9.2

Read Case Study F in Appendix D on page 276.

Question

Briefly explain why the *mean* was used instead of the *correlation* in the statistical calculations for interpreting the results of the study.

Answer

The *mean* (arithmetical average) as a descriptive device provides the scores obtained by the whole sample of managers and the whole sample of entrepreneurs for their innovative problem-solving styles. Therefore, by using this statistic (the mean), the value of the scores of the two groups can be compared with one another, whereas a statistic such as the *correlation* coefficient indicates the extent to which the individual scores of the managers change in relation to those of the entrepreneurs.

Summary

After research has been conducted according to its planned design, the obtained results must be interpreted. Therefore, the design of a study also concerns the statistical analysis and interpretation of the appropriate data obtained for investigating of the research hypothesis by measurement of variables.

A large data file can be reduced to useful information, which can facilitate the interpretation of data and the drawing of conclusions by means of descriptive and inferential statistics.

If the scores of the entire population under investigation were available, the use of descriptive statistics would be sufficient. If,

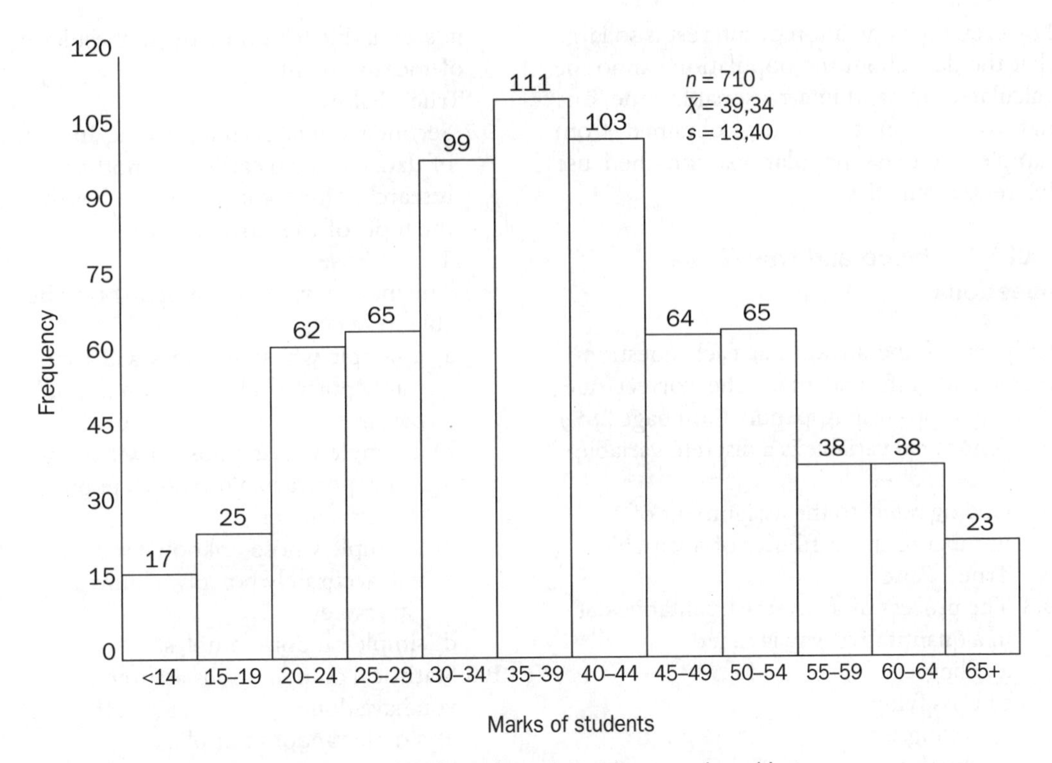

Figure 9.7 Academic performance of 710 students in public speech making

Table 9.4
Correlations between speech quality and other variables

	Speech quality
Speech preparation time	0.75
Speech anxiety	0,03

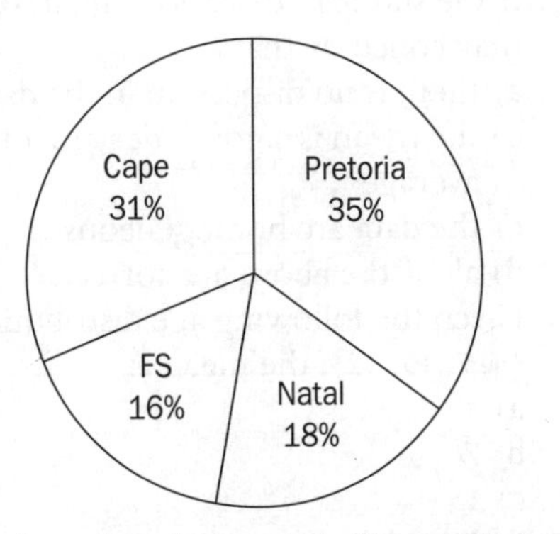

Pie chart numbers in rounded-off percentages

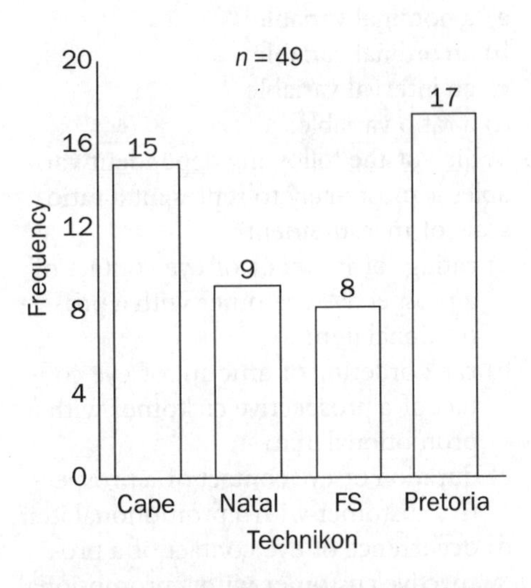

Figure 9.8 Number of students of technikons who participated in an experiment to transplant brains

however, the population of interest is so large that the data about the population cannot be calculated by hand in a reasonable time, one has to rely on the results obtained from samples of these populations and then use inferential statistics.

Multiple choice and true/false questions

Only *one* of the answers at each question is correct. Identify and mark the correct one. (Answers appear in Appendix E on page 285.)

9.1 A nominal variable is a discrete variable.
True False

9.2 Coding refers to the assignment of a number to the attributes of a variable.
True False

9.3 The process of analysing qualitative data in a quantitative way is called
a) filing
b) classifying
c) coding
d) chunking.

9.4 Classifying an electrical transmitter as working or not working treats transmitter functioning as:
a) a nominal variable
b) an ordinal variable
c) an interval variable
d) a ratio variable.

9.5 Which of the following dependent variables is most likely to represent a ratio scale of measurement?
a) ratings of intimacy of eye contact of a prospective customer with a promotional item
b) rank ordering of amount of eye contact of a prospective customer with a promotional item
c) duration of eye contact of a prospective customer with a promotional item
d) occurrence of eye contact of a prospective customer with a promotional item.

9.6 When the research purpose is not clear, it is advisable to choose the highest level of measurement.
True False

9.7 Secondary analysis refers to the analysis of data collected earlier by another researcher for some purpose other than the topic of the current study.
True False

9.8 The main purpose of sampling is to be able to select:
a) a sample whose statistics will accurately portray a known population parameter
b) a sample whose statistics will accurately portray an unknown population parameter
c) a sample whose unknown statistics will accurately portray a known parameter
d) simple random samples.

9.9 Statistical computations assume that you have done:
a) simple random sampling
b) systematic sampling
c) cluster sampling
d) stratified sampling.

9.10 Which of the following measures of central tendency can be used at any level of measurement?
a) mean
b) mode
c) median
d) standard deviation.

9.11 If the standard deviation equals 0, we may conclude that:
a) there is no dispersion in the data
b) the mean is a good measure of the average
c) the data are homogeneous
d) all of the above are correct.

9.12 Given the following age distribution {4, 7, 15, 32}, the mean is:
a) 4
b) 7
c) 15
d) 32

9.13 Descriptive statistics include both the summarisation of univariate distributions and the summarisation of associations between two or more variables.
True False

9.14 Pearson's product moment correlation indicates how much of the variance in the dependent variable has been explained.
True False

9.15 If, from the same sample of people, events, or objects two variables are measured and they seem to vary together, then these two measurements are:
a) contingent
b) redundant
c) dependent
d) correlated.

9.16 The absolute size of a correlation coefficient indicates the following about a relationship:
a) complexity
b) strength
c) direction
d) refusion.

9.17 If the points on a scatterplot go from the upper left to the lower right along a line, then the correlation between the two variables is:
a) zero
b) negative
c) positive
d) diminutive.

Self-evaluation question

1 **List,** after identifying according to the technique of **content analysis**, the *five* most important/key words/sentences (variables) that highlight your interviewees' opinion as collected by doing the last self-evaluation question at the end of Chapter 8.

2 Use your answer to the above question do the following:
a) Indicate the number/frequencies of the identified key words used by each individual you have interviewed on the spreadsheet (matrix) provided on page 220 and/or on the CD-ROM's spreadsheet.
b) Choose an appropriate statistical technique (see Section 9.4) to help make sense of the data in the spreadsheet. Be sure to explain your choice of statistic to a lay person.
c) Present the result according to your chosen technique graphically by means of a hand drawn diagram or by means of the CD-ROM's printout procedure.

SPREADSHEET FOR ANALYSING INTERVIEWS

Names of interviewees	Frequency of key words......	Frequency of key words......	Frequency of key words......	Frequency of key words......	Frequency of key words......
TOTALS					

Fill in the five words in the space provided at the top of each column of this spreadsheet according to your answers given in Question 5 (a) of the second assignment.

10 Report writing

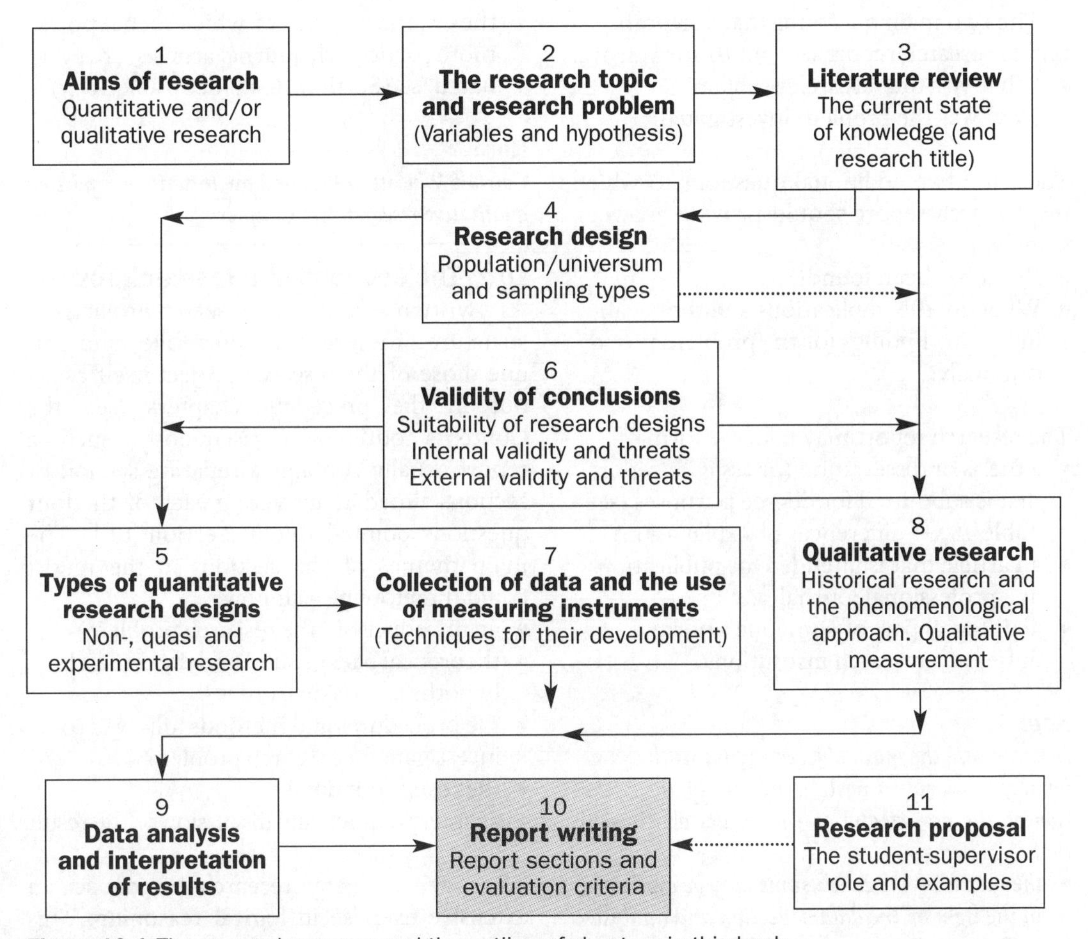

Figure 10.1 The research process and the outline of chapters in this book

Learning Outcomes

After studying this chapter, you should be able to:
write a report on your own research project.

10.1 Introduction

If we have taken the trouble to carry out a research project, then it deserves to be reported. If we do not release the findings of a project, they cannot serve the real purpose for which we undertook the research in the first place, namely to expand scientific knowledge. Writing the research report rounds off the research project.

The two main questions that a hypothesis-testing research report sets out to answer, are:
- What was the research problem?
- How was the problem investigated?

There are two additional questions to which the research report should provide answers, namely:
- What has been found?
- What are the implications and the meaning of the findings for the problem posed originally?

The research report may take the form of:
- a thesis or dissertation (or essay or report) that is submitted for degree purposes (see Table 10.1 – differences of explanation)
- an article that is intended for publication in a professional journal
- an integral part of someone's normal duties at a research institution.

Note

In every case the main objective remains the same, namely to provide a written account of the execution of the project and of the results obtained so that:
- *the merits of the conclusions may be evaluated in the light of the data collection and analyses;*
- *sufficient information is available for the possible replication of the study or for a re-analysis of the data obtained.*

These two considerations tie in with the principle of public scrutiny and the requirement of replicability, respectively (see Section 1.2).

In this chapter we will focus on general guidelines regarding the writing of reports on hypothesis-testing research, namely:
- the sections of a research report (see Section 10.2);
- certain conventions to follow in writing a research report (see Section 10.3; the reference system – see Sections 3.4 & 10.2.9);
- its editorial revision in respect of grammar and style (see Section 10.3); and
- the criteria in terms of which such reports, more particularly journal articles, are evaluated (see Section 10.4). (See Table 10.1.)

Note

Consult Wolcott (1990) on how to write a report on qualitative research (see Chapter 8).

10.2 The sections of a research report

As a written account of a research project, the structure of a research report follows in outline those of the research project itself as set out in the preceding chapters (see the Contents outline). Consequently, such a report usually contains a separate section or sections aimed at answering each of the four questions pointed out in Section 10.1. The main themes of the sections in the report could therefore be as follows:
- an introduction (the research problem)
- theoretical background and the research hypotheses arising from it
- the procedures and methods followed to investigate the research problem
- the results obtained
- an interpretation and discussion of the results.

We may view any research project as an extensive exercise in logical reasoning. This logical train of thought, from the formulation

Table 10.1
The differences between reports written for dissertations and theses and those for professional journal articles

Dissertations and theses	Professional journal articles
Students may be expected to state things explicitly.	Things are not stated explicitly because of the journals' considerable publication costs.
Students will devote at least a separate chapter to each of the sections indicated.	These sections will be distinguished only appearing in capital letters and/or that is centred on the page. As a result of this and the above-mentioned cost factor, journal articles are much more condensed than dissertations and theses.

of the research problem up to the interpretation of the data obtained, should be reflected in the research report.

When writing the research report, we should be careful not to get so bogged down in details that we disrupt this logical train of thought.

The extensiveness of a research report depends largely on the nature of the research project.

10.2.1 The title

The title of the research report should concisely yet unambiguously reflect the exact topic of the project It should include the important variable(s) and, preferably, the population (see Chapters 2 & 4).

> **Example**
> The title of the journal article on which RESEARCH EXAMPLE II (page 14) (see Section 2.2) is based, reads:
>
> *Transmission of management style through imitation of iron-fisted supervisory models.*
>
> That for RESEARCH EXAMPLE III (page 84) (see Section 5.4) is titled:
>
> *Relationship of television viewing habits and aggressive behaviour in children.*

10.2.2 The abstract

The abstract is a very brief summary (usually consisting of no more than 200 words) of a journal article that usually appears immediately after:

- the title (of the article); and
- the name(s) of the author(s).

In an abstract we should preferably answer each of the following questions, so we can only properly compile the abstract once we have completed the research.

- What was the research problem?
- How was the problem investigated?
- What has been found?
- What are the implications and the meaning of the findings for the problem posed originally?

In some respects, the abstract is the most important section of the report.

- It is the part, apart from the title, that future researchers will scan with a view to determining whether they should study the entire report.
- Only the title and the abstract are stored for information retrieval purposes and published in journals (such as *Psychological Abstracts*).

Because it is so extremely condensed, the abstract may require several revisions in an attempt to capture the essence of the report in the required number of words (which may vary from one publication to another).

Note

Exercises concerning writing an abstract follow at the end of Section 10.2.8.

10.2.3 The introduction

The research report begins with a chapter that stands/acts as an *introduction*. The purpose of this chapter is to describe the objective of the particular research project and its importance (see Sections 2.1, 2.2 & 2.2.2).

Although this section is known as the introduction, it usually does not have this title in a journal article.

Irrespective of its scope, the introduction (in the case of a journal article) or introductory chapter(s) (in the case of dissertations or theses) begins with a wide, general description of the problem area and progresses from there to a formulation of the specific problems and/or hypotheses investigated (problem statement and hypotheses – see Section 10.2.5).

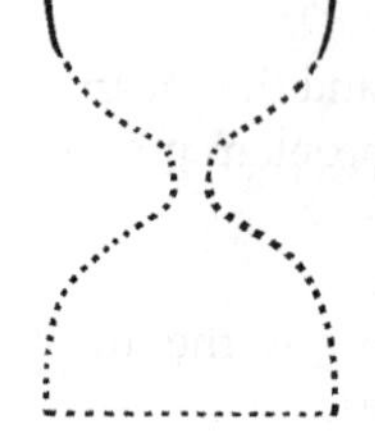

In this respect, Bem (1986) likens it to an hourglass.

The introduction begins with a general statement. Subsequently, the description gets increasingly specific (for example, in the description of a specific model) up to the point where the research hypotheses are formulated.

10.2.4 The literature review

The literature review is usually presented in a research report (for dissertations or theses) in one or more chapters following the introductory chapter.

In a journal article, the introductory comments and the literature review (here condensed into a literature survey) are usually combined in the first section.

10.2.5 Problem statement and hypotheses

The section on the literature review culminates in the formulation of the research hypothesis(es) or research question(s) in a journal article and may even occupy a separate chapter entitled *Statement of problem* in dissertations and theses. In dissertations and theses it is especially important to give the rationale for each research hypothesis.

10.2.6 Methods and procedures

The purpose of this section relates to the requirements of controllability and replicability, which are part and parcel of the scientific method (see Section 1.2).

Although the presentation of this section is adapted to the specifics of a given project and so may differ from project to project, it usually contains information on the following:

- units of analysis (humans, groups, organisations or institutions, human products or outputs, or events (see Section 4.2.1)
- research design, experimental and/or data-collection procedures (see Chapters 4, 5 & 7)
- apparatus and/or measuring instruments (see Chapter 7).

Few, if any, literature references are allowed in this section, but we should remember to give enough information on the execution of the project so that readers may be able to evaluate the appropriateness of the methods (in terms of the research objectives) and the results eventually obtained.

In addition, such a careful description of the research procedures makes it possible for anyone who may care to do so, to replicate the study (see Section 1.2). Consequently, it is important to provide sufficient information on each of the above-mentioned topics (units of analysis, and so on). This usually occupies a separate subsection in the report (conventions – see Section 10.3).

Concerning the units of analysis, we should clearly describe:

- the way in which the units of analysis/ subjects (see Section 4.2) were obtained (for example, by random sampling, and so on);
- from which experimentally accessible population (see Sections 4.2.1 & 6.4.2) they were drawn (for example, from factory workers between 20 and 40 years of age); and
- how many of them were involved.

We should describe the eventual sample in terms of relevant biographical, demographic, socio-economical or other particulars such as:

- sex (how many of each), age and educational level (mean and range – see Section 9.4.1) in the case of human subjects; or
- type of industrial sector (how many in manufacturing, distribution, retail, finance, etc.) in the case of organisations; and so on for any of the other characteristic units of analysis.

Note

In describing the ages and educational levels or the types of industrial sectors, we could consider using a frequency table (see CD-ROM manual, Box 5).

Next, we should describe the design and experimental and/or data-collection procedures. Among other things, we should clearly indicate (in the case of experimental research – see Section 5.2) how the subjects were assigned to the respective treatment groups (see Section 6.3.6). The procedure by means of which the independent variable was operationalised (for example, how the treatments, if any, were administered – see Sections 2.2, 2.3, 6.1 & 6.3.3) and how the measurements on the dependent variable were collected (see Sections 5 & 6), should be set out clearly.

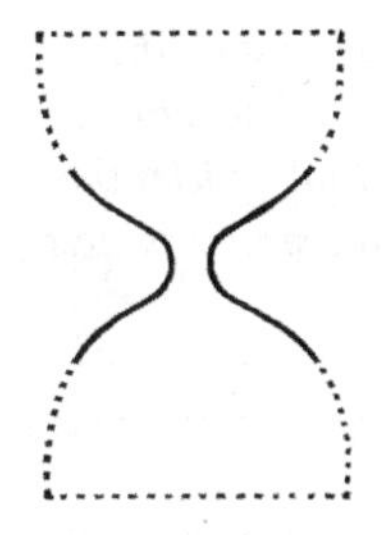

In this section (and the one on the results), the picture of the hourglass reaches its centre.

The exact instructions given to subjects (except those for standardised tests) should also be provided in this subsection.

Note

In the case of an extensive programme of instructions we could consider giving only an abridged version here and including the complete version as an appendix.

If a nuisance variable has been controlled experimentally, it should be pointed out (see Section 5.2). Any unforeseen events that have to be taken into consideration in interpreting the ultimate results, should be reported. By the same token, indications of the success or failure with which the independent variable was operationalised and the response rates (see Section 7.7.3.1) achieved in postal surveys, should be cited.

In dissertations and theses, the statistical procedures (see Section 9.4) by means of which the data obtained were analysed and, if appropriate, the significance level adopted, are also often mentioned in the procedures section.

Note

Some supervisors and promoters require their students to provide the reason for using a particular statistical method.

In journal articles this is usually required only in the case of relatively unknown methods of analysis, or unusual adaptations of regular methods (especially if there may be doubts about whether their assumptions have been proven).

Likewise, only some supervisors and promoters require that the mathematical-statistical derivation of statistical methods is given.

By the same token, whereas dissertation or thesis

students are often required to explicitly state the statistical hypotheses inferred from their operationally defined research hypotheses, in journal articles these are usually taken to be implied in the statistical tests used.

Example

If the *t*-test for independent groups has been used, the null hypothesis $\mu_1 - \mu_2 = 0$ is implied (μ_1, being a population's average score).

Instead of explicitly stating the null hypothesis and the alternative hypothesis, some supervisors and promoters prefer the expected statistical findings to be given.

Example

The mean/average decision-making score of the management learning group exposed to the high-level emergency situation will be statistically significantly higher than that of the group exposed to the low-level emergency situation.

A statement like the one above is more concise than the null and alternative hypotheses, and has the added advantage of reflecting the research hypothesis (see Section 2.3).

It should be emphasised that such a statement (in respect of whether or not the expected results will be significant) refers to the values of the sample statistics and not to the population parameters (see Section 9.4 – "Statistical techniques").

In journal articles the statistical analysis procedures are usually not identified in this subsection, but in the next one, *Results.* A possible exception to this rule occurs when the research project is devoted in its entirety to the development of a measuring instrument and the analyses occupy a central position in the project.

Lastly, if commercially available apparatus or other measuring instruments have been used, it is sufficient only to provide their names and references dealing with their development, reliability and validity. If the researcher has developed his or her own apparatus or measuring instrument, its development, reliability and validity should be completely described.

Questionnaires or paper-and-pencil tests that have been compiled in this manner should be placed in an appendix to the dissertation, thesis or research report. Preferably, a few items from such an instrument should nevertheless be given in the Procedures section so that the reader may form an idea of its general nature without having to consult the appendix.

10.2.7 The results

In this section, we simply present the results of the statistical tests performed on the data without discussing or interpreting them. (In some cases, it may indeed be more appropriate and permissible to combine the results and their discussion in the same section.) If data are presented that were collected in a pilot study (see Section 7.6) and that affected the course of the subsequent main study, they should be identified as such. Normally, this section should not contain any references to other publications.

Tables and graphs may be used as concise and well-organised summaries of results.

Example

If an analysis of variance (see Section 9.4.2.2) was performed, a table with the sample means and the summary table would provide a sufficient description of the results. However, if the results may be conveyed adequately in a sentence or two, it is preferable to report them in this manner rather than in a table.

We should not present tables or graphs if we do not refer to them somewhere in the text of the report. On the other hand, we should not describe the tables and figures in such detail in the text that it amounts to a duplication. (Similarly, tables and graphs should not duplicate each other.) On the other hand, we should not refer to tables and graphs in an incidental manner (for example, by only placing their numbers between parentheses) and then expect the reader to ferret out the necessary information.

> **Example**
>
> Give the specific number in a table that is referred to and, if necessary, the row and column in which it appears.

A separate series of Arabic numerals (for example 1, 2, 3, etc.) is generally used to number the tables and figures, respectively. (Compare the practice in this book.) References to tables and figures are made in terms of their numbers. In other words, one should refer to "Table 3" or "Figure 2" rather than to "the following table".

If there is not sufficient space (on the page) immediately following the reference to a table or figure, the remainder of that page does not have to be left blank. Instead, we could continue with the text on that page even if the table or figure appears on the next page. Each table and figure should have a concise yet clear title so that its contents may be understood without having to refer to the table or figure itself. The title of a table appears at its top; the title of a figure appears below it.

Note

If tests of statistical significance (see Section 9.4) have been performed, indicate the following:

- *the calculated values of the test statistics*
- *their degrees of freedom (between parentheses)*
- *the levels of significance; and*
- *whether one-tailed or two-tailed tests (where appropriate) were involved.*

10.2.7.1 **Presenting the results**

(a) Letter symbols

Write letters used as symbols for statistical concepts such as t or F in italics (or underline them in typewritten manuscripts). Never begin a sentence with an abbreviation or a symbol.

(b) Numbers

Write out numbers smaller than 10 as words unless they represent percentages, decimal numbers, sample sizes, ages and the numbers of tables, graphs and groups, in which case figures should be used, irrespective of the size of the number. The same applies to fractions, except common ones such as "half", "quarter", "one-third", etc., which are written out in full. If a comparison between numbers smaller than 10 and numbers larger than 10 appears in the same sentence, it is recommended that you express both in figures (for example, the ages varied between 9 and 11 years). On the other hand, clarity may often be enhanced if numbers are alternately expressed in figures and words (for example, there were 6 five-minute intervals).

If a sentence has to begin with a number, write it out as a word rather than as a numeral. If it is a long number, consider rewriting the sentence so that the number no longer appears at the beginning of the sentence. Leave a space between a number and the measurement unit to which it refers (for example, 3 kg and 4 m), except in the case of percentages and the degrees of angles (for example, 21% and 14°).

(c) Capital letters

It is customary to refer to:

- Table 1, Figure 3, Variable 5, Factor 6, Group B, but to both tables, figures, variables, factors, groups;
- the Verbal and Non-verbal factors in a factor analysis; and
- the Sex × Ethnicity factor in an analysis of variance where the × refers to a situation

where one variable (Sex) is investigated in relation to another (Ethnicity).

10.2.8 The discussions and conclusions

In this section, the hourglass-shaped format of the research report widens again.

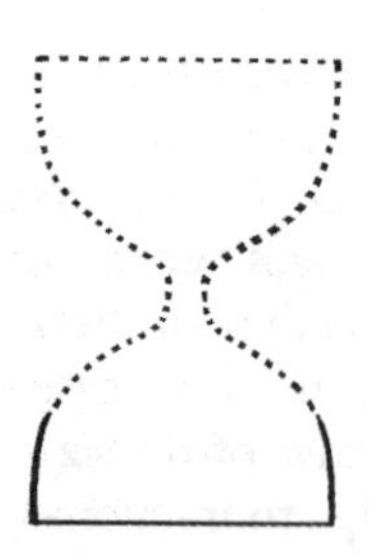

In this section, the statistical results presented in the preceding section are interpreted in terms of the research problem introduced at the beginning of the report (see Section 10.1). By this we do not mean merely repeating the results in the preceding section, but explaining their meaning and implication in the light of the purpose for which the research was undertaken in the first place.

For the sake of perspective, one can begin this section of a report with a summary of the main findings (see Section 10.2.7). In the case of dissertations and theses, each statistical hypothesis should preferably be repeated with an indication of whether it was rejected or retained and of the implications of these decisions for the respective research hypotheses.

Note

If the purpose of the project was:

- *to test a hypothesis derived from some theory, we should point out the implications of the results for the tenability or untenability of that theory*
- *to fill a gap in our knowledge left by previous studies, we should point out to what degree the results obtained succeeded in achieving this.*

In the same manner, we should discuss whether we agree or disagree with the findings of previous research projects. We should consider alternative interpretations of the results obtained and evaluate them objectively.

We should keep in mind that we should point out possible practical implications of the results. This aspect is of special importance if the research involved the implementation of some programme and especially so if the research was funded by some or other agency or research institution.

We need not dwell unnecessarily on results that have turned out to be statistically non-significant. (Statistically non-significant differences and correlations should, in any case, never be interpreted as the absence of such relationships.) Negative results do not necessarily mean that a study was useless. *For example*, if we have found that the relationship between two variables (such as Sex and Ethnicity) is non-significant, such a finding represents an extension of our knowledge about this relationship. In addition, such a finding may prevent future researchers from wasting their time and resources on this topic.

We should be careful throughout not to draw conclusions that we cannot justify by the study. Similarly, we should mention any restriction on the population and internal validity (see Sections 6.3 & 6.4.2) of the results due to:

- shortcomings in the sampling procedure (see Section 4.2)
- the assignment to samples (see Section 6.3.6)
- the inadequate control of nuisance variables (see Section 5.2)
- anything that possibly may have influenced the results.

Of course, such a *post hoc* listing of flaws does not compensate for not having carefully prevented them in the first place. However, it may serve a purpose in that it may recommend new ways of tackling the problem in future studies.

Usually, we will find that the findings of one research project suggest problems or hypotheses that we may pursue in further research projects. It is not uncommon to discover that the findings of one study raise more new questions and problems than they originally set out to answer. Consequently, we usually conclude the report with some suggestions for further research that could be carried out profitably.

Activity 10.1

Read Case Study A; Case Study B; Case Study C; Case Study D; Case Study E and Case Study F in Appendix D on page 276.

Question

Complete each case study by writing the last section, namely *Discussions and conclusions*. Pay particular attention to the possibility of causal aspects in the study. Measured against the objectives of the research study – do the results answer the research questions of the investigation; support or reject the research hypothesis? (see Section 2.3).

Answer

CASE STUDY A

Discussion: As appears from Table A (page 277), there is only one significant correlation, namely that between "Attitude towards prostitution" and "Attitude towards AIDS".

"Attitude towards AIDS" correlates quite strongly with "Attitude towards prostitution" ($r = 0{,}60$). It seems that these two variables are intrinsically connected. The stigma of prostitution is possibly aggravated by the association of prostitutes with AIDS, through their identification as a high-risk group. The weak correlation between "Knowledge of AIDS" and "Attitude towards AIDS" ($r = 0{,}22$) could indicate that the attitudes of the group of health professionals at the hospital concerned are determined by negative associations rather than by factual information.

Conclusion: The research hypothesis cannot be accepted in its entirety, owing to the absence of a connection between "Knowledge of AIDS" and "Attitude towards AIDS"; and although the correlational findings cannot be interpreted as an indication that attitudes towards AIDS are determined by attitudes towards prostitution, the findings do indicate a tendency towards a connection between negative attitudes in the one area and negative attitudes in other areas. In the case of this group of health professionals, the findings indicate that existing attitudes towards the perceived high-risk group (prostitutes) and their sexual practices probably influence their attitudes towards AIDS more strongly than objective knowledge.

It would appear that educational programmes in South Africa should focus on prostitution as well, and particularly on the sexual practices of prostitutes, if more enlightened and objective attitudes towards AIDS are to be brought about. In so doing, educational programmes will have to investigate and counter prejudice against high-risk groups and their sexual behaviour, as well as provide factual information.

CASE STUDY B

Discussion: The results in Table B (page 279) indicate that the apprentices' judgement of supervision became increasingly negative, as is reflected in the evaluation factor of the semantic differential (SD). These findings of changes before role induction correspond with predictions made at the beginning of the study, namely that the apprentices' uncertainty and lack of knowledge of the supervision process would lead to negative change in time.

It appears from the change in the SD between the second and the third evaluations that the role induction procedure did not have the predicted effect of causing the apprentices to evaluate supervision more favourably. Results show that no significant changes occurred as a result of the role induction initiative (a positive change in the mean from 3,24 to only 3,19).

Conclusion: It is notable that no significant changes are found in the SD after the role induction procedure. Since the SD evaluates attitudinal changes, one possible interpretation of the findings is that the role induction strategy used in this study was an intervention focusing on a change in thinking and in the processing of information instead of on attitudinal change. Because the questionnaires were given to the apprentices only one week after the role induction procedure, and there was therefore little intervening supervision, the changes that occurred may well have entailed a reinterpretation of their previous experience of supervision. It could be that the time that elapsed between the second and third tests was inadequate to bring about a change in attitude.

Finally, any conclusions drawn from this investigation must be qualified by an acknowledgement of the limitations inherent in the design of the study. These limitations include the use of self-description instruments to evaluate changes, and the relatively small sample sizes. With a larger sample, it would be possible to investigate the effect of role induction in training at different points in time, so as to determine whether there is an optimal period during which the procedure is the most effective.

CASE STUDY C

Discussion: Table C (page 280) indicates that there was no significant difference between the results of the two groups before the start of the course. The average / mean mark of the experimental group was 57% and that of the control group, 58%. The subjects (first-line supervisors) therefore performed equally with regard to their knowledge of management principles before the training intervention.

Table C also indicates that after the experimental group received their training, their knowledge test scores improved significantly – from 57% to 78%. This is an improvement of 21%, while the knowledge test scores of the control group (who did not attend the training course) remained more or less the same (58% – 56%).

Conclusion: According to the results in Table C, the hypothesis is thus accepted. It can be accepted with certainty that the significant difference in the pre- and postmeasurement of the experimental group, but not of the control group, is the result of the training intervention. The application of the independent variable (training course) indeed had an influence on the dependent variable (knowledge of management principles) and caused a significant change.

We can therefore accept that the course did indeed comply with its objectives in the short term with regard to the improvement in knowledge, and it is recommended that the remaining first-line supervisors of the population of 60 attend the training course. For future research it is recommended that the influence of the training course be evaluated over a longer period of time and be investigated at different kinds of agricultural organisations.

CASE STUDY D

Discussion: The results of this study provide a temporary quantitative answer that confirms the personal experience of coaches and the previous perceived relationship between preparation time and speech quality. Although no significant correlation ($r = 0{,}03$) could be found between speech quality and speech anxiety, Table D (page 282) shows that there is a high correlation between speech quality and speech preparation time ($r = 0{,}75$). The results thus support the first hypothesis that there is a high positive relationship between the speech quality and the total preparation time of a group of public speech-making technikon students and reject the second hypothesis of a high negative relation between speech quality and speech anxiety.

Conclusion: It appears that the students who spend more time preparing get higher marks for their speeches. This does not, however, mean that manipulating the one variable (speech preparation time) will cause a change in the other variable (speech quality). As the results of the previous research indicate, more preparation time contributes to greater self-confidence and this in turn may lead to a better speech.

From the results it is not clear, however, whether the preparation time of various students differs in quality. Such investigation is recommended for further research. One student could, for example, have sat in the library and paged through magazines while another student searched methodically for specific information on a specific topic, but both spent an equal amount of time searching for information and thus preparing for their speech. Future research will therefore have to use better methods of measuring the quality of preparation time, but also make use of a more representative sample in order to increase the population validity of such a study.

CASE STUDY E

Discussion: From the results of the study it seems that the bankrupt small businesses in comparison to non bankrupt businesses tend to exceed their bank overdraft limits to significantly greater amounts and experience cash flow problems to a significantly greater extent. However, no significantly high correlation ($r = 0,45$) could be found between cash flow problems and bankruptcy status. This means that businesses that experienced serious cash flow problems do not necessarily go bankrupt, and vice versa.

Table E (page 283) shows that there is a significantly high correlation between cash flow problems and bank overdraft usage ($r = 0,83$), and especially so between bank overdraft usage and bankruptcy status ($r = 0,94$). This means that businesses that depend heavily on exceeding bank overdraft limits tend to go bankrupt and tend to have more cash flow problems. The results of this study show that cash flow problems combined with bank overdraft usage may in turn predict bankruptcy. This implies that cash flow problems do not in themselves promote bankruptcy but do so in combination with seriously exceeded bank overdraft limits.

Conclusion: The results support the hypothesis that, during the past two years, bankrupt small businesses have exceeded their bank overdraft limits with significantly greater amounts per month and experienced more cash flow problems than non bankrupt small businesses.

This does not, however, mean that manipulating the one variable (bank overdraft usage) and/or cash flow problems will cause a change in the other variable (bankruptcy status). The results of the previous research indicate that management skills also contribute to bankruptcy.

If we consider the relatively small size of the samples used, the significant results become more noteworthy. However, because the research was limited for practical reasons to small businesses in a specific geographic region (Pretoria), the sample could have been biased. Replication of these findings is nonetheless needed and future research will have to use a more representative sample in order to increase the population validity of such a study.

CASE STUDY F

Discussion: The results show that the mean score obtained by the entrepreneurs was 113,9 and the mean score of the managers 96,0. By comparing these mean scores with the highest possible score of 160, it is evident that the entrepreneurs obtained a significantly higher mean than the managers. This difference means that the entrepreneurs are definitely more innovative than the managers of big businesses.

The sample of business people in this investigation was not representative of all members of the relevant population of South African entrepreneurs / managers because an accidental sample was used. Therefore, one cannot confidently generalise the results of this study to other business people in South Africa.

Conclusions: The results support the notion of the research hypothesis that entrepreneurs will be significantly more innovative in their problem-solving style than managers of big businesses.

However, nuisance (third) variables such as age, sex, intelligence, etc. could still have an influence on the research results. Future research should also take these variables into consideration by using a stratified random sample to ensure the representativeness of the different strata in the study and to enhance the population validity of the study.

Once we have written the conclusion and discussion sections of a research report, we can write its abstract (see Section 10.2.2). For this reason you can now do Activity 10.2.

Activity 10.2

Read the answers given above respectively together with Case Study A; Case Study B; Case Study C; Case Study D; Case Study E and Case Study F in Appendix D on page 276.

Question

Write an *abstract* of no more than 120 words of each report (taking the answers to Activity 10.1 above into account).

Answer

CASE STUDY A: The results of an investigation into attitudes towards and knowledge of AIDS in a group of 74 South African health professionals are described. The researchers attempted to determine the degree to which attitudes towards AIDS correlate with knowledge of AIDS, and the degree to which such attitudes correlate with attitudes towards the sexual practices of a high-risk group, namely prostitutes. It appears that attitudes towards AIDS correlate more significantly with attitudes towards prostitution than with knowledge of AIDS. The implications are that educational programmes in South Africa should also focus on prostitution, and particularly on their sexual practices, if more objective attitudes towards AIDS are to be brought about.

CASE STUDY B: The effect of a role induction procedure on goldsmith apprentices was investigated by means of a 10-minute video summary of Bernard's (1979) supervision model. The role induction procedure was applied to twenty apprentices on three occasions during their training period. By means of a self-description scale, the apprentices' attitudes towards the supervision process were evaluated. Results showed that apprentices evaluated supervision more negatively in the period after role induction than before the role induction.

CASE STUDY C: In order to evaluate a training course for first-line supervisors regarding their knowledge of management principles, a research design consisting of an experimental and control group was used. The sample consisted of 40 first-line supervisors at a South African agricultural corporation who were randomly drawn from a population of 60. The subjects' knowledge of management principles was measured with an hour-long written test before and after the training. The course significantly improved the knowledge of supervisors in the experimental group, while the control group's knowledge remained constant.

CASE STUDY D: The relationship between preparation and performance in public speech-making was investigated by video taping the speeches of 49 students from four technikons who had completed seven speech-making assignments. Speech quality was rated on a 5-point scale and its relationship with the subjects' preparation time (measured as the total number of minutes spent on different activities) and degree of anxiety (measured on an existing 21-item self-evaluation questionnaire) was calculated using the product moment correlation. Speech quality and preparation time had a high positive correlation, while anxiety did not show a relationship to speech quality. It appears, therefore, that with a group of technikon students there is a positive strong relationship between preparation and performance in public speechmaking.

CASE STUDY E: This research investigates whether bankrupt small businesses in Pretoria exceeded their bank overdrafts limits significantly and largely experienced cash flow problems more than non bankrupt small businesses during a two-year period. Thirty-six bankrupt and 36 non bankrupt small businesses indicated on a questionnaire their bank overdraft usage and the extent to which they experienced cash flow problems. The results showed that bankrupt small businesses exceeded their bank overdraft limits significantly and experienced serious cash flow problems. Future research should use a more representative South African sample.

CASE STUDY F: The purpose of the investigation was to compare the innovative problem-solving styles of entrepreneurs and managers of big businesses. An accidental sample of 222 business people was used, consisting of 112 entrepreneurs and 110 managers. The level of innovation of the respondents was measured using the KAI scale. According to the results, the entrepreneurs obtained a significantly higher mean on the KAI than the managers. The research hypothesis can be accepted as true, but the sampling did not take into account the different strata, and the sample was not representative. Consequently, one cannot confidently generalise the results in respect of all business people in South Africa.

10.2.9 **The list of references**

A research report should include a list of the sources (see Section 3.4) referred to in the report. The purpose of the LIST OF REFERENCES is to enable the reader to consult these sources. Only sources that have been consulted and that have been referred to directly in the report, should appear in this list.

Note

In textbooks, such lists are often substituted by bibliographies in which it is permissible also to list sources that have not been cited directly but that may have influenced the author's way of thinking.

There are different systems according to which the list of references may be compiled and none of them is necessarily more correct than the others. However, the important point is that whichever system we choose, we should apply it consistently (see Chapter 3).

10.2.10 **Appendices or annexures**

Material such as tests, questionnaires and stimulus materials that have been designed specifically for the research project and that may detract from the main line of thought of the report, may be placed in one or more appendices immediately after the *List of references.*

These materials are made available to enable other researchers to evaluate the research project properly and even to replicate it, if they should care to do so. Because of the restriction on their length, journal articles generally prefer to avoid appendices. Usually, a NOTE is included for the benefit of readers, indicating where material or apparatus used in the study may be obtained (for example, from the author).

Nonetheless, the research report should form a self-contained source in itself so that it should not be necessary for readers to consult the appendices or even the author(s) themselves to get clarity on the methods and procedures used. As indicated (see Section

10.2.8), a few examples of items of a self-developed questionnaire, for instance, should be given in the procedures section.

10.3 Conventions, grammar and style

10.3.1 Conventions

We can follow several conventions when we write a research report. Although it is not necessarily incorrect to deviate from such conventions, adherence to them does suggest a measure of insight. Moreover, it facilitates the editing of articles that are accepted for publication and displays courtesy towards the editor.

(a) Headings and titles

In a journal article, section titles (such as "Participants") usually appear on the left-hand side of the page and section headings (such as "Method and Procedure") in the centre of the text. In the case of dissertations and theses it will be presented as shown on page 235.

(b) Person, voice and tense

It is customary to use the past tense when we describe the research of previous researchers and the procedures they used and discuss the results and the implications of the research on which we report.

(c) Abbreviations

When such a name or word appears for the first time, we should write it out in full and place its abbreviation between parentheses immediately following it. Compare the use of the abbreviation for Statistics South Africa (Stats SA) in Section 7.7.

(d) Sex

The use of male nouns and pronouns when both sexes are referred to is seriously discouraged. Usually this problem may be avoided by using the plural form.

Example

Instead of saying:

After each individual has completed his or her questionnaire.

we may write:

After all individuals have completed their questionnaires.

When our intention is indeed to emphasise individuality, "he or she" or "him or her" may be used, provided that this is done sparingly and preferably not more than once or twice in the same sentence. In all contexts in which males are referred to as men (rather than gentlemen), females should be referred to as women (rather than ladies).

10.3.2 Grammar and style

(a) Accuracy

Remember that the scientific approach requires accuracy, also as far as writing of the research report is concerned. Regardless of how ingenious or creative researchers may be in planning and executing their research, if they are not capable of conveying its importance and implications to the scientific community, they cannot do justice to their research. Editors may edit a manuscript so that it is grammatically correct. However, if there is something amiss with the content, there may be no way of detecting it.

(b) Clear yet concise

Apart from all the grammatical rules and conventions, the most important things to bear in mind when committing anything to paper are:

- accuracy;
- optimal clarity; and
- unambiguity.

Example (Academic journal article)

THE INTERRELATIONSHIP BETWEEN JOB SATISFACTION AND ACADEMIC ACHIEVEMENT OF DISTANCE EDUCATION STUDENTS

JC WELMAN & PA BASSON

ABSTRACT

In terms of the..

....

The aim of this study.. etc.

Experiential learning

There appear to be ....

.... etc.

METHOD AND PROCEDURE

Participants

One hundred students.. etc.

Example (Dissertation/thesis)

CHAPTER 2

LITERATURE REVIEW

2.1 Experiential learning...etc.

When we write the report on the completed research, we should bear in mind that the meaningfulness and appropriateness of the entire research project will be judged solely on the basis of its report.

Keep sentences as short as possible. This will make the text more readable and lessen the chances of ambiguity. Sentences with more than 30 words should preferably be shortened. This can be done by either rephrasing the text or by breaking the sentence up into two shorter sentences.

On the other hand, short staccato-like sentences that crackle like automatic rifle fire, may be adequate in only the most simple material. Where appropriate, the length of sentences should thus preferably be varied. Moreover, the use of short sentences may go a long way in achieving clarity, but may not prevent ambiguity entirely.

As soon as a sentence has to be read more than once to puzzle out its meaning, it is usually an indication that it should be rewritten.

Note

Good advice is to file away the report for at least a week after it has been completed and then to reread it.

(c) Logical flow

There should be a logical train of thought from one sentence to the next and from paragraph paragraph.

Example

It is advisable to vary the choice of words. Instead of saying:

> *...A has found something, B has found something, C has found something, ...*

we can replace the word "found" with words such as "maintain", "suggest", or whichever best conveys the author's contribution.

It may be worthwhile to take note of the manner in which the news media alternate the word "beat" (in "the one team beat another" at whatever margin) with "thrash", "defeat", etc., when they report sports results.

The contents of a paragraph should preferably focus on a single idea, but paragraphs containing a single sentence should be avoided. (An exception occurs when different points are enumerated, each of which is regarded as important enough to warrant a separate paragraph.)

(d) Adjectives and adverbs

Adjectives and adverbs such as *only* should appear next to the word or phrase to which they refer. Thus, in the following two sentences almost opposite meanings are conveyed by placing this word in different positions:

> *It took* only *five minutes to complete the first test.*
> *It took five minutes to complete the first test* only.

When pronouns such as *this, that, these, those* and *there* are used it should be clear what their referents are. Consider the following:

> *A correlation was computed between the violence ratings of workers' favourite television programmes and their aggressiveness.*

From this formulation it is not clear whether the second variable was the aggressiveness of the television programmes or the aggressiveness of the workers. One way to avoid this problem would be to replace *their* with *the workers'*.

Publication manuals generally recommend that *while* should not be used as a synonym for although, whereas, and or but, but that it should be restricted to references to time.

10.4 Evaluation criteria for a research report

In Table 10.2 we give a brief collection of questions in terms of which researchers may evaluate their research reports. This checklist mainly draws on Tuckman (1990) and Zuber-Skerritt (1998). In respect of each of these questions, scores may even be assigned, where appropriate, as shown in Table 2.

Table 10.2

Evaluation criteria for a research report

Key to score:

N	Not applicable
1	Unacceptable and leaves much room for improvement
2	Has much merit; leaves a little room for improvement
3	As good as possible

CHECKLIST QUESTIONS	SCORES			
The title:	N	1	2	3
• is a true reflection of the contents of the report. • is not too long yet descriptive. • contains the important variables.				
The statement of the problem:	N	1	2	3
• is formulated clearly and understandably. • is formulated adequately in terms of defined concepts relevant to the topic and field of study. • does not relate to something trivial, but is of scientific theoretical and/or practical significance (so that it holds the prospect of an expansion of subject knowledge). • the theory, practical problem or previous research from which it proceeds logically, is clearly described. • explicitly sets out different points of view and assumptions. • is congruent with the title as well as the aim of the study (addresses the same issue/s). • culminates in research hypotheses or research questions which are formulated clearly in terms of the relationship between the important variables.				
The literature review:	N	1	2	3
• is relevant to the aim and problem statement of the study. • is sufficiently comprehensive and uses essential information sources. • offers a logically organised and integrated summary (in the researcher's own words, of course). • notes theories relevant to the aim of the study. • presents previous research technically correctly and provides justified criticisms of flaws in it.				
The research design:	N	1	2	3
• is appropriate for the problem in question (survey or experimental or case study design, and so on).				

• is described clearly in respect of the following aspects (so that it is replicable): i) sampling procedures (so that, for example, the experimentally accessible population is clear); ii) the way in which the respondents will be classified or the participants are to be assigned to groups; and iii) interventions (if appropriate) and/or measuring instruments administered to subjects; • takes care of threats to internal validity (for example: nuisance and third variable problems, pre-existing differences between groups, and so on). • takes care of threats to external validity (for example: the generalisability of the results from the sample to the target population and/or to other situations, and so on).				
The measuring instrument's:	N	1	2	3
• contents are described briefly. • administering and/or data gathering procedures are described. • reliability is discussed. • validity is discussed.				
The analytical/statistical techniques:	N	1	2	3
• are appropriate for the given problem (descriptive and/or inferential). • have been applied properly.				
The results:	N	1	2	3
• are clearly and properly presented. • are interpreted correctly.				
The discussion:	N	1	2	3
• provides necessary and valid interpretations and conclusions. • covers appropriate and reasonable theoretical and/or practical implications. • is unbiased and considers whether or not alternative explanations of the obtained results are appropriate. • takes unforeseen restrictions on the internal and external validity into consideration.				
The write-up of the report in its entirety:	N	1	2	3
• follows a logical structure and train of thought. • is concise without being ambiguous or foregoing clarity and readability.				

Self-evaluation questions

Evaluate any research article published in any professional journal (see the literature sources at the end of Chapter 3) in the human behavioural sciences in terms of the checklist given in Section 10.2. An article (Welman & Basson, 1995) is hereby provided for this exercise.

Appendix

THE INTERRELATIONSHIP BETWEEN THE WORK EXPERIENCE OF DISTANCE EDUCATION STUDENTS, JOB SATISFACTION, AND ACADEMIC ACHIEVEMENT

JC WELMAN & PA BASSON

In terms of the cooperative education strategy of technikons, students are expected to do subject-relevant work in the industry/commerce to gain practical experience. The degree of subject-relevant work performed by 166 distance education students, and how this is related to their academic performance, was investigated. It was found that in contrast to older Afrikaans- and English-speaking male students, it was mainly students who speak a black language who do not gain subject-relevant work experience, have minimal job satisfaction and do not earn high marks in the third-year subject (Organizational Behaviour). It is suggested that the State integrate the issues of work provision, education and training for the success of cooperative education in South Africa.

INTRODUCTION

The aim of this study, supported by the background given by the various perspectives on cooperative education, is to explore and confirm the implications of cooperative education for third-year students studying via distance education at technikon.

If the goal of cooperative education is to equip the student to attain occupational competence and economic independence, how is this goal accomplished in distance education, where the academic institution is not in a position to offer real work experience?

Given the differences that exist between cooperative and non-cooperative jobs and their relation to achieving learning objectives (Stern, Stone, Hopkins, McMillion & Cagampang, 1992), and keeping in mind that there are many elements in the cooperative experience that are vital to success (Laycock, Hermon & Laetz, 1992), the question arises as to how the participation of the academic institution in cooperative education will be affected if students are unemployed or hold non-cooperative jobs. Examined in more detail: how will the employed student's extent of academic subject-related work experience (Kaupins & Warberg, 1992), and job satisfaction influence his/her academic achievement?

Perspectives on cooperative education

There appear to be different perspectives concerning cooperative education in South Africa (Du Plessis, 1994). These are as follows:

1. The student and industry are partners alongside each other on a horizontal plane, with the academic institution playing some part in preparing the student for efficient service.
2. There is a symmetrical relationship between the student (the important partner), the academic institution and the student's employer.
3. The State, as a fourth partner, acts as mediator for industry/commerce and the academic institution with the aim of ensuring that each individual has knowledge about the manufacturing process.
4. The academic institution helps to bring about contact between the student and employer.

According to Du Plessis (1994), the role of the academic institution in the first three perspectives mentioned above is limited to the period of academic training and culminates in the delivery of the career-mature student as an employee to industry/commerce. It is only in the last (fourth) perspective mentioned that the academic institution fulfils its contribution to cooperative education.

In ascertaining whether the academic institution satisfies the expectations of the market (Coldstream, 1988), graduation rates (progress, drop out and completion rates), overall placement rates (employability) and career achievement of graduates can be used as indicators. The employer's role in this process is, inter alia, to provide job descriptions, criteria, job specifications and other requirements for inputs, processes and outputs of the education system (Van Wyk, 1993).

Problem statement and research hypothesis

At Technikon SA, because of the limitation that distance education places on the above-mentioned role, the onus rests on the student to make contact with (potential) employers. For that matter, it is assumed that students are employed while studying towards a specific and specialized career (Tothill, 1993a). Bearing this problem in mind, what are the implications of cooperative education within a distance education environment such as Technikon SA?

Given that the general supportive and facilitative environment of the academic institution influences what is accomplished in terms of academic, personal, and vocational gains (Davis & Murrell, 1993) and that work factors are related to the failure rate for part-time students (Snelgar, 1990), students whose jobs are not in the field in which they are studying may well not have suitable facilities in their place of work to acquire practical experience (Aslanian, 1993).

In this regard Laycock et al. (1992) found that the student's perception of the job is not related to his/her overall perception of the quality of the cooperative education experience. This may be so because cooperative education jobs (which are often first learning experiences in a professional setting) do not contain all the dimensions of a highly motivating position.

The perception of employees of how well their jobs provide for and meet their expectations has an effect on their attitude towards the job. Employees who are satisfied with their job may, for example, feel that they are being treated well and are being rewarded with a good salary – and so have a positive attitude towards the job (that is, the work, the boss, and/or coworkers) (Luthans, 1992).

In examining the outcomes of job satisfaction, it seems that low job satisfaction leads to high employee turnover and absenteeism, while high job satisfaction results in fewer on-the-job accidents, work grievances and less time needed to learn job-related tasks (Luthans, 1992).

The following research hypothesis was examined:

There is a significant positive relationship between the extent of subject-related work experience of distance education students (degree of academic subject-relatedness), job satisfaction, and academic achievement.

METHOD

SUBJECTS

One hundred and sixty-eight (168) students in Personnel Management III (Organizational Behaviour) at Technikon SA participated in the study. These students had submitted the required two assignments out of three containing exercises and questionnaires used to sample the data needed for this study. Two (2) students were unemployed and their data could not be used, since it was based on previous jobs they had held.

INSTRUMENT

In the exercises, which formed part of the assignments, the students had to complete questionnaires presented in the prescribed book by Luthans (1992). One of these questionnaires was used as an instrument in this study, namely the Minnesota Satisfaction Questionnaire (MSQ), on which the students rated the extent to which they are satisfied with various aspects of their present job.

The Minnesota Satisfaction Questionnaire

The Minnesota Satisfaction Questionnaire (MSQ) is a rating scale for measuring job satisfaction. The rating scale used in this study is a short form of the MSQ consisting of 20 items, that is, the items with the highest factor loadings on each of the 20 subscales of the MSQ. It provides a detailed picture of the specific satisfactions and dissatisfactions of employees (Luthans, 1992).

The MSQ measures satisfaction and dissatisfaction with ability utilization, achievement, activity, advancement, authority, company policies and practices, compensation, co-workers, creativity, independence, moral values, recognition, responsibility, security, social service, social status, supervision – human relations, supervision – technical, variety, and working conditions (Gillet & Schwab, 1975).

Gillet and Schwab (1975) reported validity coefficients (by using multitrait-multimethod analysis) of four scales of the MSQ ranging from 0,49 to 0,70 (Kerlinger, 1986, p. 424, describes a value of 0,53 as "fairly substantial"). Using a South African sample of 1 791 professional people, Kaplan (1990) examined the validity of the instrument and found the factors of the short-form MSQ to be conceptually meaningful and distinct. Kaplan reported a reliability coefficient of 0,90 of the sum of the 20 items.

Because the instrument was administered only once in the present study, it was decided to examine the reliability of the instrument (its accuracy or precision) by way of Cronbach's alpha coefficient. This method was used to determine the internal consistency of the instrument (the homogeneousness of the 20 items of the instrument).

Unfortunately the construct validity of the instrument could not be determined by way of factor analysis because the sample size was too small (Kerlinger, 1986).

PROCEDURE

Academic achievement

All Personnel Management III students at Technikon SA were required to complete two of three assignments (consisting of case studies and exercises). If a student submitted all three assignments, the two highest marks were used to calculate the average which represented the student's year mark. A student had to obtain a minimum of 40% to write the two open book examinations (comprising a case study problem to be solved with the help of the prescribed textbook) in November 1993. The final mark was calculated (as indicated in the Calendar of Technikon SA) as the sum of 40% of the year mark and 60% of the examination mark.

Criterion groups

The students were rated into nine (9) groups according to how closely their area of work experience was related to the academic subject area (Organizational Behaviour). This was done by comparing the extent to which the aspects covered by the syllabus for Organizational Behaviour were present in the student's job title and work experience (the exercises that the students had to do as part of their assignments consisted, inter alia, of writing down their present job title and what work they were doing).

The syllabus of the subject Organizational Behaviour comprises the following units:

Introduction to organizational behaviour; Job satisfaction; Motivation; Change in organizational behaviour; Informal organization; Conflict; Leadership; Communication; Decision-making; Organizational development.

The rated area of work experience of group 9 was closely related to the syllabus content of the subject Organizational Behaviour and involved management and administration of organizational behaviour, while the rated area of work experience of group 1 was not related at all (it involved no participating in or experience of organizational behaviour). A typical member of group 9 would be the Personnel Manager in charge of organizational development in a big corporate organization, while a night watchman is a good example of a member of group 1. The distribution of participants according to this rating is presented in Table 1.

Table 1
Distribution (frequency) of the students in terms of subject-related work experience

	Work experience group									
	1	2	3	4	5	6	7	8	9	Total
Number of students	19	32	39	17	31	12	11	3	1	166
Percentage of total	11	19	23	10	19	8	7	2	1	100

Statistical techniques

Descriptive statistics (frequency distributions, central tendency and variability) were used to compile a student profile. The Product Moment Correlation was used to examine the inter-relationship between the variables and to establish whether the hypothesis was acceptable (Huysamen, 1990).

Cronbach's alpha coefficient was used to examine the reliability of the Minnesota Satisfaction Questionnaire (MSQ). The computer package SPSS for Windows (release 6.0) was used for the calculations.

RESULTS

To construct a student profile, the following variables with alpha codes and values were included in the study:

AGE: Age group of the student at enrollment for the subject (0 = 17 – 23 yrs, 1 = 24-30yrs, 2 = 31 – 44 yrs, 3 = 45 + yrs)
SEX: Sex of the student (0 = female, 1 = male)
LANGUAGE: Home language of student
(0 = Afrikaans, 1 = English, 2 = Other, 3 = North Sotho, 4 = South Sotho, 5 = Swazi, 6 = Tsonga, 7 = Tswana, 8 = Venda, 9 = Xhosa, 10 = Zulu)

Values for the item choices of the Minnesota Satisfaction Questionnaire (MSQ) were coded as follows: "Very dissatisfied" was assigned the value 1, and items ranged as far as "Very satisfied", which was assigned the value 5. The minimum and maximum scores that any respondent could obtain were 20 and 100 respectively.

Means and standard deviations

Table 2 shows that students in the subject-related work experience groups (groups 5 to 9) obtained relative high marks in the subject. It seems that the older students and more male than female students had the more closely subject-related work experience (groups 6 to 9).

From Table 2 it seems that the majority of students in all language groups except Afrikaans and English had work experience not closely related to the academic subject (groups 1 to 3).

Table 2 indicates that the students with the more academic subject-related work experience had a higher degree of job satisfaction.

In brief, the means and standard deviations of the variables presented in Table 2 shows that students with closely subject-related work experience obtained higher marks in the academic subject, are older, male and tend to be Afrikaans- and English-speaking and experience a high degree of job satisfaction.

Table 2
Group means and standard deviations of variables

Group	n		MARK	AGE	SEX	LANG	SATS
			Variables				
1	(19)	$\overline{X}$	47,42	1,00	0,58	4,42	66,26
		s	19,59	0,58	0,51	4,02	14,51
2	(32)	$\overline{X}$	53,00	1,09	0,50	1,38	73,84
		s	15,91	0,53	0,51	2,54	13,09
3	(39)	$\overline{X}$	53,13	1,49	0,64	1,90	73,18
		s	10,38	0,68	0,49	2,86	14,18
4	(17)	$\overline{X}$	56,88	1,53	0,76	1,41	72,41
		s	6,53	0,80	0,44	2,69	17,49
5	(31)	$\overline{X}$	58,32	2,03	0,71	1,41	75,77
		s	7,73	0,66	0,46	2,61	14,63
6	(13)	$\overline{X}$	58,31	2,08	0,85	0,77	74,62
		s	9,35	0,86	0,38	2,20	13,40
7	(11)	$\overline{X}$	61,18	2,09	0,91	0,27	73,00
		s	10,78	0,70	0,30	0,47	12,73
8	(3)	$\overline{X}$	55,67	2,33	0,67	0,33	90,67
		s	13,50	0,58	0,58	0,58	6,43

9	(1)	$\overline{X}$	73,00	2,00	1,00	0,00	65,00
		s	0,00	0,00	0,00	0,00	0,00
Total	166	$\overline{X}$	54,91	1,56	0,67	1,72	73,29
		s	12,68	0,77	0,47	2,89	14,37

$\overline{X}$ (read "X-bar") is the symbol representing the arithmetic mean, or average, of the sample (**n**).
s is the symbol representing the standard deviation expressed in the same units as those of the original measurements.
n is the symbol representing the group size.

Correlation matrix
The intercorrelation matrix presented in Table 3 confirms what was shown in Table 2 and shows that there is a positive relationship between the rated work experience (degree of academic subject-relatedness), job satisfaction, and academic achievement. It also shows that students who experience high job satisfaction obtained higher marks in the academic subject.

Table 3
Intercorrelations between all variables in the study

Variable	MARK	AGE	SEX	LANG	SATS
GROUP	0,29°°	0,51°°	0,22°°	–0,28°°	0,14∞
MARK		0,11	0,00	–0,39°°	0,18°°
AGE			0,24°°	–0,09	0,03
SEX				–0,03	0,03
LANG					–0,22°°

°p<0,05 for one-tailed significance.
°°p<0,05 for two-tailed significance.

Reliability of the measuring instrument
An alpha coefficient of 0,9233 for the Minnesota Satisfaction Questionnaire (MSQ) was found. Each of the 20 items contributes not less than a coefficient of 0,9169.

CONCLUSION

There is a positive relationship between the rated work experience (degree of academic subject-relatedness) of students studying via distance education, job satisfaction, and academic achievement.

The cooperative education experience differs for the rated different work experiences and thus different employers. This makes a cooperative education programme (where administrators and placement staff of the academic institution perform support functions in developing practical experiences for students) invaluable if cooperative education is to succeed as an educational strategy in South Africa or any other part of the world.

From the research results it seems clear that a student who had work experience that is closely subject-related obtains a high mark in that academic subject and experiences a high degree of job satisfaction. However, it seems that it is mostly older, male, Afrikaans-speaking and English-speaking (home language) students who had the closely subject-related work experience.

Young black language-speaking students need subject-related work experience opportunities.

In order for students to make a link between theory and practice, cooperative education is the answer. Academic institutions are, of course, obliged to ensure the vocational relevance of their courses (Tothill, 1993b), but if organizations (potential employers) continue to scale down and/or restrict their recruitment to "experienced" candidates in order to be internationally competitive in the short term, cooperative education in South Africa will not succeed.

Policy decisions about the practical role of industry/commerce in employing students who have no work experience must be considered a priority by the Government of the "new South Africa". In this regard it may be necessary to stipulate the role of the academic institution (in conjunction with the State department of Manpower) in having the power to, and taking the responsibility for the administration (or coordination) of the placement of students, in legislation. Perhaps an amalgamation of the areas of employment, education, and training into a single State department of "Higher Education and Employment Services" is the answer?

REFERENCES

Aslanian, C.B. (1993). Organizations as students – the challenge for education. *Industry and Higher Education*, 7(2), 98–103.

Coldstream, P. (1988). Industry finds its voice – and higher education an unexpected ally. *Higher Education Quarterly*, 42(4), 370–377.

Davis, T.M. & Murrell, P.H. (1993). A structural model of perceived academic, personal, and vocational gains related to college student responsibility. Research in Higher Education, 34(3), 267–289.

Du Plessis, W.S. (1994). Die ko-operatiewe onderwysstrategie. *Suid-Afrikaanse Tydskrif vir Hoër Onderwys*, 8(1), 57-60.

Gillet, B. & Schwab, D. P. (1975). Convergent and discriminant validities of corresponding Job Descriptive Index and Minnesota Satisfaction Questionnaire scales. *Journal of Applied Psychology*, 60(3), 313–317.

Huysamen, G.K. (1990). *Introductory statistics and research design for the behavioural sciences:* Volume I (2nd ed.). Cape Town: H&R Academica.

Kaplan, R.A.L. (1990). *The career anchors, job involvement and job satisfaction of professional people.* Unpublished doctoral thesis, University of Cape Town, Cape Town.

Kaupins, G. & Warberg, W. (1992). Course prerequisites for personnel cooperative education students. *Journal of Cooperative Education*, 28(1), 48–55.

Kerlinger, F.N. (1986). Foundations of behavioral research (3rd ed.). New York: CBS Publishing.

Laycock, A.B., Hermon, M.V. & Laetz, V. (1992). Cooperative education: Key factors related to a quality experience. *Journal of Cooperative Education*, 27(3), 36–46.

Luthans, F. (1992). *Organizational behavior* (6'th ed.). New York: McGraw-Hill.

Snelgar, R. J. (1990). Stress and the part-time student: Work factors associated with failure rate. *South African Journal of Psychology*, 20(1), 42–46.

Stern, D., Stone, J.R., Hopkins, C., McMillion, M. & Cagampang, H. (1992). Quality of work experience as perceived by two-year college students in co-op and non-co-op jobs. *Journal of Cooperative Education*, 28(1), 34–47.

Tothill, A. (1993a). Distance education in the workplace. *People Dynamics*, 11(8), 27–32.

Tothill, A. (1993b). Higher education and employment in the OECD: Lessons for South Africa? *Africa* 2001, 2(1), 40–45.

Van Wyk, J.J. (1993). The role of the employer in curriculum development and quality assurance. *Pro Technida* (Port Elizabeth Technikon), 10(2), 51–64.

Summary

As indicated in this Chapter, a research report should have a clear, simple writing style and clearly defined sections so that the reader of the report finds all the information readily accessible. Spelling and grammatical errors should be avoided.

11 The research proposal

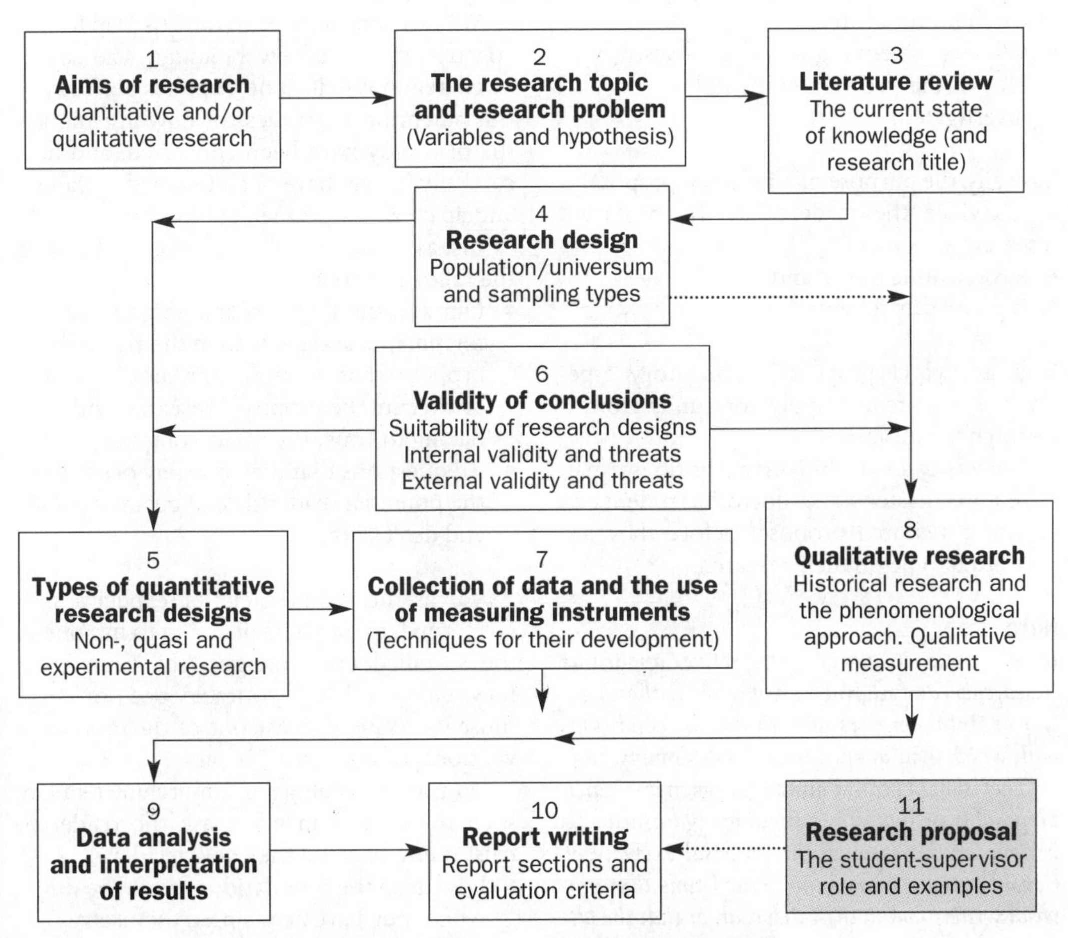

Figure 11.1 The research process and the outline of chapters in this book

Learning Outcomes

After studying this chapter, you should be able to:

1. plan a research project
2. list the sections of a research proposal
3. write a research proposal relevant to your study field.

11.1 Introduction

The main objective of a research proposal is to clearly and unambiguously convey the plan in terms of which our proposed research is going to be carried out. Therefore, the two main questions that should be answered by a research proposal are:

- Which problem is going to be investigated?
- How is this problem going to be investigated?

Basically, the purpose of a research proposal is to convince the reader that the proposed research:

- has scientific merit; and
- is practically feasible.

Such a research proposal is obligatory, especially if researchers apply for funds from a research institution.

University and technikon authorities usually require master's and doctoral students to submit a research proposal before they are permitted to begin their research.

Note

In all these instances, prospective applicants (researchers and students) are advised to thoroughly acquaint themselves with the precise conditions with which their applications should comply.

They should bear in mind that when a research proposal is evaluated by a funding organisation, it is done on the basis of the proposal exclusively. Considerations such as the limited time that proposal writers had at their disposal, or that the latter's competence should ensure that any problems cropping up during the research process will be dealt with, cannot be taken into consideration. The evaluators are restricted to what they have in print in front of them and this should be the deciding factor. Researchers should also bear in mind that the project is not going to be evaluated in terms of its good intentions (for example, to eradicate poverty, and so on) but on the basis of the manner in which it intends to achieve such admirable objectives, whatever they may be.

Even if a research proposal is not required for official or formal reasons, it remains an essential element in the research process because it represents the blueprint or ground-plan for the proposed research.

We can liken it to an architect's plan for the construction of a new building. The saying "well begun is half done", applies perfectly to this blueprint. Regardless of how ingeniously the plan may have been conceived, and how carefully it may have been planned, it cannot anticipate all unforeseen complications.

Just as in the case of an architect's drawing, the following apply:

- Our aim should be so unambiguously formulated and detailed in the research proposal that someone else should be able to execute the proposed research without having to consult with its compiler.
- All questions that may possibly occur to the potential reader should be anticipated and dealt with.

As far as the requirement of explicitness is concerned, researchers planning to use one of the so-called open designs (see Chapter 8) may be in a less favourable position than those who intend to use one of the more conventional designs (see Chapter 5).

To use the analogy of an architect's plan, such researchers in effect ask the reader to trust them, because they will decide:

- how deep the foundations should be dug when they have acquainted themselves with the soil formations; and

- what the slope of the roof should be once they have learnt more about the average annual rainfall.

We can understand why funding organisations are less inclined to provide financial support for open design proposals, because such designs cannot provide preliminary plans as discussed above.

Naturally, the research proposal should have a title that concisely yet unambiguously identifies the exact topic of the proposed research. In other words, the title should not reflect the general field of study in which the research is to be carried out, but the exact topic. In the case of experimental research, at least the independent variable (and preferably the dependent variable, too) (see Section 2.2) should be reflected in the title.

Example

The title of the research in Appendix A, page 272 reads:

A laboratory study of the effects of situation redefinition in spatial crowding

Here the independent variable is SITUATION REDEFINITION and the dependent variable is SPATIAL CROWDING.

Note

Often, students do not obtain a research problem directly from theories, everyday observation or practical problems (see Section 2.2.1). A lecturer, for example, (who has obtained it directly from one of those sources) may suggest it to them.

11.2 Requirements of a research topic

Prospective researchers should acquaint themselves with previous research on a particular topic before they start planning research on it. We have already dealt with the topic of a literature search and review (see Chapter 3).

The research topic should meet certain requirements, namely:

- originality
- topicality (actuality)
- replicability
- practical feasibility
- value-free topics.

(a) Originality

We could easily recognise that some topics lack ORIGINALITY in that they immediately elicit a reaction of "So what?".

Example

Consider the difference in psychological adjustment of individuals whose bedroom windows face north and south, respectively.

Previous research projects are seldom repeated in practice unless there is convincing evidence to suggest that there was something methodologically wrong with them. However, researchers frequently set out to improve on the design (see Section 4.2.5) or statistical analysis (see Section 9.4) of previous researchers. Rather than simply duplicate these projects, they may examine the role of a variable that was previously ignored, or operationalise (see Sections 2.3, 6.1 & 6.3.3) the relevant variables more adequately.

Example

We have shown (see Section 6.3.2.3) how the findings of one project on the relationship between television viewing and feelings of safety were put in a totally different perspective by an investigation in which the residential area of the participants was taken into consideration.

Another possibility we can consider is to repeat a research project on a different population which, technically speaking, does not result in a simple duplication, but which might be lacking in originality.

Especially in the case of doctoral research, the prospective research is usually required to represent a meaningful contribution to the particular field of study. (Doctoral students, in particular, should realise that using a research problem suggested by a lecturer provides less room for demonstrating originality.)

Note

A word of caution: If you plan a project with an overly grandiose scope, the chances are that it may prove to be practically unfeasible (compare the requirement of practical feasibility), or you may have to abandon it for some or other reason. The topic should preferably be sufficiently limited in scope without being trivial (compare the requirement of topicality).

(b) Topicality (actuality)

Often research is undertaken simply because data (typically psychometric test data), collected for another purpose, are available. The research topic is then formulated to fit the available data, rather than the other way around. The problem with such existing data sets is that there may be a lack of data on key variables necessary for investigating topical and interesting problems. As a result, the researcher is restricted to the available information, a situation that may be likened to putting the cart before the horse.

To be able to formulate hypotheses and questions of scientific merit, experience and a sound knowledge of the stage of research development in the area involved are required. As a superficial indication of the topicality of the proposed research, the dates of the references (see Section 3.4) are often checked to see how recent the majority of them are. (For example, notice that in the research in Appendix A all the references are all older than 23 years.) Naturally, not all references need to be of a recent publication date.

(c) Replicability

We have already seen (see Section 1.2) that the core feature of scientific research is its controllability or replicability. By this we mean that future researchers should be able to repeat the proposed research by means of the same operationalised variables (see Sections 2.3, 6.1 & 6.3.3) on a new sample from the same population (see Section 4.2). In some cases the intervention (see Section 5.2) cannot be made to occur again on purpose, for example, earthquakes, the El Niño effect, the crash (collapse) of the share markets (stock exchanges) or riots, but in such an event the data collected originally should be available for possible re-analysis (see Section 9.4).

(d) Practical feasibility

When we choose a research topic for a master's degree or doctorate, certain practical considerations, mainly its feasibility, should be taken into account. For example, the problem should preferably not be so comprehensive that it cannot be investigated in a single project.

Note

It is often advisable to study only a single aspect of an extensive research problem. For example, it would have been impossible to investigate Latané and Darley's research into the helping behaviour of bystanders (RESEARCH EXAMPLE VI, page 109 – see Section 6.3.3.1).

A sufficiently large sample of the kind of subjects required for the investigation should be available without exorbitant costs being incurred.

Example

It would be impractical to compare a large group of South African companies over 50 years of existence with a control group if only a few such companies are readily available to the prospective researcher.

Furthermore, we should be certain that we can complete the proposed research within the time available or permitted. Obviously, a longitudinal study (see Section 5.4.3) extending over five years would be less suitable for a master's dissertation.

Apart from the time required for the execution of a research project, the writing, technical preparation and editing of the report (see Chapters 3 & 8) usually require much more time than we originally anticipate. In addition, we should budget for costs that will be incurred by the following:

- hiring staff (research assistants, typist)
- the procurement of the necessary literature (computer searches, photocopying, translating in the case of sources in foreign languages)
- the purchase or even development of apparatus (for operationalising variables)
- telephone accounts (in telephone surveys)
- travelling expenses (for visiting participants)
- computer time and translation (if applicable)
- duplication and binding of the report (project report, dissertation or thesis).

Note

In applications for funding, the details mentioned above serve to convince the funding organisation that the researcher knows what is at stake and that he or she is the right person to be funded for the research.

It should be clear that the facilities (laboratories, apparatus, and so on) and the assistance necessary for the execution of the project, are available. In such proposals, a detailed budget is also required. The expenditures that might be questioned, must be justified especially carefully.

Furthermore, some research institutions have to be persuaded of the practical value of the eventual results so that funding will not amount to a waste of their money. They wish to be satisfied that the project will yield dividends for their expenditure. We should thus point out possible practical applications of the expected results.

In addition, we should be sure to point out how the proposed research relates to matters of interest to the funding organisation. If the funding organisation favours certain topics because of particular sociopolitical considerations, we should obviously keep this in mind.

We must also consider the feasibility of the proposed project in the light of possible ethical objections (see Section 7.9) and the prevailing political climate.

Finally, we should take into consideration our own preferences, training, skills and limitations. It would serve little purpose to select a topic with which we cannot identify and/or for which we lack the necessary training and skills.

Note

If a student has no training and experience in the application of statistical methods, the choice of a topic requiring multivariate statistical techniques (see Section 9.4), may prove to be disastrous.

Example

Someone conducting research on the incidence of emotional outbursts among middle-aged male managers may possibly be accused of considering the lives of middle-aged male managers of greater importance than those of middle-aged female managers.

If someone develops a programme to improve the assertiveness of disabled employees, it may be taken to mean that this kind of behaviour is regarded as desirable.

(e) Value-free topics

It is difficult to conceptualise instances of entirely value-free research.

Values may prejudice researchers to such an extent that their ability to examine phenomena without bias is impaired.

11.3 Designing a research project

After we have identified a general research area, and delineated a more limited research problem, we have to plan or design a project to investigate the relationships we postulated in the research hypothesis(es) or research question(s) (see Section 2.3). In this connection, we should bear in mind that statistical techniques (see Section 9.4), however sophisticated, cannot compensate for inept theorising (see Section 2.2.1), design flaws (such as inadequate operationalisation of variables – see Sections 2.3, 6.3 & 6.3.3) or for unsatisfactory data (see Chapters 5, 6 & 7).

(a) Statistical analysis

We could correct faulty statistical analysis (see Section 9.4) by means of re-analysis, but no statistical analysis can compensate for, or rectify, the omission of key variables in the collection of data, for example. The research design (see Chapter 5) occupies a central component in the proposal that is planned at this stage.

(b) Defining the variables

In planning a research project, we must operationally define (see Sections 2.3, 6.1 & 6.3.3) the relevant variables (for example, independent and dependent variables (see Section 2.2) in experimental research) and identify possible nuisance variables (in experimental research – see Section 5.2.1) or third variables (in survey research – see Section 6.3.2).

Therefore, if we plan an experiment, we must decide which manipulations (interventions), if any, are required to create the independent variable appearing in the research hypothesis (see Section 2.3). As we have indicated (see Section 6.3.3), it is usually desirable to consider the ways in which variables have been operationalised in previous research. If the variables in the research hypothesis cannot be defined operationally, it means that the research hypothesis cannot be investigated empirically.

In the case of a single QUALITATIVE INDEPENDENT VARIABLE, the minimum number of levels that is required is usually dictated directly by the research hypothesis.

Example

Suppose the research hypothesis states:

> *Typists learn to type faster by means of a computer program method than with a written manual instruction method.*

Then we have to include at least these two methods in the experiment (see Figure 11.2).

We do not determine the appropriate number of levels of a QUANTITATIVE INDEPENDENT variable by means of the research hypothesis only, but in the light of:

- previous research; or
- the researcher's experience.

Kerlinger (1986) emphasises that the variance (see Section 9.3.1) of the independent variable should be maximised and this recommendation is probably relevant only in the case of quantitative independent variables. In terms of this recommendation, it will be advisable to use values that are spread across the widest possible range of the quantitative scale, rather than values that are close to each other.

Example

The practice schedules used in RESEARCH EXAMPLE I (page 6) (learning in a distributed fashion versus massed learning – see Section 1.2.2.1) should not differ in terms of hours only, but also in terms of weeks.

Note

It is not the role of research hypotheses to make value judgements. For instance, in RESEARCH EXAMPLE I (page 6) (see Section 1.2.2.1), the research hypothesis did not suggest that one practice schedule was better than another, but simply that it would result in a higher addition proficiency. Therefore the researcher did not make any value judgements.

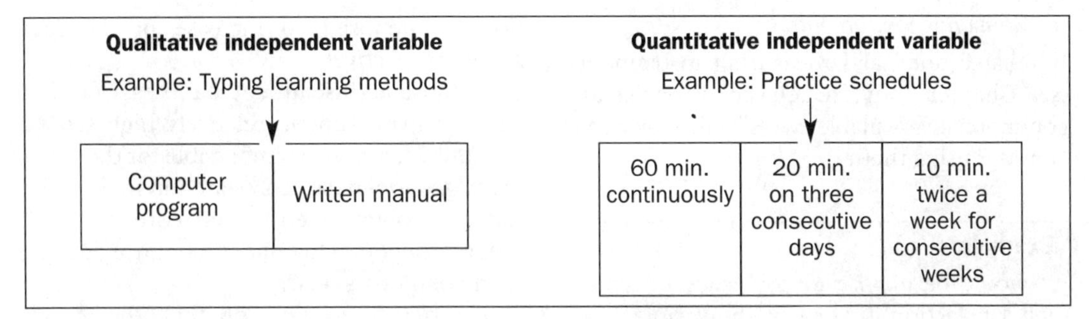

Figure 11.2 The difference between qualitative and quantitative variables

Refer to Figure 11.2 for an explanation of the difference between qualitative and quantitative independent variables.

(c) Nuisance variables

If we should find that there are one or more nuisance variables that may be relevant in a proposed experiment, we should consider ways of eliminating or controlling them. In this connection, the literature survey (see Chapter 3) may suggest nuisance variables that previous researchers in the particular area have considered necessary to control and how they have gone about doing it. In the discussion of their findings, previous researchers possibly also may have indicated nuisance variables that should preferably be taken care of in future research in the area involved.

Note

As we have indicated before, there are various ways in which we can keep nuisance variables at bay, including:

- *matching groups (see Section 6.3.7);*
- *creating blocks (see Section 9.3.2.3) of individuals who are homogeneous in terms of such variables;*
- *randomly assigning participants:*
  - *to all levels of the independent variable (see Section 6.3.6); or*
  - *to all possible combinations of the levels of two or more independent variables (see Section 9.4).*

If the research hypothesis deals with the effect of repeated exposure to a task or stimulus, such as in solitary confinement studies, and if there are no non-additive sequencing effects, the repeated measures design (see Section 9.3.2.3) may be considered to control nuisance variables pertaining to differences among individuals.

(d) Dependent variable

If the dependent variable is a physical attribute, such as mass or blood pressure, then the operational definition of its measurement does not present insurmountable problems.

However, the operational definition of the dependent variable (see Sections 2.3 & 7.3) usually does not follow directly from the research hypothesis.

Example

If the dependent variable is *creativity* or *leadership*, there is no obvious measure. In other cases, again, there may be more than one measure of the dependent variable. For example, there are at least five methods to measure the retention of verbal learning. (The recall method, for example, requires that subjects reproduce the material they have learnt, whereas the recognition method requires them to select from among several items the one which is the response which they have learnt.)

(e) Measuring instruments

If reliable and valid measuring instruments (see Chapter 7) of the relevant variables are commercially available, we should obviously consider using them.

> **Example**
>
> It would be unwise to construct a test of job satisfaction in view of the various job satisfaction tests currently available in South Africa. (See the list of Internet sites on page 292.)

Of course, we should satisfy ourselves that the reliability coefficients (see Section 7.5) reported in the test manual of published tests have been determined for a group similar to the one we intend using. If we plan to use an instrument for a group for which no such information is available, the reliability of the instrument should be investigated for such a group, or for a similar one.

We should also ensure that the available instrument is valid for the purpose for which we are considering using it (see Section 7.4). A measuring instrument that has been found to be valid for one particular purpose need not necessarily be valid for measuring the particular dependent variable in the research hypothesis.

Note

If a questionnaire or attitude scale is translated from another language into English, Brislin's (1970) backward translation procedure is recommended. In this procedure, two people translate the material into English, independently of each other, and then two other individuals translate the resulting version back into the original language. Differences between the original and the translated versions may be eliminated through discussion.

Measuring instruments should neither be too difficult nor too easy if the intended intervention is supposed to increase or decrease scores, respectively.

Suppose an instrument is too easy, so that all participants obtain relatively high scores. In this case, it may be impossible for the treatment group whose scores are intended to be raised, to obtain even higher scores than the other group(s). This phenomenon is known as the CEILING EFFECT.

The FLOOR EFFECT, on the other hand, occurs when the test is so difficult that all participants obtain relatively low scores. In this case, we cannot discern any differences between groups if a group has been subjected to a treatment designed to lower scores.

11.4 Sections of a research proposal

It is recommended that a research proposal contain (at least) the following sections:

- an introduction containing references to the relevant research literature (see Chapter 3) and pointing out the importance of the proposed research;
- the statement or formulation of the research problem (hypotheses or questions) (see Sections 2.2 & 2.3);
- the proposed method (see Chapter 7), procedures (see Chapter 5) and statistical analyses (see Section 9.4); and
- a short list of references (see Chapter 3 & Section 10.2.9).

11.4.1 The introduction

The objective of the introduction is to orient the reader towards the topic of the proposed research, in other words, to pave the way for the description of the topic. The importance, meaningfulness or relevance of the proposed research, in other words, the reasons why the topic justifies research in the first place, should be spelled out clearly.

To achieve this, it may be necessary to provide a concise review of the relevant literature in which we refer briefly to the theories or research from which the intended research proceeds. If an extended literature survey has already been completed, a meaningful summary of the literature most directly relevant to the proposed research and required for understanding the formulation of the objectives of the research project, will suffice.

Note

The library is no longer our only source of information. The development of the Internet, electronic publishing and its effect on research supervision, peer review of publications and general communications capabilities have all changed the way in which researchers work. (See the list of Internet sites on page 292.)

Example

The *Researchers Networking Database* is published with the *Nexus Database System*. It contains biographical profiles of individual researchers in South Africa, including their fields of interest and areas of specialisation in the social sciences and the humanities. Visit the website at:

http://www.hsrc.ac.za/nexus.html

This will provide you with a list of experts in various fields. You can also view the *TALK* conference database.

11.4.2 The statement or formulation of the research problem

Here we should identify the variables (see Section 2.2) and specify the target populations (see Section 4.2).

The formulation of the research problem, research hypothesis(es) or research question(s) (or central thesis in the case of analytical studies – see Section 2.2.3 & Chapter 6) should follow from the introduction.

The problem statement may take the form of:

- a testable research hypothesis (for example, *Typists learn to type in a shorter period of time by means of Method A than by Method B);* or
- an exploratory question (for example, *To investigate to what extent the top management success of junior managers may be predicted by means of matriculation achievement, intelligence and achievement motivation).*

If there is more than one research hypothesis or research question, we should state them all, and make the rationale of each, as it arises from the concise literature survey, clear. As we have indicated (see Section 2.3), such a hypothesis or question deals with the relationship between variables in one or more population(s) (see Section 4.2).

11.4.3 The proposed method, procedures and statistical analysis

11.4.3.1 Research method and procedures

The research procedures by means of which we intend to investigate the stated problem should be scientifically well-founded and describe the following aspects:

- the population(s) (see Section 4.2) from which the participants are actually going to be obtained
- the manner in which, and how many of, the participants are going to be obtained
- the manner in which, and how many, groups are going to be formed
- the way in which the data are going to be collected and the specifications of any apparatus (see Chapter 7) including:
  - in the case of experimental research, the manipulations (interventions – see Section 5.2.2) intended to create the independent variables (see Section 2.2);
- the measurement of the variables (see Chapter 7); and
- the statistical methods for processing and analysing the data obtained (see Chapter 9).

The description of the above-mentioned points should clarify why the proposed course of action will assist in finding answers to the formulated problem. If new or modified methods are proposed, these should be justified. It should be clear to the reader that the proposed research methods are the most appropriate for the intended research.

11.4.3.2 Statistical analysis

In respect of the statistical methods, it will not be sufficient to simply say that we will analyse the data by means of some computer programe (for example, SPSS, BMDP, SAS or MoonStats on the CD-ROM included on the back cover of this book) as if such a program can decide by itself which analyses should be performed.

We should identify not only the name of the statistical technique(s) but also the variables to which they are to be applied.

Example

If we are going to use the *t*-test for independent groups, we should identify the two groups (including the unit of analysis) and the dependent variable:

"The *t*-test for independent groups will be used to investigate whether the experimental group of workers has shown significantly more aggressive responses than the control group."

In the case of multiple regression, we should similarly identify the predictor variables (see Section 5.4.4) and the criterion variable.

By indicating the why and the how of the proposed statistical procedures, the candidate aims to convince the reader that he or she understands why a particular statistical technique is going to be used.

11.4.4 The list of references

We conclude the research project with a list of a few (say, five or six) core references. The conventions related to compiling such a list are indicated in Chapter 3.

Note

The six references in the research in Appendix A were completely sufficient to accommodate all the necessary references in the proposal.

Finally, the entire proposal should be well-thought-out, logically coherent and grammatically flawless. The evaluators (of the proposal) should be convinced that the researcher (prospective student) has mastery over that particular study field, both as far as terminology and methodology are concerned, and that he or she should be able to complete the project successfully.

11.5 Evaluation criteria for a research proposal

In this section, there is a brief collection of questions in terms of which supervisors and prospective students (researchers) may evaluate their research proposals. This checklist mainly draws on Tuckman (1990) and Zuber-Skerritt (1998). In respect of each of these questions, scores may even be assigned, where appropriate, as follows:

Key to score:

N	Not applicable
1	Unacceptable and leaves much room for improvement
2	Has much merit; leaves a little room for improvement
3	As good as possible

PROPOSED CHECKLIST QUESTIONS	SCORE			
The title:	N	1	2	3
• is a true reflection of the contents of the proposal • is not too long yet descriptive • contains the important variables.				
The statement of the problem:	N	1	2	3
• is formulated clearly and understandably • is formulated adequately in terms of defined concepts relevant to the topic and field of study • does not relate to something trivial, but is of scientific theoretical and/or practical significance (so that it holds the prospect of an expansion of subject knowledge) • clearly describes the theory, practical problem or previous research from which it proceeds logically • explicitly sets out different points of view and assumptions • is congruent with the title as well as the aim of the study (addresses the same issue/s) • culminates in research hypotheses or research questions which are formulated clearly in terms of the relationship between the important variables. • notes theories relevant to the aim of the study • includes key words/concepts used in a computer literature search with a copy of its results				
The literature review:	N	1	2	3
• is relevant to the aim and problem statement of the study • is sufficiently comprehensive and uses essential information sources • offers a logically organised and integrated summary (in the researcher's own words, of course).				
The research design:	N	1	2	3
• is appropriate for the problem in question (survey or experimental or case study design, and so on) • is described clearly in respect of the following aspects (so that it is replicable): i) sampling procedures (so that, for example, the experimentally accessible population is clear); ii) the way in which the respondents will be classified or the participants are to be assigned to groups; and iii) interventions (if appropriate) and/or measuring instruments administered to subjects. • takes care of threats to internal validity (for example: nuisance and third variable problems, pre-existing differences between groups, and so on) • takes care of threats to external validity (for example: the generalisability of the results from the sample to the target population and/or to other situations, and so on).				

The measuring instrument's:	N	1	2	3
• contents are described briefly • administering and/or data gathering procedures are described • reliability is discussed • validity is discussed.				
The analytical/statistical techniques:	N	1	2	3
• are appropriate for the given problem (descriptive and/or inferential).				
The proposal:	N	1	2	3
• is limited to 10 typed pages • includes a time schedule for the writing of different chapters.				

Thus, mainly the research proposal should satisfy the following criteria:

1 The purpose of the research (see Section 2.2.2) should be clearly defined.
2 The research procedure (Chapters 4, 5, 7 and/or 8) to be used should be described in sufficient detail to permit another researcher to continue or repeat the research.
3 Possible flaws in procedural design and an estimate of their effects upon the research findings should be reported (compare Chapter 6).

The acceptability of a research topic for study purposes may be judged by giving consideration to its feasibility and value. FEASIBILITY involves the following aspects:

- availability of, and access to, information/data
- opportunity to pursue a particular research design
- time needed to complete the research
- technical skills needed
- financial support.

VALUE entails demonstrating a measure of research competence or problem-solving ability (see Chapter 1) and, to a lesser degree, adding to the body of knowledge in a field of science.

11.6 The student-study supervisor role

The first step in designing a research project is to prepare a research proposal for approval by your study supervisor (study leader) or promoter. The supervisor/promoter must have the necessary insight and understanding to lead you and help you reach a high standard in your research.

Ultimately it is your responsibility to do the following:

- select the research topic
- develop a proposal
- execute and manage the research project
- write the research report.

Student/study supervisor relation

You may call on your supervisor for advice and support and contact with him/her is important and should happen frequently. To enhance this relationship, each may be required to play the following roles.

SUPERVISOR/STUDY LEADER	STUDENT
Be available at specified times	Initiate contact and explore study field
Have in-depth knowledge of study field	Follow up guidelines given by the supervisor
Help student to plan research	Plan research
Give support in the development of the research proposal	Develop the research proposal
Guide the student's thinking and provide feedback on submitted work Be involved and show interest in student	Obtain new perspectives Show flexibility and dedication
Give constructive criticism	Follow up on suggestions and ideas
Give guidelines and support on the structure and form of the research report	Develop the research report and follow the provided guidelines
Give support and suggestions regarding: • obtaining the sample selection; • the questionnaire application; • doing fieldwork; and • analysing the results.	Has to: • draw the sample; • administer the questionnaire; • do the fieldwork; and • analyse the results.
Ensure availability and access to research facilities	Use the available research facilities and explore new ones if necessary
Should terminate the candidature if student does not make progress	Should terminate the relationship if personal conflict occurs
Give advice on prerequisites of publication acceptance	Take full responsibility for grammar and spelling
Encourage	Be enthusiastic

11.7 Research proposal evaluation example

In this example the research proposal by a prospective master's degree student in Human Resource Management is presented. Normally, it would be followed by the comments and evaluation by the supervisor, but in order to show and compare these comments in connection to the relevant sections of the prospective student's proposal, both scripts are presented in two columns (this way of supervising can be followed if the student's draft is available on floppy disk, stiffy, e-mail, or the Internet).

PERCEPTIONS ON TRADE UNION INVOLVEMENT
IN AFFIRMATIVE ACTION PROGRAMMES

by

U. WILLBESORRY

RESEARCH PROPOSAL

submitted in preliminary fulfilment
of the requirements for the

MAGISTER TECHNOLOGIAE

Human Resource Management

TECHNIKON BEPREPARED

Supervisor: Dr C. Youhavenot
Co-Supervisor: Dr U. Haveto

April 2002

Note

This should be a full page – the first page of the proposal.

Note

The prospective student's research appears in the left-hand column of the table on the following pages. The supervisor's comments appear in the right-hand column, and will usually be presented in the form of a letter to the student.

In order for you to read the proposal and completed checklist, several general comments by the supervisor are presented here first.

General comments

Dear student

Your research proposal is, in general, well structured. You have obviously considered the structural elements in the development of a research proposal. In addition, there is definitely a need for this study, and you deserve recognition for having identified the importance of considering trade union perceptions of affirmative action. However, due to serious shortcomings with regard to methodology and content, you will have to do some more work and then resubmit this proposal. The following general comments are therefore pertinent:

- Your proposal (draft) is based on an over dependence on secondary sources. You should do further reading on studies by leading South African corporate and academic South African experts such as L. Human, M. van Wyk, K. Hofmeyr, E. Charoux and P. Madi. In addition, you should consult scientific journals such as the *Industrial Relations Journal of South Africa* and the *SA Journal of Labour Relations* in order to enhance the scientific value of your proposal and, ultimately, your master's manuscript itself.
- You make no reference to the Employment Equity Act. You should study this Act in detail and identify its impact on the field of study.
- Furthermore, you should attempt to obtain policy documents and position papers on affirmative action published by trade unions and union federations. You should also read the union views in the *SA Labour Bulletin*. See also Patel (in Innes, 1993) in your presented list of sources (references).
- You should specify the limitations of the study and indicate how these limitations will be addressed.
- The conceptual framework of your research proposal is not well developed. Your proposal raises many questions that need further clarification. The how, what, why, where, when and who need to be addressed during the planning phase of this study in order to prevent problems during the research process.
- The discrepancy between the current title and the content of your research proposal is highly problematic. You could either change the title or amend the content of the proposal in order to ensure congruency.
- You should correct the spelling and grammatical errors.

	SPECIFIC COMMENTS FROM THE SUPERVISOR
1 TITLE "Perceptions of Trade Union involvement on Affirmative Action Programmes"	Another suggested title that may be suitable for the topic to be studied may be presented here.
2 INTRODUCTION Affirmative Action began in America in the early 1950s as a basis for formal equality in education, employment and welfare. However, this was not a guarantee for equal treatment because it could not eradicate inequalities deriving from economic, cultural and environmental factors. In Australia, representation can be achieved by a legally registered union. In colonial Africa, it is noted that whenever Africans took over higher posts without the necessary experience and qualifications, productivity would be very poor as has been the case in Ghana, Angola and Guinea. In the Sub-Sahara, Zimbabwe has never precisely formulated or implemented Affirmative Action.	Your fleeting reference to a few isolated countries is neither correct nor complete. Although not a legal requirement, affirmative action (AA) has been, and still is being, practised by large companies in Zimbabwe. See Strachan (1993) and Gatherer & Erickson (in Innes, 1993) which you consulted according to your list of sources (references).

In the South African context various factors affecting success and failures of Affirmative Action as a reactive process to address discrimination in job need to be analysed and this is the basis for the research.	What are the various factors you referred to?
3 MOTIVATION FOR THE INVESTIGATION	
Affirmative action is an issue that continues to arouse interest and demand attention and deliberations in the content of a changing South Africa. To date, much has been debated and written on the issue, particularly on the philosophy of the policy and the implementation.	The purpose of this paragraph is not clear. It does not form part of the motivation for the research.
However, these arguments and deliberations have focussed primarily on the need to address imbalances emanating from the apartheid era, as Griffin (1990:25) contends. Ironically, the South African society is engaged in a multiparty democracy with diversified political persuasions. It is this dichotomy that arouses interest in the project since their viewpoints on affirmative action differ significantly.	
The practical and fundamental importance of the study, therefore, is to attempt to evaluate whether or not external consultancy has a bearing on the quality of people employed and the resultant production.	It is not clear why external consultancy is considered important.
The assumption is made that rationalization necessitates union involvement as a result of the Government's open-door policy	Why does rationalisation necessitate union involvement?
4 AIMS OF THE RESEARCH	
Whilst affirmative action is a major focus in the 1990s, Innes (1993:1) sees it as a priority which will pave the way for a truly democratic society. The main aim of the investigation is to establish perception concerning the role of trade unions on affirmative action.	There is no link between these two sentences. In addition, why do you want to establish perception concerning the role of trade unions on affirmative action? What is the significance of this? How can organisations benefit from the research?
This aim may be supported by secondary aims in an attempt to explain why people join the unions.	The secondary aim must also relate to the title of the research.
These objectives may be considered as indirect methods of maintaining the welfare of union members.	This statement does not make sense.
At the end of the research, it will be clear to everybody that on a macro level, addressing the imbalances of the past is the ideal objective, but such efforts should not be executed in a dogmatic manner without taking cognisance of the practical implications.	Phrases such as "... it will be clear to everybody ..." are too sweeping. Yes, it is important to consider the practical implications. At this stage, can you identify some of these?

5 THEORETICAL GROUNDING OF THE INVESTIGATION	
Theoretical grounding of the investigation should emphasise the following themes: • An explanation of the concept affirmative action as well as its operation. Affirmative action is best described by Rosenfeld (1991:42) as an attempt to bring members of under represented groups, that have suffered discrimination into a higher degree of participation in some beneficial programme. – Beneficiaries: This is a controversial issue as beneficiaries are described in political and racial overtones. – Moral, political and constitutional arguments for and against affirmative action • An explanation of the concept Trade Union. – Section 25 of the New Labour Relations Act (LRA) 66 of 1995 provides for workers representation in the workplace.	Consider South African definitions of affirmative action, especially by the Department of Labour. Rosenfeld s definition is not the best one. The phrase '...some beneficial program.' is vague. Give your own interpretation of the term after you have provided a formal definition. In addition, your theoretical basis for terms such as 'beneficiaries' is not clear. Be specific. Who are the beneficiaries? Please read the Employment Equity Bill. What is the relevance of moral, political and constitutional arguments for and against affirmative action? The fact that affirmative action will need to be compatible with the Constitution and the above-mentioned Bill makes some of these issues somewhat irrelevant. Also, the concept trade union is not explained. Yes, the Labour Relations Act (LRA) makes provision for worker representation in the workplace, but you should indicate the relevance of this for your study.
– Why workers join trade unions (Finnemore & Van der Merwe 1992:95–97).	Why do workers join trade unions – relevance?
6 AN OVERVIEW OF RELATED STUDIES	
There is not enough literature to address issues related to affirmative action.	This statement is incorrect. There is a vast amount of literature available on issues related to affirmative action. According to the Human Sciences Research Council, more that 100 theses are being written on affirmative action.
Available literature with regard to this current issue can be categorised as follows: • Studies that are generally well executed: Some books written within an American context are generally well executed. In the American context, affirmative action was aimed mainly at blacks (Qunta, 1995:29). Nevertheless, there are some American indicators for the South African situation. For example, the book by	Your discussion of available literature is inadequate. You are not required to do book reviews. Rather, take the most relevant literature and indicate how your study will build on it. In addition, when criticising other studies, make sure that your criticism is valid, objective and well

Conrad P.J. and Maddur R.B. sets a comprehensive and practical guidelines about equal employment and affirmative action which may well be executed in South Africa. • The second category are those studies with some shortcomings which invalidate findings: Some books written within the South African context are marred by shortcomings. For instance, Maphai seems to be biased against other racial groups in dealing with beneficiaries for affirmative action whilst Hugo favours the whites. It is therefore, a matter of black and white syndrome. Test samples are taken from their respective communities and they rely on their empirical observation and subjective interpretation of important issues. Books written under these circumstances cannot depict a clear and objective picture of employment problems in South Africa.	substantiated from a scientific perspective.
• Areas where little or no systematic knowledge exists: Klug (1993:25) is of the opinion that all along the National Party (NP) has been practising affirmative action.	Klug's statement bears no relevance to your topic.
• Well conducted studies: Christine Qunta's book, Who is Afraid of Affirmative Action is unique. While most of the provision for worker representation in the workplace, but you should indicate the relevance of this for your study.	Your review of Qunta's book does not relate to the topic of your research either. Yes, the author does focus on the role of the black professional, but how will you integrate this with the perceptions of trade unions?
7 STATEMENT OF PROBLEM AND ITS PRACTICAL RELEVANCE	
The research problem can be formulated as follows: "To what extent will trade unions have an effect on affirmative action programmes?" This problem may be elucidated by the following hypotheses:	The problem statement is not well formulated. Check your grammar as well. Elaborate more on the problem in a paragraph or two prior to formulating your hypotheses.
H_0 There is no significant difference in the perceptions of government-, trade union and academic respondents that trade unions must be involved in affirmative action programmes.	
H_A There is significant difference in the perceptions of government-, trade union and academic respondents that trade unions must be involved in affirmative action programmes.	
Rationale: Affirmative action will pave the way for racial integration. This means that the traditional rule that certain jobs are reserved for Whites will disappear. Unions will no longer be aggressive towards the management.	Your rationale does not relate to the hypothesis. The hypotheses must flow logically from the theoretical rationale and review of the literature.

Problems facing civil service centre around the following: • Psychological and symbolic level (Hugo & Scheire, 1990:133). The September Commission of Cosatu in Kempton Park exposed deep rooted mistrust between the government and COSATU (Adler, 1997:38). • The economic role of civil service (Walton & Handy, 1997:210) • On political level, civil service is strongly partisan and top echelon in the civil service should represent a major political power block.	What is the relevance of the mistrust between the government and COSATU? Please explain. What do you mean when you state that the civil service is strongly partisan and should represent a major political power block? The emphasis you place on the civil service gives the impression that you intend to focus your study on the civil service, but this not explicitly mentioned anywhere in your proposal.
8 THE INVESTIGATION The investigation will be carried out, very broadly in the following way: 8.1 Method According to Huysamen (1993:26) the survey method is generally used when the researcher wishes to elicit opinions. Since the objective of the research will be to measure perceptions concerning the impacts of trade union on affirmative action, the survey method is deemed to be most appropriate. It will also be practically impossible to exercise control over the variables. As a sensitive project, participants will be able to voice their opinions without being recognized. 8.2 Test Samples The target population for this research will be the top management in the Government service, Trade unionists and the academics. This will be done by approaching informants in a simple random sample. The number required for the whole exercise will be one hundred and fifty (150). The said procedure will be conducted irrespective of age distribution, level of education, socio-economic status, gender or creed. Data collected will be used to test the hypothesis. 8.3 Measuring Instruments It is important that measuring instruments used should ensure some measure of reliability and validity. Most appropriate measuring instruments are survey questionnaires. According to Huysamen (1993, p.128) these are used to obtain information from respondents about	Why are academics to be included, which academics are going to be included, and from which institutions or departments? Which trade unions will be used? What problems do you foresee? Will all groups complete the same questionnaire, and if so, how many questionnaires for each group? Have you considered alternative data collection methods and sampling procedures? More information is needed on your questionnaire. What do you plan to include in the questionnaire? How and where will the questionnaires be administered and distributed? How will reliability and validity be

biographical particulars (age, educational qualification, etcetera) typical behaviour (what they favour) opinions and attitudes. Structured and unstructured question-naires and these will conform to the Likert Scale.	ensured? Why have you referred to structured and unstructured questionnaires? How will the Likert scale be used?
8.4 Statistical analysis An appropriate statistical technique is the *t*-test. Illustrations in the form of diagrams will be demonstrated.	Why is the *t*-test appropriate, and how and where will this analysis be done?
9 EXPECTED RESULTS It is expected trade unionists will favour dominating role in affirmative action involvement whereas the majority of top management in the public service will favour no role of trade unionists because of frequent conflicts with the government policies. The academics will not favour any trade union involvement. In fact, affirmative action should pave the way for equal opportunities	How do these statements relate to your hypotheses? What is your rationale for stating that academics would not favour trade union involvement?
10 A LIST OF EQUIPMENT AND FACILITIES THAT WILL BE REQUIRED A computer is most appropriate to analyse data in this regard.	This statement does not constitute a list. Which computer package will be used? Any other equipment and facilities?
11 PROGRAMME/SCHEDULE Progress reports will be submitted per chapter per month after Ist March 2002 until the whole project is completed.	A detailed research plan is required. When will the literature study be conducted? When will the survey instrument be compiled? When will it be distributed? When will data be collected and analysed? When will results be discussed? When will language editing be done? When will the manuscript be typed? When will the final product be completed?
12 THE POSSIBLE IMPACT ON INDUSTRY AND/OR COMMUNITY Affirmative action practice has a bearing on national economic reconstruction issues. Production by well satisfied and qualified employees will result in increased production and subsequent economic increase. Economics often shudder at the costs affirmative action will demand to compensate for the inefficiencies that are likely to follow from some irregular affirmative action initiatives.	This paragraph is one of the most important parts of your proposal. You should clearly indicate the value of your study for industry and the community. Once again, this discussion should be directly related to your topic.

13. LIST OF SOURCES	
ADLER, GLENN. 1977. Cosatu s Fine Balancing Act. Mail Guardian.19–25 September: 38. CONRAD, P.J. & MADDUX, R.B. 1988. Guide to Affirmative Action: A Primer for Supervisors and Managers. Menlo Park: CA Crisp. FINNERMORE, M. & VAN DER MERWE, R.1992. 3rd ed. Introduction to Industrial Relations in South Africa. Johannesburg: Lexicon. GRIFFIN, R.W. 1990. Management. Boston: Hougton. HUGO, P. & SCHRIRE, R. 1990. Affirmative Action in the Public Service: Critical Choices for South Africa – Agenda for the 1990's. Cape Town: Oxford. HUYSAMEN, G.K. 1994. Methodology for the Social and Behavioral Sciences. Halfway House: Southern. INNES, D. 1993. Affirmative Action: Issues and Strategies. IN Kentridge, M. & Perold, H. (Eds). Reversing Discrimination Affirmative Action in the workplace: 4–21. Cape Town: Oxford. KLUG, H. 1993. Affirmative Action in Action. Suid-Afrikaan: 20–25.May/Jun. ROSENFELD, M. 1991. Affirmative Action & Justice – A philosophical and Constitutional Enquiry. London: Yale. QUNTA, C. 1995. Who's Afraid of Affirmative Action. Cape Town: Kwela Books. ROGENFELD, M. 1991. Affirmative Action and Justice – A Philosophical and Constitutional Inquiry. London: Yale. WALTON, M. & HENDY, J. 1997. Individual Right To Union Representation in International Law. International Law Journal, 26(3) 207–210. SEPT.	There are a number of mistakes in your list of references (you named it "sources"!), for example incorrect dates, the omission of subtitles, and incorrect alphabetical sequence.

PROPOSAL CHECKLIST QUESTIONS	SCORE			
The title:	N	1	2	3
• is a true reflection of the contents of the proposal • is not too long yet descriptive • contains the important variables.		X	 X X	
The statement of the problem:	N	1	2	3
• is formulated clearly and understandably • is formulated adequately in terms of defined concepts relevant to the topic and field of study • does not relate to something trivial, but is of scientific theoretical and/or practical significance (so that it holds the prospect of an expansion of subject knowledge)		X X		 X

• clearly describes the theory, practical problem or previous research from which it proceeds logically		X		
• explicitly sets out different points of view and assumptions		X		
• is congruent with the title as well as the aim of the study (addresses the same issue/s)		X		
• culminates in research hypotheses or research questions which are formulated clearly in terms of the relationship between the important variables.		X		
The literature review:	N	1	2	3
• is relevant to the aim and problem statement of the study		X		
• is sufficiently comprehensive and used essential information sources		X		
• offers a logically organised and integrated summary (in the researcher's own words, of course)		X		
• notes theories relevant to the aim of the study		X		
• includes key words/terms/concepts used in a computer literature search with a copy of its results.		X		
The research design:	N	1	2	3
• is appropriate for the problem in question (survey or experimental or case study design, and so on)		X		
• is described clearly in respect of the following aspects (so that it is replicable)		X		
i) sampling procedures (so that, for example, the experimentally accessible population is clear)		X		
ii) the way in which the respondents will be classified or the participants are to be assigned to groups		X		
iii) interventions (if appropriate) and/or measuring instruments administered to subjects		X		
• takes care of threats to internal validity (for example: nuisance and third variable problems, pre-existing differences between groups, and so on)		X		
• takes care of threats to external validity (for example: the generalisability of the results from the sample to the target population and/or to other situations, and so on).		X		

The measuring instrument's:	N	1	2	3
• contents are described briefly • administering and/or data gathering procedures are described • reliability is discussed • validity is discussed.		X X X	 X	
The analytical/statistical techniques:	N	1	2	3
• are appropriate for the given problem (descriptive and/or inferential).		X		
The proposal:	N	1	2	3
• is limited to 10 typed pages • includes a time schedule for the writing of different chapters.		 X		X

Key to score:

N	Not applicable
1	Unacceptable and leaves much room for improvement
2	Has much merit; leaves a little room for improvement
3	As good as possible

CONCLUSION

In the light of the above comments it is evident that you need to redevelop your research proposal. By taking cognisance of the comments and suggestions made, the scientific quality of this proposal will be improved and you will get a clear picture of the research plan and its implications.

A well-developed research proposal will not only guide you during the research process, but will also prevent frustration when problems do occur. It will make it easier for you to achieve the objectives of your study and complete the dissertation.

Please reconsider answering the following questions in rewriting your research proposal:

- What is the central question or problem?
- Why is this problem important and worthy of studying?
- What research methods will you use and why?
- What is the time structure for each stage of your proposed research methods and writing process?

Activity 11.1

Evaluate the following research proposal according to the example above and the checklist (Section 11.5.)

RESEARCH PROPOSAL

by

X.X. WHYBESOBER

submitted in partial fulfilment of the
preliminary requirements for the

MASTER'S DEGREE IN COMPUTER SCIENCE

UNIVERSITY OF NOT SO STUPID

Supervisor: Dr C. Omputer

April 2004

Note

This should be a full page – the first page of the proposal.

Research title

A description of Object Oriented design implementation problems in the software engineering industry.

Motivation

Due to the difficult nature of the software engineering industry there is a constant move to new methods for solving design problems. More specifically there is a move towards the Object Oriented (OO) methods, presumably because of the various advantages offered in terms of maintainability, and changeability of code produced this way.

As with various other aspects of the software industry there are, however, also problems encountered in this transition and lessons to be learned from the experience of companies who have already performed this change.

The aim of this study therefore is to know what these problems are and how to avoid them in order to make a success of Object Oriented (OO) projects, so that the advantages offered by OO can indeed be utilised. Also, before making this change, it is useful to find out if indeed the change should be made to OO and if there are not even newer options available.

Problem

The research done will look at the general change in methods, but will concentrate on two areas:

- where change was undertaken from a previously structured design to an OO design; and
- where informal or no design principles were previously used.

Possible contribution to study field

The final report will provide guidelines for companies who are currently contemplating a change to the OO methodology, covering important issues one should know about prior to this change.

It will also summarise the problems faced in the transition so far, the reasons for these problems and suggest possible solutions.

Planned approach and proposed solution

The target population that the study will concentrate on is the situation in the South African market place.

While researching this transition, a questionnaire will be developed and circulated to selected companies, in conjunction with interviews addressing the following issues:

- the role of CASE tools
- budget size of the project undertaken, number of people involved as well as company size (according to taxable profits) and area of work (military, banking, and so on)
- skills base of developers used (years of experience and qualifications), permanent or contracting, in house skills, consultants, and so on
- specific method used the past two years, if any, and reasons for specific choice of method
- influence of the need for obtaining ISO 9000 or similar accreditation within the same department or company
- cost and time implications of existing method
- resistance faced internally when changing methods
- the role of cost effective software project management
- the situation companies in South Africa face, in contrast with the global situation: is there anything to be learnt from the development done overseas.

Depending on the results obtained, some of the above areas will be studied more carefully, if it is found to have an important influence on the progress of projects.

Draft work plan

The following chart demonstrates the tasks and their proposed duration during 2004:

Plan of action	Feb–Mar	Apr–May	Jun–Jul	Aug–Sept	Oct
Literature study	X				
Data collection		X	X		
Interviews		X	X		
Data interpretation			X	X	
Interim report		X	X		
Evaluation				X	
Final report					X

Literature study

A literature search and review will be conducted to find out what work has already been done in this research area, and what type of data will need to be collected. Where possible data from the Internet will be collected and all other possible resources will also be explored.

Units of analysis

The emphasis throughout will be on South African companies and projects, since the constraints are often localised, and may be different from those experienced overseas.

It is important to note that the word transition is used in this proposal to refer not only to the change made from other methods (such as structured methods) but also to refer to those situations where no design method was previously used. Companies that fall in the latter category will therefore also be included in the study.

Data collection

A list of companies will be compiled. Selection will be done such that all the main business sectors are covered, including banking, retail, military and mining, using stratified sampling procedures. Selection will also be done in such a way that the entire range from small to large enterprises is covered. Questionnaires will be sent to all the selected companies that are willing to assist in the research, ensuring a high response rate.

Interviews

Once the questionnaires have been sent out, interviews will be arranged and conducted with the selected companies to discuss the questionnaire (either telephonically or personally), as well as any additional information these companies can supply that could be of assistance.

Data interpretation

Data collected will be interpreted to find any similarities between design methods and the companies that use it.

The data acquired will be evaluated in conjunction with all other information acquired via resources such as the Internet and literature available, followed by suggestions. This will include profiles of companies that made the transition.

In addition, the transition process that takes place will be classified to determine what was or is a successful or unsuccessful method of change.

Evaluation

Once all the necessary data have been obtained and evaluated, the results will be interpreted and written up and possible guidelines formulated.

Requirements at the University

For the literature study and data collection, the library facilities as well as access to the Electrical Engineering network will be required.

Costs involved in the research include photocopying, fax and telephone costs, as well as the cost of travelling to the various companies.

Activity 11.2

Do Activity 3.1 and the self-evaluation exercise given at the end of Chapter 10.

Note

See pages 42-43 for a list of academic journals (periodicals) that contain mostly good articles that may be used as information sources for the literature review (introduction) of your research proposal.

Summary

In general, the research proposal refers to the preconceived plan according to which the number of, and manner in which the individual units of analysis should be formed and information is to be collected as well as analysed for the envisaged investigation of the research hypothesis or research question/central theme.

Appendices

Appendix A

A laboratory study of the effects of situation redefinition on spatial crowding

There is an increase in the stress that accompanies the present population explosion and increased urbanisation, overcrowded situations (for example, overpopulated residential areas, crowded trains and buses). Although various researchers (among others, Proshansky, Ittelson & Rivlin, 1973) are of the opinion that coping mechanisms may play a significant role in respect of stress during spatial crowding, little research on this relationship has been reported in the literature.

According to Sundstrom (1975), cognitive and/or perceptual adjustment processes may reduce the experience of stress situations. Research by Holmes and Houston (1974) suggests that the redefinition of an expected stressful situation may serve as a successful coping mechanism in the stressful situation itself. For example, they told one experimental group to think of electrical shocks which they were about to receive as "a vibration sensation" and to tell themselves that "These aren't shocks: they are vibrations" (p. 214).

McFall and Twentyman (1973) found that audiotape recordings on which different test situations were defined, and according to which subjects could model their own reactions, were just as effective as audiovisual tape recordings.

The purpose of the present study is to investigate the effectiveness of a similar situation-redefinition technique as a coping mechanism in a more diffusely stressful situation such as spatial crowding.

The following research hypotheses are formulated:

- A high-density spatial crowding situation will result in a higher degree of negative effect and more negative experiences of interpersonal relationships and of the physical conditions of the experimental situation than will a low-density spatial crowding situation.
- These adverse effects of crowding will be less severe for the experimental group, which employs an externally-induced coping mechanism, namely situation redefinition, than for the control group, which does not employ this mechanism.

Subjects

To hold constant the effect of sex, only male students will be used. About 64 first-year student volunteers from the Rand Afrikaans University will participate.

Experimental design

The effect of the two independent variables of spatial crowding (with two levels: high density and low density) and situation redefinition (with two levels: presence versus absence of it) will be investigated in a design in which these two variables will be completely crossed and in which there will be two groups nested in each of the resulting four combinations (of the two levels of each of the two variables). Subjects will be assigned randomly to eight groups of eight each who will meet separately in one of the Psychology laboratories. The dimensions of the latter are similar to those used in previous research on spatial crowding [for example, that of Sundstrom (1975)], namely, 1,65 m x 3 m with no exterior windows for the high-density situation, and 6 m x 6 m for the low-density situation. In each room eight plastic chairs with no arm supports will be arranged in a circle.

After the eight groups have been assigned randomly to the eight rooms, two people will be selected randomly from each group to switch on the tape recording and distribute the questionnaires, respectively. On the tape to be played to the four groups that are going to be exposed to the situation redefinition, a density situation similar to the one to which they are exposed, and in which the subjects are discussing Jourard's (1971) self-disclosure topics positively, will first be sketched. Next all eight groups will discuss the same self-disclosure topics for 45 minutes. Finally, all eight groups will be given instructions by means of the tape recording to complete the questionnaires.

Measuring instruments

The Mood Adjective Check List of Nowlis (1965) will be used to measure intrapsychic behaviour in terms of a series of seven-point rating scales (for aggression, anxiety, cheerfulness and exhaustion, among others). Interpersonal behaviour (experience of the friendliness, pleasantness, social affect and genuineness, among others, of fellow participants) will also be assessed by means of a series of seven-point rating scales. The experience of the physical conditions of the experimental rooms will be measured by having the subjects complete seven-point rating scales (of the pleasantness, interestingness, duration of experiment, comfortableness, temperature and ventilation of the experimental rooms) and by having them estimate the size of these rooms.

After completion of the questionnaires, the subjects will be informed about the nature of the experiment.

Statistical analysis

The intercorrelations among the various dependent variables will be computed to investigate the discriminant validity of the various measures. A two-factor analysis of variance will be performed to investigate the significance of the two main effects. In the case of significant interaction effects, Tukey's HSD test will be carried out to determine the significance of the differences between cell means.

References

Holmes, D.S. & Houston, B.K. (1974). Effectiveness of situation redefinition and affective isolation in coping with stress. *Journal of Personality and Social Psychology*, **29**(2), 212–218.

Jourard, S.M. (1971). *Self-disclosure: An experimental analysis of the transparent self.* New York: Wiley & Sons.

McFall, R.M. & Twentyman, CT. (1973). Four experiments on the relative contributions of rehearsal, modeling, and coaching to assertion training. *Journal of Abnormal Behaviour*, **81**, 199–218.

Nowlis, V. (1965). Research with the Mood Adjective Check List. In S.A. Tomkins & C. Izards (Eds). *Affect, cognition and personality.* New York: Springer.

Proshansky, H.M., Ittelson, W.H. & Rivlin, L.G. (1976). *Environmental psychology: People and their physical settings.* New York: Holt, Rinehart & Winston.

Sundstrom, E. (1975). An experimental study of crowding: Effects of room size, intrusion, and goal blocking on nonverbal behavior, self-disclosure, and self-reported stress. *Journal of Personality and Social Psychology*, **32**(4), 645–654.

Compiled retrospectively from Van Staden and Viljoen (1980) which had been based on an M.Sc. dissertation submitted by the first author to the RAU in 1978. Used with the kind permission of Dr Van Staden.

Appendix B

Answers to some self-evaluation questions

1.1 layperson's knowledge; accidental observation

1.2 layperson's knowledge; authority

2.1 There are more cars with GP registration numbers than any other registration numbers on that route. Consequently one may expect more careless drivers with GP registration numbers than with other numbers on this route.

2.2 There may be other reasons which play a role in a decision to go to university, such as social pressure of parents or peers.

2.4 a) sex, race and ability of applicant
b) success of application

5.1 a) experimental research
b) field study

5.2 a) i) Pre-experimental research
ii) Premeasurement and postmeasurement design

5.3 interrupted time-series design

5.4 interrupted time-series design

5.5 a) non-experimental research
b) correlational design

5.8 panel study

6.1 This design would be regarded as internally valid to the extent that an increase in assertiveness may be unambiguously ascribed to the assertiveness training programme rather than anything else. Possible threats include: Historical events possibly occurring concurrently with the programme, spontaneous development of assertiveness as students become more familiar with their new environment, measurement reactivity and the regression effect.

6.2 None of the threats under 6.1 applies.

6.3 Lecturers are usually older than students. With increasing age comes poorer vision. Those with poorer eyesight probably sign their names larger than those with better eyesight.

6.4 Population validity is suspect because only employees of a particular insurance company, who are not necessarily representative of all individuals with an unhealthy Type A behaviour, were used.

Ecological validity is hampered because of the artificiality of the situations to which subjects were exposed in a specially-equipped room.

6.5 Because the students were aware of the fact that they were participating in an experiment, their behaviour possibly might not have been representative of their behaviour in similar real-life situations of spatial crowding.

7.1 a) interval (approximately)
b) ordinal
c) nominal
d) nominal.

7.3 Semantic differential

7.8 Again there is a difference of opinion. It could be argued that it is difficult to see how someone's dignity could be impugned if neither the person whose dignity is so affected nor the person who does this to him or her, is familiar with the former's identity.

7.9 Construct validity of the operationalisation of the independent variable is subject because of the possibility of subject effects (the so-called control group does not meet the definition of such a group) and experimenter effects (raters know which of the subjects were in the experimental group and which were in the control group).

7.9 Systematic, direct observation

7.10 a) direct observation
b) journal articles
c) intercoder reliability

Appendix C

Table of random numbers (Huysamen, 1989a)

97	76	75	66	21	32	99	04	37	80	15	28
49	70	78	25	05	11	26	50	66	42	58	76
61	80	34	80	70	02	75	34	24	33	34	12
82	93	22	90	42	38	44	22	38	22	56	73
92	50	70	65	59	62	39	79	17	89	67	54
80	80	56	13	73	21	69	27	36	73	36	90
11	04	24	07	26	93	22	97	78	98	04	89
80	01	79	63	68	41	29	09	84	27	47	34
00	55	27	65	42	68	32	75	57	70	46	79
02	76	38	45	26	52	76	84	20	59	88	65
74	08	77	92	54	91	64	60	81	48	15	56
56	06	25	94	43	07	51	42	95	88	35	82
74	49	24	99	77	72	37	73	02	55	63	50
04	30	44	90	42	36	38	97	41	73	71	41
66	39	34	52	01	40	28	04	76	15	47	98
05	95	21	69	18	87	63	89	67	00	81	26
97	80	04	01	64	71	50	61	14	28	99	09
46	20	02	29	59	89	03	12	42	43	99	04
74	56	71	17	63	21	61	74	92	86	94	76
99	51	13	12	58	36	93	28	27	13	74	81
26	43	21	34	14	77	30	87	51	24	41	81
79	60	42	11	85	11	97	82	17	62	29	89
20	62	87	64	01	31	74	64	22	48	73	96
93	22	94	63	28	98	38	46	31	66	28	19
14	91	17	79	20	05	46	31	70	42	06	66
20	40	63	12	03	14	55	95	78	08	61	85
48	13	42	32	11	79	75	36	34	80	29	38
73	17	45	12	65	79	90	24	34	83	64	03
90	92	43	30	91	67	88	19	19	42	31	48
79	94	51	57	78	53	13	01	89	20	02	27
19	33	26	50	70	66	63	80	11	48	16	66
85	73	73	84	43	99	85	30	41	80	09	29
02	95	49	36	71	02	68	85	98	24	67	04
55	11	76	51	21	61	79	21	13	88	53	70
06	42	96	94	01	58	37	00	65	86	54	59
27	87	75	66	22	35	12	58	40	15	13	98
29	30	22	58	48	65	53	34	23	32	86	20
81	99	59	59	27	27	15	40	06	76	21	95
00	12	71	18	69	53	92	78	38	22	39	76
87	19	27	91	03	95	42	93	80	40	40	10

Note

Compare Section 4.2.2.2 as well as the random number generator on the CD-ROM attached to the back cover page of this book.

Appendix D
Case Study A

AIDS: Knowledge and attitudes of a group of South African health professionals

Introduction

Over the last decade there has been growing concern about the rapid spread of acquired immune deficiency syndrome (AIDS) throughout the world. AIDS was first diagnosed in South Africa in 1982 and is spreading steadily. By December 1990, 613 full-blown AIDS cases had been diagnosed positively. The average doubling time for AIDS in South Africa is 11,4 months (Ijsselmuiden et al., 1988). There is therefore an urgent need to continue with research and to plan for the management and prevention of the syndrome.

This study is an attempt to investigate attitudes towards AIDS among a group of South African health professionals. Since doctors and nurses are often the first-line staff who deal with AIDS cases, their attitudes towards these patients are meaningful for treatment and prevention purposes.

One of the greatest obstacles in the case of AIDS is the moral censure and prejudice surrounding the syndrome. Because negative stereotypes tend to characterise the high-risk groups that have been identified, namely, homosexuals, prostitutes and users of intravenous drugs, they have influenced the general social perceptions of AIDS sufferers (Levi, 1987). We must understand these attitudes if we want to implement effective educational programmes (Ijsselmuiden et al., 1988).

It was widely accepted that effective education on AIDS requires people to learn about the facts of the syndrome, and that this knowledge is adequate to eliminate the prejudices and misconceptions regarding the virus and its sufferers. However, recent psychological research (Furnham, 1988) suggests that knowledge of AIDS is perhaps not the main determinant of attitudes towards AIDS. Educational initiatives may therefore be necessary to pay attention to the dominant attitudes towards high-risk groups and provide information at the same time. This study investigated the relationship between attitudes towards AIDS and knowledge of AIDS, as well as attitudes towards the sexuality of an observed high-risk group, namely prostitutes.

The study investigated the extent of correlation between a measurement of subjects' attitudes towards AIDS and the following two variables:

- knowledge of AIDS
- attitude towards prostitution

Subjects

Permission was obtained to conduct the study in a general hospital that served mainly white and coloured population groups. Participation in the study was voluntary. In total, 80 subjects were approached to participate in the study, and 74 completed the questionnaire on which the analysis was based.

Of the 74 subjects:

- 43 were nursing sisters and 31 were doctors
- 48 were female and 26 male
- 61 were white, 7 were coloured, 4 were Indian and 2 were black
- the ages ranged from 22 to 64 years (an average of 38 years).

Instrument

The questionnaire used in this study was based on a scale developed by McManus and Morton (1986). This scale incorporates three basic areas of involvement: knowledge of AIDS, attitude towards AIDS and attitude towards prostitution. The three sections of the questionnaire contained the following broad dimensions:

1 Knowledge of AIDS (18 items):
   1.1 General knowledge of AIDS, for example: *AIDS was first diagnosed in the previous decade.*

1.2 Questions on transmission, symptoms and appearance of AIDS, for example: *One must assume that all people with antibodies against HIV are infected.*
1.3 Questions on AIDS in the South African context, for example: *The occurrence of AIDS is highest among prostitutes in South Africa.*

2 Attitudes towards AIDS (12 items):
2.1 Moral judgement, for example: *AIDS is a punishment for immoral activities.*
2.2 Prejudice based on fear, for example: *AIDS patients must be avoided if possible.*

3 Attitude towards prostitution (12 items):
3.1 The normality or deviation of prostitution, for example: *Prostitution is a psychological disturbance.*
3.2 Moral judgement, for example: *Prostitution is immoral.*
3.3 The rights of prostitutes, for example: *Prostitutes must have job opportunities.*

The first part of the questionnaire comprised 18 knowledge questions and the last part contained the 24 attitude items in random order. It took approximately 30 minutes to complete the questionnaire. Knowledge questions required a true/false or correct/incorrect answer, while the attitude questions were evaluated on a 5-point Likert scale, from DO NOT AGREE AT ALL (1) to AGREE FULLY (5).

Procedure

A pilot study was done to ensure that the questionnaire was effective. After small amendments, the questionnaire was given to the subjects individually. Subjects were assured that the questionnaire was confidential and they were encouraged to answer as honestly as possible. The data were collected over a period of two weeks in 1988.

The questionnaires were marked individually and then analysed statistically. Each question was analysed individually in terms of validity, content and the frequency of responses. In addition, Pearson's product moment correlation was used to calculate the correlation between the three dimensions of the questionnaire.

Correlations were based on the average score of each subject for each of the three sections of the questionnaire which concerned the variables being studied.

Results

Only the correlative data are given below, since they were the most convincing for the article. The correlations between the three variables are illustrated in Table A.

Table A
Correlative findings

	Attitude towards AIDS	Attitude towards prostitution
Knowledge of AIDS	0,22	0,03
Attitudes towards AIDS		0,60

References

Furnham, A. 1988. *The relationship between knowledge of, and attitudes to AIDS.* Unpublished manuscript. London: Department of Psychology, University College.

Gottlieb, M. 1987. *AIDS in Africa: an agenda for behavioural scientists.* In N. Miler & R.C. Rockwell (Eds). AIDS in Africa: The Social and Policy Impact. Queenston: Edward Mellen.

Ijsselmuiden, C.B., Steinberg, M.H., Padayachee, G.N., Schoub, B.D., Strauss, S.A., Buch, E., Davies, J.C.A., De Beer, C., Gear, J.S.S. & Hurwitz, H.S. 1988. AIDS and *South Africa – towards a comprehensive strategy*: Part I-III. South African Medical Journal, **73**: 455–467.

McManus, I. & Morton, A. 1986. Attitudes to and knowledge about the acquired immune deficiency syndrome: Lack of a correlation. *British Medical Journal*. **293**: 67–71.

Case Study B

The effect of role induction on goldsmith apprentices' perceptions of supervision

Introduction

Supervision over goldsmith apprentices is essential because the incorrect use of precious metals and stones in the creation of jewellery leads to large financial losses. However, the supervision is often stressful, partly because of the apprentices' lack of knowledge of the supervision process (Cohen, 1980; Schauer, Seymour & Green, 1985). Goldsmith apprentices receive theoretical and applied training, but there are few training programmes that prepare apprentices in any way for the supervision experience. It therefore limits the effectiveness of the supervision interaction.

It is clear that if apprentices were better informed of what supervision entails, the period of adaptation could be shorter and less stressful, and the quality of the supervision relationship could therefore be improved.

Role induction (by showing a video) is one method of informing apprentices of the supervision process. The current investigation examined the effectiveness of a role induction procedure during the adaptation process of goldsmith apprentices. The role induction procedure is designed to provide the apprentices with a conceptual framework to understand the roles, expectations and objectives of the supervision process. For the specific role induction, the apprentices were shown a video of Bernard's (1979) supervision model. This model defines the supervisor role (for example, adviser) and the objectives of supervision (for example, to improve diamond setting skills). The ideal is that the apprentices' needs determine the choice of the supervision objective and the supervisor role that must be fulfilled.

Two hypotheses were investigated in the study. The first hypothesis was that if no role induction is offered, the apprentices' evaluations of supervision will become increasingly negative over time. This hypothesis is based on the belief that the apprentices' lack of understanding of the expectations and roles of supervision will lead to confusion, stress and increasing dissatisfaction with the supervision interaction. The second hypothesis was that the implementation of the role induction procedure will lead to a more favourable evaluation of supervision.

Subjects

The subjects were 20 goldsmith apprentices with no previous experience of supervision, and who were enrolled for a course in goldsmith work at a large jewellery firm. Of the 20 subjects:

- 10 were women and 10 were men
- six were white, seven were black and seven were coloured
- nine were 19 years old, eight were 20 years old and three were 21 years old.

Role induction

For the role induction procedure, the subjects studied a 10-minute video recording describing Bernard's (1979) supervision model. The video briefly outlined the objectives of supervision, such as improving goldsmith skills in various areas. The skills dimensions were described in order to explain the concepts. After the presentation of the goldsmith skills areas, a brief overview was given of the supervisors' roles.

The subjects were told that the video had been compiled to promote communication in the supervision process. The video was shown in a small-group situation during an ordinary scheduled practical class.

Questionnaire

The semantic differential (SD) was used as a measure of the subjects' attitudes towards supervision. The questionnaire comprised six bipolar word pairs where subjects had to indicate their associations with the key concept "supervision". Osgood (1952) indicated test-retest correlations of 0,85 for group averages in the SD.

Procedure

All the subjects completed the questionnaire (SD) on three occasions. The questionnaire was given to all the apprentices at the beginning of the training period to obtain a baseline measure of attitudes towards supervision before the process was begun. The second and third evaluations were done immediately before the role induction (showing of the video) and one week after role induction. It was assumed that differences in the subjects' responses that became evident between the first and second evaluations could be attributed to the effect of time on supervision. It was also assumed that differences in subjects' responses from the second to the third application reflected changes stemming from the role induction procedure.

All the apprentices received group and individual supervision by licensed and different supervisors during the entire training period. None of the individual and group supervisors was aware of the aim or nature of the role induction intervention.

Results

All 20 subjects in the sample completed the questionnaire from which data on the early, middle and late role induction groups were obtained. This data were used to make comparisons between the first and second application (changes as a result of time in supervision) and between the second and third application (changes as a result of role induction). Table B summarises the averages and standard deviations for the dependent measures over the three evaluation periods.

Table B
Averages and standard deviations over time for the semantic differential (SD)

		Time 1	Time 2	Time 3
Evaluation of supervision	$\bar{X}$	2,76	3,24	3,19
	s	0,73	0,83	0,96

Note: Higher scores on the SD reflect more negative evaluations.

References

Bernard, J. 1989. Supervision training: A discrimination model. *Education and Supervision*, **2**(19):60–68.

Cohen, L. 1990. The new supervisee views supervision. New York: Wiley.

Osgood, C.E. 1952. The nature and measurement of meaning. *Psychological Bulletin*, **49**:197–237.

Schauer, A.H., Seymour, W.R. & Green, R.G. 1993. Effects of observation and evaluation on anxiety in apprentices. *Journal of Development*, **6**(3):26–47.

Case Study C

Evaluation of a training course in management principles for first-line supervisors at a South African agricultural corporation

Introduction

Because unskilled supervisors often learn negative behaviour that is difficult to change, it is important that supervisors learn the skills of supervision before they are introduced into supervisory situations (Jacobs, 1985). To emphasise the urgency of offering evaluated management courses, Nortjé and Crous (1990) point out that supervisors in Southern

Africa must be trained to meet the increasing challenges and higher expectations.

According to Heunis (1981), it is important that when time and money are invested in training needs, training interventions are not launched without the necessary evaluation. Flippo (1981) supports this thought when he mentions that the only answer to the evaluation of management courses lies in the scientific evaluation of training results.

The aim of this research study is therefore to evaluate the above management course for first-line supervisors on a scientific basis with regard to their knowledge in order to determine the effectiveness of the course for the agricultural corporation.

Problem statement

The problem, according to the formulation of the aim of this study, is whether a significant increase in the knowledge of first-line supervisors will occur because of their attendance of a management course.

Subjects

An experimental group and a control group were used. The sample group consisted of 40 supervisors (experimental $n = 18$, control group $n = 22$), randomly drawn from a population of 60 supervisors working for the agricultural corporation from the following provinces and distributed as follows:

- Free State: 9
- Mpumalanga: 6
- North West: 14
- Northern Cape: 11.

Measuring instrument

The measuring instrument consisted of a one-hour written test that was used to evaluate the knowledge of management principles of the experimental and control group in the pre- and post-phases.

Procedure

A non-equivalent control group design was used in this study. The researcher trained a group of first-line supervisors in management principles. These principles included study objectives such as leadership skills, the presentation of a programme and schedule, organisation of planned actions, guidance and control. The evaluation was carried out before and after the training course to evaluate the nature of the changes in knowledge.

Results

The results of the experimental and control groups were compared with regard to the two phases of evaluation. In Table C, the results of the total group in respect of knowledge (scores on the test presented in percentages) are compared before and after the course was offered to the experimental group.

Table C

Differences in averages between the experimental and control group before and after the training intervention

	Knowledge test scores	
	Before training	After training
Experimental group	57%	78%
Control group	58%	56%

References

Flippo, E B. (1981). *Personnel management*. 5th edition. Auckland: McGraw-Hill.

Heunis, D.F. (1987). *The task of the first-line supervisor in the South African public service.* Unpublished master's dissertation, University of Port Elizabeth, Port Elizabeth.

Jacobs, W. (1985). Training of supervisors. *Human Resource Management*, **1** (1): 35–36.

Nortjé, J D & Crous, M J. (1990). *The changing role of management*. Bloemfontein: University of the Orange Free State.

Case Study D

The relationship between preparation time and actual performance in public speech-making.

Introduction

Public speech coaches have long taken for granted that there is a positive relationship between preparation time and actual performance in public speech-making. They stress the importance of preparation to their students; but what about the student who reports spending hours in preparation and yet makes a poor speech? What about the student who admittedly does very little preparation but is a superb speaker? Hayes (1978) found, for example, that good speakers had lower anxiety levels – this is a factor outside the realm of preparation.

A survey of public speech-making students (Hayes, 1978) showed that nearly all perceived a positive relationship between the time they spent preparing for a speech and the quality of the speech that followed. Reisch and Ballard (1985) encourage coaches of speakers to emphasise practice, writing that "practice at any time, in any place will do more to bolster the self-confidence of a novice speaker than any other factor" (p. 13).

One factor that may diminish the effectiveness of preparation is the amount of anxiety that the speaker feels. Students in basic communication courses who experience speech anxiety, reported being more concerned about audience size and speech length, than preparation procedures (Hayes & Marshall, 1984).

Research questions

This study examined the relationship between preparation time and speech anxiety with respect to the quality of public speaking. The two specific questions addressed in the research were as follows:

1 What is the relationship between speech quality and total preparation time?
2 What is the relationship between speech quality and speech anxiety?

Subjects

The subjects in this study were 49 students from four technikons and they were distributed as follows:

- Cape Technikon: 15
- Technikon Natal: 9
- Technikon Free State: 8
- Technikon Pretoria: 17

The subjects' ages ranged from 18 to 48, with a mean age of 23.

All subjects had completed seven speech-making assignments prior to the final video-taped speech upon which this study is based.

Procedure

Speech preparation time

The subjects were asked to indicate, in minutes, the time they spent on the following activities: discussion with coach, library research, audience analysis, preparation of speaking notes, silent rehearsal, oral rehearsal, and other activities. The times were added to get the total time spent in preparation.

Speech quality

A speech rating scale was used to measure the following: the introduction, conclusion, overall organisation and structure of arguments, eye contact, gestures and movement, voice usage, energy and enthusiasm. Each of these eight elements was evaluated on a 5-point scale (5 – done exceptionally well; 4 – done well; 3 – average; 2 – done poorly; 1 – not done well at all) and the values were added to get a total score for each subject.

Speech anxiety

Speech anxiety was evaluated with a questionnaire developed by Booth and Gould (1986). The questionnaire consists of 21 items pertaining to the subject's general feelings of anxiety about communication. Subjects assign values for all items (for example, "I am short of breath before I begin a speech") on a 4-point scale ranging from 1 (almost never) to 4 (almost always). The responses were added to get a single speech anxiety score for each subject.

Data analysis

The data were analysed with the Statistical Package for Social Sciences (SPSS). To determine the relationship among variables, the product moment correlation was used.

Results

Table D displays the results of this study. It is a summary of the results as they relate to the two research questions.

Table D
Correlations between speech quality and other variables

	Speech quality
Speech preparation time	0,75
Speech anxiety	0,03

Booth and Gould (1986) used Cronbach's coefficient alpha as a reliability estimate for the communication anxiety questionnaire and reported a coefficient of 0,89.

References

Booth, S. & Gould, M. (1986). The communication anxiety questionnaire. *Communication Quarterly*, **34**, 194–205.

Hayes, B.J. & Marshall, W.L. (1984). Generalization of treatment effects in training public speakers. *Behavior Research & Therapy*, **22**, 519–533.

Hayes, D.T. (1978). *Nonintellective predictors of public speaking ability and academic success in a basic college-level speech communication course.* Unpublished doctoral thesis, University of Missouri, Missouri.

Reisch, R.J. & Ballard, D.S. (1985). *Coaching strategies in contest persuasive speaking: A guide to coaching the novice.* Paper presented at the annual meeting of the Speech Communica-tion Association, Denver.

Case Study E

The role of bank overdraft usage and cash flow problems in the prediction of bankruptcy

Introduction

From the claims records in judicial courts ("Third of claims", 1992), it appears that the non-availability of cash is still the predominant cause of bankruptcy in all small businesses in South Africa. Research on possible contributory causes of bankruptcy therefore remains of the utmost importance.

Friedman and Rosenman (1974) came to the conclusion that risk factors for bankruptcy (such as poor credit control and debt collection) were predictors of fewer than half the cases of bankruptcy. According to these authors, businesses that exceed their bank overdraft run a greater risk of becoming bankrupt.

During the eighties, the findings on the importance of bank overdraft usage as predictor of bankruptcy were contradicted in several prominent investigations, and enthusiasm for this topic waned. These investigations tended to take bankruptcy into consideration on the basis of bank overdraft usage without taking other risk factors, such as cash flow problems into account.

Levy (1998) believes that, statistically, bank overdraft usage is a less important predictor of bankruptcy than management skills, and that there is a mutually operative relationship between bank overdraft usage and management skills in this regard. As a possible explanation of the data they obtained in investigating the opinion of Levy above, Kreitler and Brunner (1997) suggest that "in a business where management skills such as co-ordination of enterprise functions is highly developed... tends more to business where management skills such as co-ordination of enterprise functions is highly developed...

tends more to make use of bank overdrafts as a means for controlling cash flow problems" (p. 493).

There are various means by which management skills and cash flow problems might combine with bank overdraft usage to give rise to bankruptcy. Accordingly, overextension of bank overdraft need not represent a risk on its own; it can become a risk only if it is linked to specific levels of other variables (Maticek, 1998). Thus bank overdraft usage and cash flow problems do not have to be played off against each other regarding their ability to predict bankruptcy, because this ability to predict is in fact increased by viewing these factors jointly.

The purpose of the present research thus was to investigate the role of bank overdraft usage and cash flow problems in predicting bankruptcy status (bankrupt versus non-bankrupt).

Subjects

The names and telephone numbers of small businesses that employed between 40 to 60 employees that had been declared bankrupt in the preceding two years were obtained from the Receiver of Revenue in Pretoria. The owners of small businesses situated in Pretoria were contacted by telephone to secure their co-operation in completing the questionnaire. Only three refused to participate in the project. Appointments were made with 36 owners, during which they were given the questionnaires and told how to complete them. A control group of an equal number of small business owners who were prepared to participate in the project of corresponding sizes (number of employees) and comparable business sectors (for example, bakeries, second hand car sales, and so on) but without any record of bankruptcy completed the questionnaire in the same manner.

The average size of the bankrupt group was 50 employees and that of the control group was 49.

Procedure

Apart from the business owners having to indicate the size of the small business (number of workers employed) and business sector they also had to indicate the amount by which they exceeded their overdraft limit on average per month. They also had to indicate on a 4-point scale the extent to which they are/were prone to having cash flow problems by marking the letters **F** (completely false), **f** (more false than true), **t** (more true than false) or **T** (completely true). **T** was scored a 4 (four).

Bankruptcy was scored a 1 (one) and non-bankrupt a 0 (zero).

Results

The correlations between the predictor variables and bankruptcy-status (bankrupt/non-bankrupt) are given in Table E.

Table E
Correlation matrix of variables

	Bank overdraft usage	Bankruptcy
Cash flow problem	0.83	0.45
Bankruptcy status	0.94	

Bank overdraft usage (reported amount by which bank overdrafts were exceeded) correlated significantly high ($r = 0{,}94$) with bankruptcy status and also showed a significantly high positive correlation of 0,83 with cash flow problems. Cash flow problems showed a correlation of 0,45 with bankruptcy status (bankrupt/non-bankrupt).

References

Third of claims (1992, 18 December). *The Star*, p. 8.

Levy, H.J. (1998). The perspective importance of management skills, bank overdraft and interaction effects for the genesis of bankruptcy. *Management skills and small businesses*, **9**, 453–464.

Friedman, M., & Rosenman, R.H. (1974). Association of bank overdraft usage patterns with increase in bankruptcy. *Journal of the American Business Association*, **44**, 525–553.

Maticek, R. (1998). Synergetic effects of bank overdraft, cashflow problems and risk factors in bank overdraft usage. *Financial Business Skills*, **34**, 267–272.

Kreitler, S, & Brunner, D. (1997). The relation of bank overdraft to financial risk factors for bankruptcy. *Management Skills and Small Businesses*, **12**, 487–495.

Case Study F

The differences in innovative problem-solving styles of entrepreneurs and managers of big businesses in South Africa

Introduction

Research done on the skills of business people has recently shifted to an examination of entrepreneurs' cognitive styles and innovative abilities in terms of problem solving. It also focused on the differences in management styles of managers and entrepreneurs.

Begley and Boyd (1986) found, for example, that entrepreneurs exhibited a higher risk-taking propensity than small business managers. In a comparison of the decision-making approaches used by entrepreneurs and managers of larger firms, Smith, Gannon, Grimm and Mitchell (1988) found that the managers used a more rational approach than did entrepreneurs. Swayne and Tucker (1973) argued that entrepreneurs are more innovative than managers in seeking ways to expand their business or start new ones.

Research by Sexton and Bowman-Upton (1986) shows that entrepreneurship students tend to be more innovative than other business administration students. Similarly, the research of Chaganti and Chaganti (1983) suggests that entrepreneurs will be more innovative than managers.

A theoretical framework for identifying problem-solving styles is the Kirton Adaption-Innovation (KAI) theory (Kirton, 1987). Kirton (1976) developed a measuring-instrument (KAI scale) based on the above-mentioned theory.

The purpose of the current study was to compare the innovative problem-solving styles, as measured by the KAI scale, of entrepreneurs and managers of big businesses.

Method

Respondents

A sample of 222 business people was used in the research project. They were located in the following way:

A sample of 300 respondents (entrepreneurs) located in Gauteng and the Western Cape was selected from two entrepreneurial networking groups. An introductory letter was sent to each respondent inviting him or her to participate in the research project. A hundred and sixty respondents returned the response forms, indicating their willingness to participate in the research project. The KAI measurement questionnaires were mailed to the 160 respondents and 112 completed questionnaires were returned. The 112 respondents (entrepreneurs) consisted of:

- 100 males, and
- 12 females.

The average age of the entrepreneurial group was 28.

A sample of 300 respondents (managers) of 30 large companies located in Gauteng and the Western Cape was also selected. An introductory letter was sent to each respondent, inviting him or her to participate in the research project. A hundred and thirty respondents returned the response forms, indicating their willingness to participate in the research project. The KAI measurement questionnaires were mailed to the 130 managers and 110 completed questionnaires were returned. The 110 respondents (managers) consisted of:

- 70 males, and
- 40 females.

The average age of the group of managers was 42.

Measuring instrument

The measuring instrument used in the project to measure the difference in the innovative problem-solving styles of the respondents was the Kirton Adaptation-Innovation (KAI scale). The KAI is a 32-item self-report measuring instrument with scores ranging from 32 (lowest level of innovation) to 160 (highest level of innovation).

Results

For the purpose of the study, the mean KAI score for the entrepreneurs was compared with the mean KAI score for the managers. The KAI scores for the two groups are as follows (Table F):

Table F
Mean scores and standard deviation scores of managers and entrepreneurs on the KAI scale

	Mean scores on KAI	Standard deviation
Managers	96,0	13,0
Entrepreneurs	113,9	13,2

The results of the *t*-test comparing the means of the two groups indicated that the entrepreneurs were significantly more innovative than the managers.

References

Begley, T. & Boyd, D. (1986). Psychological characteristics associated with Entrepeneurial Performance, in *Frontiers of Entrepreneurship Research*, red. R. Ronstadt, J. Hornaday, R. Peterson, & K.Vesper, Wellesley, Mass.: Babson College, Center for Entrepreneurial Studies, 146–166.

Chaganti, R. & Chaganti, R. (1983). A Profile of profitable and Not-so-profitable Small Business. *Journal of Small Business Management*, **21** (July), 26–31.

Kirton, M. (1976). Adaption and Innovation: A description and Measure, *Journal of Applied* Psychology, **61** (October), 622–629.

Smith, K.M., Gannon, M., Grimm, C. & Mitchell, T. (1988). Decision making behaviour in Smaller Entrepreneurial and Larger Professionally Managed Firms, *Journal of Business Venturing*, **3** (Summer), 223–232.

Sexton, D. & Bowman-Upton, N. (1986). Validation of a Personality Index: Comparative Entrepreneurial Analysis of Female Entrepreneurs, Managers, Entrepreneurship Students and Business Students. In *Frontiers of Entrepreneurship Research*, (red.) R. Ronstadt, J. Hornaday, R. Peterson & K. Vesper, Wellesley, Mass.: Babson College, Center for Entrepreneurial Studies, 40–51.

Swayne, C. & Tucker, W. (1973). *The Effective Entrepreneur*. Morristown, N.J.: General Learning Press.

Appendix E

Answers to multiple choice and true/false questions

1.1 d 1.2 c 1.3 a 1.4 d

2.1 T 2.2 c 2.3 F 2.4 b 2.5 d 2.6 b 2.7 b 2.8 d 2.9 T 2.10 F

3.1 b 3.2 d 3.3 b 3.4 c 3.5 c

4.1 b 4.2 c 4.3 c 4.4 T 4.5 T 4.6 T 4.7 d 4.8 c 4.9 c 4.10 b

5.1 c 5.2 d 5.3 T 5.4 d 5.5 c 5.6 T 5.7 b 5.8 b 5.9 b

6.1 b 6.2 d 6.3 T 6.4 d 6.5 d 6.6 c

7.1 F 7.2 T 7.3 a 7.4 a 7.5 c 7.6 d 7.7 T 7.8 T 7.9 T 7.10 F 7.11 d
7.12 d 7.13 T 7.14 T 7.15 d 7.16 d 7.17 T 7.18 c 7.19 d

8.1 F 8.2 T 8.3 T 8.4 c 8.5 d 8.6 c 8.7 b 8.9 a 8.10 T

9.1 T 9.2 T 9.3 c 9.4 a 9.5 c 9.6 T 9.7 T 9.8 b 9.9 a 9.10 b 9.11 d
9.12 c 9.13 T 9.14 T 9.15 d 9.16 b 9.17 b

References

American Psychological Association (APA). (1982). *Ethical principles in the conduct of research with human participants.* Washington, D.C.: APA.

Arnold, D.O. (1982). Qualitative field methods. In R.B. Smith & P.K. Manning (Eds), *A handbook of social science methods, Vol. II: Qualitative methods.* Cambridge, Mass.: Ballinger.

Babbie, E., & Mouton, J. (2001). *The practice of social research.* Cape Town: Oxford University Press.

Bachrach, A.J. (1981). *Psychological research: An introduction* (4th ed.). New York: Random House.

Bailey, K.D. (1987). *Methods of social research* (3rd ed.). New York: The Free Press.

Bales, R.F. (1970). *Personality and interpersonal behavior.* New York: Holt, Rinehart & Winston.

Bandura, A., Ross, D. & Ross, S.A. (1961). Transmission of aggression through imitation of aggressive models. *Journal of Abnormal and Social Psychology,* **63**, 575–582.

Barlow, D.H. & Hersen, M. (1984). *Single-case experimental designs* (2nd ed.). New York: Pergamon.

Bassa, F.M. & Schlebusch, L. (1984). Practice preferences of clinical psychologists in South Africa. *South African Journal of Psychology,* **14**, 118–123.

Bem, D.J. (1986). Writing the research report. In L.H. Kidder & C.M. Judd (Eds), *Research methods in social relations* (5th ed.). New York: CBS Publishing.

Berkowitz, L. & Donnerstein, E. (1982). External validity is more than skin deep. *American Psychologist,* **37**, 245–257.

Bluen, S.D. & Goodman, E.R. (1984). The stigmatization of ex-political detainees in employment practices. *South African Journal of Psychology,* **14**, 137–139.

Botha, J. (1987, 3 May). VSA se ergste TV-reekse ook hier uitgesaai [Worst USA TV series also broadcast here]. *Rapport,* p. 3.

Botha, M.P. (1990). *Televisieblootstelling en aggressiwiteit by hoërskoolleerlinge: 'n Opvolgondersoek oor vyf jaar* [*Television exposure and aggressiveness among high-school pupils: A follow-up study over five years*]. Unpublished doctoral thesis, University of the Orange Free State, Bloemfontein.

Bracht, G.H. & Glass, G.V. (1968). The external validity of experiments. *American Educational Research Journal,* **5**, 437–474.

Brislin, R.W. (1970). Back translation for cross-cultural research. *Journal of Cross-cultural Research,* **1**, 185–216.

Brown, S.R. (1980). *Political subjectivity: Applications of Q methodology in political science.* New Haven: Yale University Press.

Campbell, D.T. & Fiske, D.W. (1959). Convergent and discriminant validation by the multitrait-multimethod matrix. *Psychological Bulletin,* **56**, 81–105.

Campbell, D.T. & Ross, H.L. (1968). The Connecticut crackdown on speeding: Time-series data in quasi-experimental analysis. *Law and Society Review,* **3**, 33–53.

Cannell, C.F. & Kahn, R.L. (1986). Interviewing. In G. Lindzey & E. Aronson (Eds), *Handbook of social psychology* (2nd ed.). Reading, Mass.: Addison-Wesley.

Carlsmith, J.M. & Anderson, C.A. (1979). Ambient temperature and the occurrence of collective violence: A new analysis. *Journal of Personality and Social Psychology,* **37**, 337–344.

Carlsmith, J.M., Ellsworth, P.C. & Aronson, E. (1976). *Methods of research in social psychology.* Reading, Mass.: Addison-Wesley.

Christensen, L.B. (1985). *Experimental methodology* (3rd ed.). Boston: Allyn & Bacon.

Cleaver, G. (1988). A phenomenological analysis of victimization. The experience of having one's house attacked and damaged. *South African Journal of Psychology,* **18**, 76–83.

Cohen, J. (1988). *Statistical power analysis for the behavioral sciences* (2nd ed.). Hillsdale, N.J.: Erlbaum.

Cook, T.D. & Campbell, D.T. (1979). *Quasi-Experimentation: Design and analysis issues for field settings.* Chicago: Rand McNally.

Cronbach, L.J. (1951). Coefficient alpha and the internal sturcture of tests. *Psychometrika,* **16**, 297–334.

Cronbach, L.J. (1980). Validity on parole: How can we go straight? *New Directions for Testing and Measurement*, **5**, 99–108.

Cronbach, L.J. & Furby, L. (1970). How we should measure "change" – or should we? *Psychological Bulletin*, **74**, 68–80.

Cronbach, L.J. & Meehl, P.E. (1955). Construct validity in psychological tests. *Psychological Bulletin*, **52**, 281–302.

De Vetta H.M. (1980). Raised in the wrong sex: A case study. *South African Journal of Psychology*, **10**, 89–95.

Dillman, D.A. (1978). *Mail and telephone surveys*. New York: Wiley.

Doob, A.N. & MacDonald, G.E. (1979). Television viewing and fear of victimization: Is the relationship causal? *Journal of Personality and Social Psychology*, **37**, 170–179.

Du Preez, P. (1991). *A science of mind: The quest for psychological reality*. London: Academic Press.

Ehrenreich, B. (1991, 3 June). Science, lies and the ultimate truth. *Time*, **137**(22), p. 60.

Ekman, P., Davidson, R.J. & Friesen, W.V. (1990). The Duchenne smile: Emotional expression and brain physiology II. *Journal of Personality and Social Psychology*, **58**(2), 342–353.

Ennis, R.H. (1973, June). On Causality. *Educational Researcher*, 4–11.

Eron, L.D. (1963). Relationship of TV viewing habits and aggressive behavior in children. *Journal of Abnormal and Social Psychology*, **67**(2), 193–196.

Feather, N.T. (1964). Acceptance and rejection of arguments in relation to attitude strength, critical ability, and intolerance of inconsistency. *Journal of Abnormal and Social Psychology*, **69**(2), 127–136.

Flanders, N.A. (1970). *Analyzing teaching behavior*. Reading, Mass.: Addison-Wesley.

Fullagar, C. & Barling, J. (1983). Social learning revisited: A psychological approach to advertising effectiveness? *South African Journal of Psychology*, **13**(1), 18–22.

Gage, N.L. (1989). The paradigm wars and their aftermath: A "historical" sketch of research on teaching since 1989. *Educational Researcher*, **18**(7), 4–10.

Gerbner, G. & Gross, L. (1976, April). The scary world of TV's heavy viewer. *Psychology Today*, p. 41–45.

Glass, G.V. (1968). Analysis of data on the Connecticut speeding crackdown as a time-series quasi-experiment. *Law and Society Review*, **3**(1), 55–76.

Glass, G.V., Willson, V.L. & Gottman, J.M. (1975). *Design and analysis of time series*. Boulder, Colo.: Laboratory of Educational Research Press.

Gottschalk, L. (1969). *Understanding history: A primer of historical method*. New York: Knopf.

Grosof, M.S. & Sardy, H. (1985). *A research primer for the social and behavioral sciences*. Orlando, Florida: Academic Press.

Guilford, J.P. (1954). *Psychometric methods*. New York: McGraw-Hill.

Haertel, E.H. (1987). Review of 'Foundations of behavioral research' (3rd ed.) by F.N. Kerlinger. *Contemporary Psychology*, **32**, 249–250.

Hays, W.L. (1988). *Statistics for the social sciences* (4th ed.). New York: Holt, Rinehart & Winston.

House, E.R. (1991). Realism in research. *Educational Researcher*, **20**(6), 2–9.

Huysamen, G.K. (1989a). *Introductory statistics and research design for the behavioural sciences, Vol. II*. Bloemfontein: Author.

Huysamen, G.K. (1989b). *Psychological and educational test theory*. Bloemfontein: Author.

Huysamen, G.K. (1990a). *Introductory statistics and research design for the behavioural sciences, Vol. I*. Bloemfontein: Author.

Huysamen, G.K. (1990b). *Psychological measurement: An introduction with South African examples*. Pretoria: Academica.

Huysamen, G.K. (1991). Steekproefgroottes in plaaslik gepubliseerde psigologiese navorsing [Sample sizes in locally published psychological research]. *Suid-Afrikaanse Tydskrif vir Sielkunde*, **21**(3), 183–190.

Huysamen, G.K. (1994). *Methodology for the social and behavioural sciences*. Halfway House: Southern.

Huysamen, G.K. (1997). Qualitative and quantitative research cycles. *South African Journal of Psychology*, **28**(1), 183–190.

Kaestle, C.F. (1988). Recent methodological developments in the history of American education. In R.M. Jaeger (Ed.). *Complementary methods for research in education*. Washington, D.C.: American Educational Research Association.

Kahn, R.L. & Cannell, C.F. (1957). *The dynamics of interviewing: Theory, technique, and cases.* New York: Wiley.

Kazdin, A.E. & Wilson, G.T. (1978). *Evaluation of behavior therapy.* Cambridge, Mass.: Ballinger.

Kemmis, S. (1985). Action research. In T. Husen & T.N. Postlethwaite (Eds). *The International Encyclopedia of Education,* Vol. I. Oxford: Pergamon.

Keppel, G. (1991). *Design and analysis: A researcher's handbook* (3rd ed.). Englewood-Cliffs, N.J.: Prentice-Hall.

Kerlinger, F.N. (1979). *Behavioral research: A conceptual approach.* New York: Holt, Rinehart & Winston.

Kerlinger, F.N. (1986). *Foundations of behavioral research* (3rd ed.). New York: CBS Publishing.

Kidder, L.H. & Judd, C.M. (1986). *Research methods in social relations* (5th ed.). New York: CBS College Publishing.

Koocher, G.P. (1977). Bathroom behavior and human dignity. *Journal of Personality and Social Psychology,* **35**, 120–121.

Kraemer, H.C. (1981). Coping strategies in psychiatric clinical research. *Journal of Consulting and Clinical Psychology,* **49**(3), 309–319.

Kratochwill, T.R. (1978). *Single subject research: Strategies for evaluating change.* New York: Academic Press.

Lalumiére, M.L. (1993). Increasing the precision of citations in scientific writing. *American Psychologist,* **48**, 913.

Latané, B. & Darley, J.M. (1968). Group inhibition of bystander intervention in emergencies. *Journal of Personality and Social Psychology,* **10**, 215–221.

Lazarus, S. (1985). Action research in an educational setting. *South African Journal of Psychology,* **15**, 112–118.

Linn, R.L. & Slinde, J.A. (1977). The determination of the significance of change between pre- and posttesting periods. *Review of Research in Education,* **47**, 121–150.

Middlemist, R.D., Knowles, E.S. & Matter, C.F. (1976). Personal space invasions in the lavatory: Suggestive evidence for arousal. *Journal of Personality and Social Psychology,* **33**, 541–546.

Middlemist, R.D., Knowles, E.S. & Matter, C.F. (1977). What to do and what to report: A reply to Koocher. *Journal of Personality and Social Psychology,* **35**, 122–124.

Murphy, K.R. & Balzer, W.K. (1989). Rater errors and rating accuracy. *Journal of Applied Psychology,* **74**, 619–624.

Naude, C.M.B. (1990). Execution patterns in the USA and South Africa in terms of race of offenders, types of crimes committed, race and gender of victims, and sentences commuted. *Acta Criminologica,* **3**(2), 5–10.

Osgood, C.E., Suci, C.J. & Tannenbaum, P.H. (1957). *The measurement of meaning.* Urbana, IL: University of Illinois Press.

Page, B. (1976). *Reactions to disaster: Two studies in South Africa.* Grahamstown: Rhodes University.

Pedhazur, E. (1982). *Multiple regression in behavioral research: Explanation and prediction* (2nd ed.). New York: Holt, Rinehart & Winston.

Perold, S. (1983, 31 Oktober). Reg in die kol! [Right on target!] *Rapport,* p. 11.

Peter, R.S. (1973). *The philosophy of education.* Oxford: Oxford University Press.

Piliavin, I.M., Rodin, J. & Piliavin, J.A. (1969). Good samaritanism: An underground phenomenon? *Journal of Personality and Social Psychology,* **13**(4), 289–299.

Pitts, M. & Phillips, K. (1991). *The psychology of health.* London: Routledge.

Polkinghorne, D.E. (1989). Phenomenological research methods. In R.S. Valle & S. Halling (Eds), *Existential-phenomenological perspectives in psychology.* New York: Plenum.

Prinsloo, R.J. (1982). The control of psychological tests by the Test Commission of the Republic of South Africa (TCRSA). *South African Journal of Psychology,* **12**, 106–110.

Preston-Whyte, E. (1982). Why questionnaires are not the answer. In South African Labour and Development Research Unit (SALDRU) (Ed.), *Questionnaires are no short cut.* Cape Town: SALDRU, University of Cape Town.

Psychological Association of South Africa (PASA). (1987). *Guide to authors.* Pretoria: SAPA.

Reed, H.B. (1924). Distributed practice in addition. *Journal of Educational Psychology,* **15**(4), 248–249.

Rhoodie, N.J. (1986). Die wortels van wit-swartkonflik in Suid-Afrika vanuit die perspektief van John Galtung se teorie oor revolusionêre aggressie [The roots of white-black conflict in South Africa from the perspective of John Galtung's theory on revolutionary aggression]. *Suid-Afrikaanse Tydskrif vir Sosiologie*, **17**, 117–133.

Rizo, F.M. (1991). The controversy about quantification in social research: An extension of Gage's "'historical' sketch". *Educational Researcher*, **20**(9), 9–12.

Rosenthal, R. (1976). *Experimenter effects in behavioral research* (rev. ed.). Hillsdale, New Jersey: Erlbaum.

Rosenthal, R. & Jacobson, L. (1968). *Pygmalion in the classroom: Teacher expectation and pupils' intellectual development*. New York: Holt, Rinehart & Winston.

Schuman, H. & Presser, S. (1981). *Questions and answers in attitude surveys*. New York: Academic Press.

Saal, F.E., Downey, R.G. & Lahey, M.A. (1980). Rating the ratings: Assessing the psychometric quality of rating data. *Psychological Bulletin*, **88**, 413–428.

Saling, M., Abrams, R. & Chester, H. (1983) A photographic survey of lateral cradling preferences in black and white women. *South African Journal of Psychology*, **13**(4), 135–136.

Schmitt, N.W. & Klimonsky, R.J. (1991) *Research methods in human resources management*. Cincinatti, Ohio: South Western College Publishing.

Scriven, M. (1988). Philosophical inquiry methods in education. In R.M. Jaeger (Ed.), *Complementary methods for research in education*. Washington, D.C.: American Educational Research Association.

Sears, D.O. (1986). College sophomores in the laboratory: Influences of a narrow data base on social psychology's view of human nature. *Journal of Personality and Social Psychology*, **51**, 515–530.

Sidman, M. (1960). *Tactics of scientific research*. New York: Basic Books.

Snook, I.A. (1972). *Indoctrination and education*. London: Routledge & Kegan Paul.

Soltis, J. (1987). *An introduction to the analysis of educational concepts* (2nd ed.). Reading, Mass.: Addison-Wesley.

Spector, P.E. (1981). *Research designs*. Beverly Hills, Cal.: Sage.

Stake, R.E. (1988). Case study methods in educational research: Seeking sweet water. In R.M. Jaeger (Ed.), *Complementary methods for research in education*. Washington, D.C.: American Educational Research Association.

Sternberg, R.J. (1990). *Methaphors of mind: Conceptions of the nature of intelligence*. Cambridge: Cambridge University Press.

Stevens, S.S. (1951). Mathematics, measurement and psychophysics. In S.S. Stevens (Ed.), *Handbook of experimental psychology*. New York: Wiley.

Strümpfer, D.J.W. (1980, September). *Een honderd-en-een jaar na Wundt* [*One hundred and one years after Wundt*]. Paper presented at the National Psychological Congress, Johannesburg.

Strümpfer, D.J.W. (1989). Do white South African managers suffer from exceptional levels of job stress? *South African Journal of Psychology*, **19**, 130–137.

Taft, R. (1985). Ethnographic research methods. In T. Husen & T.N. Postlethwaite (Eds), *The International Encyclopedia of Education*, Vol.3. Oxford: Pergamon.

Te veel bier lei tot tydelike impotensie [Too much beer leads to temporary impotence]. (1991, 8 Nov.). *Die Burger*, p. 15.

Tuckman, B.W. (1990). A proposal for improving the quality of published educational research. *Educational Researcher*, 19(9), 22–25.

Tyack, D.B. (1976). Ways of seeing: An essay on the history of compulsory schooling. *Harvard Educational Review*, **46**(3), 355–389.

Tyson, G.A. & Turnbull, O. (1990). Ambient temperature and the occurrence of collective violence: A South African replication. *South African Journal of Psychology*, **20**(3), 159–169.

Valle, R.S., King, M. & Halling, S. (1989). An introduction to existential-phenomenological thought in psychology. In R.S. Valle & S. Halling (Eds), *Existential-phenomenological perspectives in psychology*. New York: Plenum.

Van Staden, F.J. & Viljoen, H.G. (1979). Hanteringsmeganismes tydens ruimtelike oorbesetting [Coping mechanisms in spatial crowding]. *Suid-Afrikaanse Tydskrif vir Sielkunde*, **10**, 11–17.

Viney, L.L. (1983). The assessment of psychological states through content analysis of verbal communications. *Psychological Bulletin*, 94, 542–563.

Visser, D. & Van Staden, F. (1990). Analysis of sample selection, sample composition and research design: A review of the past decade's contributions to the South African Journal of Psychology. *South African Journal of Psychology*, **20**, 111–119.

Walster, E., Cleary, T. & Clifford, M. (1971). The effect of race and sex on college admission. *Journal of Educational Sociology*, **44**, 237–244.

Webb, E.J., Campbell, D.T., Schwartz, R.D. & Sechrest, L. (1966). *Unobtrusive measures: Nonreactive research in the social sciences*. Chicago: Rand McNally.

Webb, E.J., Campbell, D.T., Schwartz, R.D., Sechrest, L. & Grove, J.B. (1981). *Nonreactive measures in the social sciences* (2nd ed.). Boston: Houghton Mifflin.

Weitzman, E. & Miles, M. (1995). *Computer software for qualitative analysis.* London: Sage.

Welman, J.C., & Basson, P.A. (1995). The interrelationship between the work experience of distance education students, job satisfaction, and academic achievement. *Journal of Industrial Psychology*, **21**(1), 14–17.

Willitt, J.B. (1988). Questions and answers in the measurement of change. *Review of Research in Education*, 15, 345–422.

Wilson, J. (1969). *Thinking with concepts*. Cambridge: University Press.

Wolcott, H.F. (1990). *Writing up qualitative research*. San Francisco: Sage.

Zelger, J. (1991). GABÉK – a new method for qualitative evaluation of interviews and model construction with PC-support. In E.A. Stuhler & M.O. Suileabhain (Eds.) *Enchanting human capacity to solve ecological and social-economic problems* (pp. 14–35) Munchen, Germany: Rainer Hampp Verlag.

Zietsman, P.H. (1990, 19 Des.). "Oriëntering" disorienteer [Brief aan die redakteur]. ["Orientation" disorientated (letter to the Editor)] *Beeld*, p. 14.

Zuber-Skerritt, O. (1998). *Postgraduate research training and supervision* (Workshop notes). Gordon's Bay: Centre for Higher and Adult Education – University of Stellenbosch.

Zweigenhaft, R.L. (1970). Signature size: A key to status awareness. *Journal of Social Psychology*, **81**, 49–54.

Internet resources

(One may register for a small fee per year with Technikon SA's excellent library. Visit http: / /www.tsa.ac.za. or contact per e-mail: mailto:cll@tsa.ac.za to gain access to sites where user-name and password are required.)

General sites

Visit the first site for a general overview of research. Use the other addresses to access information for specific purposes, as indicated by the headings. (Note: Although all these addresses were correct at the time of going to press, websites and Internet addresses are subject to change.)

General overview of the research process
http: / / trochim.human.cornell.edu / kb / rel&val.htm

Specific important issues in conducting research
African Digital Library – access to about 8 000 full text books for people living in Africa:
http: / / AfricaEducation.org / adl /
http: / / www.netlibrary.com

Agriculture in South Africa
http: / / www.uovs.ac.za / data / input / kovsagric / kovsagrig-in.asp

Bursaries and funding – National Research Foundation
http: / / www.nrf.ac.za / funding / guide /

Business abstracts / indexing
About 15 080 business journals & dictionary of financial terms
http: / / search.epnet.com / login.asp?site=ehost
User ID: technikon Password: ebsco

Business Credit News
http: / / www.creditman.co.uk

Business Day
http: / / www.bday.co.za

Code of standards for survey research in the United States
http: / / www.casro.org /

Conferences database
http: / / www.hsrc.ac.za / nexus.html
http: / / www.apa.org / science / bulletin.html

Constitutions – database on modern
http: / / www.hsrc.ac.za / databases.html

Emerald (MCB) Library
More than 20 000 full-text management articles
http: / / www.emerald-library.com / EMR / EMR.html

Username: tsa1 Password: bird
tsa2 ant
tsa3 fly

Ethical issues for research involving humans
http://www.sshrc.ca/english/programinfo/policies/ethics.htm

Ethics, teaching thereof in research
http://medicine.ucsd.edu/research/ethics/resources/index.htm

Ethnographical studies
http://www.ualberta.ca/~jrnorris/qual.html

Genetics – research for the US Human Genome Project, 1998-2003
http://www.nhgri.nih.gov/ELSI/

Government website
http://www.polity.org.za

Guidelines for post-graduate training in doing research (United Kingdom)
http://www.esrc.ac.uk/ptd/guidelns/postgradguidelines.htm

Harvard method of referencing
http://www.unisanet.unisa.edu.au/SubjectInfoBooklet/06385/Appendix.Harvardmethodofreferencing-9.htm

Human – life in South Africa – bio-information
http://www.sanbi.ac.za/Dbases.html

Human Resource Management Practice – profession's standards
http://www.sabpp.co.za

Human Rights – South African organisations database
http://www.hsrc.ac.za/sahro/sahro.html

Industrial Psychology & Human Resource Management – SGB/NQF
http://www.hrsgb.org.za

Internet research
http://www.nrf.ac.za/yenza

Labour, SA Department of
http://www.labour.gov.za

Libraries on-line
http://AfricaEducation.org/adl/
http://www.sabinet.co.za
http://innopac.tsa.ac.za
http://oasis.unisa.ac.za/search/
http://www.lib.ouhk.edu.hk/
http://www.emerald-library.com/EMR/EMR.html

Username: tsa1 Password: bird
tsa2 ant
tsa3 fly

Management articles MCB Library
More than 20 000 full-text management articles
http://www.emerald-library.com/EMR/EMR.html
Username: tsa1 Password: bird
tsa2 ant
tsa3 fly

Methods of research – The National Research Foundation
http://www.nrf.ac.za/methods/archmeth.htm

Monetary issues – European
http://www.cfp-pec.gc.ca/english/emu.htm
http://www.europe.ibm.com/euro/european_monetary_union_consultancy_bw.html

National Academy of Sciences' booklet on being a scientist
http://books.nap.edu/catalog/4917.html

National Research Foundation (NRF)
Tel. (012) 481-4000; e-mail (info@nrf.ac.za)
http://www.nrf.ac.za.

NEXUS – current & completed research in South Africa
77 000 projects listed
http://www.hsrc.ac.za/nexus.html
Username: ztsa Password: tsa5

NQF (National Qualifications Framework) – Business, Commerce & Management Studies – SGB 03
http://www.hrsgb.org.za

Open University of Hong Kong
1 000 databases & 500 000 volumes of books
http://www.lib.ouhk.edu.hk/

Political information – South Africa
http://www.idasa.org.za/

Post-graduate guidelines – Economic & Social Research Council (United Kingdom)
http://www.esrc.ac.uk/ptd/guidelns/postgradguidelines.htm

Programme evaluation
Best practice & meta-evaluation:
http://www.mande.co.uk/best.htm
http://www.mapnp.org/library/evalatn/fnl_eval.htm

Search: McNamara, C.(1998). Basic guide to program evaluation – St.Paul, MN.

Proposal – writing of the research proposal from the NRF's workshop kit
http://www.nrf.ac.za/yenza/research/proposal.htm

Psychological Assessment Initiative (PAI) – measuring instruments
http://sunsite.wits.ac.za/conferen/psychology/pai/pai.html

Qualitative research conjunctions and divergences with quantitative research
http://qualitative-research.net/fqs/fqs-eng.htm

Qualitative research computer package – ATLAS.ti
http://www.atlasti.de

Recognition of research courses (United Kingdom)
http://www.esrc.ac.uk/ptd/recogn/recogn.htm

Reference to information sources
The Harvard method:
http://www.unisanet.unisa.edu.au/SubjectInfoBooklet/06385/Appendix.Harvardmethodofreferencing-9.htm
The APA (American Psychological Association) method:
http://www.apa.org/science/bulletin.html
On-line citing sources:
http://www.quinion.com/words/articles/citation.htm

Researchers in South Africa – profiles, interests & specialisation
http://www.hsrc.ac.za/nexus.html

Research proposal writing from the NRF's workshop kit
http://www.nrf.ac.za/yenza/research/proposal.htm

Research topic/titles registered with the Human Sciences Research Council
http://www.hsrc.ac.za/nexus.html
Username: ztsa Password: tsa5

Sabinet high quality database
http://www.sabinet.co.za
Contact per e-mail for password: cll@tsa.ac.za

South African academic journals
http://www.nrf.ac.za/yenza/research/sajourn.htm

Simulations of conducted research
http://www.vrnews.com

SGB (Standards Generating Body -03) for Industrial Psychology & HRM
http://www.hrsgb.org.za

Statistics South Africa – for information and results of Census 1996 & 2001/other
http://www.statssa.gov.za/

Supervision of post-graduate research students
University of the Witwatersrand:
http://www.wits.ac.za/supervise/

University of Manchester – Pat Cryer:
http://www.iah.bbsrc.ac.uk/supervisor_training

Survey research
South African and international (SADA):
http://www.nrf.ac.za/sada
Commercial in the USA:
http://www.casro.org/

Textbooks on Research Methodology – reviews
http://www.nrf.ac.za/yenza/research/reviews.htm

Theses and dissertations
African Universities – database:
http://www.aau.org./datad/
Australian – full textb from seven universities:
http://adt.caul.edu.au/

Workshops – Research and Academic Development
http://www.radct.co.za/

Writing guidelines – reports
University of Wisconsin-Madison:
http://www.wisc.edu/writing/Handbook/AcademicWriting.html

Search engines

Explanation of how search engines work
http://www.calvin.edu/library/searresco/internet/as

Peer reviewed academic articles
17 scientific domains of – paid subscription required
http://www.scirus.com/

Global search engine
There are many search engines – one example listed
http://www.yahoo.com

South African search engines
There are a number of search engines – one example listed
http://www.aardvark.co.za
http://www.anazi.co.za

Index

absolute sample size (n) 64
absorbing of anti-positivist researcher 181
abstract, research report 223
academic journals 42–43
  electronic sources in 43
accidental observation as a source of knowledge 4–5
accidental sampling (incidental sampling) 62–63
accuracy 234
acquiescence 136–137
action research 21, 22, 190,191
  as democratic 191
  purpose of 21
active involvement of participants 190
activity
  2.1 15
  2.2 20
  2.3 27
  2.4 27
  3.1 40
  3.2 41
  4.1 52
  4.2 65
  5.1 78
  5.2 78
  5.3 83
  5.4 85
  5.5 89
  5.6 91
  6.1 105
  6.2 105
  6.3 121
  7.1 133
  7.2 134
  7.3 148
  7.4 152
  7.5 157
  7.6 172
  8.1 191
  9.1 209
  9.2 216
  10.1 229
  10.2 232
  11.1 268
  11 2 270
additional independent variable 72
adjectives and adverbs 236
aggression, components *example* 154
agreement or disagreement with previously published findings 228
alternative hypothesis 197
ambiguity alternative questions to avoid *example* 168
  alternative words to avoid 168
  sources of 168
ambiguous question *example* 168
analogy to validity and reliability 142
analytical
  notes 187
  research 20
    and explanatory study 21
annexures 233
anonymity 147, 159
  ensuring for future 185
  of prospective participants 188
anti-positivists 7
anti-positivist view, quantitative approach *illustration* 8
apartheid 21
apparatus and / or measuring instruments used 142, 224
apparatus or other measuring instruments, commercially available 226
appendices or annexures, in research report 233
Appendix A 272
Appendix A: A laboratory study 272
Appendix B 273
Appendix C: Table of random

numbers 275
Appendix D: Case Studies A to E 276
Appendix E: Answers to multiple choice and true/false questions 285
applicable questions, problem of 171
applied research in industry 21–22
appreciable, questions to all respondents 171–172
archival information 144–145
article
abstracts *examples* 235
articles in newspapers, reference to 40
artificiality of situation 78
assignment 70, 79, 90
in field studies 78
random 114
attitude scales 149–150
commercially available 150
attitudes 150
audiotape recorder, use of 35, 187
see *also tape recorder*
authority as a source of knowledge 3
authors
authenticity of 179
publications by different 38
publications by same 38
average 208

bar diagram 208
basic types of research design 84
basis of comparison 99
lack of 101
behaviourally anchored rating scale 154
biased samples 61
bibliography see *list of references*
biographical particulars 146
biographical variable *example* 90
book reviews
references to 40
books and chapters in books, references to 39
box/square 26
branching 171

capital letters 227
captive audience 62
case studies, purpose of 21
Case Study
A 276
B 278
C 279
D 281
E 282
F 284
case study research 21, 182
causal
explanations 179
factors 74, 77, 102
nature 97
relationships 18, 74, 79, 98
conclusions about 79
validity 97
causality 180
in human behavioural sciences 73–76
cause 18
and effect *example* 73
CD-ROM reference in source in the reference list 40
ceiling effect 252
census 19, 46
versus survey 91, 93
versus telephone survey *example* 93
central tendency, error of 156
central thesis or main theme 20
ceteris paribus principle 76, 79, 104
CHAID-analysis 203, 205
changing and controlling human behaviour 19
Chi-squares 203, 205, 212, 213
of homogeneity 203, 205
of independence 203, 205
of McNemar 203, 205
classification factor 86, 104
cluster sampling 60–61
and sample size 61
co-constitute individuals and their world 181
coding 200, 201
selected behaviours 163
systems 196
coefficient alpha 141
cohort design 88
collection of questions/items 145
communication
between treatment groups 117
by telephone 158–161
comparable results of research 6
comparisons 208–209
computer
programmes and packages 197, 215
search for references 34
computer-administered surveys 171
computer-assisted telephone interviews 159, 164
conceptual analysis 23
conclusions 96–125
validity of 97–125
conclusions and discussion in research report 228–229
concrete variables 23
concurrent validity 17, 106–136, 137
dominance 142
of the independent variable *example* 120
of the operationalisation of independent variable *example* 107
valid indicator *example* 138
construct 17
in human behavioural sciences 17, 129
validity 17, 26, 135
of a measuring instrument 135, 136
of the dependent variable 135–138
constructs, irrelevant 135
consumers and research
content analysis 89, 144, 183, 195–197
example 89
context of the study, importance of 181
continuous observation 164
contradiction *example* 137
contradictory
explanations 180
findings 35
contrast error 155, 156
control 70, 106
of scientific knowledge 5
of the third variable, 74–75, 90
over nuisance variables 70–71, 77, 101, 228
l over the independent variable 70
control group 8, 11, 70
example 70
not qualifying as such *example* 108–109
convergent validity 136
corporate law 21
correlation 73
coefficient 203

of original attitude scores with criterion status to predict future behaviour 91
correlational
design 85, 86
relationship 18
correspondence analysis 203
counter hypothesis 22, 23, 28
covariant as independent variable
example 85
covary 85
credibility of information 179
crime 19
criterion
groups
design 86
variables 91, 203, 254
criterion related validity 135, 137–138
critical evaluation of scientific conclusions 6
cross-lagged panel design 88
cross-sectional design 86
cross-tabulations 209
cyclic progress of scientific expansion of knowledge 28–30

data
collecting, methods and measuring instruments in quantitative research 126
obtained from focus-groups 189
debating as a source of knowledge 4
debriefing interview 110
deception 109
experiments 109
deductive
inference 23
of conclusions or hypothesis 23–24, 62–63
reasoning 23
empirical cycle in expansion of knowledge *figure* 11
deductively, infer 23
defined case 183–184
demand characteristics 110
demarcated case 183–184
dependent variable(s) 13, 14 69, 103–104
division into sub categories
example 163–164
example 88
in research project 262
measurement of 26–28
description
and nature of study object 18
of object of research 18–19
descriptive
statistics 183, 208
study 20
design
and experimental and/or data collection procedures 224
research 224
designing a research project 249–252
detached observation vs. complete participation 187
Dewey Decimal System 41
difference(s) between articles written for dissertations and theses and those for professional journal articles *table* 223
differential attrition of participants 117
direct observation 162–165
disclosure of objectives of observation 185
discriminant analysis 205
discriminant validity 136
disguised experiment 109
dissertations 16, 33, 222–225, 227, 233–234, 244, 254
distinghuisability 130
distributed versus massed learning, Research Example 1 6, 70, 73, 138, 250
dominance construct 142
double-barreled question 168
double-blind experiment 111

earth quakes 183
ecological validity 120, 121
education system 79
effect of sample size and proportion sample on standard error of mean, *table* 64
effect of television viewing on the aggressiveness of teenagers, Research *Example* IV 87
electronic publishing 253
e-mail 257
emergent designs 182
empirical cycle 11
equal intervals 130
equating groups 115
estimating reliability 139
ethical
considerations 171
principle 110
demand characteristics 108–110
evaluation criteria
for research proposal 246–249, 254, 256
for research report table 237–238
evaluation, interpretation of results 222
event sampling 164
ex post facto design 79
exhaustive measurement 132, 165
experience life-world of interviewed through unstructured interviews 187
first-hand 182
of having one's house attacked by fire bombs Research *Example* VIII 185–186
experimental and control group
example 70
experimental
intervention 99
of cause of effect 101
research 69-79
and internal validity 97
basic purpose of 72
experimentally accessible population 119
example 119
experimenter effect 110
experimenter's expectations see *researcher, expectations of*
experiments
deception and subject effect 109
disguise and subject effect 109
explanation and relationships between things in research 17–18
explanatory study 18–20
exploratory/explorative research 12, 18, 23
and research hypotheses 23
and specific problem 12
purpose of 18
unstructured interviews in 160–161, 187
external criticism 179
external validity 180
and threats 118–124
example 191
low priority of 191

F-test 198, 207, 213
factor analysis 197, 227
factors beyond the researcher's

control 99–106
faking responses 136, 143
falsification principle 28
fear of disapproval (or condemnation) 188
feasibility of a research proposal 248, 257
field experiment(s)
  and participant-observational studies, ethical considerations 171
  on the number of bystanders and help behaviour, Research *Example* VII 171–172
  versus laboratory experiment 77, 121
field research 77, 84
field situations 77
field studies (or field surveys) 77
fieldwork 183
filter questions 146, 170
firsthand experience, participants' 188
flaws
  in measurement procedures, detecting possible 142
  of historical sampling
floor effect 261
focus groups 189, 190
  phases in conducting 189
form of research report 222
forms of research 20–22
frames of reference *example* 180
frequencies 169
frequency
  distribution control 116
  table, use of 216
friendship with groups studied, danger of 186
funding, application for 249
funnel order of questions 170

general level of communication *example* 135
generalisation 139
generalising results 119-120
generic survey research 85
goals in defining explaining and predicting behaviour 19–20
grammar and style, conventions 234–236
graphical rating scale 153–155
grounded theories 29
group contacts 145–157
group differences 113
grouping together related questions 170
groups, variation in and between 113, 190–191

halo effect 155
  prevention of 155
Harvard method 37
Hawthorne effect 108
headings and titles 234
Health Professions Council of South Africa 149
histogram 208
historical events 81, 178–179
  flaws of 180
  in history and criminology 178
  in history and education 178
  in history and law 178
  in history and sociology 178
  key problems 180
  principles of 178–180
  purpose of 20–21, 35
historical sampling, disadvantages ` of 180
history 99
homogenous population 65
human behaviour in everyday life 120
human behavioural sciences
  constructs in 17, 129
  units of analysis 48
Human Sciences Research Council (HSRC) 149
hypotheses
  and explanatory questions 253
  and well-defined research problem 12
  or statistical analysis for research proposal 253
hypothesis 11, 22–30
  alternative 197
  confirmation of *example* 108
  counter 22, 23, 28
  definition 11
  example 89
  null 197
  research 25, 222
  rival 11, 28, 98, 104, 199
  statistical 216
  testing in research 183

identification
  of causal relationships 98
  of unclear or ambiguously formulated items 140
ideographic research 29
idiosyncrasy of a particular case 181
idiosyncratic conclusions, risk of participant observer's 186
inappropriate responses 166
incidental sampling 62
incomparable data *example* 145
incorrect conclusions *example* 82–135
incorrect impression through postal survey *example* 147
increasing reliability of measurements/tests 156
independent variable(s) 13–14, 89, 104–105
  in light of theory of 24
  construct validity of operalisation of 26
  control over 70
  example 72
in-depth interviews 187, 188
indicators 129, 142
  financial 142
  of success 129
individual apparatus (measurement/tests) 162
individual as representative of a particular population 183
individual units 18
inductive
  logic 180
  process 29
  reasoning 29
  search 184
industry and research 22
infer 129, 147, 180
influx control 79
informed versus uninformed subjects about reasons for research 172
inspection of scientific research 6
instructions given to subjects 225
instrumentation 112–113
instruments to collect data, ways of *figure* 128
intact group 88
  design 70, 88
integrating studies into literature review 35
interaction
  between selection and spontaneous change 113
  of selection and regression 81
  with individual being interviewed

187–188
inter-library loans 34
internal consistency 140
internal criticism 179
internal validity 79, 97, 99, 123, 180
  and threats 97–121
  critical importance of 98
  example 99
  of conclusions reached, threats to *example* 117
Internet 34, 43, 253, 292
  and library 253
  source, reference to 40
interpreted reality 188
interrater/intercoder/tester/test or measurement-scorer reliability 140, 160, 164
interrupted time series design 79–83
  example 144
  figure 81
  figure 82
interval
  measurement 132–133
  time sampling 164
intervention 69, 70, 80–82, 99–101
  and cause of effect 101
  experimental 99
  measurements before and after 80
interviewers, rules and recommendations for 158–159
interviewing, source of valuable advice 161
interviews 161
  analysis for unstructured 183
  guide 161
  guidelines for telephonic 159
  in-depth 188
  schedule 159, 182
    among rural people 168
  unstructured 183
intimidation 188
introduction
  of research proposal 252
  of research report 224
involvement of all participants in action research 190–191
IQs, difference(s) in size between successive 133
irrelevant sources of systematic variations in measurement 138–139
Islam 170
John Henry effect 108
joint involvement in research project 190
journal articles 223
  in list of references 39
journals 42, 222–224
juvenile delinquency 90–91

KAI scale 135, 173
keeping abreast research reported 34–35
kinds of reliability 138–141
knowledge
  scientific and non-scientific 3–6
  scientific expansion 28–30
Kruskal-Wallis test 205

laboratory 77–78
  experiment on the number of bystanders and helping behaviour, see Research *Example* VI
  experiments 77, 84, 121
  or natural environment 77
  study 272
  surveys 77
  versus field studies 77–78
language of reference 38–39
larger samples than desired, drawing 65
large-scale survey(s)
  and cluster samples 60
  and stratified samples 65
  research, sampling frame problems 51
law 21
leading questions 169, 188
length, variable *example* 130
lengthening measurements/tests 156
letter symbols 227
letters to a newspaper editor, references to 40
library 34
  Internet 253
  using a 41
Likert scale 134, 150–152
  negatively formulated item *example* 151
  positively formulated item, *example* 151
list of references
  in research proposal 254
  in research report 233
literary sources academic sources
  with good articles 42-43
literature
  findings of previous research 228
  references 224
  review 33
    compiling a 35-36
    in research report 224
    searches 33-34
    searches planning of 34–35
  sources, list of 42–43
  surveys, writing up 35
  tracing and recording 33
loaded questions 169
logical error 156
  prevention of 156
logical positivism 7
logical reasoning as a source of knowledge 4
logical train of thought 236
longer measurement/test and internal consistency 141
longitudinal design(s)/investigations 86–89

main objective, of research report 222
main steps in the research process *figure* 29
Mann-Whitney U test 205
margin for error 63
matched group design 115
matching 114
  participants 114
  technique *example* 116
mean 208
measurement
  form 139
  nature of 130
  occasion 139
  of changes in the dependent variable 112–113
  of human abilities 140
  problems 112
  reactivity 112–113
  reactivity *example* 112–113
measurement instruments/apparatus 142
  development of 226
  in the index of the research report 226
  items in the research report 226
measurement
  test
    readiness *example* 139
    reliability *example* 138

theory 128
user 139
measures
for preventing threats to internal validity 100
of accretion 140
of erosion 140
measuring
different samples 88
instruments 142–143
and their translation 252
reliability of, in research reports 226
same sample at different times 88
median 205
medical studies 107–109
methodological notes 187
methods and procedures research report 224–226
mode 186, 203
multi-dimensional attitude scale 151
example 151
multiple-choice item(s)
example 166
with only two alternatives 166
versus open ended questions 165–166
multiple choice and true/false questions, Answers to 285
multiple choice questionnaire, open ended question in a 165–166
multiple regression 199
multivariate nature of human behavioural research 101
multivariate statistical analyses 104
multivariate statistical methodology 104
mutual relationship 74
mutually exclusive measurement 132
mutually influencing variables 102

naive knowledge 2–5
natural environments research in 77–79
natural-scientific method 7
nature 188
necessary cause 74
figure 76
negative results 228
negatively formulated item, Likert scale *example* 151
neutrality 169–170
Nexus Database System 34
nominal measurement 132, 165
example of 133
exhaustive 132
mutually exclusive 132
nomothetic research 29
non-experimental research 83–90
non probability samples/sampling 46–47, 61–63
non-equivalent control group design 79, 101, 122
non-experimental hypothesis-testing research 84
non-experimental research conclusions 103
non-experimental research designs involving measurements at a single time 85
non-experimental research *example* 84
non-scientific knowledge 3–5
non-verbal behaviour 141
normal distribution 208–209
nuisance variable(s) 72–73, 79, 101, 115, 225, 228
control over 70–71, 77, 101, 200, 228
example 72
failure to find a difference in it for two groups 91
in research project 250–252
in the control group 108–109
uncontrolled *example* 78
null hypothesis 197, 198, 226
numbers at beginning of sentence 227
numerical rating scale 154

objective of a case study 182
observable variables
constructs in terms of *figure* 98
testing relationship between *figure* 25
observation
continuous 164
of behaviour 195
of behaviour *example* 98
observer's notes 187
offence, avoiding 167
offensive question *example* 167
official statistics and archival sources 144
one-shot case study 100, 101, 183
open ended question(s) 165–167, 195
avoidance of inappropriate responses *example* 166
example 165
in unstructured interviews 165–166
versus close ended questions 165–167
operational definition 24
operationalised construct 23–26
operationalised independent variable 119
opinion
of peers as a source of knowledge 3–4
poll about AIDS, Research *Example* V 91
polls 65, 91
surveys 60, 84
beliefs and convictions 146
order of rank 132
ordinal measurement 132
original sources 35
originality and research project 24–248
overlapping example 133
overlapping variables 101–102

panel design 87
paper-and pencil
examination 138
notes for reporting 190
questionnaires 137
test 226
parallel-forms reliability 140
parametric test 205
partial correlation 200
participant
demand characteristics of 108
observation 181, 183, 184–185
example 184
process/course of 185
participant observer as research instrument 186
participant-observational studies, ethical considerations 171
participation, degrees of 185
participatory research 190–191
path analysis 199
Pearson's product moment correlation 233
permission to observe groups 185
person, voice and tense 234
personal documents 183

personal documents and mass media material 144
personal interviews, advantages and disadvantages 158–159
personal visits and communication by telephone 158–161
phases in cluster sampling 60
phenomenological approach 181–182
phenomenologist aim of research 181
phenomenologist emergent designs 182
phenomenology 7
phi coefficient 203
physical traces 143–144
pilot studies in the development of an instrument 141
pilot study 62, 141, 226
placebo 107–108
  use of in human behavioural sciences 109
point time sampling 164
point-biserial correlation 203
political violence 188
population (universe) (*N*) 17, 18, 28, 48, 49, 63–34
  experimentally accessible 119
  of individuals under a universe of settings 18
  target 118–120
  validity 118–120, 124
  validity *example* 119
positive research design 182
positively formulated item, Likert scale *example* 151
positivist aim of research 182
positivist approach 7
possible flaws in procedural design 256
possible results in an interrupted time-series design *figure* 82
post hoc listing of findings 228
post test scores, difference(s) in *example* 113–114
postal surveys 146–148
  advantages and disadvantages 147
  guidelines 142, 165
postmeasurement 69
postulated relationships in one or more populations 118
practical feasibility and research project 248–249
practical implications of findings 228
practical problems as source of research problems 16
precision control 115
  method 116
prediction 89
  of phenomena in research 19
  studies 89–91
predictive
  study 20
  validity 137
    of a selection measurement *example* 137
predictor variables 89–90
pre-existing groups, use of as experimental and control groups 79
pre-existing, heterogeneous groups 60
pre-experimental
  designs 99
  intervention 99
  research 70, 99, 114
    one-shot case study 100, 101, 183
    post-measurement single group design 82, 100
    pre-measurement single group design 82, 100
preference for television programmes and aggressiveness of prisoners, Research *Example* III 84, 86, 105
premeasurement 69
  and postmeasurement design 80, 100
  single-group design 100
pretest sensitisation 111–112, 121
pretesting
  and planning for surveys 171
  example 112
previous research
  as source of research problems 17, 33
  tracing and recording relevant literature 33–34
primary and secondary sources 35
primary data 142
primary source 35
primary versus secondary sources 179
principles of historical research 179–181
probability samples and sampling 46–47
  types of 56–61
problem(s)
  formulation of 33–34
  statement and hypothesis, research report 224
  suggested and hypotheses to pursue 228
  technique of defining 12–13
procedures of scientific research 6
process/course of participant observance 185
process/course of the interview(s) 188
products and research 22
promoters 225
proportion(s)
  and frequencies 92
  and percentages 92
  and strata *figure* 57–58
  of population in particular categories of some variable 93
  of sample (*N*/*n*) 63–64
proposed method, procedures and statistical analysis, in research proposal 253
prospective design 91
proximity error 150
  prevention of bias of 156
Psychological Assessment Initiative (PAI) 49
psychological reality 181
psychometric research 26–27
  example 25
public scrutiny of scientific research 6
purposive sampling 63

qualitative and quantitative research cycles 6
  a sequence of *figure* 31
qualitative and quantitative variables, difference(s) between *figure* 251
qualitative
  independent variable 250
  methods 182–191
  research 6–9, 177–192
    data collecting and measuring instruments 126–172
    designs types of 177–192
    report writing 244
quantitative independent variable 250
quasi-experimental
  intervention 99

research 79–83
conclusions 103
questionnaire items *examples* 227
questionnaires 62, 65, 148, 233 see also *questions/items*
and paper-and-pencil test 226
interview schedules and attitude items techniques and hints 165–171
questions
about sensitive and highly emotional issues 169, 188
concise and unambiguous 168–170
dealing with contentious issues 188
questions/items
in interview schedules
filter 146, 170
guidelines 165
in interview schedules probes 162
in questionnaires
branching 171
filter 146, 170
guidelines 161, 165
quota sampling 63
quotations 36

random assignment 114
of participants *example* 114
of units of analysis to groups 70–72
to groups 113–114
random measurement error 135
random numbers 275
how to use a table of 54
table of, example of using *figure* 55
random sample *example* 53
random sampling 53–56
random selection versus random assignment of participants 120
randomised groups design 70–71, 116
diagrammatic representations of *figure* 71
randomised multigroup design 71–72
randomised two groups *example* 71
randomised two-group design 71
extension of 71
randomised-block design 200
randomly assigned participants 99
range of acceptable responses 169
rapport 170
rating errors
correction of 151
research on 156
rating scales 142, 153
and situational tests 153–155
ratings to assess dependent variable 111
ratio measurement 133
ratio reaction time *example* 133
reactivity of research 107
recording
of selected behaviours
paper-and-pen 190
tape 184, 189
records 20, 163
reference 20, 21
reference list see *literature sources, list of* 38–39
reference system 36–38
references
in the text 37–39
to a table 226
to appendices/annexures 233
to bibliographies 233
to figures 226–227
to males and females 234
regression 80–81
regular randomised groups design 116
relationship (correlation) 25
between two variables *example* 86
between two variables in a single population *example* 85–86
between variables 18, 23, 73–74
reliability 138, 139
coefficient 141
internal 140, 152
of measuring instruments in research reports 226
replicability 180
and research project 248
and scientific knowledge 6
of study 224
report on qualitative research 228
report writing 227–252
reporting 190
reports
articles in 222–224, 234
dissertations 222–224, 235
evaluation criteria 222
journals 222–234, 235
results 226–227
theses 222–224, 228
representative sample *figure* 48
representativeness 48
research 2
aims of 1–9, 181
clear purpose of the 256
design 46
designs and methods 182
Example I 5, 6, 73, 138, 250
Example II 14, 17, 18, 19, 23, 24, 25, 26, 28, 71, 77, 97, 98, 99, 100, 113, 118, 119, 163, 170, 223
Example III 84, 85, 103
Example IV 87
Example V 92
Example VI 110, 129, 130, 248
Example VII 171–172
Example VIII 185, 188
Example IX 195
findings, review of 33
historical 20, 178–179
hypotheses 22–27, 108, 118, 119, 224
in the human sciences 107
formalised in terms of operational constructs 22–25
formulating the 22–23, 24
instrument, participant observer as 186
population and sampling types 45–66
problem 10–31
and its variables statement of 11–23
examples of 11–12
origin of 16–18
procedures 224
for research proposal 253
to be used 256
process
aims of research *figure* 1
evaluation *example* 258
psychometric research *example* 25
three main steps in *figure* 29
proposal 245–270
purpose of 18, 256
question(s), research proposal 253
report, form of 222
suitability of 97
topic 10–31
requirements for a 247–248
quasi-experimental 79–83
researcher
biographical attributes of 111

control 99
control factors influencing 106
dependence of, on participation of community members 190
expectations of 111
involvement of *example* 11
role of 181–182
role of positivist versus phenomenologist view of 181
Researchers Networking Database 253
respondents' literacy level 167
response rate 159
non-respondents 65, 145, 147
response styles and how to prevent them 155
responses indicative of unacceptable attitudes *example* 155
responsibility for changes in dependent variable 169
results
in research report 226
interpretation of 228
negative 228
of statistical tests performed 232–234
practical implication of 228
presentation in reports 226–227
retest reliability, investigation of 164
retrospective design 89
main problem of 90
meaningfulness of 90
review of research findings 33
revolution 21
risk of idiosyncratic conclusions by participant observer 186–187
rival hypothesis 22, 76, 100, 103, 104, 199
and statistical procedure 199
roles of researcher and participants 189
rules and recommendations for interviewers 158

same group examined at different times 86
sample 46, 87, 88, 89
size (n) 61, 63–65
statements statistics 226
illustrations *figure* 50
samples
assignment to 228
biased 61
initial 61
margin of error 64
phases in cluster sampling 60–61
representative of the relevant population 88
representative of the relevant population response rate 65
representative of the relevant population restrictions 228
representative of the relevant population sampling error 64
sampling 46–65, 180–181, 189
captive audiences 62, 145
error 47
event 164
focus groups 187
frame 47–51, 54
historical 178
interval time 164
point time 164
unstructured interviews 187
satisfactory interrater 164
scale points number of 154–155
scatterplot 213
science, lay concept of 2
scientific
community 6
knowledge 5–6
expansion of 29–30
as not a private matter 6
core features of 5
methods 2
versus non-scientific knowledge 3–6
secondary data 142
secondary sources 35
dangers of *example* 179
sections
of research proposal 252
of research report 22–23
segment 21
selected behaviours, recording or coding of 163
selection 113
selective observation 5
self-evaluation questions
chapter 1 6
chapter 2 16, 30
chapter 4 53, 66
chapter 5 93
chapter 6 117, 124
chapter 7 173
chapter 8 192
chapter 9 219
chapter 10 239
answers to some 273
self-selected participants *example* 104
semantic differential 151–152
semi-structured interviews 161
sensitive issues, questions about 170
sensitive topics 170–171
sentence or two preferred to a table 226–227
sequence of questions, justified 170
severity or stringency error and the leniency error 156
sex 234
significance and satisfactory 164
simple random sample 55
figure 53
simple random sampling 52–53
simplest *example* of randomised two-group design 71
single dependent variable 85
single independent variable 85
single time research designs 85–86
single-group design 69, 81, 99–100
single-sample pre-experimental designs 99
situational tests 153
snowball sampling 63, 189
social acceptability 136
social desirability 136
social status 90
social unacceptability *example* 136
socially desirable responses 136
socially errors, correction of 151
socio-economic status 129
socio-economic status *example* 136
sources
in reference list, alphabetical order of 38
of non-scientific knowledge 3–5
summarising 34
South African Journal of Psychology (SAJP) 36–37
Spearman rank order correlation 205
Spearman-Brown formula 140
special target populations 148
specific questions *example* 165
spontaneous change (development, maturation, recovery or deterioration) 100
spontaneous development 81–100
of interaction between interviewer and research participant 187

spreadsheet 212, 220
standard deviation 208
standard error of mean 64
standardised measuring instruments 142
standardised test 149
statement or formulation of research problem 216, 226–227, 253
statistical
analysis procedures 197, 206, 213
and the interrupted time-series design 79
regression and accidental fluctuations 81
significance, tests of 227
techniques 225
validity 197
Statistics South Africa 142
example 144
statistics, required training and experience 249
strata 57–60
stratified random sampling 55–56
stratified, systematic sample with a random start *figure* 59
stratum 21, 65
stringent criticism of sources 179
structural equation modelling 199
structured interviews 160, 189
structuredness of different types of interview *figure* 161
student/study supervisor role 256
subject effect(s) 107–110
subject mortality 117
subjects/elements/units of analysis
subjects/elements/units of analysis instructions 216
subpopulations 62
success of failure, indication of 225
sufficient cause
example 74
figure 76
sufficiently limited project 248
suitability of research designs 97
summary
of main findings 228
of sources 34
summated or Likert scale 150
supervisor role 256
survey
designs (relationships between variables) 84–85
questionnaires 142
and postal dispatch 146–148
research 91
generic 85
versus census 91–93
surveys, large-scale 51, 60, 65
symbols 227
systematic
coding through content analysis 189
observation 128
and quantitative measurement 128
and scientific knowledge 5
sampling 58-60
source of variation *example* 114

t-test 207, 212–213
in proposal 212, 226
for independent groups 213, 226, 254
table of random numbers, example of using *figure* 55
tables and graphs 226, 233
references to, in a research report 226
tape recording 189 see also *audiotape*
target population 119
telephone survey versus census *example* 93
telephonic interviews 159–161, 170, 188
advantages and disadvantages 160
guidelines for 159, 170
impossible *example* 93
temperature scales (Centigrade and Fahrenheit) *example* 133
test-retest reliability 139
tests, one and two tailed 227
theories as source of research problems 17–18
theory 11–17, 22, 24
theory procedure and components in testing 24
theses 32, 223
thesis, references to 40
third variable 73, 74, 90
control of 74–76, 90
example 73, 102, 105
problem 101–105
threat
of history 100
of instrumentation *example* 112–113
threats to internal validity 99, 122–123
of conclusions reached *example* 117
title, research report 223
topic
and research report titles 223, 233
of research 223
topicality (actuality) and research project 248
tracing and recording relevant literature 33–34
tradition as a source of knowledge 4
traffic deaths in an interrupted time-series design *figure* 81
training of raters 152
tramps 184
transcription
of a tape recording 189
of pen and paper notes 189
transition from one topic to the next 170
translations 179
of measuring instruments 252, 273
transmission of management style, Research Example II 14
trend design 87, 88, 89
and panel and cohort designs *figure* 88
triangulation 184
true experimental intervention 99
true experimental research 70–73, 114
true meaning 181
trust, researcher and position of 186
types of longitudinal designs 86
types of research and their correspondence to external and internal validity, table 125
typical behaviour 146

unacceptable responses, questions to avoid *example* 169
understanding 181
undesirable side-effects of researcher's presence 163
uni-dimensional scale *example* 151
uniqueness of a particular case 183
units of analysis 48–49, 224

description in research report 224–225
elements 48, 58
figure 50
illustrations of *figure* 50
in human behavioural sciences 52
member 48
universe of circumstances 62–63
universe of indicators 129
unjustified conclusions 228
unobtrusive measurement 143
unobtrusive measurement and historical research 178
unplanned developments within and between groups 116–117
unpublished papers, references to 40
unrepresentative sample *figure* 49
unstructured and in-depth interviews (and focus groups) 187–190
unstructured interviews 160, 187–188
example 188
using more than one measurement of the same construct 136

validity
construct 26
construct validity of the dependent variable 135
investigation of 164
internal 79, 97, 99, 101, 123, 180
threat to 99, 122–123
of conclusions 97–128
of measuring instruments in research reports 226
value of a research proposal 256
value(s) 226
value-free project 249
variable(s) 13–14, 84–85
caused by other variable(s) 14
concrete 23
constructs 17
of research project, defining of 250–251
relationships between 18
relationships between relevant in a particular research area 104
variance (heterogeneity) of variable 64, 227–228
variation
in and between groups 116, 198–199
in measurement systematic 139–140
source in experiments 109
versatile design of action research 190
verstehen 181
video studies 120
volunteers 119
volunteers and population validity
example 119

Western Electric Company 108
Wilcoxon rank test 205
withdrawal of positivist researcher 181
workers' awareness 108
writing the report, by participant observer 187
writing, clear yet concise 234

Z-scores 206

User guide to MoonStats

This "User Guide" is adapted and reproduced with the permission of the copyright holder MoonStats CC, (c) 2001, all rights reserved.

1 What does MoonStats do?

MoonStats (c) is a stand-alone statistical software program that operates in Windows 95 or higher. It has been designed for the novice computer user and provides the statistical tools for data exploration and data description, as described in Chapter 9. Users can gain experience in the most commonly used statistics with the aid of an intuitive user interface. All statistical routines are complemented by graphs to enhance the user's visual understanding of the statistic. MoonStats enables students, researchers and professionals to gain a solid foundation in statistics, and to confidently manage basic statistics.

MoonStats allows for data entry of numeric values into a data sheet of up to 50 variables and 500 cases (units of analyses). It performs the standard descriptive statistical computations and a selection of bivariate descriptive and inferential statistics as listed below:

Descriptive statistics: mode, median, mean, standard deviation, the 95% confidence interval for the mean, minimum, maximum, range, skewness, kurtosis, and frequency tables

Graphs: bar charts, pie charts, histograms and scatterplots.

Bivariate statistics: cross-tabulation with chi-square; Pearson's product moment and Spearman's rank order correlations; and *t*-tests for independent and dependent groups

Each statistic is accompanied by *result-specific comments* on the interpretation of the statistical result, and provides suggestions on how to report the results (as described in Chapter 10 of the textbook). The program also incorporates a *pseudo-random number calculator* to generate sampling lists (as described in Chapter 4 of the textbook).

2 System requirements

- A Pentium level personal computer.
- Windows 95 or higher.
- 32 Mb RAM.
- At least 3 Mb of hard disk space.
- A CD-ROM driver (or 1.44 Mb floppy diskette – see Installation Procedure for more information on this option).

3 End-user licence agreement

3.1 Read the terms and conditions of the licence carefully before opening the CD-ROM package. By using the software as supplied on the CD-ROM or other storage device you acknowledge that you have read and accept the following terms and conditions of the MoonStats software and the "User Guide". This is an agreement between you and the MoonStats Close Corporation (hereafter MoonStats CC). If you do not agree with the terms and conditions do not open or use the CD-ROM package and immediately return it to the publisher to the address supplied below.

3.2 MoonStats CC grants you a nonexclusive licence to use one copy of the enclosed software program solely for your own personal or business purpose on a single computer (whether a standard computer or a workstation component of a multiuser environment). This license to use the software is conditional upon your compliance with the terms of this agreement. The software is in use on a computer when it is loaded into temporary storage (RAM) or installed into permanent memory (hard disk, CD-ROM or other storage device). You agree you will only copy the software into any machine-readable or printed form as necessary to use it in accordance with this license or for backup purposes in support of your use of the software.

3.3 MoonStats CC is the owner of all rights, title and interest, including copyright of the software recorded on the CD-ROM or storage device, and copyright of the "User Guide" supplied as the Appendix in the textbook *Research Methodology* (2nd edition, 2001 edition) by Welman & Kruger, published by Oxford University Press Southern Africa (hereafter referred to as "the textbook"). Ownership of the MoonStats software and the "User Guide" and all proprietary rights relating thereto remain with MoonStats CC. MoonStats CC reserves all rights not expressly granted in this licence.

3.4 The legal owner of the textbook (hereafter referred to as "the owner"), may make only one copy of the MoonStats software for backup or archival purposes, or transfer the software to a single hard disk. The owner may not (a) rent or lease the software, (b) copy or reproduce the software through a LAN or network or other system, or (c) modify, adapt, decompile, disassemble, reverse engineer, translate, or create derivative works based on the software. Any attempt to do so (whether or not successful), terminates this license to use the software without refund of any fees paid. The owner may transfer the software and user documentation with the textbook on a permanent basis provided the transferee agrees to accept the terms and conditions of this agreement and the previous owner retain no copies of the software nor of the "User Guide".

3.5 The software media (CD-ROM) is warranted for a period of 60 days from the date of the first purchase or receipt of the textbook. If the CD-ROM is damaged and Oxford University Press Southern Africa receives notification of defects in the CD-ROM within the warranty period and valid proof of purchase is supplied, Oxford University Press Southern Africa will replace the defective CD-ROM.

3.6 MoonStats CC, Oxford University Press Southern Africa and the authors of the textbook disclaim all other warranties, express or implied, including without limitation implied warranties of merchantability, fitness for a particular use, and/or noninfringement of third-party rights, with respect to the software, the programs, the source code contained therein, and/or the techniques described in the textbook, and also do not warrant that the functions contained in the software will meet the owner's requirements or that the operation of the software will be error free. This software and accompanying written materials (including instructions for use) are provided "as is" without warranty of any kind. MoonStats CC does not warrant, guarantee, or make any representations regarding the use, or the results of use, of the software or written materials in terms of correctness, accuracy, reliability, currentness, or otherwise. The entire risk as to the results and performance of the software is assumed by you. If the software or written materials are defective you (and not MoonStats CC or its dealers, distributors, agents, or employees) assume the entire cost of all necessary servicing, repair, or correction.

3.7 MoonStats CC's and Oxford University Press Southern Africa entire liability and exclusive remedy for defects in materials and workmanship shall be limited to replacing the software media by writing and returning the defective media with valid proof of purchase to: Client Services – *Research Methodology*, Oxford

University Press Southern Africa, PO Box 12119, N1 City, Goodwood 7460, South Africa. This limited warranty is void if failure of the software media has resulted from accident, abuse or misapplication. Any replacement software media shall be warranted for thirty days after postage to the user.

3.8 In no event shall MoonStats CC or Oxford University Press Southern Africa or the book authors be liable for any damages whatsoever (including without limitation damages for loss of business profits, business interruption, loss of business information, or any other pecuniary loss) arising from the use of or inability to use the book and/or the software.

3.9 By using the software you acknowledge that you have read this limited warranty, understand it, and agree to be bound by its terms and conditions. You also agree that the limited warranty is the complete and exclusive statement of agreement between the parties and supersedes all proposals or prior agreements, oral or written, and any other communications between the parties relating to the subject matter of the limited warranty.

4 Software support

For software questions and support visit our website at http://www.moonstats.com or e-mail us at moonstats@iafrica.com. Alternatively you can write to us via: Client Services – "MoonStats – Research Methodology", Oxford University Press Southern Africa, PO Box 12119, N1 City, Goodwood 7460, South Africa. If your CD-ROM is defective and covered under the limited warranty return the CD-ROM to Oxford University Press Southern Africa (see previous section "End user licence agreement").

5 Installing MoonStats

- Insert the CD-ROM (label side up) into your CD-ROM drive.
- Click the Start button to display the Start menu, and then choose Run.
- Type D:\setup.exe in the dialog box's Open text box and then press Enter.
- (If your CD-ROM uses a different letter than D, replace D with the correct letter.)
- (Alternatively you can go to Windows Explorer, and then select the drive called "Moonstats" and run the setup file.)
- Follow the directions that appear on your screen. You must agree with the licensing agreement in the initial window in order to continue with the installation program and to use the program.

6 Getting started – a quick overview of MoonStats

MoonStats was designed to make the process of data entry and data analysis on computer as simple as possible. We suggest that you first play around with the program, and explore it by using the following easy steps.

First, install the software as described in Section 5 of this User Guide. Then start the program by clicking on the MoonStats icon on the Windows Desktop (or selecting MoonStats from the Windows Programs menu). When it starts (see Box 1) you can open any data set (such as the data set "BUS.MON") that was supplied with the program by clicking on the "Open a data set" button (see Box 2).

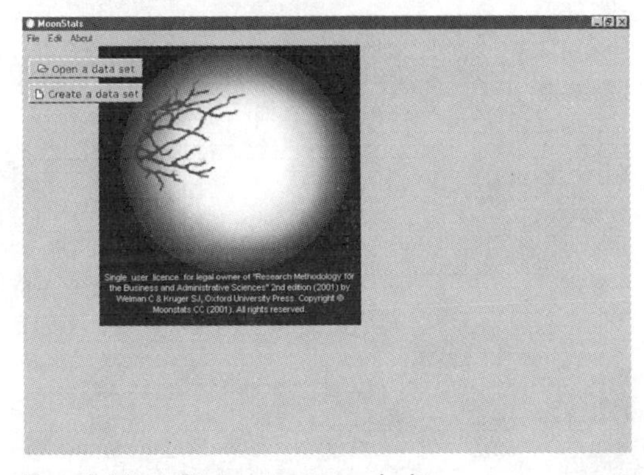

Box 1 MoonStats start up window

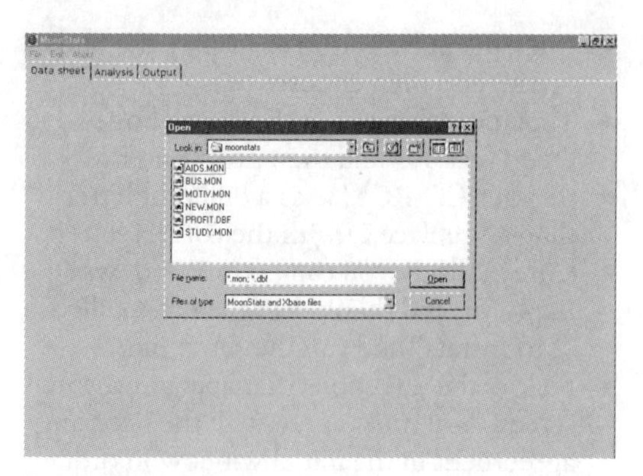

Box 2 Open data set

Box 1 and Box 2 show the first two screens that you get when starting Moonstats and opening a data set. Once you have opened a data set, the data will be displayed in the Data sheet window.

MoonStats consists of three windows:

1 A **Data sheet window** where you can enter and edit data (see Box 3).
2 An **Analysis window** where you choose which analytical procedure to use (see Box 4).
3 An **Output window** where the results are displayed as text or as graphs (see Box 5).

MoonStats C:\moonstats\BUS.MON

File Edit About

Data sheet | Analysis | Output

	REFNUM	AGE	SEX	EDUC	INCOME	BUSROUTE	BUSTIME	BUSRECK	BUSFARE
1	32	26	1	4	4900	1	5	2	1
2	28	26	1	5	4700	1	5	2	2
3	112	34	2	5	4500	1	3	2	2
4	44	29	1	4	4500	1	3	2	1
5	20	25	1	4	4500	1	4	3	1
6	86	26	2	5	4400	1	4	2	2
7	11	23	1		4400	1	5	2	3
8	88	28	2	5	4300	1	4	3	1
9	27	26	1	4	4300	1	4	2	1
10	22		1	5	4300	1	2	1	2
11	54	32	1	4	4200	1	5	3	1
12	24	25	1	4	4200	1	4	2	2
13	9	22	1	4	4200	1	4	2	1
14	36	27	1	4	4100	1	3	3	2
15	31	26		5	4100	1	3	3	1
16	101	31	2	5	4000	1	3	3	1
17	14	24	1	5	4000	1	5	2	2
18	13	23	1	4	4000	1	5	3	2
19	1	16	1	3	3900	1	3	2	1
20	39	27	1	3	3700	1	4	2	2

Box 3 The Data sheet window

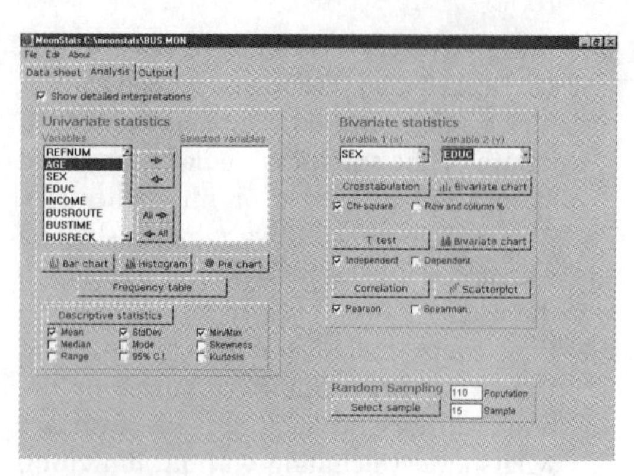

Box 4 The Analysis window

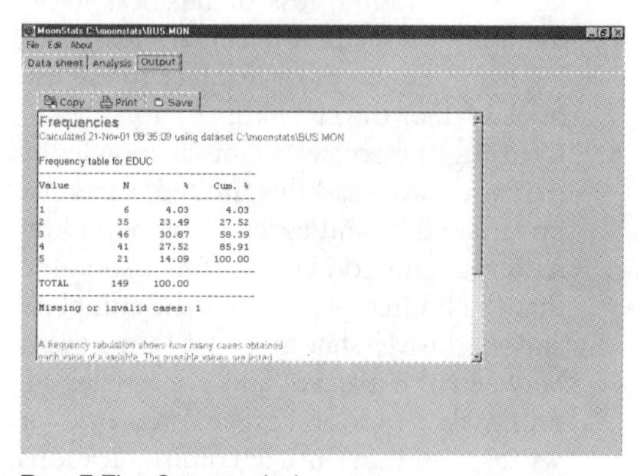

Box 5 The Output window

You can move between these windows by clicking on the TABS labelled Data sheet, Analysis and Output.

6 Enter or edit data using the MoonStats Data Sheet

Data can be entered or edited using the data sheet.

6.1 What is a data sheet?

A **data sheet** presents a clear and easy way to handle a large data set. A **data sheet** is also called a **data matrix** or a **spreadsheet**. The following picture shows that a data sheet consists of **columns** (running vertically from top to bottom) and **rows** (running horizontally from left to right).

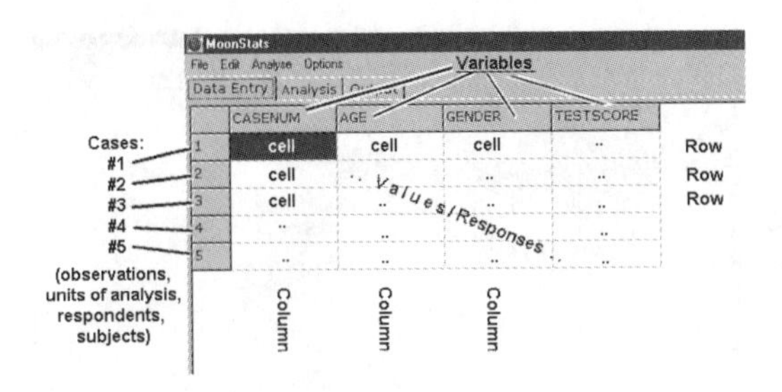

Box 6 Detailed data sheet

Each column is occupied by a **variable** (in this instance the variables are: casenum, age, gender, testcore) that relates to an item or question in the data collection instrument (questionnaire/interview/etc.) that was used to collect the data.

Each row is occupied by a **case** or **unit of analysis**, also called an **observation**, respondent, subject, individual, or element. A case can be a person, a household, a school, etc., depending on the research. There are 5 cases in this example, from case #1 to case #5. (See section 4.2.1 of textbook.)

The **cell** or box where each row and column meet represents the specific **response** or **value** or **score** or **datum** (datum is the singular of data) that the respondent or subject gave for that question or item. In this example the 5 rows and 4 columns result in 20 cells or values.

6.2 Open a data set in the data sheet

When MoonStats starts you have the option to "Open a data set" or to "Create a data set". You can also find Open and Create options on the File menu. The default (the selection automatically chosen by the computer) extension of MoonStats data files is *.MON. You can open MoonStats data files (*.MON) or import data files in the widely available Xbase/Dbase format (*.DBF).

Note that MoonStats data files can contain *numerical* values only. Convert any *alphabetic* values (a, b, c, etc.) to numeric (1, 2, 3, etc.) prior to data analysis. Open the desired data set or any of the data sets, such as "BUS.MON", that is provided with MoonStats, or incorporate your own data from other software programs such as Excel, Quattro Pro, SAS, SPSS, etc. by converting them to Xbase/Dbase (*.dbf) and importing them to Moonstats.

6.3 Create a new data set in the data sheet

If you want to create a new data set you should select the option "Create a data set" on the MoonStats start screen or choose Create from the File menu. Remember that MoonStats data files can contain numerical values only. Convert any alphabetic values (a, b, c, etc.) to numeric (1, 2, 3, etc.) prior to entering the values or doing data analysis. Make a note of the variable names that you assign to each item and to keep track of your data entry process. Moonstats allows a maximum of 10 characters for a variable name. Use variable names that are a descriptive of the question or item, as the variable names appear in the output tables and graphs.

6.3.1 Define the data set

When you choose to create a data set the "define a data set" dialog box (see Box 7) will appear.

- ↗ The variables in your new data set will be listed here.
- ↙ A few example variable names are provided by default, i.e., REFNUM, AGE, SEX, TESTSCORE1, but these can be changed to suit your needs. You should always have a REFNUM that corresponds to the unique number written on top of each data collection measure (questionnaire, interview, etc.) so that you can easily check the data on the physical data collection measure (the questionnaire, interview, etc.) against the data entered for that case/subject on the Data sheet.

Change a variable name by clicking on it and editing it.

You can add additional variables by using the down arrow ↓ on your keyboard to go to the blank area below the last variable (the area below TESTSCORE1).

↘ A dialog box will appear asking you to: "Click OK if you want to add another variable." Click OK to continue.

⇐ When you have defined all the variable names, click on CREATE to create the data set. You will be prompted to supply a file name for the data set. The default (automatic choice) data set or file name will be "NEW.MON" unless you change it. Use an appropriate name for your data set that accurately describes your research topic.

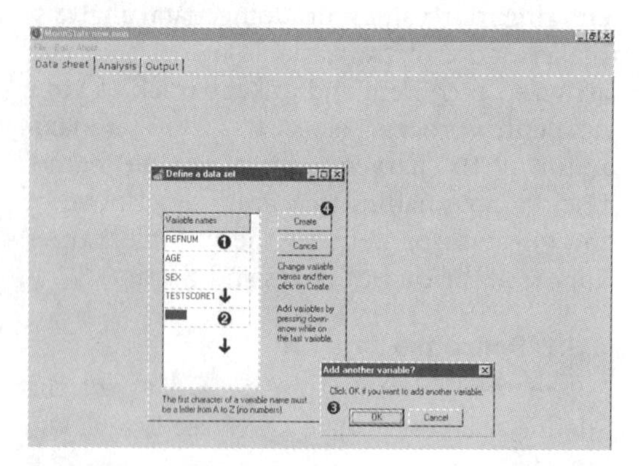

Box 7 Define a new data

You can now enter the data. If you wish to add another variable at a later stage, simply go to the MENU BAR at the top of MoonStats, select EDIT. Then select CHANGE/ADD VARIABLES and follow the steps as described in the previous paragraph.

6.3.2 **Enter the data**

Data entry is done by clicking on the first empty cell (case 1, variable 1) and typing in numeric data. Moonstats saves each data entry while you are busy entering the data.

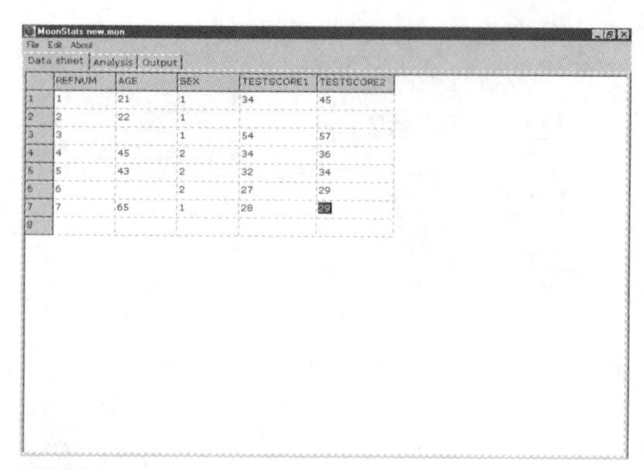

Box 8 Enter the data

When a question or item has not been completed by a respondent you have "missing data". This might be because the question is not relevant to the person, for a personal reason such as sensitivity of the information, failure to complete the questionnaire, entry of an invalid code, etc. MoonStats handles missing data by excluding the missing data from univariate analysis. In bivariate analysis the case/person/unit of analysis is simply ignored.

If a value is missing you can simply leave that cell in the data sheet empty. MoonStats will treat empty cells as missing data during statistical analysis. Because Moonstats only recognises numerical values, all alphabetical values are also treated as missing values. Do not use a zero (0) as a missing value. Zero is an actual value!

TIP: MAKE BACKUP COPIES!

Remember to make a backup of your data on 1.44 Mb stiffy (floppy) diskette or other removable storage media such as CD-RW, tape streamer, etc. If your computer breaks down or disappears you need to have access to your backup data. Always store 2 or more copies of your data in a safe place, preferably in a different venue away from the computer. When in doubt ask yourself what it will cost you in time, energy and money to recreate the data set.

7 Analysing the data

To perform statistical analyses you should go to the Analysis window (click on the Analysis tab). Select one or more variables and then click on the various statistics.

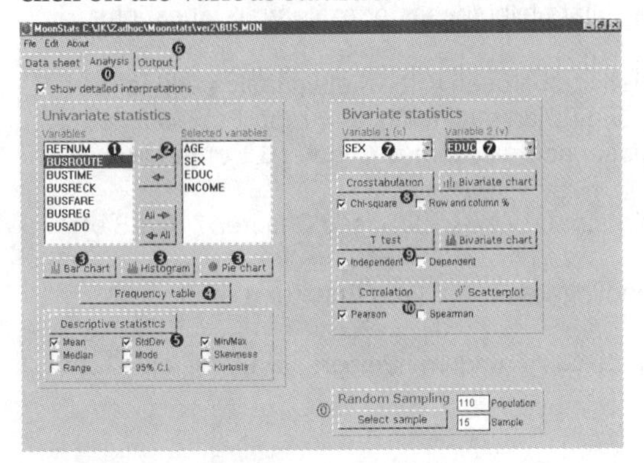

Box 9 Analysis window – step by step

Univariate statistics

⓿ Click on the Analysis window tab (Box 9).

❶ Select a variable by clicking on it.

❷ Click on the right arrow to move it to the "selected variables list". (To deselect, click on the left arrow to return the variable to the list on the left.)

❸ Click on bar charts, histograms and pie charts. The results will appear automatically in the ❻ Output window. To return to the Analyses window click on the Analysis tab ⓿.

❹ Click on frequency table. The results will appear automatically in the ❻ Output window.

❺ Select descriptive statistics (mean, standard deviation, minimum-maximum, kurtosis, etc.) and then click on descriptive statistics.

❻ The results appear automatically on the output window.

Bivariate statistics

❼ Select the two variables from the two drop down lists.

❽ A crosstabulation will provide a Chi-square statistic for nominal and/or ordinal variables with a limited range. The bivariate chart gives a visual representation of the relationship between the variables.

❾ A correlation (Pearson's product moment for interval/ratio data or Spearman's rank-order for ordinal data) gives the relationship between variables. The scatterplot gives a visual representation of the relationship between the variables.

❿ The *t* test is used to evaluate the differences in means between two groups. An example of independent groups are a randomly selected experimental/treatment and control groups. Dependent groups are based on related subject samples, for instance when a group of subjects are tested before and after an intervention to see if there is an improvement in their scores. The bivariate chart gives a visual representation of the relationship between the variables.

Random number calculator:

⓪ A list of pseudo-random numbers can be created, based on sampling without replacement so that there are no repeat numbers in the sampling list. The default setting automatically selected by Moonstats is for a population of 110 (i.e., your sampling frame or list of all possible cases) and a sample of 15 cases, but you can change these values as desired.

8 Using MoonStats

8.1 MoonStats and the research phases

By now you are perhaps wondering how to start your research project, or you may have collected research data and need to analyse the results and write the report. The following table gives an overview of the research phases and how MoonStats can help you. The ways in which MoonStats can assist are indicated with a black arrow (➔) below. The other stages are discussed in the textbook and indicated with a normal arrow (→).

Table 1
Overview of research phases

→ Decide on a topic that you want to investigate (see Chapter 2 of the textbook).
→ Do a literature review of the topic and consult key stakeholders (see Chapter 3 of the textbook).
→ Define the research problem and objectives. Formulate hypotheses or exploratory questions (see Chapter 2 of the textbook).
→ Develop a data analysis plan, i.e., (a) what statistic to be used with what variables and for what purpose (see Chapter 2 and 9 of the textbook), and (b) an outline for your report to indicate what statistic will be reported where in the proposal and report (see Chapter 11 of the textbook).
→ Design data collection instruments (questionnaires, interviews, etc.) (see Chapter 7 and 8 of the textbook).
→ Decide on, and draw the sample in terms of sampling frame/list (see Chapter 4 of the textbook).
→ If the study requires RANDOM SELECTION create a list of random numbers for the sample with the RANDOM NUMBER CALCULATOR.

Data entry and analysis with MoonStats

➔ CODE the data into numerical format and create a (hand-written) CODE SHEET on a separate page (see Chapter 9 of the textbook), and keep this page safe.
➔ ENTER the data using the MoonStats Data sheet.
➔ CLEAN the data of errors and make data backups.
➔ EXPLORE the data using charts and descriptive statistics.
➔ UNIVARIATE STATISTICS:
- Charts: bar chart, histogram and pie chart.
- Frequency tabulation.
- Descriptive statistics: mode, median, mean, standard deviation, 95% confidence interval of the mean, minimum/maximum, range, skewness, kurtosis.

➔ BIVARIATE STATISTICS:
- Cross tabulation, Chi-square, and bivariate chart.
- *T* test for dependent or independent groups and bivariate chart.
- Correlation and scatterplot.

→ Write report (see Chapter 10 of the textbook).
→ Disseminate report and implement findings.

8.2 CODE the data into numerical format and create a CODE SHEET

MoonStats accepts only numerical data – therefore if you have alphabetical data you have to code your data to make it numerical. You may for example have a question with response values that ranged from A to E as is the case in the example in Table 2. This should be recoded so that an A = 1, B = 2, C = 3, D = 4, E = 5. You can then enter the numbers in the data sheet/spreadsheet, remembering that a value of "1" on this variable represents an A, and a value of "5" represents an E. Coding is also described in the chapter on statistical techniques (see Section 9.4 in Chapter 9 of the textbook).

Let us work through an example data set provided with MoonStats (compare Section 7.7.3.3 of Chapter 7 of the textbook). The following questionnaire was used to collect the data in the "Bus Service" study (in the "BUS.MON" data file). This is a fictitious research study of bus passengers' perceptions of their bus service, and was designed to introduce users to MoonStats as an example data set.

Table 2
Questionnaire used in the "Bus Service" study (see "BUS.MON" data file)

Dear Sir/Madam, please help us improve our bus service by completing the following anonymous questionnaire. Write your answers or indicate with a cross on the appropriate answer how much you agree or disagree with the statements.

Reference number for administrative purposes

1 What is your age?...............

2 Indicate your sex. [(1) male / (2) female]

3 What is the highest educational level that you have successfully completed?
[(1) Below Grade 10 or Std. 8 / (2) Grade 10 and 11 / (3) Grade 12 (Matric) / (4) Post-matric Diploma or Degree / (5) Post graduate degree]

4 Indicate your monthly income R.............. per month

5 What bus route do you normally use? [(1) Rietvlei .... / (2) Kwa-Thema...............]

6 Our local buses are usually on time.
[a. Strongly disagree / b. Disagree / c. Sometimes / d. Agree / e. Strongly Agree]

7 Our local bus drivers are reckless.
[a. Strongly disagree / b. Disagree / c. Sometimes / d. Agree / e. Strongly Agree]

8 Our local bus fares are too high.
[a. Strongly disagree / b. Disagree / c. Not sure / d. Agree / e. Strongly Agree]

9 Our local bus services care for their passengers
[a. Strongly disagree / b. Disagree / c. Not sure / d. Agree / e. Strongly Agree]

10 Would you like to add anything about the bus service?
....

Thank you. Your participation is greatly appreciated!

Create your own code sheet for the "Bus Service" data set

A code sheet provides a summary of the questions or items in the data collection instrument (questionnaire/ interview/etc.), the names of the variables in the data set, the coding or meaning of values, the minimum and maximum values, the range and the measurement levels. A code sheet can be made using pen and paper.

Some of the questions in the questionnaire (Table 2) have numeric responses (1, 2, 3, ...) and others have alphabetical responses (a, b, c, ...). As MoonStats accepts only numeric data you have to convert the alphabetical values to numeric values. Therefore we strongly encourage you to work out a detailed CODE SHEET of your data set on a piece of paper.

The following code sheet relates to the questionnaire in the previous section on the "Bus Service" study (in the "BUS.MON" data file).

Table 3
Code sheet for the bus study

CODE SHEET				
Data set: BUS.MON		**Date: 1/10/2005**		
Question/Item and variable name	**Coding**	**Minimum – Maximum**	**Range**	**Measurement level**
Reference number of questionnaire completed by passenger (refnum) **	Unique number on each questionnaire.	1–150	150	Ratio (could be zero)
Age. (age)	Exact age as supplied by respondent	16 – 48	30	Ratio (could be zero)
Sex. (sex)	m : 1 = male f : 2 = female	1 – 2	2	Nominal/ categorical
Monthly income level. (income)	Exact income as supplied in Rands	500 – 4900		Ratio (could be zero
Educational level (educ)	1 = Below Grade 10 (below Std 8) 2 = Grade 10 and 11 (Std 8 – 9) 3 = Grade 12 (Matric) 4 = Diploma/Degree 5 = Post graduate degree	1 – 5	5	Ordinal
Busroute (busroute)	1 = Rietvlei 2 = Kwa-Thema	1 – 2	2	Nominal/ categorical

Our local buses are on time (bustime)	Likert scale *** a = 1, b = 2, c = 3, d = 4, e = 5	1 – 5	5	Ordinal (but can for practical purposes be treated as interval)
Our local bus drivers are reckless (busreck)	Likert scale a = 1, b = 2, c = 3, d = 4, e = 5	1 – 5	5	Ordinal (but can for practical purposes be treated as interval)
Our local bus services care for their passengers (buscare)	Likert scale a = 1, b = 2, c = 3, d = 4, e = 5	1 – 5	5	Ordinal (but can for practical purposes be treated as interval)
Open ended question: Would you like to add anything about the bus service? (busadd) (See textbook section 7.8 – consideration number 1, and Section 9.2 – content analysis)	These themes were identified after the data was collected and the following codes assigned to each theme: 1 "The bus service is very good" 2 "The buses don't wait for passengers." 3 "Do something about the reckless driving of the bus drivers." 4 "Start a bus service at 21h00 when we work late." 5 "The bus drivers make detours to pick up their friends and then we work late."	1 – 5	5	Nominal/categorical

* You don't have to type in the data of this research – just open the file "bus.mon".

** Variable names in MoonStats are limited to 10 characters or fewer. In this case "reference number" (15 characters) is reduced to the variable name "refnum" (6 characters) in the data set.

*** The Likert type item responses were worded as follows: a = Strongly disagree, b = Disagree, c = not sure or sometime, d = Agree, e = Strongly Agree.

Note: The Code Sheet is not on the MoonStats program or CD-ROM – you will have to create the code sheet on your own on a separate paper !!!

8.4 **Clean the data set**

Most data sets initially have some errors in them. These errors could be due to typing errors, misreading the raw data, computer errors or other human errors. It is vital that you "clean" the data before doing statistical calculations. If the data have errors your statistical output will reflect these errors. In computer terminology this is called *gigo* (garbage in – garbage out). It is therefore imperative that your data are "clean" and 100% correct before you start doing statistical analyses!

The following easy steps are recommended to clean the data:

- Compare the original questionnaires with the data in the Data sheet

- Check the minimum and maximum values
- Check for outliers – values in the data set that are substantially different from the other observations. They are much higher or lower than the bulk of the values in the distribution.

8.4.1 **Compare the original questionnaires with the data in the data sheet**

Select a random sample of 10% to 15% of the original questionnaires (questionnaires/interviews/etc.). Now compare these against the data entered in the Data sheet, using the reference number to trace the original questionnaire on the Data sheet. (When entering the data you should always write a unique reference number on top of each questionnaire, and enter this number in the first column of the Data sheet. In MoonStats the first default variable "refnum" is supplied automatically for this very reason.)

One way to select the random sample is by selecting say every 7th (or every nth number that will lead to a sample of between 10 and 15%). Then take the sample of questionnaires and double check that the correct values for each variable have been entered in the Data sheet. If you encounter errors you should fix them.

It would be prudent to try and determine why these errors occurred (i.e., was it a person who did the data entry who always made the same errors or who did poor quality work? Are the errors always on a specific place in the data set?) You need to consider what the chances are that there are many of these errors in the remaining 85% or 90% of the questionnaires that you have not checked. You need to be 100% sure that the data are error free and clean before you start with any statistical analysis, otherwise you will have *gigo*! If you find that the data have been unreliably entered you have the option to either re-enter all the data correctly, or to check each and every value in the Data sheet against the original questionnaire. When the data have been cleaned in this way, you should make backups before continuing.

8.4.2 **Check the minimum and maximum values**

The following procedure will produce an Output window with minimum and maximum values, which you can then compare to the minimum and maximum values as indicated on the Code sheet that you have created:

After entering the data (and making back-up copies of the data set) go to the Analysis window in MoonStats. Now use the *univariate statistics* and select all the variables by clicking *select all*. Then click on the *descriptive statistics* button. The Output window will appear to show the variable names, means, standard deviations, minimum and maximum values.

Carefully study the descriptive statistics in the Output window. Some of the invalid data can be detected here because their values are outside the permissible range of minimum or maximum values. Invalid values are lower than the prescribed minimum value or higher than the prescribed maximum value on the data set Code sheet that you created (see section 8.3 for an example code sheet). If you find invalid values you have to return to the Data sheet (click on the Data sheet window), and search the variable for the incorrect value (go to the top menu, select *edit* and scroll down to select *find*). Find and then delete the invalid value and replace it with the correct value by referring to the original questionnaire.

8.4.3 **Outliers**

An outlier is a score/observation/value that is substantially different from the others. Outliers can be a result of: (a) incorrect data entry; (b) because of an extraordinary event that can be explained (in which case you can decide whether it is representative of the sample or should be ignored); (c) because of an extraordinary event that can not be explained (again you can decide to include or ignore the data); and (d) observations that fall within the ordinary range of values on each of the variables but are unique in their combination across the variables (Hair et al, 1998; Howell, 1989; Welman & Kruger, 2001).

Some outliers which were the result of (a) incorrect data entry will have been fixed in the previous section by checking the minimum and maximum values.

The remaining outliers are most easily detected in MoonStats by using the appropriate graphical methods of representation as described in the next section on distribution, i.e., bar charts, pie charts, histograms, scatter plots or *t* test group histograms. Refer to the next section for the appropriate graphical methods. Within each of these you should look for exceptionally high bars or plots, or clearly isolated bars/plots on the left or right of the distribution. If you find outliers you should return to the Data sheet (click on the Data sheet window), and search the variable for the outlier value (go to the top menu, select *edit* and scroll down to select *find*). Compare the outlier values with the values on the original questionnaire by matching the unique reference number on the questionnaire to the value in the *refnum* variable. If the outliers are invalid due to data entry errors you can now correct them.

TIP: Make a backup of the cleaned data

Now, after spending some time and energy to clean the data, is the ideal time to update the backups of the data you made on diskette or other removable storage device! Store the updated backups in a safe and accessible place.

8.5 Univariate statistics

The univariate statistics available in Moonstats include: mode, median, mean, standard deviation, the 95% confidence interval for the mean, minimum, maximum, range, skewness, kurtosis, and frequency tables.

- Mode: The most common occurring value or score.
- Median: The score corresponding to the point in the exact middle of the values, so that 50% of the values are below it when the scores are arranged from low to high.
- Mean: The average value obtained for a variable by adding all the values and dividing by the number of values.
- Standard deviation: The standard deviation – an indication of how closely values are clustered around the mean. Approximately 68% of cases lie between one standard deviation below and one standard deviation above the mean. The variance is the standard deviation squared.
- 95% Confidence Interval (95% CI): If you are working with a sample, there is a 95% probability that the actual mean of the larger population from which your sample was drawn lies within the range indicated by this value – either above or below your sample mean.
- Minimum: The smallest value obtained for a variable.
- Maximum: The largest value obtained for a variable.
- Range: The distance from the lowest to the highest values. Obtained by subtracting the highest from the lowest values.
- Skewness: An indication if the distribution of values are symmetrical or not. A negatively skewed distribution has a mean that tends toward the higher values.
- Kurtosis: Kurtosis measures the "peakedness" of a distribution by looking at the flatness of the tail-ends of the distribution. If the kurtosis is high, then the distribution has a heavy-tailed distribution with a

large number of scores that are very high and very low. If the kurtosis is low, then the distribution is more "peaked" and has relatively few values that are very high and very low.
- Frequency tables: A table listing the values or scores and the frequencies with which they occur.

The following graphs can be used with univariate statistics: bar charts, pie charts, and histograms.

- *Bar chart*: A graph in which disconnected rectangles are used to represent frequencies of values.
- *Pie chart:* A graph in which the slices of a circle are used to represent frequencies of values.
- *Histogram:* A graph in which connected rectangles are used to represent frequencies of values.

Univariate statistics, frequency tabulation and charts can be classified according to the measurement level of the variable as listed in Table 4 (see Section 9.4 of the textbook).

8.6 Bivariate statistics

The bivariate statistics available in MoonStats are: cross-tabulation with chi-square; Pearson's product moment and Spearman's rank order correlations; and *t*-tests for independent and dependent groups.

- A crosstabulation shows how many cases with particular values on one variable have particular values on another variable. If you ticked the "percentages" box, you will also see tables showing these frequencies as row and column percentages. You can also select a chi-square statistic for nominal and/or ordinal variables with a limited range (no more than 25 categories in Moonstats). The chi-square test shows if

Table 4

List of univariate descriptive statistical techniques and measurement level

	Categorical		**Continuous/Quantitative**	
	Nominal	Ordinal	Interval	Ratio
Descriptive statistic (in MoonStats)	Frequency tables Min-maximum Mode – – – –	Frequency tables Min-maximum – Median – – –	Frequency tables Min-maximum – – Mean and Standard deviation 95% confidence interval of the mean Skewness & Kurtosis	Frequency tables Min-maximum – – Mean and Standard deviation 95% confidence interval of the mean Skewness & Kurtosis
Graphical method (in MoonStats	Pie chart Bar chart –	Pie chart – Histogram	Pie chart – Histogram	Pie chart – Histogram
Examples of variables	*Sex, gender, marital status,*	*Social class, attitudes, any*	*Attitudes, calendar time, scores of*	*Age, cost, exact income, number of*

work status, disability status, province, city, day of week, month, cultural group, cultural language.	*ranking of high/middle/low, or junior/mid-level/senior.*	*abilities (verbal, numerical, 3-dimensional insight, memory, artistic, writing, empathy)*	*children, exam result as a percentage.*

there is a relationship between two categorical variables. Simply look at the *p*-value to see if the relationship is statistically significant. The bivariate chart gives a visual representation of the relationship between the variables.

- A correlation (Pearson's product moment for normally distributed data or Spearman's rank-order for not-normally distributed data or when the distribution is unknown) gives the relationship between variables. The *p*-value provides an indication of the significance of the relationship. The scatterplot gives a visual representation of the relationship between the variables. Correlations are relatively sensitive to outliers.
- The *t*-test is used to evaluate the differences in means between two groups. An example of independent groups are randomly selected experimental/treatment and control groups. Dependent groups are based on related subject samples, for instance when a group of subjects are tested before and after an intervention to see if there is an improvement in their scores. The bivariate chart gives a visual representation of the relationship between the variables. The *p*-value reported with a *t*-test represents the probability of error involved in accepting the research hypothesis about the existence of a difference in the means. The *t*-statistic assumes normality of the group distributions or variance. However, if the variances are unequal a different formula is used to perform the *t*-test.

9 **Write a report**

Each Output window has a copy and save option. You can copy and paste the results and charts to a word processor, or save the results and then import them into the word processor.

REFERENCES

Hair, J.J.; Anderson, R.E.; Tatham, R.L. & Black, W.C. (1998) *Multivariate data analysis*, 5th ed. New Jersey: Prentice-Hall International.

Howell, D.C. (1989) *Fundamental statistics for the behavioural sciences* (2nd ed). Massachusetts: PWS-Kent.

Moonstats (2001) *MoonStats User Manual.* Typeset Document. Pretoria.

Welman, J.C. & Kruger, S.J. (2001) *Research Methodology*. (2nd ed), Cape Town: Oxford University Press Southern Africa.